中英双语

The Wisdom of Confucius

孔子的智慧

林语堂 /著

黄嘉德 /译

湖南文艺出版社
HUNAN LITERATURE AND ART PUBLISHING HOUSE

博集天卷
CS-BOOKY

The Wisdom of Confucius

Copyright © 1938 by Lin Yutang

This edition arranged with Curtis Brown Group Ltd.

through Andrew Nurnberg Associates International Limited

著作权合同登记号：图字 18-2016-161

图书在版编目（CIP）数据

孔子的智慧：汉、英 / 林语堂著；黄嘉德译 . --
长沙：湖南文艺出版社，2021.1
书名原文：The Wisdom of Confucius
ISBN 978-7-5404-5918-5

Ⅰ. ①孔… Ⅱ. ①林… ②黄… Ⅲ. ①孔丘（前 551 ~
前 479）—思想评论—汉、英 Ⅳ. ①B222.25

中国版本图书馆 CIP 数据核字（2020）第 180668 号

上架建议：名家经典·文化

KONGZI DE ZHIHUI: HAN、YING

孔子的智慧：汉、英

作　　者：林语堂
译　　者：黄嘉德
出 版 人：曾赛丰
责任编辑：丁丽丹
监　　制：邢越超
策划编辑：王　维
特约编辑：王　屿
版权支持：辛　艳　张雪珂
营销支持：文刀刀　周　茜
版式设计：李　洁
封面设计：棱角视觉
出　　版：湖南文艺出版社
　　　　　（长沙市雨花区东二环一段 508 号　邮编：410014）
网　　址：www.hnwy.net
印　　刷：三河市兴博印务有限公司
经　　销：新华书店
开　　本：880mm × 1270mm　1/32
字　　数：207 千字
印　　张：12.5
版　　次：2021 年 1 月第 1 版
印　　次：2021 年 1 月第 1 次印刷
书　　号：ISBN 978-7-5404-5918-5
定　　价：59.80 元

若有质量问题，请致电质量监督电话：010-59096394
团购电话：010-59320018

孔子
的
智慧

The

Wisdom

of Confucius

目录

CONTENTS

2

第一章　导言

实际上，儒家思想所持的是人道主义者的态度，对全无实用虚无缥缈的玄学与神秘主义完全弃之不顾，而是只注重基本的人际关系，灵异世界神仙不朽又有何用？这种独具特色的人道主义中最有力的教义，是"人的标准就是人"。

一、孔子思想的特性

时至今日，还能有人热衷儒家思想吗？若说是有，岂非怪事。其实这全系于人对善念是否还肯执着，而一般人对善念是不会有一股狂热的。更重要的，似乎是今日之人是否对儒家思想还存有信心。这对现代的中国人特别重要。这个问题是直接指向现代的中国人，挥之不去，也无从拒绝。因为现代有些中国人，甚至曾经留学外国，思想已趋成熟，他们对儒家所持的态度与观点，都显得心悦诚服。由此我认为儒家思想是具有其中心性，也可以说有其普遍性的。儒家思想的中心性与其人道精神之基本的吸引力，其本身即有非凡的力量。孔子去世后数百年间政治混乱、思想分歧的时期，儒家思想战胜了道家、墨家、法家，自然派思想及共产派思想，以及其他林林总总的学派。在两千五百年内中国人始终奉之为天经地义，虽然有时际遇稍衰，但终必衰而复振，而且声势益隆。与儒家思想抗衡者，除道家在公元后第三至第六世纪盛行之外，其强敌莫过于佛教。佛教多受宋儒所宗仰，佛教虽无玄妙精微，在儒家人道精神及知识论的阐述上，也只能予以修正，然后即将重点移至儒家经典所已有之的某些观念上，而予以更充分之重视，但也并不能将儒家思想根本推翻。这也许是纯粹由于孔子个人多年来的声望地位使然，但是儒家心中非凡的自负，对本门学说精当之信而不移，因而鄙弃佛教理论而侧目视之，或者给予宽容，当时的情形可能正是如此。儒家也以平实的看法否定了庄子的神秘思想，也以此等平实的思想鄙弃了佛教的神秘思想。今天，儒家思想遇到了更大的敌手，但并不是基督教，而是整套的西方思想与生活以及西方新的社会思潮，这种西方文明全是工业时代所引起的。儒家思想，若看作是恢复封建社会的一种政治制度，在现代政治经济的发展之前，被人认为陈旧无用，自是；若视之为人道主义文化，若视之为社会生活上基本的观点，我认为儒家思想仍不失为颠扑不破的真理。儒家思想，在中国人生活中，仍然是一股活的力量，还会影响我们民族的立身处世之道。西方人若研究儒家思想及其基本的信念，他们会了解中国的国情民俗，会受益匪浅的。

在西方读者看来，孔子只是一位智者，开口不是格言，便是警语，这种看法，自然不足以阐释孔子思想其影响之深而且大。若缺乏思想上更为深奥的统一的信念或系统，纯靠一套格言警语而支配一个国家，像孔子思想之支配中国一样，是办不到的。孔夫子的威望与影响如此之大，对此一疑难问题之解答，必须另自他处寻求才是。若没有一套使人信而不疑的大道理，纵有格言警语，也会久而陈腐令人生厌的。《论语》这部书是孔学上的圣经，是一套道德的教训，使西方人对孔子之有所知，主要就是靠这部书。但是《论语》毕竟只是夫子自道的一套精粹语录，而且文句零散，多失其位次，因此若想获得更为充分之阐释，反须要依赖《孟子》《礼记》等书。孔子总不会天天只说些零星断片的话吧。所以，对孔子的思想之整体系统若没有全盘的了解，欲求充分了解何以孔子有如此的威望及影响，那真是缘木求鱼了。

简捷说，孔子的思想是代表一个理性的社会秩序，以伦理为法，以个人修养为本，以道德为施政之基础，以个人正心修身为政治修明之根柢。由此看来，最为耐人深思之特点是在取消政治与伦理之间的差异。其方法为一伦理性之方法，与法家以讲严刑峻法为富国强兵之道截然不同。孔子的学说也是断然肯定的，要求人对人类与社会负起当负的责任，所谓以天下国家为己任，此点与道家的适世玩世又大有不同。实际上，儒家思想所持的是人道主义者的态度，对全无实用虚无缥缈的玄学与神秘主义完全弃之不顾，而是只注重基本的人际关系，灵异世界神仙不朽又有何用？这种独具特色的人道主义中最有力的教义，是"人的标准就是人"。就凭这条教义，一个常人只要顺着人性中的善去行，就算初步奉行儒家的为人之道了，并不必在什么神祇上去寻求神圣理想中的完美。

更精确点说，儒家思想志在重新树立一个理性化的封建社会，因为当时周朝的封建社会正在趋于崩溃。儒家思想当然主张阶级分明。要了解这种情形，我们必须回溯到孔子当时封建制度崩溃以及此后数百年内的状况。当时中国领土内有数百大大小小公侯伯子男等级的国家，各自独立，其强者则国土与国力日增，时常与他国兵连祸结。周朝皇帝名为华夏君王，统治全国，实则徒拥虚名，衰微已极。甚至孔子及以后之孟子，虽周游列国，干谒诸侯，求其施仁政，拯百姓于水火，但亦不屑于一朝周帝。这颇与其所主张之建立理性社会，尊崇周王之学说相矛盾。因当时国内情势纷乱已极，周室衰微，帝国荏弱，纵然前往朝见，终无大用。各国间虽订有条约，转眼粉碎，结盟和好，终难持久。养兵日众，捐税日增，强凌弱，众暴寡。国与国间随时会商，真是舌敝唇焦，不见成功。学人智者开始定攻守之计，和战之策，别利害，辨得失。说来也怪，当时学者智士之间，国界之分渐渐混灭，周游列国，朝秦暮楚，亲疏无常。而古礼失，尊卑乱，贫富悬殊，政教乖误，此等混乱失常遂使思想锐敏之士，劳神苦思以求拨乱反正之道。在此种气氛中，更兼以思想之极端自由，智慧明敏之士遂各抒己见，如百花齐放，竞妍争香，乃形成中国哲学之黄金时代。或蔑弃礼教如老庄；或主张人人当亲手工作以谋生，如萌芽期之共产主义，如许行及其门人；墨子则倡单一神祇，崇爱上帝，教人重人道，勿自私，甚至窒欲苦行，竟趋于极端而排斥音乐；此外尚有诡辩家、苦行家、快乐主义者、自然主义者，等等，不一而足。于是，不少人，如今日之欧洲人一样，开始对文化表示怀疑，而想返回太古之原始生活，正如今日若干思想家要返回非洲丛林中或到爪哇以东之巴厘岛一样。孔子则如现代的基督徒，他相信道德力量，相信教育的力量，相信艺术的力量，相信文化历史的传统，相信国际间某种程度的道德行为，相信人与人之间高度的道德标准，这都是孔子部分的信念。

在《礼记·儒行》篇里，我们可以看出儒家与其他各派的差异。"儒"这个字，在孔子时便已流行。而称为儒的一派学者，大概是特别的一批人，他们在观点上持保守态度，精研经史，其儒冠儒服正表示他们对古代文化的信而不疑。下面的几段摘录文字足以表示儒家的高度道德理想。

鲁哀公问于孔子曰："夫子之服，其儒服钦？"孔子对曰："丘少居鲁，衣逢掖之衣。长居宋，冠章甫之冠。丘闻之也，君子之学也博，其服也乡。丘不知儒服。"

哀公曰："敢问儒行？"孔子对曰："遽数之，不能终其物。悉数之乃留，更仆未可终也。"哀公命席，孔子侍曰："儒有席上之珍以待聘，夙夜强学以待问，怀忠信以待举，力行以待取。其自立有如此者。

"儒有衣冠中，动作慎。其大让如慢，小让如伪；大则如威，小则如愧。其难进而易退也，粥粥若无能也。其容貌有如此者。

……

"儒有可亲而不可劫也，可近而不可迫也，可杀而不可辱也。其居处不淫，其饮食不溽，其过失可微辨而不可面数也。其刚毅有如此者。

……

"儒有今人与居，古人与稽。今世行之，后世以为楷。适弗逢世，上弗援，下弗推。谗谄之民，有比党而危之者。身可危也，而志不可夺也。虽危，起居竟信其志，犹将不忘百姓之病也。其忧思有如此者。

"儒有博学而不穷，笃行而不倦，幽居而不淫，上通而不困。礼之以和为贵，忠信之美，优游之法，举贤而容众，毁方而瓦合。其宽裕有如此者。"

在此等列国纷争、王室陵夷、封建制度日趋崩溃之际，孔子的教义自然不难了解，尤其是孔子以礼乐恢复封建社会的用心之所在。孔子的教义我认为含有五项特点，对了解儒家教义至为重要。

政治与伦理的合一

孔子特别重视礼乐，关心道德这些方面，西方人往往不甚了解。可是把孔子心目中的社会秩序表现得更好，再没有别的字眼比"礼乐"一词更恰当了。孔子回答弟子问为政之道时说（子张问政，子曰）："师乎，前，吾语汝乎？君子明于礼乐，举而错之而已。"（谓举礼乐之道而施之于政事。见《礼记》第二十八篇《仲尼燕居》）听孔子说这种话，似乎过于幼稚天真。其实从孔子的观点看，这也容易了解。我们若记得孔子对"政"的定义是"政者正也"，自然不难了。换言之，孔子所致力者是将社会之治安置于道德基础之上，政治上之轨道自然也由此而来。《论语》上有这样的对话：

或谓孔子曰："子奚不为政？"子曰："《书》云：'孝乎，惟孝。友于兄弟，施于有政。'是亦为政，奚其为为政？"

换言之，孔子差不多可算作一位无政府主义者，因为他的最高政治理想在于社会上大家和睦相处，因此管理社会的政府已然没有必要。这个意思在这几句话里，也暗示出来，他说："听讼，吾犹人也。必也，使无讼乎？"但是如何才可以达到此等无讼的地步呢？他在后文里另有说明。但是切莫误解的是，孔子为政最后的目的，与刑罚礼乐的目的是相同的。在《礼记·乐记》中说："礼以道其志，乐以和其声，政以一其行，刑以防其奸。礼乐刑政，其极一也，所以同民心而出治道也。"

孔子从不满足于由严刑峻法所获致的政治上的秩序，他说："道之以政，齐之以刑，民免而无耻。道之以德，齐之以礼，有耻且格。"在政治上孔子认为有两种等级，他曾说，齐国再往前进步，就达到了鲁国的文化程度，也就是达到了第一阶段的治世；鲁国若再往前进一步，就达到了真正文明的地步，也就是达到了第二阶段的治世。

礼——理性化的社会

儒家思想，在中国被称为"孔教""儒教"或是"礼教"。西洋的读者会立刻觉得礼字的含义比纯粹的礼仪要复杂得多，或者觉得孔子的思想是一套假道理。我们对这个问题必须严正从事，因为"礼乐"一词在孔门著作里屡见不鲜，似乎包括孔子对社会的整套制度，正如"仁"字似乎包括了孔子对个人行为的教训精髓一样。"礼乐"一词的精义及其重要性，在本书第六、七、八三章将有详细的讨论。现在只需要指出孔子自己对"政"与"礼"的定义是一而二，二而一的。政是"正"，而礼则是"事之治也"（见《礼记》第二十八篇）。中国这个"礼"字是无法用英文中的单词表示的。在狭义上看，这个字的意思是"典礼"（ritual），也是"礼节"（propriety），但从广义上看，其含义只是"礼貌"（Good Manners）；在最高的哲学意义上看，则是理想的社会秩序，万事万物各得其宜，所指尤其是合理中节的封建社会。如前所述，当时的封建社会正在崩溃当中。

孔子力求实现自己的理想，乃致力于恢复一种社会秩序，此种社会必须人人相爱，尊敬当权者，在社会上公众的拜祭喜庆，必须表现在礼乐上。当然，这种拜祭的典礼一定是原始的宗教典礼，不过我们所谓的"礼教"，其特点为半宗教性质。因为皇帝祭天，这是宗教性质的一面，但在另一面则是教导百姓在家庭生活上要仁爱守法敬长辈。在祭天、祭当权者的祖先、祭地、祭河川、祭山岳，这等宗教性的祭祀则各有不同。在《论语》与《礼记》上有若干次记载，记孔子并不知道这些祭拜与皇室祖先的意义，如果知道，则治天下便易如反掌了。在这方面，儒家的思想类似摩西大部分的戒律，若在儒家的教义上把孔子与摩西相比，则较与其他哲学家相比容易多了。儒家所倡的礼也和摩西的戒律一样，包括宗教的法规，也包括生活的规范，而且认为这二者是不可分的一个整体。孔子毕竟是他那个时代的人，他是生活在正如法国哲学家孔德（Comte）所说的"宗教的时代"。

再者，设若孔子是个基督徒，毫无疑问，他在气质上，一定是个"高教会派"的教士（High Churchman——英国国教中，重视教会权威及仪式之一派），不然便是圣公会教士（Episcopalian），或是个天主教徒。孔子喜爱祭祀崇拜的仪式，所谓"我爱其礼"，当然不只是把仪式看做缺乏意义的形式，而是他清楚了解人类的心理，正式的礼仪会使人心中产生虔敬之意。而且，正像圣公会教士和天主教教士一样，孔子也是个保守派的哲人，相信权威有其价值，相信传统与今昔相承的道统。他的艺术的美感十分强烈，必然是会受礼乐的感动，《论语》上此种证明很多（参看本书第五章第二节"孔子的感情与艺术生活"）。祭天与皇室的祭祖会引起一种孝敬之感，同样，宴饮骑射在乡村举行时，伴以歌舞跪拜，会使乡人在庆祝之时遵礼仪守秩序，在群众之中这也是礼仪的训练。

所以，从心理上说，礼乐的功用正复相同。儒家思想更赋予礼乐歌舞以诗歌的优美。我们试想孔子本人就爱好音乐，二十九岁就从音乐名家学弹奏乐器，并且虽在忧患之中，也时常弹琴自娱，因此他将礼乐并重，也就不足为奇了。孔子时代的六艺，在孔门经典中清清楚楚指出为礼、乐、射、御、书、数。孔子在六十四岁时，删订《诗经》，据说经过孔子编辑之后，其中的诗歌才算分类，各得其所，而且各自配上适当的音乐。事实上，据记载，孔子自己讲学的学校，似乎不断有弦歌之声。子游为武城宰时，开始教百姓歌唱，孔子闻之欣然而笑，并且向子游开玩笑。见《论语·阳货》：

> 子之武城，闻弦歌之声。夫子莞尔而笑曰："割鸡焉用牛刀？"子游对曰："昔者偃也，闻诸夫子曰：'君子学道则爱人，小人学道则易使也。'子曰：'二三子，偃之言是也。前言戏之耳。'"

礼乐的哲学要义由《礼记·乐记》可见：

"观其舞，知其德。"（见一国之舞，知其国民之品德。）

"乐自中出，礼自外作。"（音乐发自内心，礼仪生自社会。）

"乐者，乐也。人情之所不能免也。"（音乐表喜乐之感，此种情绪既不能抑而止之，又不能以他物代替之。）

"乐由天作，礼以地制。"（音乐代表天，是抽象的；礼仪代表地，是具象的。）

国不同，其乐不同，正足以见民风之不同。

先王制礼乐，不只以餍百姓耳目口腹之欲，亦所以教民正当之嗜好，明辨邪恶，民生和顺。

礼教的整个系统是包括一个社会组织计划，其结论是一门庞大的学问，其中有宗教祭祀的典礼规则，宴饮骑射的规则，男女儿童的行为标准，对老年人的照顾，等等。将孔子的这门真实学问发扬得最好的莫若荀子。荀子与孟子同时，在学术上为孟子的敌人，其哲学思想在《礼记》一书有充分之阐述，足以反映荀子之见解（见本书第六、七、八章）。

对礼之重要有所了解，也有助于对孔子另一教义的结论之了解，即"正名"一说。孔子把他的时代及他以前两百年的政治历史写成《春秋》，其用意即在以"正名"为手段，而求恢复社会之正常秩序。比如帝王处死一叛将曰"杀"之，王公或将相杀死其元首曰"弑"之。再如春秋诸国里，非王而自称王者，孔子仍以其原有合法之头衔称之，即所以示贬也。

仁

孔子的哲学精义，我觉得是在他认定"人的标准是人"这一点上。设非如此，则整个一套儒家的伦理学说就完全破产，亦毫无实行的价值了。儒家整套的礼乐哲学只是"正心"而已，而神的国度正是在人心之中。所以个人若打算"修身"，最好的办法就是顺乎其本性的善而固执力行。这就是孔子伦理哲学之精义。其结果即"己所不欲，勿施于人"（见本书第五章"《论语》"）。关于仁，孔子有极精极高的含义，除去他的两个弟子及三个历史人物之外，他是绝不肯以仁这个字轻予许可的。有时有人问他某人可否算得上"仁"，十之八九他不肯以此字称呼当世的人。在本书"《中庸》"一章里，孔子指出"登高必自卑，行远必自迩"，他有一次说，孝悌即为仁之本。

"仁"一字之不易译为英文，正如"礼"字。中文的"仁"字分开为二人，即表示其意义为人际关系。今日此字之读法同"人"，但在古代其读音虽亦与"人"相同，但只限于一些特殊词中，汉代经学家曾有引证，今日已无从辨别。在孔门经典中，"仁"这个字与今日之"人"字，在用法上已可交换，在《论语》一书还有明显的例证。在《雍也》篇，宰予问曰："仁者虽告之曰：'井有仁焉'，其从之也？"足见"仁"与"人"在这里通用。由此可见"仁"与"人"之间的联想是显然可见的，在英文里，human，humane，humanitarian，humanity这些词，其中最后一词就含有mankind和kindness两词的意思。孔子与孟子二人都曾把"仁"字解释为"爱人"。但是此事并不如此简单。第一，如我所说，孔子不肯把仁字用来具体指某个真人，同时，他也未曾拒绝举个"仁人"的实例。第二，他常把这个"仁"字描写为一种心境，描写为人所"追寻"、所"获得"的状态，心情宁静时的感受，心情中失去"仁"以后的情况，心中依于"仁"的感受。孟子则曾说"居于仁"，好像"居于室"一样。

所以仁的本义应当是纯乎本然的状态。准乎此，孟子开始其整套的人性哲学的精义，而达到人性善的学说。而荀子相信人性恶，关于教育、音乐、社会秩序，更进而到制度与德行上，则走了孔子学说的另一端，发展了"礼"字的观念，而置其重心在"约束"上。在普通英文的用语里，我们说我们的相识之中谁是一个real man或real person，此词的含义则极为接近"仁"字。一方面，我们现在渐渐了解何以孔子不肯把"仁"这个徽章给予他当代那些好人而称之为仁者，我们今天则愿意把real man，real person一词最高的含义指我们的同代人（林肯自然是当之无愧的）。另一方面，依我们看来，一个人做人接近到"仁人"的地步并不那么困难，而且只要人自己心放得正，看不起那些伪善言行；只要想做个"真人"，做个"仁人"，他都可以办得到。孔子都说人若打算做个"仁人"，只要先做好儿女、好子弟、好国民，就可以了。我们的说法不是和孔孟的说法完全相符吗？我以为，我把中国的"仁"字译成英文的true manhood是十分精确而适宜的。有时只要译成kindness就可以，正如"礼"字在有些地方可以译作ritual（典礼），ceremony（仪式），manners（礼貌）。

　　实际上，孟子的理论已然发展到人性本善，已是人人生而相同的了，他还说"人人可以为尧舜"，也正是此义之引申。儒家说"登高必自卑，行远必自迩"，将此种近乎人情的方法用在德行方面，从平易平凡的程度开始。这一点足以说明其对中国人所具有的可爱之处，正好不同于墨子的严峻的"父道"（fatherhood）与"兼爱"（兼爱之说与基督的道理那么相近）。儒家有合乎人情的思想，才演变出以人作为人的标准这条道理。这样，不仅使人发现了真正的自己，使人能够自知，也自然推论出"己所不欲，勿施于人"的恕道。孔子不仅以此作为"真人""仁人"的定义，并且说他的学说是以恕道为中心的。"恕"字是由"如"与"心"二字构成的。在现代中文里，"恕"字常作"饶恕"讲，所以有如此的引申是不难看出的。因为你若认为在同一境况下，人的反应是相同的，你若与别人易地而处，你自然会持饶恕的态度。孔子就常常自己推己及人。最好的比喻是：一个木匠想做一个斧子的把柄。他只要看看自己手中那把斧子的把柄就够了，他无须另求标准。人就是人的标准，所谓推己及人是也。

修身为治国平天下之本

　　儒家对政治问题所采取的伦理方法已然讲解清楚。最简明的说法是：孔子相信由孝顺的子孙、仁爱的弟兄所构成的国家，一定是个井井有条、安宁治安的社会。儒家把治国平天下追溯到齐家，由齐家追溯到个人的修身。这种说法颇类似现代教育家所说，现在天下大乱在于教育失败一样。把世界秩序作为最终目的，把个人修身作为基本的开始，这二者之间的逻辑关联，在本书"《大学》"一章中有详明的叙述。可再参阅第三、四、六、七、八各章。中国人对格言谚语的重视，由此看来，自然不难明白，因为那些格言谚语并非彼此独立、毫无关联，而是一套内容丰富、面面俱到的哲学。

从现代心理学上看，这条道理可以一分为二，就是习惯说与模仿说。对孝道的重视（我不妨译作"当好儿女"）是以习惯说为其基础的。孔子、孟子都分明说在家养成了敬爱的习惯，将来对别人的父母与兄长也一定会恭敬，对国家的元首也会敬爱。本书第四章中有：家家习于仁爱，则全国必习于仁爱；家家习于礼让，则全国必习于礼让；使弟子敬爱父母兄长及尊敬长辈，必能为良善国民奠定正确的心态与道德的基础。

士

模仿学说，或可称之为楷模的力量，产生了知识阶级与"贤人政治"。知识分子这个上层阶级，必须同时是道德的上层阶级，否则便失去其为上层阶级的资格了。这就是孔子所说的君子的含义，是尽人皆知的。孔子所说的君子，绝不是德国哲学家尼采所说的"超人"。君子是在道德上仁爱而斯文的人，他同时好学深思，泰然从容，无时无刻不谨言慎行，深信自己以身作则，为民楷模，必能影响社会。不论个人处境如何，无时不怡然自得，对奢侈豪华，恒存几分鄙视之心。孔子的道德教训全表现在绅士身上。中文里的君子一词，在孔子时已然流行，只是孔子另赋予新义而已。在有些地方，其过去的含义与"君王"相同，绝不可译成英文中之gentleman；在其他地方，其含义显然是指有教养的绅士。由于有士大夫这种上层阶级，君子一词的两种含义便互相混合了，其所形成的意思，颇类似希腊哲人柏拉图所说的"哲人王"。关于以身作则或者说是身教，其力量如何，这种学说在《论语·述而》有充分的讨论。对于道德行为之影响力量，孔子是过于自信的。有一次，一个贪官季康子告诉孔子，他国内盗匪横行，窃贼猖獗，他深以为忧，孔子很直率地告诉他："苟子之不欲，虽赏之不窃。"（你本人若不贪，你赏窃贼让他去偷窃，他也不会去的。）

二、孔子的品格述略

在孔子去世后数百年，以及再往后的中国历史上，孔子本人的声望之高及其遗教地位之隆，要归之三个因素。第一，孔子思想对中国人特具吸引力；第二，中国古典学术与历史知识为孔门学人所专有，当时其他学派对中国古典及历史则不屑一顾，同时，中国此等古代学问本身即极为宝贵；第三，孔子本人的人品声望使人倾慕。在我们这个世界上，有些伟大师表人物，他们影响之大多半由于其人品可爱，反倒不是由于他们的学问渊深。我们想到古希腊哲人苏格拉底、意大利圣人圣方济各，他们本人并没有写过什么重要的著作，但是给当代留下那么深厚的印象其影响乃不可磨灭，竟至历久而弥新。孔子的可爱之处正与苏格拉底可爱之处一样。苏格拉底之深获柏拉图的敬爱，就足以证明是由于他的人品与思想使然。诚然，孔子删《诗经》、著《春秋》，但是孔子谆谆教人的传统只是由弟子及日后的信徒记录下来的。

在儒家著述中，对孔子的人品有许多不同的描写。我们在本书第三章论《中庸》时，曾先提到一些。孔子的弟子颜回曾赞美孔子，把他高捧到云天之上，将他比作神秘不可知之物，颜回说："仰之弥高，钻之弥坚；瞻之在前，忽焉在后。"下面有几段文字，可算做描写孔子最好的文字。一段是："子温而厉，威而不猛，恭而安。"孔子自己的描述尤其好。一次，一位国君向孔子的一个弟子问孔子是何等人，弟子并未回答。他回来之后将此事告诉孔子。在《论语》中有这样文字："叶公问孔子于子路，子路不对。子曰：汝奚不曰：'其为人也，发愤忘食，乐以忘忧，不知老之将至云尔。'"在这段夫子自道的文字里，我们不难看出孔子生活的快乐、热情及其力行的精神。孔子有好几次说他自己不是圣人，只是自己"学而不厌，诲人不倦"而已。下面有一段文字，可以说明孔子的奋勉力行。（原书此处漏排——编者注。）这表示孔子是有其道德的理想，自己知道自身负有的使命，因此深具自信。

孔子的品格的动人处，就在他的和蔼温逊，由他对弟子说话的语气腔调就可清清楚楚看得出。《论语》里记载的孔子对弟子的谈话，只可以看做一个风趣的教师与弟子之间的漫谈，其中偶尔点缀着几处隽永的警语。以这样的态度去读《论语》，孔子在最为漫不经心时说出只言片语，那才是妙不可言呢。比如说，我就好喜欢下面这一段：一天，孔子和两三个知己的门人闲谈时，他说："你们以为我有什么话不好意思告诉你们两三个人吗？说实在话，我真是没有什么瞒你们的。我孔丘生性就是这种人。"原文是：

子曰："二三子，以我为隐乎？吾无隐乎尔。吾无行而不与二三子者，是丘也。"

还有一次，因为子贡爱批评人，孔子不是用客气话称他的号，而是叫他的名字说："喂，赐啊，你是够聪明的，是不是？我可没有那么多闲工夫！"原文是：

> 子贡方人（批评人），子曰："赐也，贤乎哉！夫我则不暇。"

还有一次，孔子说："天天吃得饱饱的，什么也不做，只知道鬼混。这太不像话了。不是有人赌博下棋吗？那也比闲着无所事事好呀。"原文是：

> 子曰："饱食终日，无所用心，难矣哉！不有博弈者乎？为之，犹贤乎已。"

又有一次，孔子对弟子的行为开了一次玩笑，听了孔子的话，弟子大惑不解。孔子告诉弟子说："前言戏之耳。"言外之意是孔子并不反对那件事，而是赞成。这因为孔子的确是个乐天派的老先生。不管谁想向他求教，他都以高雅的态度表示欢迎。由下面一件事就可见出，这件事也正像基督教《新约》上的记载，耶稣一次向门徒说："让小孩子们到我跟前来。"那件事是这样：一个村子的居民因不老实而讨人厌，村里有几个年轻人去见孔子，孔子的弟子知道孔子居然接见了他们，对此事颇不以为然。孔子说："干什么对他们那么凶？我认为，重要的是他们肯来向我请教，而不是他们走后的行为如何。人家既然诚心诚意地来见我，我就很重视他们那份诚意，当然我不能担保他们以后的行为如何呀。"

这段原文如此：

互乡难与言。童子见，门人惑。子曰："与其进也，不与其退也。唯何甚？人洁己以进，与其洁也，不保其往也。"

但是孔子可不是永远温和高雅，因为他也是一个活生生的"真人"。他能歌唱，也能十分谦恭有礼，但是他也能像普通一个真人那样恨人，那样鄙视人，正和耶稣之恨那些犹太法学家法利赛人一样。我们这个世界上从来就没有一个伟人不是疾恶如仇的。孔子有时也能十分粗野，《论语》就记载他老人家有四五次当着人面说出很刻薄的话。他那种粗野，今日的儒家都不敢表现，都办不到了。孔子恨之入骨的就是那些善恶不分的好好先生，那些伪善的"乡愿"，他说那是"德之贼"。有一次，一个乡愿式的人物叫孺悲的，要见孔子。《论语》上这样记载：

孺悲欲见孔子。孔子辞以疾。将命者出户，取瑟而歌，使之闻之。

这明明是要孺悲听见孔子在家。这段文字使所有的孔学家茫然不解。因为他们以为孔子是圣人，不是肉体凡胎的人，一向是彬彬如也恭而有礼的。这种正统的见解自然全然剥夺了孔子的人性。《论语》里另一段文字也使儒家学者感到困惑，在《孟子》一书中也有记载。那故事是这样：一个贪官名叫阳货，送给孔子一只猪蹄髈。因为阳货与孔子二人彼此毫无好感，阳货单找孔子不在家时，把一只猪蹄髈送到孔家，用以表示对孔子的敬意。孔子也特别用心，趁阳货不在家时前往道谢，留下了自己的名片。《论语》上有这样一段文字：

阳货欲见孔子，孔子不见。归孔子豚。孔子时其亡也，而往拜之……

弟子有一次向夫子问当代的王公大人为何等人物，孔子回答说："那些都是酒囊饭桶啊！"

又有一次，孔子评论一个以在母丧中歌唱出名的人。孔子斥责他说："你年轻时，狂妄不听教训。长大时，你一事无成。现在你老了，又老而不死。你简直是个祸害！"于是孔子用手中的杖打原壤的腿。在《论语》里有下列这段文字：

原壤夷俟（原壤蹲在地下等候孔子），子曰："幼而不孙弟，长而无述焉，老而不死，是为贼。"以杖叩其胫。

事实上，在孔子的所言所行上有好多趣事呢。孔子过的日子里那充实的欢乐，完全是合乎人性，合乎人的感情，完全充满艺术的高雅。因为孔子具有深厚的情感，敏锐的感性，高度的优美。孔子的得意高足颜回不幸早逝，孔子哭得极为伤心。有人问他为什么那么哭，为什么哭得浑身抽搐颤动，他回答说："我哭得太伤心了吗？我若不这么哭他，我还为谁这么痛哭呢？"原文是：

颜渊死，子哭之恸。从者曰："子恸矣！"曰："有恸乎？非夫人之为恸，而谁为？"

有一次，孔子偶然经过一个老相识的丧礼，就进门去吊祭，看见别人哭，受了那哀哭的感动，自己也哭起来。他出来之后，让弟子把他的鞍鞯上拿下一个零件来，给丧家送进去，作为祭礼，并且说："拿进去当做祭礼吧。平白无故去哭祭，不带什么礼品最讨厌了。"由此可见孔子很容易受感动，也很容易流眼泪，可见孔子的感情是多么丰富。

孔子这个人，能歌唱，能演奏乐器，如琴瑟等，并且把《诗经》重编，再配上音乐，他当然是个艺术家。我曾指出，孔子是个爱好礼乐的人。由下面一事，亦可以证明孔子是具有基督教圣公会那样宗教家的气质，雅爱礼仪音乐；但和耶稣对于律法、先知及宗教中的仪礼之不甚措意、不那么喜爱，则正好是个鲜明的对比。在安息日，耶稣曾命人到一个地洞里去救一头牛。对这种事，孔子也许赞成，也许不赞成。孔子的弟子子贡有一次提议把祭祀典礼上的羊省去，孔子说："赐啊，你爱那只羊，我爱的是那典礼啊。"《论语》上那段原文是这样：

子贡欲去告朔之饩羊。子曰："赐也，尔爱其羊，我爱其礼。"

不管怎么样，我们可以说，孔子是对动物不太关心的人。因为，还有一次，孔子听说他家的马棚着了火，他只问有没有人受伤，他不问马如何。《论语》上此一段原文是：

厩焚。子退朝，曰："伤人乎？"不问马。

由于孔子有深厚的艺术气质，他才说人的教育应当以学诗开其端，继之以敦品励行，最后"成于乐"。又据记载，孔子如果听人唱歌而自己也喜欢时，他总是请人再唱一次，而且自己也在重叠唱词之处参加歌唱。由于孔子具有此等艺术气质，他对饮食衣着也很挑剔。我曾在别处指出来，他对饮食如此挑剔，可能就是他妻子弃他而去的原因（见林语堂著作《生活的艺术》）。比如说，菜的季节不对，那种菜孔子不吃；烹调的方法不对，孔子不吃；用的作料不对，孔子也不吃。而且席位不正他还不肯坐。穿的衣裳怎样配颜色，他也很有眼光。现代的女裁缝很容易了解为什么孔子要用黑羔羊皮袍子配黑面子，白羊皮袍子配白面子，狐皮则配黄面子。孔子在衣裳上也小有发明之才。他盖的被子超过他本人的身长一半，这样好免得脚冷。为了做事方便，他要右袖子比左袖子短，他难得想到这样妙主意，但是这个妙主意可能惹他夫人生气，且气跑了（以上见《论语·乡党》，及本书第五章第二节）。孔子的贵族气质甚至使孔子趋向于休妻。孔子本人及其后的两代，他儿子及孙子不是休妻便是与妻子分居。在孔门儒家传统上，孔子本人，他的大弟子曾子，曾子的门人子思，这三代期间都不断有休妻的记载。据记载，儒学第四代大师孟子（受业于子思之门），也几乎把妻子休掉。这几位儒学大师虽非特别富有，但都是贵族，当无疑问。

孔子的最重要的若干特点之一，就是孔子的学问渊博而毕生好学。这足以真正说明为何他的声望如此之隆。孔子本人也屡次说过这种话。孔子自己承认并非那种"生而知之者"，他只是一个"学而不厌，诲人不倦"的人而已。他承认"十室之邑，必有忠信如丘者焉。不如丘之好学也"。他认为可忧愁的若干事之中有一件，那就是荒废学业。他说的话里我发现有一句，其中所显示出的遗憾，正和现代考古学家所感到的遗憾完全相同。他想重建古代的宗教礼仪，于是到杞国去求访夏代的古俗遗物，到宋国以求访商代宗教习俗礼仪，但是并无所获。他说："夏礼吾能言之，杞不足征也。殷礼吾能言之，宋不足征也。文献不足故也。足，吾能征之矣。"换句话说，孔子根本上是个历史学家，他力图从当时尚存的风俗古物以及文献之中，去研究并保存已然淹没的古代礼仪制度。他竭尽精力之所得，就是他整理编著的"五经"。严格说，正如清朝学人章学诚所说

"六经皆史"，所以"五经"就是史书，自与"四书"不同。我想孔子之如此受人仰望，并不见得怎么由于他是当年最伟大的智者，而倒是由于他是当年最渊博的学人，他能将古代的经典学问授予徒众。当时有很丰厚的古代政治制度的学问，也有更为丰富的有关古代宗教典礼的知识，那些古代神权政治有些部分已然没落，有的已日趋衰微，尤其商朝那套古礼，这些情形，由孔子手订的"五经"里即可看出。据说孔子有弟子三千人，其中七十二人精通《诗经》《尚书》《礼记》、音乐。孔子坚信历史的价值，因为他相信人类文化必然会继续。在本书第三章"《中庸》"内，可以看出孔子认为在治国平天下的大业上，有三个必要条件：个人的道德、政治地位、历史的传统，缺一而为政，不足以成功，不足以立信。政治制度不论如何好，单此一个条件，也无成功之望。孔门的学术研究，结果发展成为历史丰厚的遗产，而当时其他学派，在此方面则全付阙如。因此我个人相信，儒家之能战胜其他学派如道家、墨家，一半是由于儒家本身的哲学价值，一半也由于儒家的学术地位。儒家为师者确实可以拿出东西来教学生，而学生也确实可以学而有所收获。那套真实的学问就是历史，而其他学派只能夸示一下自己的意见与看法，"兼爱"也罢，"为己"也罢，没有具体的内容。

关于孔子和蔼可亲的风趣，必须在此一提。因为这可以说明我在前面所说孔子所过的生活是充实而快活的日子，这和宋朝理学家那种窒息生机、大煞风景的教条是大异其趣的，并且由此也可以看出孔子的单纯和伟大。孔子不是一个爱"耍嘴皮子"的人，但有时候他也不由得说几句俏皮话，像下面几句便是："凡是自己不说'怎么办呢？怎么办呢？'的人，我对这种人也没法怎么办。"《论语》的原文是：

子曰："不曰'如之何？如之何？'者，吾未如之何也已矣。"

他又说：知道自己犯了过错而不肯改，那是又犯了过错。有时孔子也用《诗经》上的句子小发风趣诙谐之词。《诗经》上有一首诗，在诗里情人说"不是不想念，而是你家离得太远了"，才没法与他相会。孔子论到这首诗时说："我看那女的心里根本就不想那个男的，否则怎么会嫌路途遥远呢。"《论语》里原文为：

"唐棣之华，偏其反而。岂不尔思，室是远而。"子曰："未之思也。夫何远之有？"

但是我们觉得孔子独具的风趣，也就是最好的风趣，那种风趣是孔子在挖苦自己时自然流露出来的。孔子有好多时候可以嘲笑自己表面的缺点，或是承认别人对他的批评正中要害。他的风趣有时只是他们师生之间偶尔轻微的玩笑而已，并无深意可言。有一次，一个村民说："孔子真够伟大的！什么都通，件件稀松。"孔子听见这样的批评，就对学生说："那么我要专攻什么呢？是射箭呢？还是驾车呢？"《论语》上的原文是：

达巷党人曰："大哉孔子！博学，而无所成名！"子闻之，谓弟子曰："吾何执？执御乎？执射乎？吾执御矣。"

和这里相关联的还有一件事。孔子一次向学生开玩笑说："若是能发财，让我去给人赶马车我都干。若是办不到，那还是从我之所好吧。"《论语》原文是：

子曰："富而可求也，虽执鞭之士，吾亦为之。如不可求，从吾所好。"

又孔子周游列国，政治的谋求终不得意，有一次，子贡说："这儿有一块宝玉，在盒子里装着出卖，是不是待高价卖出呢？"孔子说："卖！当然卖！我就是正等着高价卖出呢！"《论语》原文是：

子贡曰："有美玉于斯，韫椟而藏诸？求善价而沽诸？"
子曰："沽之哉！沽之哉！我待贾者也。"

如果评论或注解《论语》的人，不肯把这种文字看做是孔子的风趣或诙谐，那就陷入了困难，弄得十分尴尬。而事实上，孔子和弟子往往彼此开玩笑。有一次，孔子周游列国时，路途中遇到了困难。孔子被村民误认作欺负村中人而遭兵丁围困。最后终于逃出来，但是得意高足颜回却晚到了。孔子对他说："我以为你死了呢。"颜回回答说："老师您还健在，我怎么敢死！"《论语》原文是：

子畏于匡，颜渊后。子曰："吾以汝为死矣。"曰："子在，回何敢死？"

另一次，孔子及诸弟子在路途中失散。弟子后来听见一群人说，有一个人，高大个子，脑门很高，好像古代的帝王，在东门那儿站着呢，那副垂头丧气的样子，简直像个丧家之犬。弟子后来终于找到孔子，就把这些话告诉了孔子。孔子说："我像不像古代的帝王，我倒不知道。至于说我像个丧家之犬，他说得不错！一点儿也不错！"《史记·孔子世家》中有下面一段文字：

　　孔子适郑，与弟子相失。孔子独立郭东门。郑人或谓子贡曰："东门
有人，其颡似尧，其项类皋陶，其肩类子产，然自要以下，不及禹三寸。
累累若丧家之狗。"子贡以实告孔子，孔子欣然笑曰："形状，末也。而谓
似丧家之狗，然哉！然哉！"

　　这真是最富有风趣的话。而最为我喜爱的，是孔子真个在雨中歌唱
（见本书第二章"孔子生平"）。事实是，孔子带领弟子这一群学者到处漂
泊，在陈、蔡两国之间的旷野荒郊，彷徨踯躅，历时三载，饱经艰险。虽
然满腹经纶，竟找不到个安身之处，这种生不逢时，也实在令人恻然。那
些年的周游列国之后，孔子觉得无法施展政治上的抱负，乃返回山东故乡
著书立说，编辑经典。他把自己和门生比做非牛非虎无以名之的一群兽，
在旷野中流浪。他紧接着问门人，他自己到底有什么错误，有什么可非难
之处。学生中第三个人回答之后，孔子觉得满意，向这些巧于应对的门人
笑着说："颜回，是这样吗？你若家中富有，我愿到你家当个管家。"这一
段话真使我倾倒，使我好喜爱孔夫子。从这一整段看，这种师生的关系之
美、之哀感动人，真可以与《圣经》中叙述耶稣被捕时那段文字相比，只
是孔子这一段是个欢乐的收场，与耶稣不同而已。

三、本书的取材及计划

　　本书前面提到过，儒家把古代中国的史学已然是独自掌握了，这其
中包括当时已然成为古文的中国文字，而他们专精的史学就是儒家传之

于后世的"五经"。在公元前213年（秦始皇三十四年），秦始皇下令，除去医药、天文、农业诸种书籍之外，其他书籍一律焚毁。次年，因当时儒生批评这位修筑万里长城的秦始皇，他又下令活埋了儒生四百六十人。没想到秦始皇创立的这个"万世"的帝国，在屠杀儒生的五年之后，竟会溃灭，而焚书以前曾经能背诵儒家经典的儒生还有健在的。这些老儒生便凭记忆口头背诵出那些经典，大概又借着当时他们藏匿的部分竹简，算把那些经典从这一空前的文化浩劫中抢救了。那些老儒生就以自己记诵的那一套学问传授学生，又把那些经典写出来，因为中国文字在秦始皇统治期间由李斯将大篆简化成为小篆，字形上已有很大的变化，当时儒生写出经典所用的文字是当时的文字，所以叫作"今文"。此后百年间，有上面刻着古文的竹简陆续发现，总算逃过了劫难。最主要的是汉武帝末年鲁共王拆孔子宅所发现墙壁中隐藏的《礼记》《论语》《孝经》，全是秦前的籀文。因为是古文，其时群儒开始用当时的"今文"翻译阐释，此事虽然艰巨，但还可以译出。因此之故，中国古代经典便出现了古文版本，此种根据古文译出的经典便与今文版本的经典有了差异，尤其是关于古代社会、政治，与远古帝王神话性的记载。今文派与古文派的差异在汉代已然明显，当时经学大师郑玄极力想做调人，想牵合而融通之。汉后诸朝正统儒者说《诗经》与《春秋》者，皆依据古文本，而《礼记》（亦为"五经"之一）则依据今文本。直到清朝，经学家采用科学的比较方法恢复了今文本的地位，两种版本的差异才判然以分。经过运用每一片段的证据，每一种历史批评的方法与哲学研究，其最为出色的成就，则是证明《尚书》五十八章之中有二十五章为伪造，因此确定了《尚书》实为三十三篇，这正是《今文尚书》的版本。一般而论，并非是古文为伪造，而是我们现行的古文本是伪造的。

　　"儒家经典"一词，指的是"五经"和"四书"。前面已然提过，"五经"是古史，是孔门的学问，经过孔子编订，孔子也以之授诸生并传给了后代。"四书"，大体而论，则代表孔门弟子的著作，是其弟子记载孔子说的话与孔子思想的阐述。有时我们也说"十三经"。"十三经"中所包括的书名由书后的附表中可以看出。我们要知道，在孔子当年，那时说"六经"而非"五经"。所加上的一经为《乐经》，《乐经》之中今日尚存在人间的，是《礼记》中的《乐记》（见本书第十章）。

　　通常研究孔子的智慧，都是直接从"四书"下手，这是一种错误，因为这种方法没有什么结果。原因是，"四书"是一部未经编辑杂乱无章的孔子语录，往往是从别处记载的长篇论说中摘来的语句，原来在别处时，其含义清楚得多。还有，在不同的章节内也有重复的引用语句，计有二十处，这足以表示《论语》这部书是由数人动手写的，并未经一人编订。有数章显然是由曾子的门人编写，其中曾子说的语句特多。每一章中各种含义不同的语句，都未按层次种类分别编定；有时可以看出一个主旨所在，更多的时候则不能，在若干章之后，很明显地可以看出有后人的增补部分，有时不是在章节后增补，而是在正文中间插入的。本书第十章的《乐记》，显然并不完整。

　　西方人读《论语》而研究儒家思想时，最大的困难在于西方人读书的习惯。他们要求的是接连不断地讲述，作者要一直说下去，他们听着才满意。由书中摘取一行一句，用一两天不断去思索，在头脑中体会消化，再由自己的反省与经验去证实，他们根本就不肯这样。而事实上，在读《论语》时，必须把个别的格言警句分开，逐日分别去咀嚼，不要贪多，同时去思索，这才是读《论语》这部书的方法。但是对现代的读书人来说，这显然办不到。再者，谁也不能只靠读《论语》一部书，而对孔子思想的发展得到全面一贯的认识。

这就是为什么我不得不从儒家经典中选出若干章来，因为这些章代表前后连贯的思想，而这些文章是属于一个系统的，是集中于一个主题的。事实上，在《礼记》中有孔子连续一贯的对白，本书第六、七章便是明证。在第三、四章论《中庸》及《大学》时，仍然有用散文形式表达的连贯性的理论发挥。实际上，本书中我所选译的九章（《孔子世家》除外），有六章见于《礼记》，其余两章一部分选自《孟子》，另一部分是选自《论语》，而按类别排定的，还有选自《礼记》的片段。由上述可见，本书除由《礼记》中选取五章之外，还有四章（第三、四、五、十一章）表达同样内容的文字选自"四书"。"四书"在以前是儿童必读的，所以本书的编辑还是采用合乎正统的方式。"四书"中的《大学》与《中庸》，原是《礼记》中的两篇，由宋儒朱熹提升到与《论语》《孟子》并列的程度，而成为"四书"。至于《礼记》中其他各章未得升格获选，其理由就不得而知了。

通常有个问题，就是《礼记》里孔子所说的话，甚至《论语》里孔子的话，是不是精确可靠。这也引起了一个更大的问题。那就是，孔子、释迦牟尼、苏格拉底等贤哲所说的话，究竟有多少可信？比如说，柏拉图所写苏格拉底的对话，又有多少可信呢？以同样态度看《圣经》中的四福音，也发现四福音中有矛盾之处。我们也发现在《论语》《孟子》《礼记》三书之中，孔子所说的话在措辞上也微有不同。若说柏拉图在记载苏格拉底的话时，一定也染上了些柏拉图自己的笔调语气，这是无可避免的。《礼记》中好多章，一定也难免此种情形。现代政界名人曾受记者访问过的，一定深信记者笔下的文字和他自己所说的话实在不可能完全相同。除去录音之外，绝没有别的方法能使政客相信那是他亲口说的话。

我曾在前提过，《礼记》只是儒家所独自搜集的各式各样古代的记录文字，其来源一定是纷杂不一。这些篇文字（其中包括《中庸》），后人归诸孔子的孙子子思所作，其他若干篇，尤其是在《大戴礼记》中的，毫无疑问是子思或是子思的门人传下来的。论教育与音乐的文字，毫无疑问反映出荀子的思想。荀子与孟子同时，虽然也属儒家，但孟子鄙视他。另外，《礼记》中有甚多部分专论丧礼，占全书比例之大令人吃惊，而《大戴礼记》则对此等文字概付阙如，却有很多章讨论哲理、礼服与祭器。还有若干章论节庆风俗规矩，如婚礼、射箭、舞蹈、村中节庆、宴饮，及其他比赛（该书第四十章《投壶》，详记竞技的规矩，颇类似我们在射箭场上之所见）。第五章甚为重要，是今文本论古代行政制度的基础，正如《周礼》是古文本的基础一样。还有其他章文字叙述妇女与儿童的品行以及一般礼节规矩。比如第一章，除去讲礼仪的哲理之外，也包括下列的训教：

"不要滚米饭成团，不要将米饭抛弃在桌上，口边不可有汤流出。不可咂嘴出声，不可啃骨头，勿将鱼翻转，勿以骨头投予狗食，勿拼命挑取一块肉。勿翻松米饭以使之变凉，勿用筷子挑食稀粥。勿大声吞咽汤汁，勿将汤翻搅，勿剔牙，勿在汤内加酱油等物……用牙咬已煮熟之肉，但勿用牙咬干肉。"

《礼记·曲礼上》第一原文是：

毋抟饭，毋放饭，毋流歠，毋咤食，毋啮骨，毋反鱼肉，毋投与狗骨，毋固获，毋扬饭。饭黍毋以箸，毋嚽羹，毋絮羹，毋刺齿，毋歠醢……濡肉齿决，干肉不齿决。

这段文字读来如同《圣经·旧约》里的《申命记》。并且应当懂得"礼教"这个宗教，也像犹太教一样，是包括宗教崇拜与日常生活在内的，甚至连饮食也在内。

本书的计划如下：第二章首次把孔子的传记译成英文，这是孔子最早的传记，也是孔子唯一的传记，依大史学家司马迁的《孔子世家》英译的。第三章是论《中庸》，这一章给儒学系统一个完整适当的基础。第四章论伦理与政治（《大学》），虽然在伦理与政治之间，个人生活、家庭生活、国家世界之间的立论未必允当，文字则是前后一贯的论辩。第五章是经过重新排列重新选录的《论语》文本，大体而论，是本书最为隽永有味的一章。第六、七、八三章，也就是我称之为关于社会方面的"孔氏三论"，这一部分文字应当足以将"礼"的含义解释清楚。若只将礼字作礼仪或典礼讲，就大为错误了。第八章特别包括了一篇短而重要的一段文字，是孔子对世界和平与社会道德最高境界的憧憬。第九章与第十章是孔子对教育与音乐的看法，其见解、观点，是特别现代的。论音乐的第十章，也就是《乐记》，是《礼记》一书中最长的一章，实际上是从已然散失的《乐经》一书的十二章编来的。这些之后，是选自《孟子》的文字，这些文字显示了儒家哲学最重要最有影响力的发展。

Chapter One *INTRODUCTION*

I. THE CHARACTER OF CONFUCIAN IDEAS

Can one be enthusiastic about Confucianism nowadays? I wonder. The answer seems to depend on whether one can be enthusiastic about sheer good sense, a thing which people usually cannot work up very much enthusiasm for. The more important question seems to be whether one can believe in Confucianism nowadays. This is especially important to the modern Chinese of today, a question that directly challenges their minds and cannot be brushed aside. For there is a centrality or, shall I say, universality, about the Confucian attitude and point of view, reflected in a joy in Confucian belief that I see even among maturing modern Chinese who have received a Western education. The centrality and basic appeal of its humanism have a strange strength of their own. During the political chaos and battle of ideas in the centuries immediately following Confucius, Confucianism won the victory over Taoism, Motianism, Naturalism, Legalism and a host of other philosophies. It maintained this supremacy over the Chinese people for the length of two thousand five hundred years, with the exception of a few periods, and it always came back to its own stronger than even. Apart from Taoism which was in fashion in the third to sixth centuries A.D., its strongest rival was Buddhism, which attained a great vogue with the Sung scholars.

But with all its fine metaphysics, Buddhism succeeded only in modifying the interpretation of the method of arriving at knowledge and the aim of this humanist culture. It shifted the emphasis to certain ideas originally in the Confucian classics and directed a fuller attention to them, but did not replace Confucianism itself. Perhaps it was merely the old prestige of Confucius, but there was a great pride among the Confucian scholars, a belief in their own correctness, which made these scholars renounce Buddhism and look askance at it with toleration or contempt, as the case may have been. The same common sense that crushed the mysticism of Chuangtse also made them renounce the mysticism of Buddhism. Today Confucianism meets a still greater rival, not Christianity, but the entire system of Western thought and life and the coming of a new social order, brought about by the industrial age. As a political system aiming at the restoration of a feudal order, Confucianism will probably be put out of date by the developments of modern political science and economics. But as a system of humanist culture, as a fundamental viewpoint concerning the conduct of life and of society, I believe it will still hold its own. Confucianism, as a live force in the Chinese people, is still going to shape our national conduct of affairs. It is in this sense that a study of Confucianism and its fundamental beliefs will be of interest to people of the Western world, in helping them fundamentally to understand the Chinese *ethos* and Chinese *mores*.

To Western readers, Confucius is chiefly known as a wise man speaking in aphorisms or moral maxims, which hardly suffices to explain the depth of the influence of Confucianism. Without a deeper unity of belief or system of thought, no mere collection of aphorisms could dominate a nation's history as Confucianism has dominated China. The answer to the puzzle of Confucius' great prestige and influence has to be sought elsewhere. Without a fundamental system of beliefs which is accepted to be true, maxims and proverbs might easily grow stale and outworn. The *Analects*, the Confucian Bible, is such a collection of moral maxims, and it is chiefly through the

Analects that Confucianism has been made known to the West. But the *Analects* after all is only a collection of the cream of Confucius' sayings, often torn apart from their contexts, which are found with a fuller elucidation in the *Book of Mencius*, *Liki* and other books. After all, Confucius did not talk the whole day in staccato sentences. It would be impossible, therefore, to arrive at a full appreciation of the influence and prestige of Confucius without an understanding of the system of Confucian ideas as a system.

To put it briefly, Confucianism stood for a rationalized social order through the ethical approach, based on personal cultivation. It aimed at political order by laying the basis for it in a moral order, and it sought political harmony by trying to achieve the moral harmony in man himself. Thus its most curious characteristic was the abolition of the distinction between politics and ethics. Its approach was definitely an ethical approach, differing from the Legalists who tried to bring about a strong nation by a rigid enforcement of the law. It was also a positive point of view, with a keen sense of responsibility toward one's fellow men and the general social order, as distinguished from the negative cynicism of Taoism. Fundamentally, it was a humanist attitude, brushing aside all futile metaphysics and mysticism, interested chiefly in the essential human relationships, and not in the world of spirits or in immortality. The strongest doctrine of this particular type of humanism, which accounts for its great enduring influence, is the doctrine that "the measure of man is man," a doctrine which makes it possible for the common man to begin somewhere as a follower of Confucianism by merely following the highest instincts of his own human nature, and not by looking for perfection in a divine ideal.

To be more specific, Confucianism was definitely aiming at the restoration of a rationalized feudal order, with clear gradations of rank, at a time when the feudal system of the Chou Dynasty was breaking down. In order to understand this, one has to go back to a conception of the collapse of the feudal system in Confucius' days and the centuries immediately following. There were hundreds of duchies, baronies, and townships, which had emerged as independent states, with the stronger states growing in power and territory and constantly warring with one another. The power of the Emperor, still holding a theoretic sovereignty over the Chinese Empire, had dwindled to nothing; in fact to such an extent that neither Confucius in his time nor Mencius later, who went about to persuade different kings to put their doctrines into practice, did not even bother to go and see the Emperor. This was a contradiction of his own theory of a rationalized social order, upholding loyalty to the highest authority. The situation was so bad that there was no point in either one of them trying to see the weak Emperor at all. There was, therefore, an international anarchy, resembling conditions in modern Europe. Treaties were scrapped, and there were alliances and big and little ententes, which never lasted very long. Taxation was frightful, in order to keep up the growing armies, and the smaller states were constantly worried about invasions by the powerful neighboring states. Conferences were constantly held, now with the ruler of one leading state and now with that of another sitting as the chairman. Philosophers began to develop the distinction between "offensive" and "defensive" warfare and between "aggressors" and "victims." Curiously, there developed a kind of intellectual internationalism; scholars moved about and switched their allegiance from one state to another. The ancient rites and insignias of rank had fallen into a terrible confusion; there was great inequality of wealth; and this moral and political chaos set every keen mind thinking about the best way of bringing about peace and order. In this atmosphere, the greatest intellectual activity, coupled with the greatest freedom of thought, brought about the greatest richness and variety in Chinese philosophy. Some repudiated civilization entirely, as Laotse and Chuangtse did; some became budding Communists, believing that every man should work for his living with his hands; some taught the oneness of God, the love of God, and a humanitarian, unselfish and even ascetic personal life, to the extent of repudiating music itself, as Motse did; and there were

Sophists, Stoics, Hedonists, Epicureans and downright Naturalists. Many people, like modern Europeans, began to suspect civilization itself, and harked back to the primitive life, as some modern thinkers are harking back to the African jungle or the Island of Bali. Some others, like Confucius, were like the modern Christians, who believe in the force of moral ideals, in education, in the arts, in continuity with the past, and in maintaining some sort of international decencies and a high moral standard in human relationships, which were all part of the Confucian faith.

The chapter "On the Conduct of the Confucianists" in *Liki* (*Juhsing*, Ch. XLI) distinguishes this school of scholars from the rest. The term *Ju* (Confucianism is known in China as "the religion of the *Ju*" since Confucius' time) was already current in Confucius' day, and the scholars styled as *Ju* were probably a special set of people, conservative in point of view, backed by historical scholarship, and wearing a special *Ju* cap and *Ju* gown as symbols of their belief in the past. The following are a few extracts showing the high moral idealism of this group of followers of Confucius:

> The Duke Ai of Lu asked Confucius, "Is the Master's dress that of the *Ju*?" Confucius replied, "I grew up in Lu and wore a gown with broad sleeves, and stayed later in Sung and therefore wore a cap of black cloth. I have heard it said that a gentleman is broad in his scholarship, but wears the gown of his own state. I do not know if this gown that I wear may be called a *Ju* gown." "What about the conduct of the *Ju*?" asked the Duke, and Confucius replied, "I shall not be able to finish it if I were to describe all the details, and if I did, I would have to stop over here and yet not be able to cover it all, even after you have changed the attendants several times." The Duke then asked Confucius to sit down on the mat, and Confucius sat in his company and said,
>
> "A *Ju* is like one who has jewels in his keeping waiting for sale; he cultivates his knowledge morning and night to prepare himself for

requests for advice; he cherishes integrity and honesty of character against the time when he is appointed; he endeavors to order his personal conduct against the time when he shall be in office. Such is his independence!

"A *Ju* is orderly in his dress and careful in his actions; his great refusals seem like lack of respect and his little refusals seem like false manners; when he appears on public occasions, he looks awe-inspiring, and on small occasions he appears self-retiring; his services are difficult to get and difficult to keep while he appears gentle and weak Such is his appearance!

"A *Ju* may be approached by gentle manners but may not be cowed by force; he is affable but he cannot be made to do what he doesn't want; and he may be killed, but may not be humiliated. He is simple and frugal in his living, and his faults or mistakes may be gently explained but not abruptly pointed out to his face. Such is his strength of character!

"A *Ju* lives with the moderns but studies the ancients. What he does today will become an example for those in the generations to follow. When he lives in times of political chaos, he neither courts favors from those in authority, nor is boosted by those below. and when the petty politicians join hands to defame or injure him, his life may be threatened, but the course of his conduct may not be changed. Although he lives in danger, his soul remains his own, and even then he does not forget the sufferings of the people. Such is his sense of responsibility!

"A *Ju* is broad in his knowledge and not narrow-minded; he cultivates his conduct without cease; and in his private life he does not abandon himself. When he is successful, he does not depart from the truth. In his personal manners he values living in peace and harmony with others. He maintains the beauty of his inner character and is leisurely in his ways He admires those cleverer than himself and is generous toward the masses, and is flexible in principle. Such is his ease of mind and generosity of character!"

Against this background of international anarchy and a collapsing ancient feudal order, the different essential tenets of Confucian teachings will be more readily understood and appreciated, particularly Confucius' efforts to restore an ancient feudal order through ritual and music. The characteristic ideas of this body of teachings are, to my mind, five in number, and since these are also the ideas constantly to be met with in the following translations, an examination of their exact import is essential to a true understanding of Confucianism.

1. THE IDENTIFICATION OF POLITICS AND ETHICS:

The whole emphasis of Confucianism upon ritual and music and its apparent preoccupation with moral platitudes usually strikes the Western readers as queer and almost unintelligible. And yet, nothing is clearer than the fact that the so-called "ritual and music" embody better than any other phrase, the entire aim of the Confucian social order. It sounds almost childishly naive to hear Confucius say, in reply to a question about government by his disciple: "Ah Shih, didn't I tell you before? All that one needs to do is simply for the gentleman to fully understand ritual and music and then apply them to the government! (*Liki*, Ch. XXVIII)." This is easily understood, however, from the Confucian point of view, if we remember the Confucian definition of government as merely an effort to "put things right" or "put things in order." In other words, Confucius was aiming at the moral basis for peace in society, out of which political peace should naturally ensue. The *Analects* reports a conversation as follows: Someone asked Confucius, "Why don't you go into the government?" And Confucius replied, "Is it not said in the *Book of History* concerning filial piety that the King of Chen was a good son and a good brother and then he applied the principles to the government of things? This is also being in the government. Why, therefore, should I go into the government?" In other words, Confucius was almost an anarchist, believing as his highest political ideal in a society of people living in moral harmony which should make government itself unnecessary. This is implied in his saying that "In acting as a judge at lawsuits, I am as good as anyone. But the thing is, to aim so that there should not be any lawsuits at all (*Analects*, XII)." How this is to be achieved will be made clear in the following paragraphs. But it is unmistakable that Confucius held the final aim of government and the criminal law and ritual and music to be identical: "The final goals of ritual and music and the criminal law and government are the same, namely, to bring about a community of the people's aspirations and to result in social and political order" (see Ch. X "On Music"). Confucius was never quite satisfied with the kind of political order achieved by a rigorous administration or enforcement of the criminal law. "Guide the people by governmental measures," he said, "and regulate them by the threat of punishment, and the people will try to keep out of jail, but will have no sense of honor or shame. Guide the people by virtue and regulate them by *li* (sense of propriety) and the people will have a sense of honor and respect." There are then two kinds of political order, and it is in this sense that Confucius once said, "When the kingdom Ch'i moves a step forward, it will have reached the culture of the kingdom of Lu (his own state), *i.e.*, the first stage of peace that he spoke of; and when the kingdom of Lu moves a step forward, it will have reached the stage of true civilization, *i.e.*, the second stage."

2. *LI*, OR THE RATIONALIZED SOCIAL ORDER:

Confucianism, besides being known in China as "the religion of Confucius" and "the religion of the *Ju*," is further known as "the religion of *li*, or ritual." It will at once be sensed by Western readers, that there is much more to this conception of *li* than merely ritualism itself, or the entire Confucian system is a sham and a fake. We have to meet this fact squarely, for the phrase "ritual and music" occurs again and again in the Confucian texts and seems to embody the entire Confucian system of outward social order, as the conception of "true manhood" seems to embody the essence of Confucian teachings regarding personal conduct. The importance and exact meaning of the phrase "ritual and music" will be made amply clear in the *Three Confucian Discourses* (Chs. VI, VII, VIII). Here it is only necessary to point out that Confucius' own definitions of government and of *li* exactly coincide. Government is defined as putting things or people in order, but *li* is also defined as "the order of things" (*Liki*, XXVIII). The Chinese word *li* therefore cannot be rendered by an English word. On one extreme, it means "ritual,""propriety"; in a generalized sense, it simply means "good manners"; in its highest philosophic sense, it means an ideal social order with everything in its place, and particularly a rationalized feudal order which was breaking down in Confucius' days, as I have already pointed out.

To adhere to the philosophic meaning, Confucius was trying to restore a social order, based on love for one's kind and respect for authority, of which the social rites of public worship and festivities in ritual and music should be the outward symbols. Of course, the rituals of worship lead straight back to primitive religious rites and ceremonies, and it is clear that this so-called "religion of *li*" was truly semi-religious in character, being related to God at one end in the sacrifice to heaven by the Emperor, and related to the common people at the other end by the teachings of affection and discipline and respect for authority in the home life. There have existed different religious sacrifices to heaven or God, to the ancestors of the rulers, to the spirits of the earth and the mountains and rivers. Confucius, as reported several times in the *Analects* and the *Liki*, said that he did not know of the meaning of these particular sacrifices to God and the Imperial Ancestors, known as *chiao* and *t'i*, and that if he did, it would be as easy to rule the world as to turn over one's hand. In this aspect, the body of Confucian thought resembles most the laws of Moses, and it is easier to compare Confucius in the *scope* of his teachings to Moses than to any other philosopher. The *li* of Confucius, like the laws of

Moses, covers both religious laws and laws of civil life and considers the two as integrated parts of a whole. After all, Confucius was a product of his times, living in what Comte calls the "religious" era.

Furthermore, Confucius would undoubtedly have been a High Churchman in temperament, an Episcopalian or a Roman Catholic, if he were a Christian. He loved the rituals of worship, certainly not as merely ceremonial acts without meaning, but with his clear knowledge of human psychology, he saw that the proper rituals brought about in the worshipper a respectful or God-fearing state of mind. Furthermore, he was a conservative, like all Episcopalians or Roman Catholics, and believed in authority and in continuity with the past. Personally, his artistic sense was too keen for him not to be moved by the appeal of ceremonies and music, of which we have ample evidence in the *Analects* (see Ch. V, Sec. 2, "The Emotional and Artistic Life of Confucius"). And as the worship of God and the ancestors of the rulers was to bring about a state of true piety, so the ceremonies of drinking festivals and archery contests in the villages, accompanied with song and dance and kowtowing, teaching the villagers to observe form and order in their festivities, were also to bring about a sense of general order and courtesy among the masses.

Psychologically, therefore, the functions of ritual and music are the same. Confucianism gave a sort of philosophic and even poetic meaning to ritual and music and dance. This is nothing surprising, considering that Confucius himself was a great lover of music, learned to play on musical instruments from a master of music at the age of twenty-nine, and constantly sang and played on the *ch'in* (a string instrument) even amidst his troubles. It is definitely stated that the six branches of study in Confucius' time were: ritual, music, archery, carriage driving, writing and mathematics. Confucius himself edited the *Book of Songs* at the age of sixty-four, and it is said that after this job of editing, the different songs were first shifted and properly classified with respect to their accompanying music. In fact, Confucius' own school, according to reports, seemed continually to echo with the sounds of song and music, and Tsekung, when placed in charge of a town, began to teach the people to sing, which induced a smile and a joke from Confucius (Ch. V, Sec. 3). The philosophic meaning of ritual and music is fully developed in Chapter X. The gist of it is: "when you see a nation's dance, you know the character of the people"; "music comes from the heart, while ritual comes from the outside"; "music is a sense of joy—what cannot be restrained or replaced from the human heart"; "the different kinds of music in different countries are an indication of the different *mores* of the different peoples"; "music harmonizes the community, while ritual draws its social distinction"; "music represents heaven or the abstract, while ritual represents the earth or the concrete"; finally "therefore the ancient kings instituted ritual and music not only to satisfy our desires of the ear and the eye and the mouth and the stomach, but in order to teach the people to have the right taste or the right likes and dislikes and restore the human order to its normalcy."

Naturally, the whole system of *li* embodies also a concrete plan of a social hierarchy, concluding with a prodigious amount of scholarship regarding rules and ceremonies for the religious sacrifices, the festivities of drinking and archery and the conduct of men and women and children and the taking are of old people. This branch of Confucian historical scholarship was best developed by Hsuntse, a great philosopher whose books still exist and who was a contemporary and rival of Mencius, while its philosophic meaning is also fully developed in the *Liki* (see the *Three Confucian Discourses*, Chs. VI, VII, VIII), which largely reflect Hsuntse's interpretations.

This understanding of the importance of *li* helps us also to understand another corollary of Confucius' doctrines, the importance of terminology, that is, everything should be called by its right name. Therefore, when Confucius wrote the political annals of his time and the two preceding centuries, called the *Ch'unch'iu* or *Spring and Autumn*, his intention was largely to restore the social order by sharp distinctions in terminology. A ruler killing a rebellious general would be called *sha*, while a prince or a minister killing his ruler would be called *shih*. When the Baron of Wu assumed the title of "king," Confucius merely wrote down "Baron Wu," thinking that he had degraded him by that single word in his Chronicles.

3. HUMANISM:

The finest philosophic perception of Confucius, it seems to me, is his recognition that "the measure of man is man." If it were not so, the whole system of Confucian ethics would fall to pieces, and would immediately become impracticable. The whole philosophy of ritual and music is but to "set the human heart right," and the kingdom of God is truly within the man himself. The problem for any man intending to cultivate his personal life is merely to start out on a hunt for the best in his human nature and steadfastly to keep to it. That is practically the essence of Confucian ethics. This results in the doctrine of the Golden Rule, and is best explained in Chapter III, "Central Harmony." Of course as a part of this humanism, there is a high and fine conception of *jen* or "true manhood," about which Confucius constantly talked, but which, as a qualification, he consistently refused to allow to all except two of his disciples and three great men in history. Confucius was constantly reluctant to fix this concept of a "true man," and when he was asked whether such and such a good man was a "true man," in nine cases out of ten he refused to apply that epithet to a living man. But, as is made clear in the chapter on "Central Harmony," Confucius also pointed out that in order to climb high, one had to begin from the low ground, and in order to reach a distant place, one had to begin by making a first step, and once he said, "Being a good son and a good younger brother provides already the basis for being a true man."

The conception *jen* (true manhood) is as difficult to translate as the conception of *li*. In Chinese writing, this character is composed of "two" and "man," signifying the relationship between men; in its present pronunciation, it is identical with the sound for "man," but in the ancient language it had a pronunciation which was identical to that of "man" in a particular

phrase, quoted by a Han commentator, but unrecognizable today. In certain
instances in Confucian books, the word for "true manhood" is actually used
interchangeably with the common word for "man," the clearest instance of
which occurs in the *Analects*, where a disciple speaks about "a man failing
into a well," the word for "man" being written with the word for "true
manhood," usually translated as "kindness" or "benevolence." Anyway the
association of ideas is clear. In the English language in different words, such
as *human, humane, humanitarian*, and *humanity*, the last word has a double
meaning of "mankind" and "kindness." Both Confucius and Mencius also
once defined "true manhood" as the "love of man." But the matter is not so
simple. In the first place, as I have pointed out, Confucius refused to give a
concrete example of a true man, whereas certainly he would not have refused
to give a concrete example of merely "a kind man." In the second place, this
"true manhood" is often described as a state of mind, a state that one "searches
for," "attains," "feels at peace in," "departs from," "is based upon," and
(Mencius) "dwells in," as in a house.

The essential idea of *jen* is therefore a conception of the state when man
is truly himself, and from this point on, Mencius starts out on his whole
philosophy about the essence of human nature, and finds that "human nature
is good," while Hsuntse, believing that human nature is bad and taking up
the other end of Confucian teachings regarding educations and music and the
system of social order and outward forms of moral conduct, develops the idea
of *li*, with emphasis on restraint. In common English phraseology, we speak
of certain people among our acquaintances as "a real man" or "a real person,"
and this seems to come closest to the Confucian conception of *jen*. On the
one hand, we begin to understand why Confucius refused to give so many
good men of his day that label, as we can see today how many men or women
we would be willing to call "a real person," in its most ideal sense. (Abraham
Lincoln certainly was one.) On the other hand, we do find that the approach
to being a real man is after all not so difficult, and that anyone can be a real

person if he keeps his heart right and has some contempt for the artificialities of civilization—in other words, every common person can be a real man if he wants to. This fully fits in with the Confucian and Mencian statement that to be a real man, one merely needs to start out by being a good son or daughter or brother of sister, or a good citizen. I consider, therefore, my translation of *jen* as "true manhood" fully accurate and adequate. In certain places, it will have to be rendered merely as "kindness," just as the word *li* in certain places will have to be rendered merely as "ritual" or "ceremony" or "manners."

Actually, Mencius arrived at the position that men are all created equal in goodness of heart, and that "all men can be like the Emperors Yao and Shun" (the Confucian models of perfect virtue). It is this humanistic approach of climbing high from the low and reaching the distance from the nearby, and of making an easy start in virtue or the development of character that accounts for the great fascination of Confucianism over the Chinese people, as distinguished from the much more idealistic doctrine of Motse, teaching actually the "fatherhood of God" and "universal love," so akin to Christianity. The humanistic idea of measuring man by man not only forces one to discover the true self, but naturally also results in the Golden Rule, known in Chinese as *shu*, namely, as Confucius repeatedly said, "Do not do unto others what you would not have others do unto you." Confucius not only gave this as a definition of the "true man," but also said that it was *the* central thread of all his teachings. The word for *shu* (meaning "reciprocity") is written in Chinese with the two elements "a heart" and "alike." In modern Chinese, it usually means "forgiveness," but the transition is easy to understand, for if you assume that all men's reactions are the same in a particular circumstance, and if you place yourself in the other man's position, you would naturally forgive. Confucianism, therefore, constantly reverted to the personal test of how would you feel yourself or "finding it in yourself." The best analogy, as given in Chapter III, is that of a carpenter trying to make an axe-handle—all he needs to do is to look at the handle of the axe in his own band for a model.

He will not have to go far. The measure of man is man.

4. PERSONAL CULTIVATION AS THE BASIS OF A WORLD ORDER:
The ethical approach of Confucianism to the problems of politics has
already been made clear. Put in the plainest terms, Confucius believed that
a nation of good sons and good brothers could not help making an orderly,
peaceful nation. Confucianism traced back the ordering of a national life
to the regulation of the family life and the regulation of the family life to
the cultivation of the personal life. That means very much about the same
thing as when modern educators tell us that the reform of the present
chaotic world after all must ultimately depend on education. The logical
connections between a world order as the final aim and the cultivation of
the personal life by individuals as a necessary start are made perfectly plain in
the chapter, "Ethics and Politics" (Ch. IV) and also in Chapter III, Section
6, and throughout the Chapters VI, VII, VIII. The Chinese preoccupation
with moral maxims and platitudes becomes then intelligible, for they are not
detached aphorisms, but are part of a well-rounded political philosophy.

Interpreted in the light of modern psychology, this doctrine can
be reduced easily to two theories, the theory of habit and the theory of
imitation. The whole emphasis on "filial piety," more clearly translated by
myself as "being a good son," is psychologically based on the theory of habit.
Confucius and Mencius literally said that, having acquire the habits of love
and respect in the home, one could not but extend this mental attitude of love
and respect to other people's parents and elder brothers and to the authorities
of the state. As stated in Chapter IV, "when the individual families have
learned kindness, then the whole nation has learned kindness, and when the
individual families have learned courtesy, then the whole nation has learned
courtesy." The teaching of young children to love their parents and brothers
and to be respectful to their superiors lays the foundation of right mental and
moral attitudes for growing up to be good citizens.

5. THE INTELLECTUAL UPPER CLASS:

The theory of imitation, or the power of example, results in the doctrine of the intellectual upper class and of "government by example." The intellectual upper class is at the same time a moral upper class, or it fails in its qualifications to be considered the upper class at all. This is the well-known conception of the Confucian "gentleman" or "superior man" or "princely man." This princely man is not at all a super man of the Nietzschean type. He is merely a kind and gentle man of moral principles, at the same time a man who loves learning, who is calm himself and perfectly at ease and is constantly careful of his own conduct, believing that by example he has a great influence over society in general. He is perfectly at ease in his own station of life and has a certain contempt for the mere luxuries of living. All the moral teachings of Confucius are practically grouped around this cultivated gentleman. The Chinese word for this, *chuntse*, was a current term given a new meaning by the usage of Confucius. In many places, it definitely meant "the sovereign" and could not be translated as "gentleman" and still make sense; in other places, it obviously meant only a cultivated "gentleman." With the existence of an intellectual upper class of rulers, the two meanings merged into one another, and formed a concept very similar to Plato's "philosopher king." The theory of the power of example is fully developed in Chapter XII of the *Analects* (see Ch. V of this book, Sec. 9). Confucius had an overweening confidence in the power of moral example. When a rapacious rich official, Chik'angtse, told Confucius that he was worried about the prevalence of robbers and thieves in his state, Confucius bluntly replied, "If you yourself don't love money, you can give the money to the thieves and they won't take it."

II. A BRIEF ESTIMATE OF THE CHARACTER OF CONFUCIUS

The great prestige of Confucius and Confucian teachings during the centuries immediately after his death, as well as in subsequent Chinese history, must be ascribed to three factors: first, the intrinsic appeal of Confucian ideas to the Chinese way of thinking; second, the enormous historical learning and scholarship accumulated and practically monopolized by the Confucianists, in contrast to the other schools which did not bother with historical learning (and this body of scholarship carried enough weight and prestige of its own); and thirdly, the evident charm of personality and prestige of the Master himself. There are in this world certain great teachers, whose personality seems to account for their influence more than their scholarship. We think of Socrates, or of St. Francis of Assisi, who themselves did not write any books of account, but who left such a tremendous impress on their generation that their influence persisted throughout the ages. The charm of Confucius was very much like the charm of Socrates; the very fact that the latter commanded the affection and respect of Plato is sufficient evidence of the power of his personality and his ideas. It is true Confucius edited the *Book of Songs*, and it is also true that he wrote the bare skeleton of events, chronicled in the *Spring and Autumn*, but after all the great tradition of his teachings was put down by his disciples and future followers.

There are, of course, many characterizations of Confucius' personality in the various Confucian books. We get a foretaste of it at the end of Chapter III, on "Central Harmony." His disciple Yen Huei also lauded him to the skies, comparing him to a great mysterious something: "You turn up your head and look at it and it seems so high; you try to drill through it and it seems so hard; it appears to be in front of you and all of a sudden it appears behind you." Some of the best characterizations, however, are the following: It was said that he was "gentle but dignified, austere, yet not harsh, polite and completely at ease." Confucius' self-characterizations were still better. Once a king asked one of his disciples about Confucius and the disciple could not make an answer. The disciple then returned to tell Confucius of the incident, and Confucius replied, "Why didn't you tell him that I am a man who forgets to eat when he is enthusiastic about something, who forgets all his worries when he is happy, and who is not aware that old age is coming on?" In this statement, we see something of the joy of life, the enthusiasm and the positive, persistent urge for doing something. He also said of himself several times that he was not a "saint," but that he admitted he was tireless in learning and in teaching other people. As an illustration of this positive urge in Confucius, there is also the following record. One of his disciples was putting up for the night at a place, and the gatekeeper asked him where he was from. Tselu replied that he was from Confucius and the gatekeeper remarked, "*Oh, is he the fellow who knows that a thing can't be done and still wants to do it?*" There was a high moral idealism in Confucius, a consciousness of a mission, that made him completely believe in himself.

The charm of Confucius' private character really lies in his gentility, as is so clearly shown in his conversational tone with his disciples. Many of the sayings of Confucius contained in the *Analects* can only be interpreted in the light of a leisurely discourse of a humorous teacher with his disciples, with an occasional shot of witticism. Read in this light, some of his most casual remarks become the best. I like, for instance, such perfectly casual sayings as the following: He remarked one day to two or three intimate disciples talking with him, "Do you think that I have hidden anything from the two or three of you? Really, I have hidden nothing from you. There is nothing that I do that I don't share with the two or three of you. That's I." Another instance: Tsekung loved to criticize people and Confucius said, calling him by his intimate name, "Ah Sze, you are very clever, aren't you? I have no time for such things." Another instance: Confucius said, "I really admire a fellow who goes about the whole day with a well-fed stomach and a vacuous mind. How can one ever do it? I would rather that he play chess, which would seem to me to be better." In one instance, Confucius said something derisively about what one of his disciples was doing. The disciple was puzzled, and Confucius explained that he was merely pulling his leg, implying that really he approved. For Confucius was a gay old soul. His gentility and hospitality toward all desiring to learn are recorded in the following incident, resembling a story

in the Bible when Jesus said, "Suffer the little children to come unto me."
The people of a certain village were given to mischief, and one day some
young people from that village came to see Confucius, and the disciples were
surprised that Confucius saw them. Confucius remarked, "Why be so harsh
on them? What concerns me is how they come and not what they do when
they go away. When a man approaches me with pure intentions, I respect his
pure intentions, although I cannot guarantee what he does afterwards."

But Confucius was not all gentility. For he was a "real man." He could
sing and be extremely polite, but he also could hate and sneer with the hatred
and contempt of a "real man." There was never a great man in this world who
did not have some genuine good hatreds. Confucius could be extremely rude
and there are recorded in the *Analects* four or five caustic remarks made about
people in their presence. He could be rude in a way that no Confucianist
dares to be rude today. There was no class of persons that Confucius hated
more than the goody-goody hypocrites whom Confucius described as "the
thieves of virtue." Once such a person, Ju Pei, wanted to see Confucius, and
Confucius sent word to say he was not at home. When Ju Pei was just outside
the door, Confucius took up a string instrument and sang "in order to let
him hear it" and know that he was really at home. This passage in the *Analects*
has confused all Confucian critics, who proceeded upon the assumption
that Confucius was a saint and not a human being, and was always polite.
Such orthodox criticism naturally completely dehumanized Confucius.
Another passage in the *Analects*, recorded in *Mencius*, also puzzled the critics.
A corrupt official, by the name of Yang Ho, presented Confucius with a leg
of pork. As the two persons heartily disliked each other, Yang Ho found out
when Confucius would not be at home and then presented the leg of pork
at his home as a matter of courtesy. Confucius also took the trouble to find
out when Yang Ho was not at home and then went to say thanks to him and
leave his card. In reply to a question from his disciples concerning the rulers
of his day, Confucius remarked, "Oh, those are rice bags!" (i.e., good only

for filling themselves with rice). At another time he made this remark about a man who was reputed to have indulged in singing at his mother's death. "As a young boy, you were unruly; when grown up, you have accomplished nothing, and now in your old age you refuse to die. You are a thief!" And Confucius struck his shin with a walking stick.

There was, in fact, a lot of fun in Confucius. He led a full, joyous life, the full human life of feelings and artistic taste. For he was a man of deep emotionality and great sensitive taste. At the death of his favorite disciple, Confucius wept bitterly. When he was asked why he wept so and was so shaken, he replied, "If I don't weep bitterly at the death of such a person, for whom else shall I weep bitterly?" His curious sensitiveness and capacity for shedding tears was shown in an instance when he passed by casually a funeral of one of his old acquaintances. He went in, and moved by the weeping of others, he also wept. When he came out, he asked his disciple to take a part of the accoutrements on his horse as a funeral gift, and said, "Take it in as my formal present. I hated this weeping without reason."

This man, who sang and played musical instruments (*ch'in, seh,* and *hsuan*) and edited a book of songs with accompanying music, was an artist. As I have already pointed out, he was a lover of ritual and music. As an illustration of his Episcopalian temper, there was the following incident which contrasted him sharply with Jesus who had much less respect for the laws and the prophets and all the ritualism that went with them. Jesus allowed a person to save a cow out of a pit on the Sabbath. Confucius might have approved, or he might not. His disciple Tsekung once proposed to abolish the winter sacrifices of lambs, and Confucius replied, "Ah Sze, you love the lamb, but I love the ritual!" Anyway, he wasn't interested in animals. For on hearing that a stable was burnt down by fire, it was recorded that he asked whether any persons were hurt but "did not ask about the horses." The artist in him made him say that a man's education should begin with poetry, be strengthened by proper conduct, and "consummated in music." It was also recorded that when he heard another man sing and liked it, he would ask for an *encore* and then join in the refrain. The artist in him also made him very fastidious about his food and his dress. I have already pointed out elsewhere that his fastidiousness about food was most probably the cause of his wife's running away. He refused to eat when anything was not in season, or not properly cooked, or not served with its proper sauce. And he had good taste in matching colors in his dress. A modern modiste could easily understand why he would match a black lamb coat with a black covering, a white faun coat with a white covering, and a fox coat with a yellow covering. (This "covering" corresponds to the "lining" in Western fur coats, for Chinese fur coats are worn with the fur on the inside and the silk on the outside.) He was also something of an inventor in the matter of dress. His bedclothes were longer than his body by half, to avoid cold feet, and he struck upon the beautiful idea of making his right sleeve shorter than his left sleeve for convenience at work, which must have also exasperated his wife and caused this woman to run away from the crazy man. (For all these facts see Ch. X of the *Analects*, or Ch. V, Sec. 2, in this book.) The aristocracy of his taste extended even to divorce. For three successive generations, the Master, his son, and his grandson were divorced or separated from their wives. On the intellectual lineage (the Master, his great disciple Tsengtse, and Tsengtse's disciple Tsesze), the record of divorce was also unbroken for three and a half generations, it being reported that the intellectual fourth generation, Mencius (who studied under Tsesze), ahmost divorced his wife. So, although none of them was particularly rich, they were undoubtedly aristocrats.

One of the most important characteristics of Confucius which really accounted for his great prestige was simply his scholarship and love of learning. Confucius said this repeatedly of himself. He admitted that he was not one of those "born to know the truth," but that he was an indefatigable reader and teacher, tireless in his search after knowledge and learning. He admitted that in every hamlet of ten families, there were some righteous and honest men as good as himself, but one who loved learning the way he did. He counted as one of the things that would trouble him "the neglect of his studies." In one of his sayings, I note a sigh of regret which is the regret of a modern research scholar. In his efforts to reconstruct the religious practices, ceremonies and customs of the ancient dynasties, he went to the city of Chi to search for survivals of the customs of Hsia Dynasty, and to the city of Sung to learn of the surviving religious practices of the ancient Dynasty of Shang. He said, "I should be able to talk about the religious customs of the Hsia Dynasty, but there are not enough evidences in the city of Chi. I should be able to talk about the religious customs of the Shang Dynasty, but there are not enough evidences in the city of Sung. There are not enough historical documents and evidences left. If there were, I should be able to reconstruct them with evidences." In other words, he was essentially a research scholar in history, trying to salvage from existing customs as well as historical documents the ancient social and religious practices which had decayed and the theocracy which had broken down. Nevertheless, he did his best, and the result of his labors was the collection of the Confucian *Five Classics* which were strictly history (dictum of a Ch'ing scholar, Chang Hsueh-ch'eng), as distinguished from the *Four Books*. I have no doubt that people were attracted to Confucius, less because he was the wisest man of his time, than because he was the most *learned* scholar, the only one of his day who could teach them about the ancient books and ancient scholarship. There was a great body of historical learning concerning the governmental systems of ancient times, and there was still a greater body of historical learning concerning the religious rites and ceremonies of a decaying or decayed theocracy, particularly that of the Shang Dynasty, as we can see from Confucius' *Five Classics* He was reported to have had three thousand pupils in all, of which number seventy-two were accomplished in the *Book of Songs*, the *Book of History* and the theory and practice of rituals and music. He believed in history and the appeal of history, because he believed in continuity. It will be seen in the chapter on "Central Harmony" (Ch. III), that he regarded as the three essential requisites for governing the world: Character, position of authority, and the appeal to history, and that lacking any one of these things, no one could succeed with a governmental system and "command credence," however excellent it might be. The actual result was that there grew up within the Confucian school a great body of historical learning which the other schools entirely lacked, and personally I believe the victory of the Confucian school over the other schools of Laotse and Motse was as much due to its prestige in scholarship as to its intrinsic philosophic value. The Confucian teachers had something definite to teach and the Confucian pupils had something definite to learn, namely historical learning, while the other schools were forced to air merely their own opinions, either on "universal love" or on "love of oneself."

A word must be said about the genial humor of Confucius, both because it supports and illustrates what I have said about his living a full, joyous life, so different from the conventional picture of Confucius presented to us by the killjoy Sung doctrinaires, and because it helps us to see his simplicity and greatness. Confucius was not a cheap wit, but occasionally he could not resist turning a clever line, such as the following: "A man who does not say to himself 'What to do? What to do?'—indeed I don't know what to do with such a person"; or this, "Know what you know and know that you don't know what you don't know—that is the characteristic of one who knows" (or in Chinese fashion, "Know, know; don't know, don't know—that is know"); or this, "A man who knows he has committed a mistake and doesn't correct it is committing another mistake." Sometimes he was also capable of a little bit of poetic humor or occasional license. There was a passage in the *Book of Songs*, in which the lover complained that it wasn't that she did not think of her sweetheart, but that "his house was so far away." Commenting upon this passage, Confucius remarked. "She really did not think of him at all; if she did, how could the house seem far away?"

But the most characteristic humor that we find in Confucius was also the best kind of humor generally, the humor of laughing at his own expense. He had plenty of chance to laugh at his own outward failures or of admitting that other people's criticisms of him were quite correct. Some of this humor was merely casual light raillery between the Master and his disciples. Once a man from a certain village remarked, "Great indeed is Confucius! He knows about everything and is expert at nothing." Hearing this comment, Confucius told his disciples, "What shall I specialize in? Shall I specialize in archery or in driving a carriage?" (In this connection he once admitted jokingly that if wealth could be achieved entirely by human effort, he would achieve it even if he had to be a cab driver.) During the failure of his political career, Tsekung once remarked, "Here is a piece of precious jade, preserved in a casket and waiting for a good price for sale." And Confucius replied, "For sale! For sale! I am the one waiting for a good price to be sold!" Refusal to see humor in Confucius would land the critics and commentators in ridiculous difficulties over such a passage. But as a matter of fact, the Master and his disciples constantly joked back and forth. Confucius was once in difficulties while travelling. Being mistaken for a certain other man who had maltreated the people, he was surrounded by troops. He finally escaped, but his favorite disciple Yen Huei failed to turn up till later, and Confucius said to him, "I thought you were killed." Yen replied, "As long as you live, how dare I be killed!" In another story, once the Master and his disciples had lost track of each other. The disciples finally heard from the crowd that there was a tall man standing at the East Gate with a high forehead resembling some of the ancient emperors, but that he looked crestfallen like a homeless wandering dog. The disciples finally found him and told him about this remark and Confucius replied, "I don't know about my resembling those ancient emperors, *but as for resembling a homeless, wandering dog, he is quite right! He is quite right!*" This is the best type of humor, and what appeals to me most is that passage in *The Life of Confucius* (Ch. II, Sec. 5), where Confucius was actually singing in the rain. There is a deep pathos about that group of wandering scholars, roaming for three years in the wilds between Ch'en and Ts'ai, having just escaped trouble, all dressed up in their tremendous scholarship and having nowhere to go. These last years of wandering became the turning point of Confucius' career, after which he admitted his full failure in seeking a political career and returned to his native state to devote himself to editing and authorship. He compared himself and his disciples to a nondescript band of animals, "neither buffalos, nor tigers" wandering in the wilds, and began to ask his disciples what was wrong with him. After the third answer, Confucius approved and said to the disciple who made that clever answer, smilingly, "Is that so? Oh, son of Yen, *if you were a rich man, I would be your butler!*" That is a passage that completely won me over to Confucius. Taken as a whole, that passage has a beauty and pathos comparable to *Gethsemane*, except that it ends on a cheerful note.

III. SOURCES AND PLAN OF THE PRESENT BOOK

I have remarked that the Confucian school practically monopolized the historic scholarship of those days, including the ability to read what was then already an archaic script, and this body of historic learning was handed down as the Confucian *Five Classics*. In the year 213 B.C., the "burning of books" (with the exception of books on medicine, astrology and horticulture) took place, and in the following year, 212 B.C., 460 Confucian scholars were buried alive for criticizing Ch'in Shih-huang, the builder of the Great Wall. It happened, however, that this Emperor's Dynasty, founded for "ten thousand generations," collapsed five years after the massacre and many old Confucian scholars who had committed the classics to memory had survived it. These old scholars thus had salvaged the Confucian classics by an oral tradition and by sheer memory, assisted, I suspect, nevertheless by some inscribed pieces of bamboo that they had hidden away. These people then taught their disciples and had these classics written down in what was then called the "modern script," for Chinese writing went through a great process of simplification during the reign of that great Emperor. In the century following and afterwards, however, there came to light ancient bamboo inscriptions, written in the "ancient script," which had been hidden away and had escaped destruction. The most notable instance was the discovery of ancient texts by a "King of Lu," who had opened up the walls of Confucius' own house and temple and found these preserved. As they were in archaic script, scholars set about to decipher them, a difficult but not impossible job in those times. There grew up, therefore, a separate tradition, known as the "ancient script" tradition, which in part differed from the tradition of the "modern script," notably in regard to the records of the ancient forms of society and systems of government and concerning the mythological rulers. These two different traditions where noted already in the Han Dynasty, but the greatest commentator, Cheng Hsuan, for instance, tried to harmonize the two. A compromise was effected. Thus throughout the succeeding dynasties, the orthodox version and interpretation of the *Book of Songs* and the *Spring and Autumn* were based upon the "ancient script," while the *Liki*, admitted as one of the *Five Classics*, decidedly belonged to the tradition of the "modern script." The distinction between the two traditions was not sharply drawn until the Ch'ing scholars of the 17th, 18th and 19th centuries set about with their scientific comparative method to restore the tradition of the "modern script." Every available scrap of evidence and every method of historical criticism and philological research was brought to bear upon this question, the most notable achievement being the conclusive proof of forgery of twenty-five out of the fifty-eight existing chapters in the *Book of History*, thus restoring this classic to a collection of thirty-three chapters, representing the tradition of the "modern script." The general position is, not that the archaic script itself was a forgery, but that our present version of the so-called archaic script was a forgery.

The term "Confucian classics" today usually refers to the *Five Classics* and the *Four Books*. The *Five Classics* as I have pointed out formed the body of historical learning edited, taught and handed down by Confucius himself, while the *Four Books* on the whole represented the works of his followers, their records of Confucius' sayings and their interpretations or developments of Confucius' thoughts. Then at other times, we also speak of the *Thirteen Classics*. The contents of these different collections will be made plain by the Tables on pages 30 and 31. It should be remembered, however, that in Confucius' own day, there were *Six Classics* instead of *Five*, the additional one being the *Book of Music*, the remaining portions of which survive today as one of the chapters of *Liki* (Ch. X of this book). The comparative Tables on pages 30 and 31 will show the relationships. "★" indicates the "ancient script" (*kuwen*) tradition; "#" indicates the "modern script" (*chinwen*) tradition.

The usual approach to the study of Confucian wisdom by directly attacking the *Analects* is a mistake, because it leads nowhere. The *Analects* is a promiscuous and unedited collection of Confucius' sayings, often taken out of their contexts in longer discourses recorded elsewhere, which would make the meaning clearer. There are also duplicate quotations existing in different chapters, of which there are twenty, showing that the work grew by itself in separate hands and was not edited by any one man. Some of the chapters, evidently compiled by the disciples of Tsengtse, would contain more sayings of Tsengtse. The different sayings in any one chapter are not arranged at all in sequence of ideas; sometimes one can detect a main theme, but more often one cannot. There are evident later additions at the end of some chapters, and some lines in the text, for instance those at the end of Chapter X, are clearly incomplete.

But the greatest difficulty for a Western reader in approaching the system of Confucian thought through the *Analects* lies in the Western reader's habit of reading. He demands a connected discourse, and is content to listen while he expects the writer to talk on and on. There is no such thing as reading a line out of a book and taking a day or two to think about it, to chew and digest it mentally and have it verified by one's own reflections and experience. Actually, the *Analects* must be read, if it is to be read at all, by having the different aphorisms spread out on the separate days of a calendar block, and letting the reader ponder over one saying each day and no more. This is the orthodox method of studying the *Analects*, the method of taking a line or two and thoroughly mastering the thought and its implications. This evidently cannot be done with respect to modern readers. Besides, no one can get a well-rounded and consecutive view of the development of Confucius' thoughts by merely reading the *Analects*.

This is the reason why in the present plan, I am forced to select from the Confucian classics and the Four Books those chapters which represent connected essays or connected discourses on any one topic. In fact, there exist in the *Liki* connected Confucian dialogues, of which Chapters VI, VII and VIII are good examples. In Chapters III and IV, on "Central Harmony" and "Ethics and Politics," we find also a connected development of ideas in the form of essays. Actually, of the nine chapters of Confucian texts (i.e., excluding the *Life* by Ssǔma Ch'ien) selected and translated by myself in this book, seven are chapters from the *Liki*, while the remaining two chapters consist of one selection from Menctus and one collection of "Aphorisms of Confucius," arranged or classified sayings selected from the *Analects*, with a few selections from other chapters of *Liki*. By looking at the above table, it will be seen that besides introducing five new chapters from the *Liki*, it covers in four chapters (III, IV, V, XI) the same field as the *Four books*, which Chinese children were required to learn, in the elementary grades. This method is therefore orthodox. Two of the *Four Books*, "Central Harmony" and "Personal Cultivation," were taken from the *Liki* anyway and elevated into the position of parts of the *Four Books* together with the *Analects* and the *Book of Mencius* only by the Sung scholar Chu Hsi (1130-1200), and there is no reason why the other chapters of the *Liki* should not have equal authority with those two chapters which Chu Hsi selected.

There is the general question as to the validity and accuracy of records of Confucius' sayings in *Liki* and even in the *Analects*. This is the general

FIVE CLASSICS	THIRTEEN CLASSICS	COMMENTS
Book of Songs (*Shiking*)	Book of Songs (Mao*, Ch'i#, Han#, and Lu# versions)	Three hundred and five songs and sacred anthems besides six with music and title without texts, edited by Confucius.
Book of History (*Shuking*)	Book of History (33 chapters* and # 28 chapters*)	Composed of early historic documents, chiefly kings' proclamations, being the earliest of Chinese documents and most archaic in style of all the classics.
Book of Changes (*Yiking*)	Book of Changes (Pi*, Shih #, Meng# Liang# and Ching# versions)	The philosophy of mutations of human events, originally a divination system based on changing arrangements of lines of an octogram (resembling the changing combinations of dots and dashes in the Morse system), but developed into a full philosophy for human conduct in varying circumstance.
Spring and Autumn (*Ch'unch'iu*)	Spring and Autumn (Cho*, Kungyang# and Kuliang# amplifications)	The Classic itself, a bare chronicle of events of two and a half centuries (722 B.C.-481 B.C.), written by Confucius with a view to restoring correct terminology. The three *chuan* or amplifications narrate the events in detail, or elucidate the meaning of Confucius' text.
Book of Rites (*Liki*)	*Chouli* Yili(*Liking*)	Allegedly a record of governmental system of early Chou Dynasty. Different ceremonial rites.

FOUR BOOKS	THIRTEEN CLASSICS	COMMENTS
2 Chapters from *Liki*, "Ethics and Politics" (*Tahsueh*) and "Central Harmony" (*Chungyung*)	*Liki* ("Great Tai" collection 85 chapters #; "Small Tai" collection 46—subdivided, 49—chapters #, usually meant by "*Liki*")	A miscellaneous collection of different "ancient records," partly resembling the *Analects*, partly sayings of Confucius' disciples, partly elucidations of *Yili*, representing the tradition of the Confucian school.
Analects (*Lunyu*)	Analects	The cream of Confucius' sayings recorded by his disciples, often cut short from their contexts, very much like Bartlett's *Familiar Quotations*. Seven books probably
Mencius	Mencius	written by Mencius himself.
	Book of Filial Piety (*Hsiaoking*)	A later essay by a Han scholar.
	Thesaurus (*Erhya*)	The earliest Chinese Thesaurus, a help to the study of ancient classics, grouped according to ideas.

Four Books

question of what exactly Confucius or Buddha or Socrates said and to what extent we can believe, for instance, that Plato's accounts of the Socratic dialogue were literally accurate. A synoptic study of the Four Gospels of the Christian Bible reveals discrepancies enough. And we find the same variations of the sayings of Confucius, given in slightly different words in the *Analects*, the *Book of Mencius* and the *Liki*. It was inevitable that Plato colored the sayings of Socrates through his own pen, and the same was true of many of the chapters of the *Liki*. Modern politicians who have the occasion to be interviewed by reporters realize the practical impossibility of obtaining a literally accurate report of what they have said. Nothing short of a dictaphone can convince the politicians of what they actually said themselves.

The *Liki* itself, as I have already said, is only a collection of various records in the possession of the Confucian school, and is definitely of extremely diverse origin. Some of these, including the essay on "Central Harmony" are ascribed to Tsesze, the grandson of Confucius, and some others, particularly a few in the "Great Tai" collection, are undoubtedly handed down by Tsengtse or his disciples. The chapters on education and music doubtless reflect the ideas of the Confucian philosopher Hsuntse, a contemporary of Mencius who spoke of the latter with contempt ("a gutter philosopher" was the phrase used). For the rest, a shocking proportion of the *Liki* is devoted to discourses on funeral ceremonies, while the "Great Tai" collection is devoid of these discussions. A good number of chapters are devoted to the philosophic meaning and actual ceremonial robes and vessels of public worship. There are also chapters on the rules and customs pertaining to all kinds of festivities—marriage, archery contests, dance, village festivals, drinking and games (Ch. XL for instance, describes a game in detail, similar to those we see in shooting galleries). An important chapter, Chapter V, is the basis of the "modern script" school on the ancient system of administration, as the *Chouli* is the basis for the "ancient script" school. There are other chapters dealing with the conduct of women and children and ordinary points of etiquette. The very first chapter, for instance, besides giving the philosophic justification for ritualism, also covers advice such as the following:

> "Do not roll rice into a ball, do not leave rice on the table, do not let your soup run out of your mouth. Do not smack your lips, do not leave a bone dry, do not turn over the fish, do not throw bones to the dog, and do not persist in trying to get a particular piece of meat. Do not turn rice about to let it cool off, and do not take porridge with chopsticks. Do not gulp the soup up, do not stir the soup about, do not pick your teeth, and do not add sauce to your soup.... bite off boiled meat with your teeth, but do not bite off cured meat with your teeth."

This reads like Deuteronomy, and it is important that it be understood that the "religion of *Li*," like Judaism, embraces both religious worship and daily life, down to the matter of eating and drinking.

The present plan of the book is therefore as follows: Chapter II gives for the first time in English a translation of *The Life of Confucius*, the earliest and in fact the only biographical sketch of Confucius, written by the great historian Ssŭma Ch'ien. Chapter III on "Central Harmony" gives a complete and adequate philosophic basis to the whole Confucian system, while Chapter IV on "Ethics and Politics" develops a coherent argument, whether sound or not for the connection between ethics and politics, between personal life, home life, national life and world order. Chapter V then gives the "aphorisms" of Confucius, selected and re-grouped from the *Analects*, on the whole the most witty chapter of the whole book. Chapters VI, VII, VIII form what I call the "Three Confucian Discourses" on the social order, which should sufficiently explain the true meaning of *li*, erroneously represented as mere ritualism. Chapter VIII in particular contains a short but important statement of Confucius' vision for world peace and his highest ideal of a moral order. Chapters IX and X then give us the Confucian ideas on education and music, singularly modern in point of view. The chapter on music is one of the longest in *Liki* and is actually compiled from a dozen chapters from the lost book on music. After all this, the reader is given a selection from Mencius, which represents a most important and influential development of Confucian philosophy. All the chapters except VIII and X are translated in full, the two exceptions being entirely too long.

I have done the translation of all the following texts myself, with the exception of the chapter on "Central Harmony." Ku Hung Ming's translation of that chapter is so brilliant and at the same time so correct and illuminating that I am sorry he did not translate more of the Confucian texts. It makes that chapter intelligible to the modern man. I have, however, considered it advisable to leave out his own comments bringing Goethe and Matthew Arnold and the *Proverbs* from the Christian Bible to elucidate the meaning of Confucianism; readers who are interested should go to Ku Hung Ming's own book (*The Conduct of Life*—John Murray, London). I have found it necessary also to make a number of corrections where Ku departs slightly from the Chinese text; besides, I do not accept Ku's rearrangement of the chapter, and have made my own. I have generally refrained from making comments, and have confined myself to making sectional divisions and providing sectional headings which will help the reader to follow the argument or the development of ideas more readily. But comments are implied throughout in the work of translation, and I regard a translation of this kind as commenting itself, for there is no really intelligent translation without the translator's interpretation of the text to be translated. This is especially true of translation from an ancient Chinese text into modern English. In the first place, the words used are necessarily so different in their general connotation, and in the second place, the ancient texts are unusually terse and concise, almost oracular in character at places, and one has to supply the necessary connectives and other words made necessary by the English syntax. Furthermore, Chinese interpretations of the same text vary a great deal, and the translator has to choose from one of them, or make a new one himself if he is convinced that he has new light on the subject. I therefore withhold myself from adding comments in the Ku Hung Ming manner, except where such comments are strictly necessary for guiding the reader with regard to the development of ideas, or for explaining certain terms.

Finally, I have found it necessary in Chapters III and IV to rearrange or re-edit the ancient texts. I realize fully such a responsibility. On the other hand, it is generally admitted that the texts of Chapters III and IV contain possible mistakes in arrangement, due to the fact that the separate paragraphs were inscribed on different pieces of bamboo and tied together in bundles. There are signs of reshuffling when these bamboo inscriptions were transcribed on silk in the Han Dynasty. Anyway, everyone admits that succeeding paragraphs in "Central Harmony" do not follow one another logically, although the main theme is always there. Chu Hsi took the bold step to re-edit the chapter on "Ethics and Politics," resulting in the transference of a whole section to an earlier part of the essay and making the development of thought much easier to follow. He even went as far as to write a paragraph of his own, declaring that he did so in order to supply a missing paragraph, but in the process enabling him to put a bit of Sung philosophy into the sacred text about meditation of the universe. However, if one confines himself to mere reshuffling of already existing texts, with a view to establishing a more connected development of thought, without personal additions to the text itself, I believe it is justifiable on the ground of making a clearer presentation of ideas its sole aim. Naturally, I have not undertaken such reshuffling without the most careful consideration and understanding of the reason why such derangements of the original text took place.

IV. ON THE METHOD OF TRANSLATION

A little more must be said about the present method of translation. I consider a translation in this case as indistinguishable from paraphrase, and believe that is the best and most satisfying method.

The situation is as follows: The ancient texts were extremely sparing in the use of words, owing of course to the method of inscribing on bamboo sticks. Most of the important ideas and characterizations that covered a whole class of qualities were expressed by monosyllabic words, and in accordance with the general nature of Chinese grammar, the meaning was indicated by syntax or word order rather than by the usual English connectives. Here are two extreme instances in the Chinese form: "Confucius completely-cut-off four—no idea—no must—no *ku*—no I"; "Language expressive only." It is clear that unless connectives are supplied by the translator, the translation would be practically unreadable. The extent to which connectives and amplifying phrases are allowable has by necessity to be left to the discretion of the translator, and for this the translator has no other guide than his own insight into the wisdom of Confucius, assisted, of course, by the commentators.

The first job is of course to determine the scope and connotation of a term in the general classical usage and secondly its particular meaning and shade of meaning in a given sentence. In the above instance of the word *ku*, this word meant several things: "strong," "stubborn," "persistence," "narrow-mindedness," "vulgarity," "limited in knowledge," and "sometimes also." From these different possible meanings, the translator has to make his choice. That is the terrible responsibility and the latitude given to the translator of ancient Chinese texts, and it is clear that a choice of a different word would alter the sense of the line completely. In this particular instance, I have translated the passage as follows: "Confucius denounced (or tried completely to avoid) four things: arbitrariness of opinion, dogmatism, narrow-mindedness and egotism." It is, of course, open to question whether the phrase "no must" should be translated as "don't insist upon a particular course," "don't be persistent," "don't be insistent," or "don't assume that you *must* be right (or don't be dogmatic)." Any of these translations involves as much paraphrasing as the others. In translating the phrase "no idea," I have paraphrased it as meaning "don't start out with preconceived notions," or "don't be arbitrary." That is a sense or shade of meaning won from a knowledge of the general meaning of the word "idea" in the Chinese language, and from an insight into the whole character of Confucius' conduct. But the mere use of the phrase "preconceived notion" or "arbitrariness of opinion" necessarily expresses what at best was only implied in the Chinese word "idea."

In the more fundamental concepts, like *li, jen, hsin, chung*, etc., I have adopted a method of provisionally translating these words in my mind by a certain English concept and going over the body of the texts containing these words to see which one would cover the field of meaning most adequately in the majority of cases, allowing, of course, several meanings for one word. Thus I have come to the conclusion that *li* usually translated as "ritual" or "ceremony" must be translated as "the principle of social order" in the general social philosophy of Confucius, and as "moral discipline" in certain passages dealing with personal conduct. I have also come to the conclusion that the translation of the word *jen* as "kindness," "charity," or "benevolence" is completely inadequate, but represents Confucius' ideal of the "true man," or the "great man" or the "most complete man." Likewise, *hsin* cannot be translated as "honesty" or "keeping one's promise," which latter quality Confucius rather despised and actually didn't care about in his own conduct. Sometimes *hsin* means a condition of "mutual confidence in the state," and sometimes it means "faithfulness."

In the actual act of translation, the translator is faced with two jobs after he has grasped the meaning of the sentence. First he is faced with the choice of one of a number of synonyms, and failure to get at the exact word would completely fail to render the meaning of the remark clear to the reader. I found it impossible, for instance, always to translate the word *teh* as "virtue" or "character," or the meaning would be hopelessly lost for the reader.

Thus, Confucius said, "Thoroughbred, don't praise its strength praise its *character*." The meaning becomes clear only when we translate it as follows: "In discussing a thoroughbred, you don't admire his strength, but admire his *temper*." Now comes this same word for "character" in another passage: "Confucius said, 'One having virtue must have words; one having words not always has virtue.' " The meaning becomes clear only when we translate the word for "character" or "virtue" here by the word "soul" in the English language, as follows: "Confucius said, 'A man who has a beautiful soul always has some beautiful things to say, but a man who says beautiful things does not necessarily have a beautiful soul.' " Then again occurs the same word elsewhere in the phrase *teh yin*; to translate this as "virtuous sounds" may give the impression of scholarly fidelity, but merely hides the lack of understanding on the part of the scholarly translator that it means "*sacred music.*" Again Confucius said, "Extravagant than not humble; frugal than *ku* (vulgar or stubborn, etc.). Rather than not humble, be *ku*." The connection between extravagance and lack of humility must be quite vague, and becomes clear only when we realize that people who live extravagantly are liable to be *conceited*. A fully clear and adequate translation must therefore involve a sure choice of words. I believe it should be translated as follows: "Confucius said, 'The people who live extravagantly are apt to be snobbish (or conceited), and the people who live simply are apt to be vulgar. I prefer vulgarity to snobbery (or I prefer the vulgar people to the snobs).' "

In the second place, the translator cannot avoid putting the thought in the more precise concepts of a modern language. The translator does not only have to supply the connectives, but has also to supply a finer definition of ideas, or the English will be extremely bald. Thus in the example given above, "Language expressive only," the modern translator is forced to translate it as follows: "Expressiveness is the only *principle* of language," or "expressiveness is the sole *concern*, or *aim*, or *principle*, of rhetoric." It is clear that there are at least a dozen ways of translating this line in any case. But it is inevitable that the translator would have to slip in a word like "principle" or "aim" or "concern" or "standard." It simply cannot be helped, if the translation is not to become unreadable.

The use of parentheses—In the resulting text of the translation, I have to resort to the use of parentheses after dodging the above difficulties. The parentheses are used for two purposes. First, for giving an alternate translation, usually indicated by "(or...)." The situation is often such that no one can be sure that a particular interpretation is the only correct one. Secondly, the parentheses are used exclusively for explanatory matter necessary to a clear understanding of the text without reference to footnotes. Without this device, such explanatory references would be endless. In this case, the parentheses are used with the sole purpose of supplying the minimum explanations to enable the reader to read a passage smoothly and understand its meaning without difficulty. The footnotes are then reserved for my comments and other reference material.

第二章　孔子生平

自古以来，天下的君王贤人也算很多了，活着时都很荣耀，到他一死就什么也没有了。孔子仅是一个平民，他的道统家世至今传了十几代，学者们都崇仰他。从天子王侯以下，凡是中国研讨六经道艺的人，都将孔夫子的话尊奉为最高的衡断标准，他真可说是一位圣明到极点的人了！

本书的孔子生平，采用司马迁的《孔子世家》，有两项重要理由。第一，因为司马迁的《孔子世家》是中国最早的孔子传记，是中国史学名著里的文章，作者司马迁不但是中国史家之祖，而且是散文大家。《史记》的地位是不能动摇的，而作者司马迁游踪甚广，曾访问孔子故乡，亦曾与当地熟知孔子逸闻旧事之父老长谈。所以我们要打算一窥孔子生活的真面貌，实在是舍此别无他途了。第二，司马迁胸襟开阔，豁达无私。他是真正的史家，不以提倡儒道尊崇孔子之心而存偏见。他虽然极其仰慕孔子，但并不属于狭义的儒家一派。因此，他是把孔子当作一个人来描绘，不是把孔子当作一个圣人来崇拜。论孔子的人，常想曲解有关孔子生活的几段文字，他们甚至用牵强的解释，否认孔子生平某些言行的真实性，而司马迁则不然。我们相信汉代大史学家司马迁头脑中孔子的面目是可靠的，因为他生活的时代是在孔子死后的三百年左右。

《史记·孔子世家》白话

世系、童年、青年（公元前551—前523年）

孔子出生在鲁国昌平乡的陬邑（今山东曲阜县东南境鄹城）。他的先世本来是宋国的公族，到了叫孔防叔的，才因避祸逃来鲁国定居。防叔生了伯夏，伯夏生了叔梁纥。梁纥晚年再娶颜姓女子（《礼记·檀弓》云孔子母名徵在）才生了孔子，而且是到尼丘（一名尼山）去向神明祈祷才有孕生下孔子的。鲁襄公二十二年（公元前551年），孔子诞生。孔子刚生下时，头顶中间是凹下的，所以就给他取名叫丘，字叫仲尼，姓孔氏。

孔子生下不久，叔梁纥就死了（《索隐》引《家语》云生三岁而梁叔纥死），葬在防山。防山在鲁城的东边（《括地志》云在曲阜县东二十五里），因此孔子没法确知自己父亲的坟墓所在；母亲年少葬夫，照当时礼俗不能亲去送葬，所以也说不出坟墓的详细地址。

孔子小的时候游戏，常摆起各种祭器，学着大人祭祀的礼仪动作。母亲死了（《孔子世家补订》《阙里志》诸书并云在孔子二十四岁；今人钱穆先生则云在孔子十七岁以前），就暂时浅厝在五父衢（鲁城道名）的路旁，不敢贸然深葬远处，可能是他为了谨慎的缘故吧！后来同邑人挽父的母亲，指点出孔子父亲的墓地，然后孔子才把母亲灵柩运去防山和父亲合葬在一起。

孔子腰间系着孝麻还在守丧，季孙子招宴军役之士（一说文学之士，此据方苞说），孔子前往参加。季孙的家臣阳虎拒斥他说："季民招宴要服役的士卒，是不敢招待你的。"于是孔子就退了回来。

孔子十七岁那一年，鲁国的大夫孟厘子跟随鲁昭公到楚去，回来之后，深为不能襄助行好礼仪而自责，所以在他临终前（孟厘子卒于昭公二十四年。以上一段《史记》原文略有疏误，此据《左传·昭公七年》文意改译），还告诫自己的嗣子孟懿子说："孔丘这个人，是圣人（《集解》引服虔曰：圣人谓商汤）的后裔，是在宋国受到华氏之祸才逃到鲁国来的。他先祖弗父何本来可以继位做宋君，却让给了他的弟弟厉公（《集解》引杜预曰：弗父何，宋愍公之长子，厉公之兄也。何嫡嗣当立，以让厉公）。到了弗父何的曾孙正考父，他辅佐戴公、武公、宣公三朝，做了上卿。他每一受命，就更加恭谨，所以考父鼎的铭文说：'第一次受命时鞠躬致敬，二次受命时折腰弓背，到了第三次受命，我的头压得更低，腰背更加弯曲了。走路时挨着墙边走，也没有人敢来侮慢我；我就用这个鼎做些面糊稀饭来清俭度日。'他就是这般恭谨俭约。我听说圣人的后裔，虽不一定能当国继位，但必然会有才德显达的人出现。如今孔丘年纪轻轻就博学好礼，这岂不就是所谓的显达的人吗？我是不久于人世的人了，你可一定要去从他求学。"孟厘子死后，懿子和鲁人南宫敬叔（《索隐》谓敬叔与懿子皆孟厘子之子，不阙更言鲁人）便去向孔子学礼。这一年，季武子死了，平子继承了卿位。

孔子早年生活，既穷苦又没地位。成年以后，曾做过仓库管理员（季氏史，《会注考证》引诸说以为当做"委吏"，孟子亦云"孔子尝为委吏矣"，今从之），出纳钱粮算量得准确清楚，也担任过管理牧场的小职务，而场中牲口就越养越多。后来，他出任主管营建的司空。过不了多久，他离开鲁国，在齐国却受到排斥，转到宋、卫两国，生活也奔波不定，又在陈、蔡两国间遭遇困厄，最后才回到鲁国。孔子身高有九尺六寸，人家管他叫"长人"，而且以奇异眼光看他。鲁国当局最后总算又对他好了，所以他才回到鲁国来的。

鲁国的南宫敬叔对鲁君说："请帮助孔子到周去。"于是鲁君就给了一辆车子、两匹马，一个童仆随他出发，到周去学礼，据说是见到了老子。学成告别时，老子送他说："我听说富贵的人送人是用财物，仁德的人送人是用言辞。我不能够富贵，却盗取了仁人的名号，就说几句话送你，这话是：一个聪明又能深思明察的人，却常遭到困厄，几乎丧生，那是因为他喜欢议论别人的缘故；学问渊博识见广大的人，却使自己遭到危险不测，那是由于他好揭发别人罪恶的后果；做人子女的应该心存父母，不该只想到自己；做人臣属的应该心存君上，不能只顾到本身。"孔子从周回到鲁之后，门下的学生就日益增多了。

三十岁至五十岁（公元前522—前503年）

这个时候，晋平公淫乱无道，六家大臣（指范氏、中行氏、知氏、赵氏、魏氏、韩氏）把持国政，不时攻打东边的国家，楚灵王的军队很强大，也常北上来侵犯中原；齐是个大国又接近鲁。鲁国既小又弱，要是归附于楚，晋国就不高兴；依附了晋，楚国就来兴师问罪；对待齐国如果不周到，齐兵就要侵入鲁国了。

鲁昭公二十年，而孔子大约是三十岁了。齐景公同晏婴来到鲁国，景公就问孔子说："从前秦穆公，国家小又地处偏僻，他能够称霸是什么原因呢？"孔子回答说："秦这个国家虽然小，目标却很远大；地位虽然偏僻，施政却很正当。（秦穆公）亲自举拔用五张黑羊皮赎来的贤士百里奚，封给他大夫的官爵，才把他从奴隶的拘禁中救出来，就和他一连晤谈三天，随后把掌政大权交给了他。从这些事实来看，就是统治整个天下也是可以的，他称霸诸侯还算成就小了呢！"景公听了很高兴。

孔子三十五岁时，季平子因为和郈昭伯比赛斗鸡结怨的事得罪了鲁昭公，昭公带了军队来打平子。于是平子就联合了孟孙氏、叔孙氏，三家一起围攻昭公，昭公兵败了，逃到了齐国，齐国把昭公安置在乾侯（今河北成安县）这个地方。过了不多久，鲁国发生乱事，孔子来到齐国，做了高昭子的家臣，想借着昭子的关系去接近景公。孔子和齐国的荣宫长讨论音乐，听到了舜时韶乐，专心地把它学起来，三个月期间，连吃饭时的肉味都觉不出来了，齐人都很称道这件事。

齐景公问孔子为政的道理，孔子说："国君要像个国君，臣子要像个臣子，父亲要像个父亲，儿子要像个儿子。"景公听了说："对极了！果真是国君不成国君，臣子不成臣子，父亲不成个父亲，儿子不成个儿子，就是有再多的粮食，我们能平安地吃着它吗？"改天他又问孔子为政的原则。孔子说："为政最要紧的是在善用财力，杜绝浪费。"景公听了很高兴，打算把尼溪地方的田封给孔子。晏婴劝阻道："儒者这种人都能言善辩，是不能用法来约束他的，态度高傲自以为是，是很难驾驭的；他们重视丧礼，长期悲痛不止，为了使丧事隆重可以倾家荡产，这种礼俗不足取法，他们不事生产，只是到处游说求职来进行政治活动，这种人不能来掌理国事。自从文王、武王、周公这些大贤先后过去，周朝王室已经衰微，礼乐的沦丧也很有些时候了。现在孔子却对仪容服饰刻意讲究，详定各种应对进退间上下快慢的礼节规矩，这些繁文缛节，就是连续几代也学不完，一辈子也弄不清楚。君子想用这一套东西来改革我们齐国的礼俗，这不是治理百姓的好办法。"此后，景公只是很客气地接见孔子，不再问起有关礼的事情了。有一天，景公慰留孔子，说："要用像鲁国给季孙氏那样高的待遇给你，我实在做不到。"所以就以上下卿（鲁有三卿，季氏为上卿，孟氏为下卿，季孟之间，犹叔氏也）之间的礼来对待孔子。齐国的大夫有人想害孔子，孔子得到了消息。景公也说："我老啦，没法用你了。"于是孔子就离开齐国，回到了鲁国。

孔子四十二岁那一年，鲁昭公死在乾侯，定公继位。定公继位的第五年夏天，季平子死了，桓子继位做上卿。季桓子家里掘水井，掘到了一只腹大口小的瓦器，器中有个像羊的东西，就去问孔子，并且说挖得的瓦器里有只狗。孔子说："据我所知，那是羊。我听人说过，山林里的怪物是一种单足兽'夔'和会学人声的山精'罔阆'（同魍魉）；水里面的怪物是神龙和会吃人的水怪'罔象'，泥土里的怪物，则是一种雌雄未成的'坟羊'。"

吴国去攻打越国，把越都会稽城给拆毁了，发现一节骨头，长度就占满了一车。吴王派了专使来问孔子说："什么骨头最大？"孔子说："大禹王召集各地的君长到会稽山，当时有个叫防风氏的君长很迟才到。禹就把他杀了陈尸在那儿，他的骨头一节就占满一车，这就是最大的了。"吴使问道："那神又是谁呢？"孔子说："名山大川的神灵，能够兴云致雨来利益天下，负责监守山川按时祭祀的就叫做神（诸侯君长），只守社稷的叫公侯，他们都归王的统治。"使者又问："防风氏是守什么的？"孔子说："汪罔氏的君长守封山、禺山一带，是姓厘。在虞、夏、商三代叫汪罔，到了周代叫长翟，现在就叫作大人。"使者问道："人的身长有多少？"孔子说："僬侥氏身长三尺，是最短的了；最长的不过三丈，这就是身高的极限了。"吴使听了之后说:"真是了不起的圣人啊!"

季桓子的宠臣叫仲梁怀的,和阳虎有了仇怨。阳虎想把仲梁怀赶走,公山不狃阻止了他。这年秋天,仲梁怀更加地骄纵了,阳虎把他给抓了起来,季桓子很生气,阳虎就把桓子也囚禁了,等谈好条件才放他,阳虎从此更加没把季氏看在眼里。季氏也很越分,声势排场都超过鲁国公室;一个上卿的家臣(谓阳虎),就执掌了国家的政权,因此鲁国从大夫以下,都不守礼分,违背常道。所以孔子不愿出任鲁国的官职,退闲在家,专心研究整理诗、书、礼、乐这些典籍,学生越来越多,不论多远,都有人来向他求学。

掌大权时期(公元前502—前496年)

鲁定公八年,公山不狃不满于季氏,就借着阳虎来作乱,打算废掉季孙、叔孙、孟孙(三家皆鲁桓公之后,故称三桓)三家的嫡生嗣子,另外拥立平日为阳虎所喜欢的庶子来继承,于是就把桓子抓了起来。桓子用计骗他。逃了出来。定公九年,阳虎计划失败,逃到齐国去。这个时候,孔子正好五十岁。

公山不狃以费邑作据点反叛季氏,派人来召孔子去帮忙。孔子心想自己依循正道而行已经很久了,内在的学养也很深厚,却无处可以表现,没有人能用自己,不禁说道:"大抵文王、武王当年是以丰、镐那么小的地方建起王业的;现在费邑虽然是小了点,该也差不多吧!"想要应召前去,子路大不以为然,劝止孔子。孔子说:"难道召我去是毫无作用吗?如果他真能用我,我将像文王、武王一样,在东方建立一个典礼完备的周啊!"然而最后也没有成行。后来鲁定公任命孔子做中都(在今山东汶上县）地方的宰官，才到职一年就很有绩效，四方的官吏都学着他做。孔子由中都宰升任司空，又由司空升任了大司寇。

定公十年的春天，鲁国和齐国和好。到了夏天，齐国的大夫黎鉏就对景公说："鲁国用了孔丘，照情形看，这是会危害齐国的。"于是派了使者去约鲁君来做和好的会盟。会盟的地点是在夹谷（今山东莱芜县）。鲁定公就装潢好车子，毫无武装便想前往。这时孔子正好是兼理典礼会盟的事务，就对定公说："我听说有文事的必须有武备，有武事的必须要有文备。从前凡是诸侯出了自己的国境，一定带全了必要的官员随行。请你也带左司马右司马一道去。"定公说："好的。"就带了左右司马出发，和齐侯在夹谷地方相会。这个地方筑了土台，台上备好席位，上台的土阶有三级。两君就在台前行了相见礼，作揖让了一番才登上台。双方馈赠应酬的仪式行过之后，齐国管事的官员急忙前来请示道："请开始演奏四方的舞乐。"景公说："好。"于是旍旄羽祓矛戟剑拨都出了场，敲打吼叫地表演起来。孔子见了赶忙跑过来，一步一阶就往台上走，最后一阶没有跨上，便举袖一挥，说道："我们两国君主，是为了和好而来会盟的，这种夷狄的野蛮舞乐，怎么可以用在这个场合呢！请命管事官员叫他们下去！"管事的叫他们退下，他们却不肯动。孔子就朝左边的晏子看看，又朝右方的景公看看，景公心里尴尬了一阵，就命令乐人下去。过了一会儿，齐国管事官员又跑来说道："请演奏宫中的女乐。"景公应说："好。"于是许多戏子矮人都前来表演了。孔子看了又急忙过来，一步一阶往台上走，最后一阶没有跨上就说道："一个普通人敢胡闹来迷乱诸侯，论罪是应该正法的，请下令管事的执行吧！"于是管事官员依法处罚，那受罚的人就手脚分离了。景公看了孔子态度这样严正，不由得敬畏动容，知道自己道理上不如他。回国之后心里很不安，就对众臣说："鲁国是用君子的道理来辅助他们的君主，你们却仅把夷狄那套歪理告诉了我，害我开罪了鲁君，这该怎么办呢？"主事的官吏上前回话："君子有了过错，就用具体的事物来谢罪；普通人有了过错，就用虚礼大辞来谢罪。君上如果心里不安，就可用具体的事物去谢罪了。"于是齐侯就把以前从鲁国侵夺来的郓、汶阳和龟阴的田还给鲁国，来表示自己的歉疚。

鲁定公十三年的夏天，孔子对定公说："臣子的家中不可私藏兵器，大夫的封邑不能筑起三百丈的大城墙。"就派仲由去当季氏的家宰，打算拆毁季孙、叔孙、孟孙三家封邑的城墙。于是叔孙先把郈邑的城拆了。季孙也准备拆费邑的城，当时的邑宰公山不狃就和叔孙辄率领了费邑的丁众进袭鲁城，定公和季孙、叔孙、孟孙三人就躲进了季孙的住处，上了季孙武子的台（在鲁城东门内），费人围攻他们，却攻不下，但已有人逼到定公的台侧（"入及公侧"，俞樾谓入当作"矢"。则云箭矢已射至定公身旁矣）。孔子就派了申句须、乐顽下台来攻击他们，费人开始退走，国人乘胜追击，在姑蔑（今山东泗水县南）地方把他们彻底打败了。公山不狃、叔孙辄两人便逃到齐国，终于把费城拆毁了。接着准备拆成城，成邑的邑宰公敛处父对孟孙氏说："拆了成邑的城，齐人必将进逼到我们北边门户。况且成城是你们孟氏的保障，没有成城就等于没有孟氏了。我打算抗命不拆。"十二月，定公率兵包围成城，没攻下来。

鲁定公十四年，孔子五十六岁。这时他以大司寇的职位参与国家大事，脸上露出得意的神色。孔门弟子见了说："听说君子祸事临头不慌张恐惧，好事到来也不喜形于色。"孔子说："是有这个话。但是不也听说过'乐其以贵下人'的话吗？"于是就把扰乱鲁国政事的大夫少正卯给杀了。孔子参与国政才三个月，贩羊卖猪的商人就不敢哄抬价钱，行人男女都分开走路，各守礼法，路上见了别人掉落的东西也不敢捡回去；四方旅客来到鲁国的，不必向官吏请求，都会给予亲切的照顾。

　　齐国听到了这种情形就担心起来，说道："孔子主政下去，鲁国必会强大称霸；要是称霸了，我们的地方最靠近那里，必然会先来并吞我们了，何不先给他们一些土地呢？"黎鉏说："还是先设法破坏他们的改革图强；如果破坏不成，再送给他们土地也不迟呀！"于是就挑选了国内漂亮的少女八十人，都穿上华丽的衣裳，教她们学会跳康乐舞，连同身上有花纹的马一百二十匹，一起送去给鲁君。先把女乐和马匹安置在鲁城南面的高门外边。季桓子知道了，曾经穿便装偷偷地去观赏了好几回，打算接受下来，就跟鲁君说好，两人装要要环游各处，实地里是整天都到那儿观赏，把政事荒废下来。子路看了情形就劝孔子说："老师，我们可以离开了！"孔子说："鲁国不久就要春祭天地，如果当局遵守礼法，能把典礼后的祭肉分送给大夫，就表示仍有可为，那么我们还可以暂时留下。"季桓子终于是接受了齐人送来的女子乐团，整日沉迷其间，一连三天都不过问政务；而且春祭天地的大典之后，又违背常礼，没给大夫们分送祭肉，于是孔子失望地离开了鲁国，当天就在屯（在鲁城南）的地方过夜。乐师己前来送行，说道："先生就这样怪罪了？"孔子说："我唱个歌告诉你好吗？"于是唱道："听信妇人的话，可以失去亲信；过于接近妇女，可以使人败事亡身。既然如此就该离开，优游自在地安度岁月。"乐师己回去了，桓子问他说："孔子说了些什么？"乐师己照实相告。桓子长叹一声，说："孔夫子是为了那一群女乐的事怪罪我了！"

五年漂泊（公元前496—前492年）

　　孔子来到了卫国，寄住在子路的大舅子颜浊邹家里。卫灵公问孔子：

"你在鲁国的官俸是多少？"孔子回答说："官俸是六万小斗粟子。"卫国也照样给了六万小斗粟子。过不多久，有人向卫灵公说了孔子的坏话，灵公就派公孙余假带了兵仗在孔子那儿走出走进，孔子担心会出事惹祸，待了十个月，就离开了卫国。

正打算到陈国去，经过匡（在今河北长桓县西南）城，弟子颜刻（刻亦作剋）替孔子赶车，用鞭子指着一处说："从前我进这个城，就是由那个缺口进去的。"匡人听说当年和阳虎同行的颜刻出现，以为鲁国的阳虎又来了。因为阳虎曾经欺虐过匡人，匡人于是就留住孔子。孔子的模样像阳虎，所以被困在那里整整有五天。慌乱中颜渊失散了，稍后才来会合，孔子见了说："我以为你乱中遇难了！"颜渊说："老师您还健在，我怎敢轻易就死呢！"匡人围捕孔子围得越来越急，弟子们都很紧张，孔子就说："文王虽已死了，文化道统并没有丧失，现在不都在我们身上吗？上天如果要绝灭这个文化道统的话，就不会让我们能够认知并负起传承的责任。天意既然是不绝灭这个文化道统，那匡人又能对我怎么样？"于是孔子派了一个随行弟子到卫宁武子那里做家臣（此句所言与《左传》《家语》不合，恐有误），然后才得脱险离开。

从匡出来就到了蒲（在匡城北十五里），过了一个多月，又回到卫国，寄住在蘧伯玉家。卫灵公的夫人名叫南子的，派了人去对孔子说："各国的君子只要有意和我们国君攀交情的，必定会来见我们夫人；我们夫人愿意见你。"孔子托言推辞告罪一番，最后还是不得已去见了。会见时，夫人站在葛细布做的帷幕里面，孔子进了门，向北跪拜行礼，夫人在帷幕里面回拜答礼，身上的佩玉首饰触发清脆的响声。事后孔子说："我一向是不想去见她，现在既然不得已见了，就得还她以礼。"子路还是不高兴，孔子就很严正地申明道："我要不是因存着得君行道的一点希望才不得已去回见她的话，天一定厌弃我！天一定厌弃我！"过了个把月，卫灵公和夫人同坐了一辆车，宦官雍渠陪侍在右，出了宫门，要孔子坐第二部车子跟着，就大摇大摆地从市上走过。孔子感慨地说："我还没见过爱慕德行像爱慕美色一般热切的人。"于是对这里的一切感到厌恶失望，就离开卫国往曹国去了。这一年，鲁定公死了。

孔子又离开曹国，来到宋国。一天和弟子们在大树下讲习礼仪。宋国的司马桓魋想要加害孔子，把大树给砍了，孔子只好离去。弟子催促说："我们行动该快一点！"孔子说："上天既然赋了道德使命给我，桓魋他又能把我怎样！"

孔子来到郑国，却和弟子彼此失散了；孔子一个人站在外城的东门口。郑国有人看见了就对子贡说："东门那里站有一个人，他的额头像唐尧，脖子像皋陶，肩膀像子产，可是从腰以下比禹短了三寸；一副疲惫倒霉的样子，真像个失去主人家的狗。"子贡见面把这些话据实告诉孔子，孔子笑着说："一个人的状貌如何，那是不重要的；倒是他说我像只失去主人家的狗，那可真是啊！那可真是啊！"

孔子来到了陈国，寄住在司城贞子家里。过了一年多，吴王夫差来打陈国，夺取了三个城邑才撤兵。赵侯鞅来打卫国的朝歌。楚国来围攻蔡国，蔡国就请求迁到吴国的土地上去，受他保护。吴国又在会稽地方把越王勾践打败了。

有一天，许多鹰隼落在陈国宫廷前死了，身上被楛木做的箭射穿着，箭头是石头做的，箭杆有一尺八寸长。陈愍公派了人来请教孔子，孔子说："鹰隼飞来的地方是很远了，这箭是肃慎人的箭。从前武王灭亡了商纣，就和四方的蛮夷民族来往，开导他们。他恩威并施，要他们把各地的特产献给朝廷，叫他们不能忘记自己的职责义务。于是肃慎人献来楛木做的箭杆，石头做的箭头，长度是一尺八寸。先王为了表彰他的美德，就把肃慎人的箭分给长女太姬。后来太姬嫁了虞胡公，虞胡公又封来陈国。当初王室分美玉给同姓诸侯，用意是要展现亲谊，分远方贡物给异姓诸侯，是要他们不忘归服周王，所以分给陈国肃慎人的箭。"愍公听了叫人到旧府去查证一下，果然找到了这种箭。

　　孔子在陈住了三年，正好遇着晋、楚两国在争强斗胜，一再来打陈国，直到吴国攻打陈为止，陈国常常受到侵犯。孔子感叹说："回去吧！回去吧！留在我们家乡的那批孩子们，志气都大，只是行事疏略些，他们都很有进取心，也没忘掉自己的初衷。"于是孔子就离开了陈国。

　　路过蒲邑，刚好遇上公叔氏占据了蒲而背叛卫国，蒲人就留住孔子。弟子中有个叫公良孺的，自己带了五辆车子跟随孔子周游各地。他这个人身材高大，才德好，又英勇；他对孔子说："我以前跟着老师在匡的地方遇到危难，如今又在这里遇上危难，这是命吧！我和老师一再地遭难，宁愿跟他们拼死算了！"于是就跟蒲人猛烈地拼斗起来。蒲人害怕了，就对孔子说："如果能不去卫国，我就放你们走。"双方条件谈好，就放孔子一行从东门离去。孔子脱险后却一路前往卫国。子贡说："约定好的条件可以不遵守吗？"孔子说："在胁迫下订的条约，神明是不会认可的。"卫灵公听说孔子来了，很高兴，亲自出城来迎接。问道："蒲可以讨伐吗？"孔子答说："可以。"灵公说："我的大夫却认为不能去讨伐。因为现在的蒲是卫国防备晋、楚的前哨据点，我们自己发兵去打，如果蒲人干脆投靠敌方，或敌方趁机来袭，那后果不是很不好吗？"孔子说："蒲邑的百姓，男的都效忠卫国，有拼死的决心；妇女们也有保卫这块西河地方的愿望。所以我们所要讨伐的，只是领头叛乱的四五个人罢了。"灵公说："很好。"却不去伐蒲。

卫灵公年纪大了，政务废弛，也不用孔子。孔子感叹地说："如果有人用我来掌理国政，一年就可以有个样子，三年便有具体成效了。"孔子只好离开了。

佛肸做中牟（在今河南汤阴县西）邑宰。晋国的大夫赵简子要攻灭范氏、中行氏两家，中牟不服赵氏，就来攻伐中牟。佛肸就据有中牟公然反叛了，派人来召请孔子协助，孔子有意前往，子路说："我听老师说过：'一个本身做了坏事的人那里，君子是不会去的。'现在佛肸自己据了中牟反叛，您想前去，这又是为什么呢？"孔子说："我是说过这话的。但我不也说过真正坚实的东西吗？它是怎样磨都不会薄损的，不也说过真正精白的东西吗？它是怎么抹也不会污黑的。我难道是个中看不中吃的葫芦瓜（一云匏瓜为星名）吗？怎么能只供人挂着而不吃呢！"

一天孔子击着磬，有个担着草制盛土器经过门前的人听见了，说道："真是有心啊，这个击磬的人，叮叮当当地直敲着。既然世上没有人赏识自己，那就算了吧！"

孔子向鲁国的乐官师襄子学弹琴，一连十天都没有进展。师襄子说："可以进学一层了。"孔子说："我已学会了乐曲的形式，但节奏内容还不了解。"过了一些时候，师襄子又说："你已学得了曲子的节奏内容，可以进学一层了。"孔子说："我还没领会乐曲的情感意蕴。"过了一些时候，师襄子又说："你已领会了乐曲的情感意蕴，可以进学一层了。"孔子说："乐曲中那个人我还体认不出呢！"再过一段时间，孔子一副安详虔敬有所深思的样子，随又欣喜陶然，像是视野情志正与高远的目标相遇似的。最后说道："我体认出曲中的这个人啦！他的样子黑黑的，个子高高的，眼光是那样的明亮远大。像个统治四方诸侯的王者，这不是文王又有谁能够如此呢！"师襄子离开座位很恭敬地说："我就说过这是文王的琴曲啊！"

孔子既然不被卫王所用，打算往西去见赵简子。到了黄河边，听到窦鸣犊、舜华两人被杀的消息，就对着河水感叹说："河水是这样的壮美，这样的盛大啊！我不渡过这条河，也是命吧！"子贡听了趋前问道："请问这话是什么意思？"孔子说："窦鸣犊和舜华两人是晋国有才德的大夫。当赵简子还没有得志的时候，是倚仗这两人才能从政的；如今他得志了，却杀了他们来执掌政权。我听说过：一个地方的人，如果残忍到剖开动物的肚子来杀死其幼儿，麒麟是不来到郊外的，排干了池塘水来捉鱼，蛟龙就不肯调和阴阳来兴云致雨了；弄翻鸟儿的巢打破了卵，凤凰就不愿来飞翔。这是为什么呢？是君子忌讳自己的同类受到伤害啊！连飞鸟走兽对于不义的人事尚且知道避开，何况是我孔丘呢！"于是回到陬乡歇息，作了《陬操》这首琴曲来哀悼他们两人。随后又回到了卫，进住蘧伯玉的家。

有一天，卫灵公问起军队战阵的事。孔子说："关于祭祀典礼的事，我倒听说过，至于军队战阵的事，却是不曾学过。"第二天，灵公正和孔子在谈话，见有雁群飞过，只顾抬头仰望，神色间并不注意孔子。于是孔子就离开卫，又去陈国。

同年的夏天，卫灵公死了，立了灵公的孙子辄继位，他就是卫出公。六月间，赵鞅（赵简子）派人把流亡在外的卫灵公太子蒯聩（出公辄之父）强送到卫国的戚邑。于是阳虎要太子去掉帽子露出发髻，另外八个人穿麻戴孝，装成是从卫来接太子回去奔丧的样子，哭着进了戚城，就住了下来。冬天里，蔡国从新蔡迁到州来（下蔡，时属吴地）。这一年正是鲁哀公三年，而孔子已六十岁了。齐国协助卫国围攻戚城，是因为卫太子蒯聩住在那儿。

夏天里，鲁桓公、厘公的庙失火烧了起来。这时孔子在陈国，听说鲁庙失火了，说道："火灾一定发生在桓公、厘公的庙吧！"后来消息证实，果然是如他所言。到了秋天，季桓子病重，乘着辇车望见鲁城，感叹地说："以前这个国家几乎是可以强盛起来的，只因为我得罪了孔子，没有好好用他，所以才没有兴盛啊！"随即对着他的嗣子康子说："我死了，你必然接掌鲁国的政权；掌政之后，一定得请孔子回来。"过了几天，桓子死了，康子继承了卿位。丧事办完之后，想召孔子。公之鱼却说："从前我们先君（桓子）用他没用到底，最后惹来别国的笑话，现在你再用他，如果又是半途而废，别国岂不又要笑话你。"季康子说："那要召谁才好呢？"公之鱼说："应该召冉求。"于是就派了专人来召冉求。冉求正要起程时，孔子说："鲁国当局来召冉求，不会小用他，该会重用他的。"就在这一天，孔子说："回去吧！回去吧！在我们家乡的那批孩子，志气都大，只是行事疏略些；他们的文采都很美，我真不知道要怎样来调教他们才好。"子贡知道了孔子想回乡，在送冉求时，据说就叮嘱他："就职了，设法要他们来请老师回去！"

厄于陈蔡（公元前491—前489年）

冉求回去后，第二年，孔子从陈国迁到蔡国。蔡昭公要到吴国去，这是吴王召他去的。以前昭公欺骗他的臣子要把都邑迁到吴境的州来，现在即将应召前往，大夫们担心他又要搬迁，公孙翩就在路上把他射杀了。楚军来进犯蔡国。同年秋天，齐景公死了。

第二年，孔子从蔡国前往叶。叶公（楚大夫诸梁封邑在叶，僭称公）问孔子为政的道理，孔子说："为政的道理在使远方的人归附，近处的人服帖。"有一天，叶公向子路问起孔子的为人，子路没回答他。孔子知道了就对子路说："仲由！你怎么不回他说'他这个人嘛，学起道术来毫不倦怠，教起人来全不厌烦，用起功来连饭也会忘了吃，求道有得高兴起来，什么忧愁都可忘掉，甚至连衰老即将到来也不知道了'等等。"

离开了叶，在回蔡的路上，长沮、桀溺两人一起在田里耕作。孔子看出了他们是隐居的高士，就叫子路前去向他们打听渡口的方位。长沮说："那车上拉着缰绳的人是谁？"子路说："是孔丘。"长沮说："是鲁国的孔丘吗？"子路说："是的。"长沮说："那他该知道渡口在哪儿了。"桀溺遂又问子路说："你是谁？"子路说："我是仲由。"桀溺说："那你，是孔丘的门徒啰！"子路说："是的。"桀溺说："天下哪儿都是一样的动荡啊，但是又有谁能改变这种局势？况且你与其跟着那逃避暴君乱臣的人到处奔波，还不如跟着我们这种避开整个乱世的人来得安逸自在呢！"说着，就自顾自去下种覆土了。子路把经过情形报告了孔子，孔子怅然地说："人总该有责任的，怎可自顾隐居山林，终日与鸟兽生活在一起。天下如果清明太平的话，那我也用不着到处奔走要想改变这个局面了。"

有一天，子路一个人走着，遇上一位肩上挑着除草竹器的老人。子路请问道："你可看见了我的老师？"老人说："你们这些人，手脚都不劳动，五谷也分不清楚，谁是你老师我怎么会知道？"只管拄着杖去除草。事后子路把经过告诉了孔子，孔子说："那是一位隐士。"叫子路回去看看，老人却已走了。

孔子迁到蔡国的第三年，吴国进攻陈国。楚国前来救陈，军队驻扎在城父（楚邑，在今河南宝丰县东）。听说孔子住在陈、蔡两国的边境上，楚国就派了专人来聘请孔子。孔子正打算应聘前去见礼，陈、蔡两国的大夫就商议说："孔子是位有才德的贤者，凡他所讽刺讥评的，都切中诸侯的弊病所在。如今他长久留驻在我们陈、蔡两国之间，各位大夫的所作所为，都不合于仲尼的观点意思。现在的楚国是个强大的国家，却来礼聘孔子；楚国如果真用了孔子，那我们陈、蔡两国掌政的大夫就危险了。"于是双方都派了人一起把孔子围困在荒野上，动弹不得，粮食也断绝了。随行弟子饿病了，都打不起精神来。孔子却照样不停地讲他的学，朗诵他的书，弹他的琴，唱他的歌。子路满怀懊恼地来见孔子，说道："君子也会有这样困穷的时候吗？"孔子说："会有的，只不过君子遭到困穷时能够把持自己，小人遭到困穷的话，那就什么事都做得出来了。"子贡的神色也变了，孔子对他说："赐啊，你以为我是多方去学习而把学来的牢记在心里的吗？"子贡说："是的，难道不对吗？"孔子说："不是的，我是把握住事物相通的基本道理，而加以统摄贯通的。"

孔子知道弟子心中有着懊恼不平，于是召子路前来问他说："《诗》上说：'不是犀牛也不是老虎，为什么偏偏巡行在旷野之中。'难道是我的道理有什么不对吗？我为什么会落到这个地步？"子路说："想必是我们的仁德不够吧，所以人家不信任我们；想必是我们的智谋不足吧，所以人家不放我们通行。"孔子说："有这个道理吗？仲由，假使有仁德的人便能使人信任，那伯夷、叔齐怎会饿死在首阳山呢？假使有智谋的人就能通行无阻，那王子比干怎会被纣王剖心呢？"子路退出，子贡进来相见。孔子说："赐啊！《诗》上说：'不是犀牛也不是老虎，为什么偏偏巡行在旷野之中。'难道是我的道理有什么不对吗？为什么我会落到这个地步？"子贡说："老师的道理是大到极点了，所以天下人就不能容受老师。老师何不稍微降低迁就一些！"孔子说："赐，好农夫虽然善于播种五谷，却不一定准有好收成；好工匠能有精巧的手艺，所作却不一定能尽合人意；君子能够修治他的道术，就像治丝结网一般，先建立最基本的大纲统绪，再依序疏理结扎，但不一定能容合于当世。现在你不去修治自己的道术，反而想降格来苟合求容，赐啊！你的志向就不远大了！"子贡出去了，颜回进来相见。孔子说："回啊！《诗》上说：'不是犀牛也不是老虎，为什么偏偏巡行在旷野之中。'难道是我的道理有什么不对吗？为什么我会落到这个地步呢？"颜回说："老师的道术大到极点了，所以天下人就不能够容受。然而，老师照着自己的道术推广开去，不被容受又有什么关系？人家不能容，正见得老师是一位不苟合取容的君子呢！一个人道术不修治，才是自己的耻辱；至于道术既已大大地修成而不被人所用，那是有国的君主和执政大臣的耻辱了。不被容受有什么关系？人家不能容，正见得自己是一位不苟合取容的君子呢！"孔子听了欣慰地笑了，说道："有这回事吗？颜家的子弟呀！假使你能有很多财富的话，我真愿意做家宰，替你经理财用呢！"于是差了子贡到楚国去，楚昭王便派兵前来迎护孔子，才免去了这场灾祸。

楚昭王想把有居民户籍七百里大的地方封给孔子。楚国的令尹子西（即公子申，昭王之兄）阻止说："大王使臣出使到诸侯各国的，有像子贡这样称职的吗？"昭王说："没有。"子西又问："大王左右辅佐大臣，有像颜回这样贤能的吗？"昭王说："没有。"子西又问："大王的将帅，有像子路这样英勇的吗？"昭王说："没有。"子西再问："大王各部主事的臣子，有像宰予这样干练的吗？"昭王也说："没有。"子西接着说："况且我们楚国的祖先在受周天子分封时，名位只是子爵，土地是跟男爵相等的方五十里。如今孔丘遵循三皇五帝的遗规，效法周公、召公的德业，大王如果用了他，那么楚国还能世世代代公然保有几千里的土地吗？想当初文王在丰邑，武王在镐京，以百里小国的君主，两代经营终而统一天下。现在孔丘如拥有那七百里土地，又有那么多贤能弟子辅佐，对楚国来说并不是好事。"昭王听了就打消封地给孔子的念头。这年秋天，楚昭王死在城父。

楚国装狂自隐的贤士接舆，唱着歌走过孔子的车前，他唱道："凤呀！凤呀！你的品德身价怎么这样低落？过去的已经无法挽回补正了呀！可是将来的还可以来得及避免的。罢了！罢了！现在从政的人都是很危险的啊！"孔子下了车，想和他谈谈，他却快步走开了，没能跟他说上话。于是孔子从楚国回到了卫国。这一年，孔子六十三岁，也是鲁哀公六年。

再度漂泊（公元前488—前484年）

第二年，吴国和鲁国在缯（今山东峄县境）的地方会盟，吴王要求鲁国提供百牢（牛羊猪三牲俱备曰一牢）的礼献。吴太宰嚭召见季康子，康子就请子贡前去应对，经子贡据理力争才得免了。

孔子说："鲁、卫两国的政事，真是兄弟一般的情况。"这个时候，卫君出公辄的父亲蒯聩不能继位，流亡在外，这件事诸侯屡次加以指责。而孔子的弟子很多都在卫国做官，卫君辄也想要孔子来佐理政事。子路就问孔子说："卫君想要老师去帮他掌理政事。老师打算先做什么？"孔子说："那我必定要先端正名分吧！"子路说："有这回事吗？老师太迂阔不切实际了！有什么好正的？"孔子说："你真是鲁莽啊，仲由！要知道名分不正，说出来的话就不顺当；说话不顺当，政事就没法成功；政事不成功，礼乐教化就不能推行；教化不能推行，刑法就无法适中；刑罚不适中，那老百姓就不知道该怎么做才好。所以君子定下的名分，一定是可以顺当说出口；说出了的话，一定可以行得通。君子对他说出来的话，要做到没有一点的苟且随便才行。"

又过一年，冉有为季氏率领军队，和齐国在郎亭（在今山东鱼台县东北）地方作战，把齐兵打败了。季康子对冉求说："你对于军事作战的事是学来的呢，还是天生就懂的呢？"冉有说："是向孔子学的。"季康子说："孔子究竟是怎么样的一个人呢？"冉有回答说："想用他，要有光明正大的名分；即使向百姓公开宣布或明告于鬼神，都是没有遗憾的。如果是像我目前所处的这种情况，就是把千社（《索隐》：二十五家为社）这么大的地方给他，我们的老师也不会接受的。"季康子说："我想召请他回来，可以吗？"冉有回答说："如果真想召请他回来，就要信任他，不可让小人阻碍他，那是可以的。"这时卫大夫孔文子想攻打卫文公的后人太叔，向孔子问计。孔子推说不知道，随即招呼备车就离开了，说道："鸟是选择树林来栖息，树林哪能选择挽留它。"正好季康子赶走了公华、公宾、公林这几个人，备妥了周到的礼节来迎接孔子，孔子就回到了鲁国。

孔子离开鲁国后，一共经过了十四年的时间才又回到鲁国。

孔子之治学与生活习惯（公元前484—前481年）

鲁哀公问孔子为政的道理，孔子回答说："为政最重要的是选任好的臣子。"季康子也问孔子为政的道理，孔子说："举用正直的人来矫治邪曲的人，这样就能使邪曲的人也变为正直的了。"（《论语·颜渊》篇作孔子答樊迟问知之语）季康子忧虑国内的盗贼多，孔子告诉他说："如果你自己能够不贪欲，就是给予奖赏，人们也是不去偷窃的。"然而鲁国终究是不能用孔子，而孔子也不求出来做官。

在孔子的时代，周朝王室已经衰微，而礼乐的制度教化也废弛了，诗书典籍零散残缺。于是孔子探循三代以来的礼制遗规，厘定书传的篇次，上起唐尧、虞舜之间，下到秦穆公止，依照事类秩序加以编排。他说："夏代的礼制，我还能讲述个大概来，只是夏的后代杞国已经不足取证了；殷代的礼制，我还能讲述个大概来，也只可惜殷的后代宋国已经不足取证了。要是杞、宋两国保有足够的文献的话，那我就能拿来印证了。"孔子考察了殷、夏以来礼制增损的情形后，说道："以后就是经过百代，那变革的情形也是可以推知的。因承袭不移的是礼的精神本体，增损改变的是礼的文采仪节。周礼是参照了夏、殷两代而制订的，它的内容文采是那么的盛美！我是遵行周礼的。"所以《书传》《礼记》是出于孔子的。

孔子对鲁国的大乐官说："音乐演奏的过程是可以知道的。刚开始的时候，要八音五声齐全配合，接着乐音慢慢放开之后，要清浊高下和谐一致，又要宫商分明节奏清爽，更要首尾贯串声气不断，这样直到整首乐曲的演奏完成。"又说："我从卫国回到鲁国之后，才把诗乐订正了，使雅诗、颂诗都能配入到原来应有的乐部。"

古代留传下来的《诗》原有三千多篇，孔子把重选的去掉，选取可以用来配合礼义教化的部分。所取诗篇，最早的是追述殷始祖契、周始祖后稷的诗，其次是歌颂殷、周两代盛世的诗，再次是讽刺周幽王、周厉王政治缺失的诗，而一切都要以男女夫妇的家庭伦常为起点，所以说：《关雎》这一乐章是《国风》的第一篇；《鹿鸣》是《小雅》的第一篇；《文王》是《大雅》的第一篇；《清庙》是《颂诗》的第一篇。三百零五篇诗，孔子都把它人乐歌唱，以求合乎古代《韶乐》（虞舜乐）、《武乐》（武王乐）以及朝廷雅乐、庙堂颂乐的声情精神。先王礼乐教化的遗规，到此才稍复旧观而有可称述。王道完备了，六艺也齐全了。

孔子晚年喜欢《易》学，他阐述了（序，一云即《易·序卦》）《象辞》《系辞》《象辞》《说卦》《文言》等。他读《易》很勤，以至把编书简的皮绳都弄断了三次。还说过："再让我多活几年，这样的话，我对《易》

学的研究就可以文辞义理兼备充实了。"

孔子用《诗》《书》《礼》《乐》做教材来教人，就学的门生大约有三千人，而精通六艺的有七十二人。像颜浊邹一般受到孔子教诲却没有正式入籍的学生，为数也不少。

孔子教导学生有四个项目：《诗》《书》《礼》《乐》等籍典文献，生活上的身体力行，为人处世的忠诚尽心，待人接物的信实不欺。孔子戒绝了常人的四种毛病，不揣测、不武断、不固执、不自以为是。所特别谨慎的事是祭祀前的斋戒、战争、疾病。很少轻易谈及的是利、命和仁（此句异说不止一种，今从何氏《集解》暂译）。孔子教人，如果不是心求通而未通的，不去启发他；举述给他道理，却不能触类旁通的，就不再对他反复费词了。

孔子在自己的乡里，容貌恭敬温厚，好似不大会讲话的样子。他在宗庙祭祀和朝廷议政时却言辞明晰通达，只不过态度还是恭谨小心罢了。在朝中与上大夫交谈，态度中正自然，与下大夫交谈就显得和乐轻松了。

孔子进国君的宫门时，低头弯腰以示恭敬；然后急行而前，态度恭谨有礼。国君命他接待贵客，容色庄重认真。国君有命召见，不等车驾备好就尽快出发前往。鱼不新鲜，肉已发味，或切割不合规矩的都不吃。不适当的位子，不就座。在有丧事的人旁边吃饭，从没有吃饱过的。在这一天里哭过，就不唱歌。见到穿麻戴孝的人、目盲的人，即使是小孩子也必然改变面容表示同情。

孔子说："只要是有心向学，即使在同行三个人之中，必有可做我老师的。"又说："德行的不修明，学业的不讲求，听到正当的道理不能随之力行，对于不好的行为不能马上革除，这些都是我忧虑的。"孔子听人唱歌，要是唱得好，就请人再唱，然后自己跟着唱起来。

孔子不谈论关于怪异、暴力、悖乱以及鬼神的一些事情。

子贡说："老师所传授《诗》《书》《礼》《乐》等方面的文辞知识，我们还得以知道；至于老师有关性命天道的深微见解我们就不得知道了。"颜渊赞叹地说："老师的道术，我越仰慕它久了，越觉得崇高无比！越是钻研探究，越觉得它坚实深厚！看着它是在前面，忽然间却又在后面了。老师有条理有步骤地善于诱导人：用典籍文章来丰富我的知识，用礼仪道德来规范我的言行，使我想停止学习都不可能。即使是用尽了我所有的才力，而老师的道术却依然高高地立在我的面前。虽然尽想追随上去，但是无从追得上！"达巷党（五百家为党）的人说："孔子真是伟大啊！他博学道艺，却不专一名家。"孔子听了这话说道："我要专于什么呢？专于驾车，还是专于射箭？我看是专于驾车吧！"琴牢说："老师说过'我没能为世所用，所以才学会了这许多艺能'。"

鲁哀公十四年的春天里，在大野（今山东巨野县北）地方狩猎。叔孙氏的车夫商猎获了一只少见的野兽，他们认为是不吉利的事，孔子看了说："这是一只麒麟。"于是他们就把它运了回去。孔子说："黄河上再不见神龙负图出现，洛水中也不见背上有文字的灵龟浮出。圣王不再，我想行道救世，怕是没有希望了吧！"颜渊死了，孔子伤痛地说："是老天要亡我了吧！"等他见了在曲阜西边猎获的麒麟，说道："我行道的希望是完了！"孔子很感慨地说："没有人能了解我了！"子贡说："怎么没有人能了解老师呢？"孔子说："我不抱怨天，也不怪罪人；只顾从切近的人事上学起，再日求精进而上达天理，能知道我的，只有上天了吧！"

孔子说："不使自己的志气受到屈降，不使自己的身体受到玷辱，只有伯夷、叔齐两人了吧！"评论柳下惠、少连："志气降屈了，身子也玷辱了。"评论虞仲、夷逸："隐居在野，不言世务，行事合乎清高纯洁，自废免祸也权衡得宜。"又说:"我就跟他们的做法不一样。我不偏执一端,一切依情理行事,所以没有绝对的可以,也没有绝对的不可以。"

孔子说:"不成,不成!君子最遗憾的就是死后没有留下好声名。我的救世理想已经无法达成了,我要用什么来贡献社会留名后世呢?"于是根据鲁国的史记作了《春秋》一书:上起鲁隐公元年,下至鲁哀公十四年,前后一共包括了十二位国君。以鲁国为记述的中心,尊封周王为正统,参酌了殷朝的旧制,推而上承三代的法统。文辞精简而旨意深广。所以吴、楚君自称为王的,《春秋》就依据当初周王册封时的等级,降称他们为"子"爵;晋文公召集的践土会盟(事在鲁僖公二十八年),实际上是周襄王应召前去与会的,《春秋》以为这事不合法统而避开它,改写成:"周天子巡狩到了河阳。"推展这类的事例原则,作为衡断当时人行事违背礼法与否的标准。这种贬抑责备的大义,后代如有英明的君王加以倡导推广,使《春秋》的义法得以通行天下,那窃位盗名为非作歹的人,就会有所警惕惧怕了。

孔子过去任官审案时,文辞上如有需要与人共同商量斟酌的,他是不肯擅作决断的。到他写《春秋》时就不同了,认为该记录的就振笔直录,该删削的就断然删削,就连子夏这些长于文学的弟子,一句话都参酌不上。弟子们接受了《春秋》之后,孔子说:"后世的人知道我是在行圣王之道的,只有靠这部《春秋》;而怪罪我以布衣借褒贬来行王者赏罚的,也是因为这部《春秋》了。"

孔子逝世(公元前479年)及其后人

第二年,子路死在卫国(蒯聩夺位之乱)。孔子病了,子贡前来谒见,孔子正拄着手杖在门口慢步排遣，一见就说："赐啊！你怎么来得这么迟呢？"孔子随即叹了一声，口里哼道："泰山就这样崩坏吗？梁柱就这样摧折吗？哲人就这样凋谢吗？"哼完不禁淌了眼泪。稍后对子贡说："天下失去常道已经很久了，世人都不能遵循我的平治理想。夏人死了停棺在东阶，周人是在西阶，殷人则在两柱之间。昨天夜里我梦见自己坐定在两柱之间，我原本就是殷人啊！"过了七天就死了。

孔子享年七十三岁，死在鲁哀公十六年（公元前479年）四月的己丑日。鲁哀公对他悼念说："老天爷不仁慈，不肯留下这一位老人，使他抛开了我，害我孤零零地在位，我是既忧思又伤痛。唉，真伤心啊！尼父，我不再自拘礼法了！"事后子贡批评道："鲁公难道要不能终老于鲁国吗？老师的话说：'礼法丧失了就会昏乱，名分丧失了就有过愆。一个人丧失志气便是昏乱，失去所宜就是过愆。'人活着时不能用他，死了才来悼念他，这是不合礼的。诸侯自称'余一人'，是不合名分的。"

孔子死后葬在鲁城北面的泗水边上。弟子们都在心里为老师服丧三年，三年的心丧服完，大家在道别离去时都相对而哭，每人还是很哀痛，有的就又留下来。子贡甚至在墓旁搭了房子住下，守墓一共守了六年才离开。弟子以及鲁国的其他人，相率到墓旁定居的有一百多家，因而管那个地方叫"孔里"。鲁国世代相传每年都定时到孔子墓前祭拜，而儒者们讲习礼仪，乡学结业考校的饮酒礼，以及鲁君祭祀时的比射仪式，也都在孔子墓场（一云冢字当作家）举行。孔子的墓地有一顷大。孔子故居的堂屋以及弟子所住的房室，后来就地改成庙，收藏了孔子生前的衣服、冠帽、琴、车子、书籍，直到汉朝，两百多年来都没有废弃。高皇帝刘邦路过鲁地，用了太牢（牛羊猪三牲俱备）之礼祭拜孔子。诸侯卿相一到任，常是先到庙里祭拜之后才正式就职视事。

孔子生了鲤，字叫伯鱼。伯鱼享年五十岁，比孔子早死。

伯鱼生了伋，字子思，享年六十二岁。曾经受困于宋国。子思作了《中庸》。

子思生了白，字叫子上，享年四十七岁。子上生了求，字叫子家，享年四十五岁。子家生了箕，字叫子京，享年四十六岁。子京生了穿，字叫子高，享年五十一岁。子高生了子慎（子慎名或作斌，或作顺，或作彻，或作谦，疑莫能定，故史缺而不书），享年五十七岁，曾经做过魏国的相。

子慎生了鲋，鲋享年五十七岁。做了陈王涉（即陈胜，秦末与吴广首义抗秦）的博士，死在陈这个地方。

鲋的弟弟子襄（梁玉绳云名腾），享年五十七岁。做过汉孝惠皇帝的博士，后来改任长沙王太傅（长沙太守，钱大昕云：惠帝时，长沙为王国，不得有太守，《汉书》云太傅是也）。身高九尺六寸。

子襄生了忠，享年五十七岁。忠生了武，武生了延年和安国。安国做了孝武皇帝博士，又做到临淮郡太守，早年死了。安国生了卬，卬生了骧。

太史公说：《诗》上有言道："像高山一般令人瞻仰，像大道一般让人遵循。"虽然我达不到这个境地，但心中总是向往着他。我读了孔子的遗书，想见得到他为人的伟大。到鲁去的时候，参观了仲尼的庙堂，以及他遗留下来的车、服、礼器，那些读书的学生，都还按时到孔子的旧家来演习礼仪。我一时由衷敬仰，徘徊留恋地不肯离去。自古以来，天下的君王贤人也算很多了，活着时都很荣耀，到他一死就什么也没有了。孔子仅是一个平民，他的道统家世至今传了十几代，学者们都崇仰他。从天子王侯以下，凡是中国研讨六经道艺的人，都将孔夫子的话尊奉为最高的衡断标准，他真可说是一位圣明到极点的人了！

附：《史记·孔子世家》原文

孔子生鲁昌平乡陬邑。其先宋人也，曰孔防叔。防叔生伯夏，伯夏生叔梁纥。纥与颜氏女野合而生孔子；祷于尼丘，得孔子。鲁襄公二十二年而孔子生。生而首上圩顶，故因名曰丘云。字仲尼，姓孔氏。

丘生而叔梁纥死，葬于防山。防山在鲁东。由是孔子疑其父墓处，母讳之也。孔子为儿嬉戏，常陈俎豆，设礼容。孔子母死，乃殡五父之衢，盖其慎也。陬人挽父之母诲孔子父墓，然后往合葬于防焉。

孔子要绖。季氏飨士，孔子与往。阳虎绌曰："季氏飨士，非敢飨子也。"孔子由是退。

孔子年十七，鲁大夫孟厘子病且死，诫其嗣懿子曰："孔丘，圣人之后，灭于宋。其祖弗父何始有宋而嗣让厉公。及正考父佐戴、武、宣公，三命兹益恭，故鼎铭云：'一命而偻，再命而伛，三命而俯，循墙而走，亦莫敢余侮。饘于是，粥于是，以糊余口。'其恭如是。吾闻圣人之后，虽不当世，必有达者。今孔丘年少好礼，其达者欤？吾即没，若必师之。"及厘子卒，懿子与鲁人南宫敬叔往学礼焉。是岁，季武子卒，平子代立。

孔子贫且贱。及长，尝为季氏史，料量平；尝为司职吏，而畜蕃息。由是为司空。已而去鲁，斥乎齐，逐乎宋、卫，困于陈蔡之间，于是反鲁。孔子长九尺有六寸，人皆谓之"长人"而异之。鲁复善待，由是反鲁。

鲁南宫敬叔言鲁君曰："请与孔子适周。"鲁君与之一乘车、两马、一竖子俱，适周问礼。盖见老子云。辞去，而老子送之曰："吾闻富贵者送人以财，仁人者送人以言。吾不能富贵，窃仁人之号，送子以言，曰：'聪明深察而近于死者，好议人者也。博辩广大危其身者，发人之恶者也。为人子者毋以有己，为人臣者毋以有己。'"

孔子自周反于鲁，弟子稍益进焉。是时也，晋平公淫，六卿擅权，东伐诸侯；楚灵王兵强，陵轹中国；齐大而近于鲁。鲁小弱，附于楚则晋怒，附于晋则楚来伐；不备于齐，齐师侵鲁。

鲁昭公之二十年，而孔子盖年三十矣。齐景公与晏婴来适鲁，景公问孔子曰："昔秦穆公国小处辟，其霸何也？"对曰："秦，国虽小，其志大；处虽辟，行中正。身举五羖，爵之大夫，起累绁之中，与语三日，授之以政。以此取之，虽王可也，其霸小矣。"景公说。

孔子年三十五，而季平子与郈昭伯以斗鸡故，得罪鲁昭公。昭公率师击平子，平子与孟氏、叔孙氏三家共攻昭公，昭公师败，奔于齐。齐处昭公乾侯，其后顷之，鲁乱。孔子适齐，为高昭子家臣，欲以通乎景公。与齐太师语乐。闻韶音，学之，三月不知肉味。齐人称之。

景公问政孔子，孔子曰："君君，臣臣，父父，子子。"景公曰："善哉！信如君不君，臣不臣，父不父，子不子，虽有粟，吾岂得而食诸！"他日，又复问政于孔子，孔子曰："政在节财。"景公说，将欲以尼溪田封孔子。晏婴进曰："夫儒者滑稽而不可轨法；倨傲自顺，不可以为下；崇丧遂哀，破产厚葬，不可以为俗；游说乞贷，不可以为国。自大贤之息，周室既衰，礼乐缺有间。今孔子盛容饰，繁登降之礼、趋详之节，累世不能殚其学，当年不能究其礼。君欲用之以移齐俗，非所以先细民也。"后景公敬见孔子，不问其礼。异日，景公止孔子曰："奉子以季氏，吾不能。"以季、孟之间待之。齐大夫欲害孔子，孔子闻之。景公曰："吾老矣，弗能用也。"孔子遂行，反乎鲁。

孔子年四十二，鲁昭公卒于乾侯，定公立。定公立五年，夏，季平子卒，桓子嗣立。季桓子穿井得土缶，中若羊，问仲尼云"得狗"。仲尼曰："以丘所闻，羊也。丘闻之，木石之怪夔、罔阆，水之怪龙、罔象，土之怪坟羊。"

吴伐越，堕会稽，得骨节专车。吴使使问仲尼："骨何者最大？"仲尼曰："禹致群神于会稽山，防风氏后至。禹杀而戮之，其节专车，此为大矣。"吴客曰："谁为神？"仲尼曰："山川之神，足以纲纪天下，其守为神。社稷为公侯，皆属于王者。"客曰："防风何守？"仲尼曰："汪罔氏之君守封、禺之山，为厘姓。在虞、夏、商为汪罔，于周为长翟，今谓之大人。"客曰："人长几何？"仲尼曰："僬侥氏三尺，短之至也。长者不过十之，数之极也。"于是吴客曰："善哉圣人！"

桓子嬖臣曰仲梁怀，与阳虎有隙。阳虎欲逐怀，公山不狃止之。其秋，怀益骄，阳虎执怀。桓子怒，阳虎因囚桓子，与盟而醳之。阳虎由此益轻季氏，季氏亦僭于公室，陪臣执国政，是以鲁自大夫以下皆僭离于正道。故孔子不仕，退而修诗书礼乐，弟子弥众，至自远方，莫不受业焉。

定公八年，公山不狃不得意于季氏，因阳虎为乱，欲废三桓之适，更立其庶孽阳虎素所善者，遂执季桓子。桓子诈之，得脱。定公九年，阳虎不胜，奔于齐。是时孔子年五十。

公山不狃以费畔季氏，使人召孔子。孔子循道弥久，温温无所试，莫能己用，曰："盖周文武起丰镐而王，今费虽小，傥庶几乎！"欲往。子路不说，止孔子。孔子曰："夫召我者岂徒哉？如用我，其为东周乎！"然亦卒不行。

其后定公以孔子为中都宰，一年，四方皆则之。由中都宰为司空，由司空为大司寇。

定公十年春，及齐平。夏，齐大夫黎鉏言于景公曰："鲁用孔丘，其势危齐。"乃使使告鲁为好会，会于夹谷。鲁定公且以乘车好往。孔子摄相事，曰："臣闻有文事者必有武备，有武事者必有文备。古者诸侯出疆，必具官以从。请具左右司马。"定公曰："诺。"具左右司马。会齐侯夹谷，为坛位，土阶三等，以会遇之礼相见，揖让而登。献酬之礼毕，齐有司趋而进曰："请奏四方之乐。"景公曰："诺。"于是旍旄羽被矛戟剑拨鼓噪而至。孔子趋而进，历阶而登，不尽一等，举袂而言曰："吾两君为好会，夷狄之乐何为于此！请命有司！"有司却之，不去，则左右视晏子与景公。景公心怍，麾而去之。有顷，齐有司趋而进曰："请奏宫中之乐。"景公曰："诺。"优倡侏儒为戏而前。孔子趋而进，历阶而登，不尽一等，曰："匹夫而营惑诸侯者罪当诛！请命有司！"有司加法焉，手足异处。景公惧而动，知义不若，归而大恐，告其群臣曰："鲁以君子之道辅其君，而子独以夷狄之道教寡人，使得罪于鲁君，为之奈何？"有司进对曰："君子有过则谢以质，小人有过则谢以文。君若悼之，则谢以实。"于是齐侯乃归所侵鲁之郓、汶阳、龟阴之田，以谢过。

定公十三年夏，孔子言于定公曰："臣无藏甲，大夫无百雉之城。"使仲由为季氏宰，将堕三都。于是叔孙氏先堕郈。季氏将堕费，公山不狃、叔孙辄率费人袭鲁。公与三子入于季氏之宫，登武子之台。费人攻之，弗克，入及公侧。孔子命申句须、乐颀下伐之，费人北。国人追之，败诸姑蔑。二子奔齐，遂堕费。将堕成，公敛处父谓孟孙曰："堕成，齐人必至于北门。且成，孟氏之保鄣，无成，是无孟氏也。我将弗堕。"十二月，公围成，弗克。

定公十四年，孔子年五十六，由大司寇行摄相事，有喜色。门人曰：

"闻君子祸至不惧，福至不喜。"孔子曰："有是言也。不曰'乐其以贵下人'乎？"于是诛鲁大夫乱政者少正卯。与闻国政三月，粥羔豚者弗饰贾；男女行者别于涂；涂不拾遗；四方之客至乎邑者不求有司，皆予之以归。

齐人闻而惧，曰："孔子为政必霸，霸则吾地近焉，我之为先并矣。盍致地焉？"黎鉏曰："请先尝沮之；沮之而不可则致地，庸迟乎！"于是选齐国中女子好者八十人，皆衣文衣而舞《康乐》，文马三十驷，遗鲁君。陈女乐文马于鲁城南高门外。季桓子微服往观再三，将受，乃语鲁君为周道游，往观终日，怠于政事。子路曰："夫子可以行矣。"孔子曰："鲁今且郊，如致膰乎大夫，则吾犹可以止。"桓子卒受齐女乐，三日不听政；郊，又不致膰俎于大夫。孔子遂行，宿乎屯。而师己送，曰："夫子则非罪。"孔子曰："吾歌可夫？"歌曰："彼妇之口，可以出走，彼妇之谒，可以死败。盖优哉游哉，维以卒岁！"师己反，桓子曰："孔子亦何言？"师己以实告。桓子喟然叹曰："夫子罪我，以群婢故也夫！"

孔子遂适卫，主于子路妻兄颜浊邹家。卫灵公问孔子："居鲁得禄几何？"对曰："奉粟六万。"卫人亦致粟六万。居顷之，或谮孔子于卫灵公。灵公使公孙余假一出一入。孔子恐获罪焉，居十月，去卫。

将适陈，过匡。颜刻为仆，以其策指之曰："昔吾入此，由彼缺也。"匡人闻之，以为鲁之阳虎。阳虎尝暴匡人，匡人于是遂止孔子。孔子状类阳虎，拘焉五日，颜渊后，子曰："吾以汝为死矣。"颜渊曰："子在，回何敢死！"匡人拘孔子益急，弟子惧。孔子曰："文王既没，文不在兹乎？天之将丧斯文也，后死者不得与于斯文也。天之未丧斯文也，匡人其如予何！"孔子使从者为宁武子臣于卫，然后得去。

去即过蒲。月余，反乎卫，主蘧伯玉家。灵公夫人有南子者，使人谓孔子曰："四方之君子不辱欲与寡君为兄弟者，必见寡小君。寡小君愿见。"孔子辞谢，不得已而见之。夫人在絺帷中。孔子入门，北面稽首。夫人自帷中再拜，环佩玉声璆然。孔子曰："吾乡为弗见，见之礼答焉。"子路不说，孔子矢之曰："予所不者，天厌之！天厌之！"居卫月余。灵公与夫人同车，宦者雍渠参乘。出，使孔子为次乘，招摇市过之。孔子曰："吾未见好德如好色者也。"于是丑之，去卫，过曹。是岁，鲁定公卒。

孔子去曹适宋，与弟子习礼大树下。宋司马桓魋欲杀孔子，拔其树。孔子去。弟子曰："可以速矣。"孔子曰："天生德于予，桓魋其如予何！"

孔子适郑，与弟子相失，孔子独立郭东门。郑人或谓子贡曰："东门有人，其颡似尧，其项类皋陶，其肩类子产，然自要以下不及禹三寸，累累若丧家之狗。"子贡以实告孔子。孔子欣然笑曰："形状，末也。而谓似丧家之狗，然哉！然哉！"

孔子遂至陈，主于司城贞子家。岁余，吴王夫差伐陈，取三邑而去。赵鞅伐朝歌。楚围蔡，蔡迁于吴。吴败越王勾践会稽。

有隼集于陈廷而死，楛矢贯之，石砮，矢长尺有咫。陈愍公使使问仲尼。仲尼曰："隼来远矣，此肃慎之矢也。昔武王克商，通道九夷百蛮，使各以其方贿来贡，使无忘职业。于是肃慎贡楛矢石砮，长尺有咫。先生欲昭其令德，以肃慎矢分大姬，配虞胡公而封诸陈。分同姓以珍玉，展亲；分异姓以远方职，使无忘服。故分陈以肃慎矢。"试求之故府，果得之。

孔子居陈三岁，会晋楚争强，更伐陈；及吴侵陈，陈常被寇。孔子曰："归与归与！吾党之小子狂简进取，不忘其初。"于是孔子去陈。

过蒲，会公叔氏以蒲畔，蒲人止孔子。弟子有公良孺者，以私车五乘从孔子。其为人长贤有勇力，谓曰："吾昔从夫子遇难于匡，今又遇难于此，命也已。吾与夫子再罹难，宁斗而死。"斗甚疾。蒲人惧，谓孔子曰："苟毋适卫，吾出子。"与之盟，出孔子东门。孔子遂适卫。子贡曰："盟可负耶？"孔子曰："要盟也，神不听。"

卫灵公闻孔子来，喜，郊迎。问曰："蒲可伐乎？"对曰："可。"灵公曰："吾大夫以为不可。今蒲，卫之所以待晋楚也，以卫伐之，无乃不可乎？"孔子曰："其男子有死之志，妇人有保西河之志。吾所伐者不过四五人。"灵公曰："善。"然不伐蒲。

灵公老，怠于政，不用孔子。孔子喟然叹曰："苟有用我者，期月而已，三年有成。"孔子行。

佛肸为中牟宰。赵简子攻范、中行，伐中牟。佛肸畔，使人召孔子，孔子欲往。子路曰："由闻诸夫子，'其身亲为不善者，君子不入也'。今佛肸亲以中牟畔，子欲往，如之何？"孔子曰："有是言也。不曰坚乎，磨而不磷；不曰白乎，涅而不淄。我岂匏瓜也哉，焉能系而不食？"

孔子击磬。有荷蒉而过门者，曰："有心哉，击磬乎！硁硁乎，莫己知也夫而已矣！"

孔子学鼓琴师襄子，十日不进。师襄子曰："可以益矣。"孔子曰："丘已习其曲矣，未得其数也。"有间，曰："已习其数，可以益矣。"孔子曰："丘未得其志也。"有间，曰："已习其志，可以益矣。"孔子曰："丘未得其为人也。"有间，有所穆然深思焉，有所怡然高望而远志焉。曰："丘得其为人，黯然而黑，几然而长，眼如望羊，如王四国，非文王其谁能为此也！"师襄子辟席再拜，曰："师盖云《文王操》也。"

孔子既不得用于卫，将西见赵简子。至于河而闻窦鸣犊、舜华之死也，临河而叹曰："美哉水，洋洋乎！丘之不济此，命也夫！"子贡趋而进曰："敢问何谓也？"孔子曰："窦鸣犊、舜华，晋国之贤大夫也。赵简子未得志之时，须此两人而后从政；及其已得志，杀之乃从政。丘闻之也，刳胎杀夭则麒麟不至郊，竭泽涸渔则蛟龙不合阴阳，覆巢毁卵则凤凰不翔。何则？君子讳伤其类也。夫鸟兽之于不义也尚知辟之，而况乎丘哉！"乃还息乎陬乡，作为《陬操》以哀之。而反乎卫，入主蘧伯玉家。

他日，灵公问兵陈。孔子曰："俎豆之事则尝闻之，军旅之事未之学也。"明日，与孔子语，见蜚雁，仰视之，色不在孔子。孔子遂行，复如陈。

夏，卫灵公卒，立孙辄，是为卫出公。六月，赵鞅内太子蒯聩于戚。阳虎使太子絻，八人衰绖，伪自卫迎者，哭而入，遂居焉。冬，蔡迁于州来。是岁鲁哀公三年，而孔子年六十矣。齐助卫围戚，以卫太子蒯聩在故也。

夏，鲁桓厘庙燔，南宫敬叔救火。孔子在陈，闻之，曰："灾必于桓厘庙乎？"已而果然。

秋，季桓子病，辇而见鲁城，喟然叹曰："昔此国几兴矣，以吾获罪于孔子，故不兴也。"顾谓其嗣康子曰："我即死，若必相鲁；相鲁，必召仲尼。"后数日，桓子卒，康子代立。已葬，欲召仲尼。公之鱼曰："昔吾先君用之不终，终为诸侯笑。今又用之，不能终，是再为诸侯笑。"康子曰："则谁召而可？"曰："必召冉求。"于是使使召冉求。冉求将行，孔子曰："鲁人召求，非小用之，将大用之也。"是日，孔子曰："归乎归乎！吾党之小子狂简，斐然成章，吾不知所以裁之。"子赣知孔子思归，送冉求，因诫曰"即用，以孔子为招"云。

冉求既去，明年，孔子自陈迁于蔡。蔡昭公将如吴，吴召之也。前昭公欺其臣迁州来，后将往，大夫惧复迁，公孙翩射杀昭公。楚侵蔡。秋，齐景公卒。

明年，孔子自蔡如叶。叶公问政，孔子曰："政在来远附迩。"他日，叶公问孔子于子路，子路不对。孔子闻之，曰："由，尔何不对曰'其为人也，学道不倦，诲人不厌，发愤忘食，乐以忘忧，不知老之将至'云尔。"

去叶，反于蔡。长沮、桀溺耦而耕，孔子以为隐者，使子路问津焉。长沮曰："彼执舆者为谁？"子路曰："为孔丘。"曰："是鲁孔丘与？"曰："然。"曰："是知津矣。"桀溺谓子路曰："子为谁？"曰："为仲由。"曰："子，孔丘之徒与？"曰："然。"桀溺曰："悠悠者天下皆是也，而谁以易之？且与其从辟人之士，岂若从辟世之士哉！"耰而不辍。子路以告孔子，孔子怃然曰："鸟兽不可与同群。天下有道，丘不与易也。"

他日，子路行，遇荷蓧丈人，曰："子见夫子乎？"丈人曰："四体不勤，五谷不分，孰为夫子！"植其杖而芸。子路以告，孔子曰："隐者也。"复往，则亡。

孔子迁于蔡三岁，吴伐陈。楚救陈，军于城父。闻孔子在陈蔡之间，楚使人聘孔子。孔子将往拜礼，陈蔡大夫谋曰："孔子贤者，所刺讥皆中诸侯之疾。今日久留陈蔡之间，诸大夫所设行皆非仲尼之意。今楚，大国也，来聘孔子。孔子用于楚，则陈蔡用事大夫危矣。"于是乃相与发徒役围孔子于野。不得行，绝粮，从者病，莫能兴。孔子讲诵弦歌不衰。子路愠见曰："君子亦有穷乎？"孔子曰："君子固穷，小人穷斯滥矣。"

子贡色作。孔子曰："赐，尔以予为多学而识之者与？"曰："然。非与？"孔子曰："非也。予一以贯之。"

孔子知弟子有愠心，乃召子路而问曰："《诗》云：'匪兕匪虎，率彼旷野'。吾道非耶？吾何为于此？"子路曰："意者吾未仁耶？人之不我信也。意者吾未知耶？人之不我行也。"孔子曰："有是乎！由，譬使仁者而必信，安有伯夷、叔齐？使知者而必行，安有王子比干？"

子路出，子贡入见。孔子曰："赐，《诗》云：'匪兕匪虎，率彼旷野'。吾道非耶？吾何为于此？"子贡曰："夫子之道至大也，故天下莫能容夫子。夫子盖少贬焉？"孔子曰："赐，良农能稼而不能为穑，良工能巧而不能为顺。君子能修其道，纲而纪之，统而理之，而不能为容。今尔不修尔道而求为容。赐，而志不远矣！"

子贡出，颜回入见。孔子曰："回，《诗》云：'匪兕匪虎，率彼旷野'。吾道非耶？吾何为于此？"颜回曰："夫子之道至大，故天下莫能容。虽然，夫子推而行之，不容何病？不容然后见君子！夫道之不修也，是吾丑也。夫道既已大修而不用，是有国者之丑也。不容何病？不容然后见君子！"孔子欣然而笑曰："有是哉？颜氏之子！使尔多财，吾为尔宰。"

于是使子贡至楚。楚昭王兴师迎孔子，然后得免。

昭王将以书社地七百里封孔子。楚令尹子西曰："王之使使诸侯有如子贡者乎？"曰："无有。""王之辅相有如颜回者乎？"曰："无有。""王之将率有如子路者乎？"曰："无有。""王之官尹有如宰予者乎？"曰："无有。""且楚之祖封于周，号为子男五十里。今孔丘述三王之法，明周召之业，王若用之，则楚安得世世堂堂方数千里乎？夫文王在丰，武王在镐，百里之君，卒王天下。今孔丘得据土壤，贤弟子为佐，非楚之福也。"昭王乃止。其秋，楚昭王卒于城父。

楚狂接舆歌而过孔子，曰："凤兮凤兮，何德之衰！往者不可谏兮，来者犹可追也！已而已而，今之从政者殆而！"孔子下，欲与之言。趋而去，弗得与之言。

于是孔子自楚反乎卫。是岁也，孔子年六十三，而鲁哀公六年也。

其明年，吴与鲁会缯，征百牢。太宰嚭召季康子。康子使子贡往，然后得已。

孔子曰："鲁卫之政，兄弟也。"是时，卫君辄父不得立，在外，诸侯数以为让。而孔子弟子多仕于卫，卫君欲得孔子为政。子路曰："卫君待子而为政，子将奚先？"孔子曰："必也正名乎！"子路曰："有是哉，子之迂也！何其正也？"孔子曰："野哉由也！夫名不正则言不顺，言不顺则事不成，事不成则礼乐不兴，礼乐不兴则刑罚不中，刑罚不中则民无所措手足矣。夫君子为之必可名，言之必可行。君子于其言，无所苟而已矣。"

其明年，冉有为季氏将师，与齐战于郎，克之。季康子曰："子之于军旅，学之乎？性之乎？"冉有曰："学之于孔子。"季康子曰："孔子何如人哉？"对曰："用之有名，播之百姓，质诸鬼神而无憾。求之至于此道，虽累千社，夫子不利也。"康子曰："我欲召之，可乎？"对曰："欲召之，则毋以小人固之，则可矣。"而卫孔文子将攻太叔，问策于仲尼。辞不知，退而命载而行，曰："鸟能择木，木岂能择鸟乎！"文子固止。会季康子逐公华、公宾、公林，以币迎孔子，孔子归鲁。

孔子之去鲁凡十四岁而反乎鲁。

鲁哀公问政，对曰："政在选臣。"季康子问政，曰："举直错诸枉，则枉者直。"康子患盗，孔子曰："苟子之不欲，虽赏之不窃。"然鲁终不能用孔子，孔子亦不求仕。

孔子之时，周室微而礼乐废，诗书缺。追迹三代之礼，序书传，上纪唐虞之际，下至秦缪，编次其事。曰："夏礼吾能言之，杞不足征也。殷礼吾能言之，宋不足征也。足，则吾能征之矣。"观殷夏所损益，曰："后虽百世可知也，以一文一质。周监二代，郁郁乎文哉。吾从周。"故《书传》《礼记》自孔氏。

孔子语鲁太师："乐其可知也。始作翕如，纵之纯如，皦如，绎如也，以成。""吾自卫反鲁，然后乐正，《雅》《颂》各得其所。"

古者《诗》三千余篇，及至孔子，去其重，取可施于礼义。上采契、后稷，中述殷周之盛，至幽、厉之缺，始于衽席，故曰："《关雎》之乱以为《风》始，《鹿鸣》为《小雅》始，《文王》为《大雅》始，《清庙》为《颂》始。"三百五篇孔子皆弦歌之，以求合《韶》《武》《雅》《颂》之音。礼乐自此可得而述，以备王道，成六艺。

孔子晚而喜《易》《序》《彖》《系》《象》《说卦》《文言》。读《易》，韦编三绝。曰："假我数年，若是，我于《易》则彬彬矣。"

孔子以《诗》《书》、礼乐教，弟子盖三千焉，身通六艺者七十有二人。如颜浊邹之徒，颇受业者甚众。

孔子以四教：文、行、忠、信。绝四：毋意、毋必、毋固、毋我。所慎：斋、战、疾。子罕言利与命与仁。不愤不启，举一隅不以三隅反，则弗复也。

其于乡党，恂恂似不能言者。其于宗庙朝廷，辩辩言，唯谨尔。朝，与上大夫言，訚訚如也；与下大夫言，侃侃如也。

入公门，鞠躬如也；趋进，翼如也。君召使傧，色勃如也。君命召，不俟驾行矣。

鱼馁，肉败，割不正，不食。席不正，不坐。食于有丧者之侧，未尝饱也。

是日哭，则不歌。见齐衰、瞽者，虽童子必变。

"三人行，必得我师。""德之不修，学之不讲，闻义不能徙，不善不能改，是吾忧也。"使人歌，善，则使复之，然后和之。

子不语：怪、力、乱、神。

子贡曰："夫子之文章，可得闻也。夫子言天道与性命，弗可得闻也已。"颜渊喟然叹曰："仰之弥高，钻之弥坚。瞻之在前，忽焉在后。夫子循循然善诱人，博我以文，约我以礼，欲罢不能。既竭我才，如有所立，卓尔。虽欲从之，蔑由也已。"达巷党人曰："大哉孔子！博学而无所成名。"子闻之曰："我何执？执御乎？执射乎？我执御矣。"牢曰："子云'不试，故艺'。"

鲁哀公十四年春，狩大野。叔孙氏车子鉏商获兽，以为不祥。仲尼视之，曰："麟也。"取之。曰："河不出图，洛不出书，吾已矣夫！"颜渊死，孔子曰："天丧予！"及西狩见麟，曰："吾道穷矣！"喟然叹曰："莫知我夫！"子贡曰："何为莫知子？"子曰："不怨天，不尤人，下学而上达，知我者其天乎！"

"不降其志，不辱其身，伯夷、叔齐乎！"谓"柳下惠、少连降志辱身矣"。谓"虞仲、夷逸隐居放言，行中清，废中权"。"我则异于是，无可无不可。"

子曰："弗乎弗乎，君子疾没世而名不称焉。吾道不行矣，吾何以自见于后世哉？"乃因史记作《春秋》，上至隐公，下讫哀公十四年，十二公。据鲁，亲周，故殷，运之三代。约其文辞而指博。故吴楚之君自称王，而《春秋》贬之曰"子"；践土之会实召周天子，而《春秋》讳之曰"天王狩于河阳"；推此类以绳当世。贬损之义，后有王者举而开之。《春秋》之义行，则天下乱臣贼子惧焉。

孔子在位听讼，文辞有可与人共者，弗独有也。至于为《春秋》，笔则笔，削则削，子夏之徒不能赞一辞。弟子受《春秋》，孔子曰："后世知丘者以《春秋》，而罪丘者亦以《春秋》。"

明岁，子路死于卫。孔子病，子贡请见。孔子方负杖逍遥于门，曰："赐，汝来何其晚也？"孔子因叹，歌曰："太山坏乎！梁柱摧乎！哲人萎乎！"因以涕下。谓子贡曰："天下无道久矣，莫能宗予。夏人殡于东阶，周人于西阶，殷人两柱间。昨暮予梦坐奠两柱之间，予殆殷人也。"后七日卒。

孔子年七十三，以鲁哀公十六年四月己丑卒。

哀公诔之曰："旻天不吊，不憗遗一老，俾屏余一人以在位，茕茕余在疚。呜呼哀哉！尼父，毋自律！"子贡曰："君其不没于鲁乎！夫子之言曰：'礼失则昏，名失则愆。失志为昏，失所为愆。'生不能用，死而诔之，非礼也。称'余一人'，非名也。"

孔子葬鲁城北泗上，弟子皆服三年。三年心丧毕，相诀而去，则哭，各复尽哀；或复留。唯子贡庐于冢上，凡六年，然后去。弟子及鲁人往从冢而家者百有余室，因命曰孔里。鲁世世相传以岁时奉祠孔子冢，而诸儒亦讲礼乡饮大射于孔子冢。孔子冢大一顷。故所居堂弟子内，后世因庙藏孔子衣冠琴车书，至于汉二百余年不绝。高皇帝过鲁，以太牢祠焉。诸侯卿相至，常先谒然后从政。

孔子生鲤，字伯鱼。伯鱼年五十，先孔子死。

伯鱼生伋，字子思，年六十二。尝困于宋。子思作《中庸》。

子思生白，字子上，年四十七。子上生求，字子家，年四十五。子家生箕，字子京，年四十六。子京生穿，字子高，年五十一。子高生子慎，年五十七，尝为魏相。

子慎生鲋，年五十七，为陈王涉博士，死于陈下。

鲋弟子襄，年五十七。尝为孝惠皇帝博士，迁为长沙太守。长九尺六寸。

子襄生忠，年五十七。忠生武，武生延年及安国。安国为今皇帝博士，至临淮太守，早卒。安国生卬，卬生驩。

太史公曰：《诗》有之："高山仰止，景行行止。"虽不能至，然心向往之。余读孔氏书，想见其为人。适鲁，观仲尼庙堂车服礼器，诸生以时习礼其家，余低回留之不能去云。天下君王至于贤人众矣，当时则荣，没则已焉。孔子布衣，传十余世，学者宗之。自天子王侯，中国言六艺者折中于夫子，可谓至圣矣！

Chapter Two **THE LIFE OF CONFUCIUS**

(*K'ungtse Shihchia* — *Shiki*, Book XLVII)

The following is a translation of the life of Confucius in the *Shiki* by Ssŭma Ch'ien who lived about three hundred years after Confucius (145 B.C.-85? B.C.). The translation of this document is important for two reasons. First, it is the earliest and in fact the only connected biographical sketch of Confucius, and it exists in that great standard book of Chinese history, written by a man who is acknowledged to be the father of Chinese historians and a prose master. The authority of the *Shiki* is unquestioned, and Ssŭma Ch'ien himself travelled extensively and visited the birthplace of Confucius and talked with old people who kept alive the ancient tradition about Confucius. It is therefore as accurate a picture of Confucius' life as we can get. In the second place, Ssŭma Ch'ien was thoroughly open-minded and unbiased; he was strictly an historian and not an advocate of Confucianism, taking sides in questions. While he expressed his intense admiration for Confucius, he was not himself a strict adherent of the narrow Confucian school. The result was, he gave us a picture of Confucius the man, rather than Confucius the saint, and many Confucian critics have tried to distort the meaning of several passages in this life by far-fetched interpretations, and sometimes even to deny outright the correctness of the story. At any rate, we can take it as a very fair picture of Confucius as conceived in the mind of the most learned scholar of his times, living about three centuries after Confucius.

I. ANCESTRY, CHILDHOOD AND YOUTH (551 B.C.-523 B.C.)

Confucius was born in the town of Tsou, in the county of Ch'angping, in the state of Lu. His early ancestor was K'ung Fangshu (who was a ninth-generation descendant of a king of Sung and the fourth-generation ancestor of Confucius). Fangshu was the father of Pohsia, and Pohsia was the father of Shuliang Ho. Ho was the father of Confucius by extra-marital union with a girl of the Yen family. She prayed at the hill Nich'iu and begat Confucius in answer to her prayer, in the twenty-second year of Duke Hsiang of Lu (551 B.C.). There was a noticeable convolution on his head at his birth, and that was why he was called "Ch'iu" (meaning a "hill"). His literary name was Chungni, and his surname was K'ung. ("Confucius" means "K'ung the Master").

Soon after Confucius was born, his father died, and was buried at Fangshan, which was in Eastern Lu (in Shantung) Therefore Confucius was in doubt as to the place of his father's tomb, because his mother had concealed the truth from him. When he was a child, he used to play at making sacrificial offerings and performing the ceremonies. When Confucius' mother died, he buried her temporarily, for caution's sake, in the Street of the Five Fathers, and it was not until an old woman, the mother of Wanfu of Tsou, informed him of the whereabouts of his father's grave, that he buried his parents together at Fangshan. Once, a Baron of Lu, Chi, was giving a banquet to the scholars of the town, and Confucius went while still in mourning. Yang Ho, a corrupt official, berated Confucius, saying, "The Baron is giving a banquet to the scholars and is not contemplating the pleasure of inviting you." So Confucius left.

When Confucius was seventeen years old, Baron Li Meng fell sick. On his deathbed he gave his son, Baron Yi Meng the following advice: "K'ung Ch'iu (that is, Confucius) is a descendant of great noblemen. The house of the K'ungs was destroyed in the state of Sung (Confucius' ancestors were

persecuted out of the country by their rivals and migrated to the state of Lu).
His great ancestor, Fufu Ho, was the oldest son of the Duke of Sung, but
gave up the throne in favor of his brother, who became Duke Li. In a later
generation, Chengk'aofu assisted the Dukes Tai, Wu and Hsuan of Sung in
the government. His humility increased with his three successive promotions.
Hence the tripod of the K'ung house bore the inscription: 'With the first
promotion, I bend my head; with the second promotion, I bend my neck;
and with the third promotion, I bend my back. I walk along the wall, and no
one dares insult me. Herein I have my rice; and herein I have my porridge, to
feed my mouth.' Such was his humility. I have heard that philosophers must
come from the houses of great men, although they may not be in power.
Now K'ung Ch'iu is young and a great lover of historic learning. Perhaps he
is going to be a philosopher. When I die, you must go and follow him." On
his death, his son Baron Yi went to study under Confucius, together with
Nankung Chingshu (most probably his younger brother). That year Baron
Chi of Lu died, and his son Tai succeeded him.

Confucius was born of a poor and common family, but when he grew
up, he was put in charge of the granary of the house of Baron Chi, and he
was noted for the fairness of his measures. He also was made to take charge of
the cattle and sheep and the cattle and sheep quickly multiplied. He was then
promoted to be a minister of public works. But soon he left his home state
Lu, was unceremoniously sent away from the state of Ch'i, driven out of Sung
and Wei, and landed in difficulties and bodily danger in the suburbs between
Ch'en and Ts'ai. After all these wanderings he returned to Lu.

Confucius was nine feet six inches tall (the ancient unit of measure was
very much shorter, for King Wen was reputed to be ten feet tall), and people
all marvelled at his height and called him "a tall person." The government
of Lu had always been courteous to him, and therefore he later returned to
Lu. His disciple Nankung Chingshu asked permission from the ruler of Lu
to go on a trip to the Emperor's capital, Chou. The Duke of Lu gave them

a carriage with two horses and a page, and they both went to Chou to study the ancient rites and ceremonies and saw Laotse there. When Confucius was taking his departure, Laotse sent him off with the following advice: "I have heard that rich people present people with money and kind persons present people with advice, and I am going to present you with a piece of advice: A man who is brilliant and thoughtful is often in danger of his life because he likes to criticize people. A man who is learned and well read and clever at arguments often endangers himself because he likes to reveal people's foibles. Do not think of yourself only as a son or a minister at court."

II. BETWEEN THIRTY AND FIFTY (522 B.C.-503 B.C.)

Confucius then returned from Chou to his own state, Lu, and more and more disciples came to study under him. At this time, Duke P'ing of Chin was a profligate. His six ministers took the power in their hands and indulged in invasions of the state to the east. King Ling of Ch'u (whose state was to the southwest of Lu) had a powerful army which dominated China. Ch'i was a big state lying right next to Lu (on the north). Lu was a small and weak state; if it allied itself with Ch'u, Chin was angry, and if it allied itself with Chin, then Ch'u would come and invade the state; and if it failed to cement its friendship with Ch'i, Ch'i too would invade the state. In the twentieth year of Duke Chao of Lu (522 B.C.), when Confucius was already thirty years old (or twenty-nine in the English reckoning), Duke Ching of Ch'i came to visit Lu, together with his minister Yen Yang. The Duke of Ch'i asked Confucius, "How is it that Duke Mu of Ch'in was able to dominate the other countries, although his state was then small and situated at a far-away corner of the empire?" "Although Ch'in was small," replied Confucius, "its ambition was great, and although it was situated at a far-away corner, their conduct of affairs was in accordance with the main moral principle. The Duke took Poli Hsi from prison and raised him to the rank of a noble. After talking with him for three days, he put him in charge of the government. That was how the

Duke came into power. He might even have become a 'king', and not merely
a 'dictator' dominating the other states as he did." The Duke of Ch'i was
pleased at Confucius' remark.

When Confucius was thirty-five years old (517 B.C.), Baron P'ing of
Chi displeased Duke Chao of Lu because of a quarrel with Count Chao of
Hou over a cock fight. Duke Chao led his troops to attack Baron P'ing, and
Baron P'ing, together with the other two barons of Lu, Baron Meng and
Baron Shusun, fought the Duke. The Duke lost the battle and ran away to
Ch'i, where he was given a township at Kanhou. Soon after this, the state of
Lu was plunged into disorder, and Confucius went to Ch'i, where he served
as the secretary to Baron Chao Kao, in the hope of establishing a connection
with the Duke of Ch'i. He also discussed music with the Master of Music
in Ch'i. There he heard the music of *Hsiao* (symbolic dance music ascribed
to an ancient Emperor Shun, 2255 B.C.-2204 B.C.) and tried to learn
it. For three months he forgot the taste of meat. The people of Ch'i were
greatly impressed. One day the Duke asked Confucius about government,
and Confucius replied, "The king should be like a king, the ministers like
ministers, the fathers like fathers and sons like sons.""Good!" replied the
Duke. "If the king is not like a king, the ministers not like ministers, fathers
not like fathers, and sons not like sons, how can I have anything to eat even
if there is plenty of grain in the country?" On another day, he again asked
about good government from Confucius, and Confucius replied, "Good
government consists in limiting state expenditures." The Duke was pleased
and was going to give the land at Nich'i to Confucius. Then minister Yen
Ying spoke to the Duke, "The *Ju* (later identified with Confucianists) are bad
models to follow because of their garrulousness, and they make bad subjects
because of their pride and egotism. Their doctrines should hardly be applied
to the people because of their emphasis on funerals and their habit of letting
a family go bankrupt in order to provide an expensive burial. They also make
bad rulers because they go about preaching and begging and borrowing.

Since the great men have died and the imperial dynasty of Chou is in decline, our rituals and music today have degenerated or been partly forgotten. Now comes Confucius with his insistence on ceremonial robes and the details of ceremonial processions and court etiquette. One can spend a lifetime and not be able to master these studies, or spend entire years without being able to master the details of ceremonies. I rather question whether it is advisable for you to put him in power and change the customs of the country, bearing in mind the importance of considering the common people." Thereafter the Duke always received Confucius politely, but did not ask him questions regarding the historic rites and ceremonies. Another day, the Duke said to Confucius with the desire of keeping him in the state, "I'm not able to offer you the position of Baron Chi, but I will give you a position somewhere between the Barons Chi and Meng." The nobles of Chi were plotting against Confucius, which came to Confucius' eays. The Duke said to him, "I'm sorry I'm too old now to be able to put your doctrines into practice." Confucius then left and returned to Lu.

When Confucius was forty-two (511 B.C.), Duke Chao of Lu died and exile at Kanhou. Duke Ting succeeded him, and in the summer of the fifth year of Duke Ting's reign, Baron P'ing of Chi died, and his son Baron Huan succeeded him. (Here follow two brief anecdotes. Confucius was consulted as a learned historian about certain finds which had been unearthed. One was about the discovery of animal bones during the razing of a city wall. One of the bones was said to be as long as an entire carriage, apparently the remains of some dinosaur, and a king sent a messenger all the way from a distant place to ask Confucius what bones these were, and Confucius was ready with an answer from early history.)

Baron Huan had a favorite secretary by the name of Chungliang Huai who had a private quarrel with Yang Hu (also referred to in the *Analects* as Yang Ho), and the latter wanted to drive him away from the city, but stopped on the intervention of Kungshan Puniu. Yang finally arrested him and Baron

Huan angrily protested, upon which Yang put the Baron in prison and made him sign a pledge before releasing him. Henceforth Yang behaved all the more arrogantly toward the Baron, but on his part Baron Huan Chi had also usurped the authority of the Duke, so that the government of Lu fell into the hands of the Barons. The state was therefore plunged into a state of moral chaos, from the lords down to the people, and Confucius decided not to go into the government, but retired to study, or edit the books of poetry and history and ritual and music. The number of his disciples rapidly grew, and there were many who came from distant parts of the land.

III. THE PERIOD OF GREAT POWER(502 B.C.-496 B.C.)

In the eighth year of Duke Ting of Lu (502 B.C.), Kungshan Puniu did not get along with Baron Huan Chi and allied himself with Yang Hu to stir up a rebellion, displace the eldest son of the Baron and make the children of their concubines, who were friendly to Yang, their heirs. They therefore arrested Baron Huan Chi, but the latter escaped by a ruse, and in the following year, Yang was defeated and escaped to the state of Ch'i.

At this time, Confucius was fifty years old. Kungshan Puniu started a rebellion against Baron Huan in the city of Pi, and Baron Huan sent a messenger to ask Confucius to see him. Confucius had then, for a long time, devoted himself to the pursuit of learning; he was mild and mellow and did not know exactly where to begin to apply his teachings to the practice of government. He said, "The Kings Wen and Wu rose to power from the small cities of Feng and K'ao and finally established the empire of Chou. Pi, I know, is a small place, but perhaps I may try." So Confucius was about to go, but his disciple, Tselu (a kind of St. Peter), was displeased and tried to stop him. "Since the Baron asks to see me," replied Confucius, "he must have a plan in his mind, and if he would put me in power, we might achieve something resembling the work of Emperor P'ing" (who restored the power of the Chou Dynasty, beginning the so-called East Chou Period). But after all he did not go.

Later on Duke Ting made Confucius the magistrate of Chungtu. After a year the town became a model city for all its neighbors. From the magistracy of Chungtu, he was promoted to the office of the Secretary of Public Works (or Labor) and finally became the Grand Secretary of Justice. In the spring of the tenth year of Duke Ting (500 B.C.), Lu signed a treaty of friendship with Ch'i and in the summer a Ch'i minister, by the name of Li Chu said to the Duke of Ch'i, "This is getting dangerous for us with Confucius in office at Lu." They then arranged for a good-will conference at Chiaku between the two countries. Duke Ting of Lu was going to attend the good-will conference in his carriage, but Confucius in his capacity as an acting Chief Minister, said, "I have heard it said that in attending civil conferences, one must send along a military delegation, and in attending military conferences, one must send along a civil delegation. The rulers of ancient times always provided themselves with a military escort when they visited a foreign country. I recommend that we bring along the Right and Left Secretaries of War." To this the Duke gave his consent and they started out toward Chiaku with the Secretaries of War. The formal meeting place where the oath was to be taken was provided with an altar surrounded by three successive earthen terraces. The two delegations met with the usual ceremonies. They bowed to each other and went up the terrace, and after drinking the ceremonial cup of wine, an official of Ch'i came forward and requested permission for the playing of an orchestra from different lands. The Duke of Ch'i gave his approval, and then the entertainers came forward and started a big noise, the civil dancers with their banners and pennants of ox-tail and pheasant feathers, the military dancers with their spears, forks, swords and shields. Confucius then came forward up the steps, and advanced just below the first terrace; he lifted his broad sleeves and said, "Why the presence of these barbarian musicians, when the rulers are celebrating a good-will conference? I request that they be dismissed." The Ch'i official tried to send them away, but the musicians refused to go. Everybody turned his eyes toward the Duke of Ch'i and his Minister Yen Ying. The Duke was greatly embarrassed and then waved his hand for the entertainers to leave the place. After a while, the Master of Ceremonies of Ch'i came forward and requested permission for the performing of palace music, and the Duke gave his consent. The actors and dwarfs in costume then began to play, and again Confucius went forward up the steps and advancing to the first terrace, he said, "Common people who try to corrupt the rulers should be killed. I request an order from the Master of Ceremonies." The Master of Ceremonies had these actors executed and their limbs were separated from their bodies.

The Duke of Ch'i was greatly ashamed and impressed and thought that he had better return to his state. Speaking in a tone of great concern, he said to his ministers at court, "The people of Lu have helped their ruler to act like a gentleman, while you people have taught me to behave like a barbarian. And now I have committed an offense in the eyes of the Ruler of Lu. What shall I do?" An official replied, "When a gentleman repents of his mistake, he makes amends by acts, and when a common man repents of his mistakes, he makes amends by words. If you are sorry for what you have done, then I suggest that you make amends by real acts." Therefore the Duke of Ch'i returned the lands of Yun, Wenyang and Kueit'ien which they had taken away from Lu, as a token of apology. In the summer of the thirteenth year of Duke Ting (497 B.C.), Confucius said to the Duke, "A subject ought not to keep a private armour, and a lord ought not to have a town with over a hundred parapets (each parapet representing thirty feet)." The Duke then made Tselu, Confucius' disciple, Secretary of the Barony Chi, and ordered the razing of the cities of the three great Barons. First, Baron Shusun's city of Hou was razed. Baron Chi was going to raze his city Pi, but Kungshan Puniu and Sun Cheh led the people of Lu to attack the Duchy of Lu. The Duke and the three Barons went to the palace of Baron Chi and went up the Terrace of Baron Wu. The people of Pi attacked them there, but could not capture the place. The battle then raged around the Duke, and Confucius ordered the lords Shen Kouhsu and Yo Ch'i to go down and meet the attackers. The rebels were defeated and the soldiers of Lu chased them and defeated them at Kumi. The two Barons Shusun and Chi then fled to the state of Ch'i, and the city of Chi was razed down to the ground. The city of Ch'eng, the stronghold of Baron Meng, then came next in order to be razed, and the magistrate of Ch'eng said to Baron Meng, "When this city is razed, the people of Ch'i will have an open way to attack Lu from the north. Besides, Ch'eng is the stronghold of the Meng house. Without Ch'eng, there will be no Mengs. I refuse to have it razed." In December, the Duke laid seige to the city, but did not capture it.

In the fourteenth year of Duke Ting (496 B.C.), Confucius was fifty-six years old. From the position of the Grand Secretary of Justice, he was promoted to that of the Chief Minister. Confucius showed signs of evident pleasure at the news, and his disciples said, "I hear that a gentleman is not afraid at the sight of disaster and not delighted at success." "Is that so?" remarked Confucius. "Is it not said that one is happy because he rises to a position above the common people?" He then executed Shaochengmao, a minister who had plunged the government into disorder. After three months of his premiership, the mutton and pork butchers did not adulterate their meat, and men and women followed different lanes in the streets. Things lost on the streets were not stolen, and foreigners visiting the state did not have to go to the police, but all came to Lu like a country of their own.

When the people of Ch'i heard this, they were greatly worried and said, "If Confucius remains in power in Lu, Lu is certain to dominate the other states, and when it becomes a dominating power, we being the nearest neighbors would be the first to succumb. Why not cement friendship with them by presenting them with a bit of land?" The minister Li Chu said, "Let us try first to block him, and then if we fail, it won't be too late to give them some land." They then selected eighty of the prettiest girls of the state who were dressed in embroidery and could dance the *k'ang* dance. These maidens were presented together with a hundred and twenty fine horses to the Ruler of Lu, and they made a display of the girl entertainers and fine horses outside the South High Gate of Lu. Three times Baron Huan Chi went in plain clothes to see the show and thought he was going to receive this present, and told the Duke to go and see them by a circuitous route. So then the Duke and the Baron hung about the place for whole days and neglected their governmental duties. "I think it's time for us to quit," said Tselu. "Wait a minute," said Confucius, "it is near the time for the Sacrifice to Heaven now, and if the Duke should remember to send the burnt offerings to the ministers after the public worship, I will yet choose to stay." Baron Huan finally received the gift of girl entertainers of Ch'i, and for three days did not attend to his duties, nor did he remember to send the burnt offerings to the ministers. Confucius then left. While stopping over at the city of Tun, Shihchi said to Confucius on parting, "Master, I know you are not to blame for leaving Lu." Confucius replied, "May I sing a song?" Then he sang:

> "Beware of a woman's tongue,
> Sooner or later you'll get stung.
> Beware of a woman's visit,
> Sooner or later you'll get it.
> Heigh ho! Heigh ho!
> I'm going to run away."

Shihchi returned and Baron Huan asked him, "What did Confucius say?" Shihchi told him the truth, and Baron Huan heaved a sigh and said, "The Master is displeased with me on account of those wenches."

IV. FIVE YEARS OF WANDERINGS (496 B.C.-492 B.C.)

Confucius then went to the state of Wei (to the west of Lu) and stopped at the home of Yen Tutsou, who was the brother of Tselu's wife. Duke Ling of Wei asked what salary Confucius had received in Lu and he was told that he had a salary of sixty thousand bushels of rice, and the state of Wei also gave him a salary of sixty thousand bushels. After staying in Wei for a time, someone spoke evil of Confucius to the Duke, and the Duke asked a man, Kungsun Yuchia, who was dressed in full military uniform, to pass in and out of the room occupied by Confucius. Confucius took this as a gentle hint and left Wei after having been there for ten months.

He then went to the state of Ch'en (further west) and had to pass through the city of K'uang. Yenk'eh was acting as the driver. He pointed with his whip to a crack in the city wall and remarked, "You know, I went into the city through that crack the last time." This remark was overheard by the natives who then thought it was Yang Hu of Lu coming to the city. Now Yang Hu had once been very cruel to the natives of K'uang and the natives therefore surrounded Confucius. Confucius looked like Yang and was arrested for five days. Yen Yuen (or Yen Huei, his favorite disciple) turned up later, and Confucius said to him, "I thought you were killed." "How dare I be killed, so long as you live!" replied Yen.

The situation became more threatening, and the disciples were afraid, but Confucius said, "Since King Wen died, is not the tradition of King Wen (the moral tradition of King Wen, who embodied the ideal system of government according to Confucius) in my keeping or possession? If it be Heaven's will that this moral tradition should be lost, posterity shall never again share in the knowledge of this tradition. But if it be Heaven's will that this tradition should not be lost, what can the people of K'uang do to me?" Confucius then was allowed to go away by asking one of his followers, Baron Wu Ning, to go and serve in the government of Wei.

After this, he passed through P'u where he stayed for over a month and then returned to Wei. He stopped at the home of Chu Poyu (a cultured old gentleman whom Confucius respected). The Queen Nancia of Wei sent a message to Confucius, saying, "The gentlemen of foreign countries who do us the honor of visiting our state and wish to be friends of our King always see me. May I have the pleasure of your company?" Confucius tried to decline, but could not get out of it. The Queen saw Confucius from behind a curtain of linen. Confucius entered and kowtowed facing north, and the Queen made a double curtsy from behind the curtain, and her jade hangings jingled. After the interview, Confucius said, "I did not intend to see her, but during the interview, we saw each other with perfect decorum." Tselu was greatly displeased (for Nancia was notoriously loose in her morals), and Confucius swore an oath, saying, "If I had done anything wrong, may Heaven strike me! May Heaven strike me!"

Confucius stayed for over a month at Wei. One day the Duke was riding in a carriage with the Queen, the eunuch Yung Chu acting as the driver and Confucius following behind in a second carriage (or occupying the second driver's seat). Thus they paraded through the streets, attracting the people's attention, and Confucius remarked, "I have never yet seen people attracted by virtuous scholars as they are by beautiful women." Confucius regarded this as a disgrace and left Wei for Ts'ao. That year (495 B.C.) Duke Ting of Lu died.

After leaving Ts'ao, Confucius went to Sung and studied the practice of ceremony with his disciples under a big tree. A military officer of Sung, Huan Tuei, wanted to kill Confucius and uprooted the big tree. Confucius decided to leave Sung and his disciples said, "We had better hurry." Confucius said, "Heaven has endowed me with a moral destiny (or mission). What can Huan Tuei do to me?"

Confucius went on to Cheng (in modern North Honan) and the Master and disciples lost track of each other. While Confucius stood alone at the East Gate of the outer city the natives reported to Tsekung, "There is a man at the East Gate whose forehead is like that of Emperor Yao, whose neck resembles that of an ancient minister Kaoyao, and whose shoulders resemble those of Tsech'an; but from the waist down, he is smaller than Emperor Yu by three inches. He looks crest-fallen like a homeless, wandering dog." Tsekung told Confucius this story (when they met) and Confucius smiled and said, "I don't know about the descriptions of my figure, but as for resembling a homeless, wandering dog, he is quite right, he is quite right!"

Confucius then went on to Ch'en (Ch'en, Cheng, Ts'ai, and Sung were all quite close together) where he stayed for over a year at the home of the magistrate of the city Tsengtse. The King of Wu (a big state to the southeast in modern Kiangsu) invaded Ch'en and captured three of its towns. Chao Yang invaded Chuko (494 B.C.); the army of Ch'u laid siege to Ts'ai and the people of Ts'ai migrated to Wu. Wu defeated King Kouchien of Yueh (farther down southeast in modern Chekiang) at Kueich'i. A hawk, with an arrow piercing its body, descended at the court of Ch'en (where Confucius was staying) and died. The arrow was made of *k'u* wood and was provide with a flint arrowhead, a foot and an inch long. The Duke of Ch'en sent a messenger to ask Confucius about this arrow, and Confucius replied, "This hawk must have come from very far away. This is an arrow used by the barbarians of Shushen. When Emperor Wu conquered Shang and built roads across to the 'Nine *Yi*' and 'Hundred Man' barbarians, he ordered tribute from the different lands as a sign of their perpetual homage. The barbarians of Shushen then sent in tributes of arrows with *k'u* wood and flint arrowheads, a foot and inch long. The Emperor gave these arrows to his eldest princess as a sign of his love. She was married to a Duke Yuhu, who became the first Duke of Ch'en. It was the custom to present gifts of jade to the Emperor's relatives of the same surname as a symbol of affection, and to bring tributes from distant lands to the Emperor's relatives of a different surname, that they might not forget their allegiance to the Imperial House. That was how the Shushen arrows came to Ch'en. You may look in the old archives aud may be able to find some yet." Actually, they did find similar arrows in the archives, as Confucius had told them.

Confucius stayed in Ch'en for three years. It happened that the countries

Chin (modern Shensi) and Ch'u (modern Hupei) were fighting for power and often invaded Ch'en. When the state Wu invaded Ch'en and Ch'en Ch'ang was attacked, Confucius said, "Ah, let us go home! The young men of our state are either brilliant and erratic, or simple and retiring. But they have not lost their original simplicity of character." Confucius therefore left Ch'en and was passing through the city of P'u.

It happened that a certain Kungshu was starting a rebelling at P'u and the people of P'u surrounded Confucius. He had, however, a disciple by the name of Kungliang Ju who was following Confucius with five carriages. Kungliang Ju was tall, able, and distinguished for his bravery. He said, "Isn't this fate? The last time I was accompanying you at K'uang, we ran into trouble, and now we run into trouble again. I would rather fight and die this time." There was then a furious battle and the natives of P'u were afraid and said they would be willing to release Confucius if he promised not to go to Wei, and Confucius pledged an oath that he would not go there. He then left by the East Gate, but went straight to Wei. "Why, can one break an oath like that?" asked Tsekung. "Yes," replied Confucius, "it was an oath under duress, which is disregarded by the gods."

The Duke of Wei was delighted to hear that Confucius was coming back and went to the suburb to welcome him. "Do you think I could attack the city of P'u?" asked the Duke. "Certainly," replied Confucius. "But my ministers think it inadvisable," said the Duke, "for P'u serves as a buffer state to protect us against Chin and Ch'u. Isn't it inadvisable for us to attack it?" Confucius replied, "The men of P'u are ready to defend their state to the last man, and their women, too, are ready to defend their homes. What we want to punish, however, are only four or five of the rebel leaders.""Good," said the Duke. But actually he did not attack P'u.

The Duke was then old and did not attend to his duties and was unwilling to put Confucius in power. Confucius sighed and said, "If someone will put me in power, I shall need only one month (to lay the foundation for a new order), and in three years time, I shall accomplish great results."

Confucius then left Wei. A certain Pi Hsi was acting as the magistrate of Chungmou (in the state of Chin), and Baron Chien Chao was fighting with Fan Chunghsing and attacked his city. Pi Hsi then rebelled and sent a messenger to ask Confucius to come and help him. Confucius was thinking of going, but Tselu protested, saying, "Master, I have heard from you that a gentleman does not enter the state of a ruler who leads a bad personal life. How is it now that you are going to help this rebel Pi Hsi at Chungmou?""Yes, I did say so," replied Confucius. "But as the saying goes, a truly hard substance is not afraid of grinding, and a truly white substance is not afraid of dyes. Am I a dried up gourd that can stand hanging on the wall and go without food (for days)?"

Confucius was playing on a musical stone, the *ch'ing* and a man carrying a wicker basket was passing his door and said, "How can a man have the heart to enjoy playing idly on the musical stone like that? Such a stodgy person doesn't seem to know himself. What can I say about such a person?"

Confucius was once learning to play on *ch'in* (a string instrument) from the music master Hsiangtse, and did not seem to make much progress for ten days. The music master said to him, "You may well learn something else now," and Confucius replied, "I have already learned the melody, but have not learned the beat and rhythm yet?" After some time, the music master said, "You have now learned the beat and rhythm, you must take the next step.""I have not yet learned the expression," said Confucius. After a while, the music master again said, "Now you have learned the expression, you must take the next step." And Confucius replied, "I have not yet got an image in my mind of the personality of the composer." After some time the music master said, "There's a man behind this music, who is occupied in deep reflection and who sometimes happily lifts up his head and looks far away, fixing his mind upon the eternal." "I've got it now," said Confucius. "He is a tall, dark man and his mind seems to be that of an empire builder. Can it be any other person than King Wen himself (the founder of the Chou Dynasty)?" The music master rose from his seat and bowed twice to Confucius and said, "It is the composition of King Wen."

Confucius felt that he could not do anything in Wei and therefore was going west to Chin to see Baron Chien Chao. On reaching the bank of the Yellow River, he heard the news of the death of Tu Mingtu and Shun Hua. He stood on the bank and sighed, "How beautiful is the water! Eternally it flows! Fate has decreed that I should not cross this river." "What do you mean?" asked Tsekung coming forward. And Confucius replied, "Tu Mingtu and Shun Hua are good ministers of Chin. Before Baron Chien Chao got into power, he said that he would insist on taking these two men, should he get into power, and now that he is in power, he has killed them. I have heard that when people disembowel embryos or kill the young, the unicorn refuses to appear in the countryside, and that when people dry up a pond in order to catch fish, the dragon refuses to bring the *yin* and *yang* principles into harmony (resulting in famine or flood), and that when people snatch birds' nests and break birds' eggs, the phoenix refuses to come. Why? Because a gentleman avoids those who kill their own kind. If even the birds and beasts avoid the unrighteous, how much more should I do the same?" He therefore returned to the village of Tsou and composed a piece of music for a string instrument called "Tsou Ts'ao" in commemoration of the two good ministers.

Confucius then returned to Wei again and stopped at the home of Chu Poyu. One day, the Duke of Wei asked him about military tactics and Confucius replied, "I know something about the ceremonial sacrifices, but as for the science of warfare, I know nothing about it whatsoever." The next day when Confucius was talking with the Duke, the latter merely turned up his head and looked at the flying wild geese in the sky and did not seem to pay any attention to Confucius. And so Confucius left for Ch'en again.

In the summer of that year (493 B.C.), the Duke died and was succeeded by his grandson Cheh, who was known as Duke Ch'u of Wei. In June, Chao Yang gave the eldest son, Kuei Huei, refuge at Ch'i. Yang Hu then sent eight men dressed in mourning to welcome Kuei Huei, pretending that they were accompanying him directly from his own Duchy, Wei, in recognition of his rights. The welcoming delegation wailed in the usual fashion of a funeral procession, and Kuei Huei henceforth remained at Ch'i.

In the winter, the state of Ts'ai removed its capital to Choulai. This was in the third year of Duke Ai of Lu (492 B.C.), when Confucius was sixty years old. The state of Ch'i then sent an army to help Wei besiege the city of Ch'i where the exiled prince Kuei Huei was staying. In the summer, the ancestral temple of Huanli in Lu was burnt down and Nankung Chingshu led the people to fight the fire. Confucius was in Ch'en at this moment, but when he heard of the fire, he said that it must have been the ancestral temple of Huanli that was burnt (because the worship at Huanli was against the rules of the ancient feudal order). Later they found that Confucius' guess was right.

In the summer Baron Huan Chi was ill and he drove over to the city of Lu. Upon seeing the city wall, he sighed aud said, "This Lu once had a chance of becoming a strong state, but unfortunately it lost that opportunity because I had offended Confucius." Then he turned around and spoke to his heir Baron K'ang Chi and said, "I know that when I die you will become the Chief Minister of Lu, and when you do, you must call Confucius back into power." Baron Huan died a few days afterward and Baron K'ang succeeded him. After the burial ceremony, he was going to send for Confucius, when his brother Yu said, "Our deceased father once appointed Confucius to a position of power and then failed to go through with it, thus making himself a laughingstock of the other Dukes. Now, if you try to appoint him again and then change your mind, you will again make yourself the laughingstock of the other states." "Whom then would you suggest?" asked Baron K'ang. "Send for Jan Ch'iu" (a disciple of Confucius), was the reply. A messenger was therefore sent to ask for Jan Ch'iu. When Jan Ch'iu was about to depart,

Confucius said, "When the people of Lu send for Ch'iu, they are going to give him real authority, and not merely a small position." That day Confucius said, "Let us go home! Let us go home! The young men of our state are either brilliant and erratic or too simple and retiring. They make good material, and I must try to cut them into shape." Tsekung knew that Confucius was thinking of going home and on parting he spoke to Jan Ch'iu, "When you are in power, you must send for Confucius."

V. IN EXTREMITIES IN CH'EN AND TS'AI (491 B.C.-489 B.C.)

After Jan Ch'iu had left, Confucius proceeded in the following year (491 B.C.) from Ch'en to Ts'ai. The Duke Chao of Ts'ai was going to Wu in obedience to a summons from the King of Wu. Now Duke Chao had previously deceived his subjects when he moved his capital to Choulai, and when he was going to Wu, his ministers were afraid that he was going to move his capital once more, and Kungsun P'ien shot the Duke and killed him.

The next year (490 B.C.), Confucius went from Ts'ai to Yeh (another small state), and the Duke of Yeh asked Confucius about good government, and Confucius replied, "Good government consists in winning the loyalty of the people nearby and attracting the people far away." Another day, the Duke asked about Confucius from his disciple Tselu, and Tselu did not reply. When Confucius heard this, he said, "Ah Yu (familiar name of Tselu), why didn't you tell him that I am a man who pursues the truth untiringly, and teaches people unceasingly, and who forgets to eat when he is enthusiastic about something, and forgets all his worries when happy or elated, and who is not aware that old age is coming on?"

After leaving Yeh, Confucius returned to Ts'ai. Ch'angchu and Chiehni were plowing the field together. Confucius thought they were retired philosophers and sent Tselu to inquire the way of them. "Who is that fellow driving the carriage?" asked Ch'angchu. "That's Confucius," was Tselu's reply. "Is he K'ung Ch'iu of Lu?" And Tselu replied, "Yes." "Oh, then he ought to know the way." And Chiehni asked Tselu, "Who are you?" "I am Chung Yu." "Are you a disciple of K'ung Ch'iu?" Tselu replied in the affirmative, and Chiehni said, "Oh, the world is full of those people wandering about, but who is ever going to change the present state of affairs? Futhermore, rather than follow one who avoids certain types of people, why not follow one who avoids society altogether?" Tselu told this to Confucius and Confucius sighed and said, "Birds and beasts (or those who try to imitate them) are not right company for us. If there were a moral order in the present world, why should I bother to change it?"

Another day Tselu was walking on the road and he met an old man who carried a wicker basket and asked the latter, "Have you seen the Master?" The old man replied, "Who is the 'Master'? —a man who doesn't work with his arms and legs and who doesn't know how to distinguish between the different kinds of grains!" And the old man planted his stick on the ground and began to weed the field. Tselu told this story to Confucius, and Confucius said, "He must be a retired philosopher." Tselu went again to find him, but he had disappeared.

Confucius wandered in Ts'ai for three years. The state of Wu was attacking Ch'en, and Ch'u came to the rescue of Ch'en (this was in 489 B.C.). The army of Ch'u was encamping at Ch'engfu, and when they heard that Confucius was somewhere between Ch'en and Ts'ai, they sent somebody to ask for Confucius. Confucius was going to pay his respects. Then the ministers of Ch'en and Ts'ai plotted together, saying, "Confucius is a very able man. He has pointed out the weaknesses of the rulers of the different states. Now he has remained for a long time around here and he doesn't seem to like what we are doing. Now Ch'u is a powerful state and is thinking of using Confucins, and if Confucius should ever get into power in Ch'u, our countries would be in trouble and we ourselves the ministers would be in danger." They therefore sent soldiers to surround Confucius in the countryside. Confucius' party could not get away and they were short of food supplies. Many of those in the party fell sick and were confined to bed, but Confucius kept on reading and singing and accompanying himself with a string instrument without stop. Tselu come to Confucius with evident anger in his face and said, "Does a gentleman sometimes also find himself in adversity?" "Yes," replied Confucius, "a gentleman also sometimes finds himself in adversity, but when a common man finds himself in adversity, he forgets himself and does all sorts of foolish things." Tsekung was evidently impressed with the aptness of the remark and Confucius said to him, "Ah Sze, do you think that I have merely tried to learn as much as possible and store it away in memory?" "I think so. Isn't it true?" "No," said Confucius, "I have a central thread which runs through all my knowledge."

Confucius knew then that his disciples were angry or disappointed at heart, and so he asked Tselu to come in and questioned him. "It is said in the *Book of Songs*, 'Neither buffalos, nor tigers, they wander in the desert.' (A comparison to themselves.) Do you think that my teachings are wrong? How is it that I find myself now in this situation?" Tselu replied, "Perhaps we are not great enough and have not been able to win people's confidence in us. Perhaps we are not wise enough and people are not willing to follow our teachings." "Is that so?" said Confucius. "Ah Yu, if the great could always gain the confidence of the people, why did Poyi and Shuch'i have to go and die of starvation in the mountains? If the wise men could always have their teachings followed by others, why did Prince Pikan have to commit suicide?"

Tselu came out and Tsekung went in, and Confucius said, "Ah Sze, it is said in the *Book of Songs*, 'Neither buffalos, nor tigers, they wander in the desert.' Are my teachings wrong? How is it that I find myself now in this situation?" Tsekung replied, "The Master's teachings are too great for the people, and that is why the world cannot accept them. Why don't you come down a little from your heights?" Confucius replied, "Ah Sze, a good farmer plants the field but cannot guarantee the harvest, and a good artisan can do a skillful job, but he cannot guarantee to please his customers. Now you are not interested in cultivating yourselves, but are only interested in being accepted by the people. I am afraid you are not setting the highest standard for yourself."

Tsekung came out and Yen Huei went in, and Confucius said, "Ah Huei, it is said in the *Book of Songs*, 'Neither buffalos, nor tigers, they wander in the desert.' Are my teachings wrong? How is it that I find myself now in this situation?" And Yen Huei replied, "The Master's teachings are so great. That is why the world cannot accept them. However, you should just do your best to spread the ideas. What do you care if they are not accepted? The very fact that your teachings are not accepted shows that you are a true gentleman. If the truth is not cultivated, the shame is ours; but if we have already strenuously cultivated the teachings of a moral order and they are not accepted by the people, it is the shame of those in power. What do you care if you are not accepted? The very fact that you are not accepted shows that you are a true gentleman." And Confucius was pleased and said smilingly, "Is that so? Oh, son of Yen, if you were a rich man, I would be your butler!"

Confucius then sent Tsekung to Ch'u, and King Chao of Ch'u sent an army to welcome Confucius, which got him out of his difficulty. The king was going to give Confucius land of seven hundred *li* (or settlements of twenty-five families each). A minister of Ch'u by the name of Tsehsi said, "Does your majesty have a diplomat as able as Tsekung?" "No," was the King's reply. "Does your majesty have a chief minister as good as Yen Huei?" "No," said the King again. "Does your majesty have a general as good as Tselu?" "No," said the King. "Does your majesty have an administrator as good as Tsai Yu?" "No," said the King. "Besides," continued the minister, "the ancestor of the rulers of Ch'u was appointed to this state with the rank of a Baron, and its original territory was only fifty *li* (*li*, about one third of a mile). Now comes Confucius, who is talking all the time about the ancient systems of the Three Great Kings and the moral tradition of Duke Chou and Duke Shao. How do you expect our state to go on ruling thousands of square miles from generation to generation if Confucius is able to put into practice his ideal social order? King Wen rose from the city of Feng and his son King Wu rose from the city of K'ao, starting only with a territory of a hundred *li*, but they finally succeeded in establishing an empire over the whole of China. I hardly think that it is for the good of our state to put Confucius in possession of a territory, with such able disciples assisting him." This completely changed the King's mind.

In the autumn of that year (489 B.C.), King Chao died at Ch'engfu. There was a madman of Ch'u by the name of Chiehyu who sang as he passed Confucius in the following manner,

> "O phoenix! O phoenix!"
> What has happened to thy character,
> Let by-gones be by-gones,
> But make amends for what still lies ahead.
> Alack-a-day! A thousand pities for the rulers of today!

Confucius got down from his carriage in order to talk with him, but the latter ran away, and Confucius failed to have an interview with him. Therefore Confucius returned from Ch'u to Wei. That was the fifth year of Duke Ai of Lu (still 489 B.C.), when Confucius was sixty-three years old.

VI. FURTHER YEARS OF WANDERINGS (488 B.C.-484 B.C.)

The next year (488 B.C.), Wu and Lu were having a conference and a hundred sacrificial cows were offered on the altar (this being a presumptuous number and against the forms of Confucian feudal order). The Wu minister P'i asked Baron K'ang Chi to represent Lu, and, Baron K'ang being unwilling to go, got away by sending Tsekung in his place. Now Confucius had said Lu and Wei were cousins (the first ancestors of the two ruling houses were brothers), and at this time the successor to the Wei Duchy was staying abroad, unable to have himself established in his state, and the rulers of the different states were constantly considering possible future developments.

Confucius then had many disciples who were already in the government of Wei, and the ruler of Wei wanted to secure the services of Confucius. Tselu asked, "If the ruler of Wei should put you in power, how would you begin?" "I would begin with establishing a correct usage of terminology" (of ranks and titles), Confucius answered. "Do you really mean it?" asked Tselu. "How odd and impractical you are! What do you want to establish a correct terminology for?" "Ah Yu, you are simple-minded indeed!" Confucius replied. "If the terminology is not correct, then the whole style of one's speech falls out of form; if one's speech is not in form, then orders cannot be carried out; if orders are not carried out, then the proper forms of worship and social intercourse (in ritual and music) cannot be restored; if the proper forms of worship and social intercourse are not restored, then legal justice in the country will fail; when legal justice fails, then the people are at a loss to know what to do or what not to do. When a gentleman institutes something, he is sure by what terminology it should be called, and when he gives an order, he knows that the order can be carried out without question. A gentleman never uses his terminology indiscriminately."

The following year (484 B.C.) Jan Ch'iu, who was then assisting in the administration of the government of Lu, led the army of Baron K'ang Chi against Ch'i and defeated the latter at the battle of Lang. And Baron K'ang asked Jan Ch'iu, "How did you come to know the science of warfare? Did you learn it by study or by nature?" Jan Ch'iu replied, "I learned it from Confucius." "What kind of a person is Confucius?" asked Baron K'ang. And Jan Ch'iu replied, "If you should put him in power, his reputation would spread immediately. You could apply his teachings to the people and lay them before the gods, and even the gods will find no fault with them. What he is seeking is to put a state into a condition of perfect moral order. Even if you should give him the rule over 25,000 families, he would not abuse the power for his own selfish ends." "May I then summon him?" asked Baron K'ang. "No," replied Jan Ch'iu, "you should not *summon* him—that would be impolite, treating him like a common man; you should *entreat* him to come." It happened then that K'ung Wentse of Wei was going to attack T'aishu. He asked Confucius' advice about tactics, and Confucius declined politely, by saying that he didn't know about tactics. After the interview, Confucius ordered his carriage for departure, saying, "A bird can choose a tree for its habitation, but a tree cannot choose the bird." K'ung Wentse still tried to make him stay. Then Baron K'ang Chi drove away Kung Hua, Kung Pin and Kung Lin, and sent presents to Confucius to welcome him. Then Confucius returned to his own state Lu. So Confucius had left Lu and been abroad for fourteen years before he returned to Lu (in 484 B.C.).

VII. SCHOLARLY LABORS AND PERSONAL HABITS OF CONFUCIUS (484 B.C. -481 B.C.)

Duke Ai of Lu asked Confucius about government, and Confucius replied, "The secret of government lies in selecting the right ministers." Baron K'ang Chi asked Confucius concerning government, and Confucius replied, "Raise the righteous men into power and let them serve as the measure for the unrighteous, and the unrighteous will return to righteousness." Baron Kang was worried about bandits or thieves in the state, and Confucius said, "If you yourself do not love money, even though you should present the thieves with money, they won't take it."

But after all, the government of Lu did not see its way clear to putting Confucius in power, nor did Confucius desire or seek office. In the time of Confucius, the power of the Chou Emperors had declined, the forms of worship and social intercourse ("ritual and music") had degenerated, and learning and scholarship had fallen into decay. Confucius studied the religious or ceremonial order and historical records of the three dynasties (Hsia, Shang and Chou), and he traced the events from the times of the Emperors Yao and Shun down to the times of Duke Mu of Ch'in and arranged them in chronological order. And he once said, "I should be able to talk about the feudal order (*li* or "rituals") of Hsia, but there are not enough surviving customs in the city of Chi (ruled by the descendants of the Hsia rulers). I should be able to discuss the feudal order of the Shang Dynasty (noted for the rule of the priestcraft), but there are not enough surviving customs in the city of Sung (ruled by the descendants of the Shang Emperors). If there were enough surviving customs, I should be able to reconstruct them with evidence." And he surveyed the changes of customs between the Hsia and Shang Dynasties, and after noting how these customs ran on into the Chou period with modifications, he said, "I can even predict how the future historical development will be for a hundred generations." He noted how one dynasty (Shang) represented a culture with a wealth of ceremonial forms, and how the other dynasty (Hsia) represented a culture of the simple life, and how the Chou Dynasty had combined and merged the two previous cultures into a perfect, beautiful pattern, and he therefore decided that he would choose the Chou culture as the ideal. Therefore, Confucius handed down a tradition of historic records (for instance, the present *Book of History*) and various records of ancient customs and ethnology.

In discussing music with the Grand Music Master of Lu, he said, "The principles of music may be known. A performance should begin peacefully, then it develop into full harmony and clarity, and closes with a continuation or repetition of the theme." He once also said, "After my return to Lu from Wei, I have been able to restore the musical tradition and classify the music of *sung* (ceremonial anthems) and *ya* (classical music of Chou) and restore the songs to their respective original music. In the ancient times, there were over three thousand songs, but Confucius took out the duplicates and selected those that were suited to good form. The collection began with the songs of Ch'i and Houchi (mythological ancestors of the Chou Emperors), covered the great period of the Shang and Chou kings and carried it down to the times of the tyrants Yu and Li. It begins with a song of marital love, and therefore it is said "the Song *Kuanch'ih* heads the collection of *Feng*; *Luming* heads the collection of the 'Little *Ya*'; *Wenwang* heads the collection of 'The Great *Ya*,' and *Ch'ingmiao* heads the collection of the *Sung*." Confucius personally sang all the three hundred and five songs and played the music on a string instrument to make sure that it fitted in with the score of *hsiao*, *wu*, *ya* and *sung*. Through his efforts, the tradition of ancient rites and music was therefore rescued from oblivion and handed down to posterity, that they might help in the carrying out of this ideal of a king's government and in the teaching of "the six arts" (the six branches of study in the schools of Confucius' days: ceremonies, music, archery, carriage-driving, reading and mathematics; also taken as synonymous with the "Six Classics").

In his old age, Confucius developed a love for the study of *Yiking*, or the *Book of Changes*, its *Preface, T'uan, Hsi, Hsiang, Shuokua* and *Wenyuan*. He read the *Yiking* so thoroughly that the leather strap (holding the bundle of bamboo inscriptions) was worn out and replaced three times, and he said, "Give me a few more years to study the *Yiking*, and I should be pretty good at the philosophy of the mutation of human events."

Confucius taught poetry, history, ceremonies and music to 3,000 pupils, of whom 72, like Yen Tutsou, had mastered "the Six Arts" (probably referring to the Six Classics). There were a great number of people who came to study under him.

Confucius taught concerning four things: literature, human conduct, being one's true self and honesty in social relationships. He denounced (or tried to avoid completely) four things: arbitrariness of opinions, dogmatism, narrow-mindedness and egotism. He showed concern and care in three circumstances: ceremonial bath (in preparation for worship), war and sickness. He seldom talked about profit, heaven's will or destiny or fate, and the true man. If a man was not deeply concerned or determined to find out the truth, he would not try to explain and stimulate his thinking, and if Confucius told him one-fourth of what he wanted to say, and the man did not go back and reflect and think out the implications in the remaining three-fourths for himself, he would not teach him again.

In his private life, in his native village or with his own people, he was gentle and refined, like one who could not talk much, but at the places of public worship, and at the courts, he was eloquent, yet very careful in his choice of words. At court, he would talk very serenely and respectfully with his superiors, and quite affably with his inferiors. On entering a public hall, he would bow and hasten forward respectfully. When a king's messenger came, he would at once assume a serious demeanor, and when a king summoned him, he would go without waiting for the carriage. When fish or meat were not fresh, or when they were not cut neatly, he would not eat them. When the mat was not laid out properly, he would not sit down. When he ate in the company of people in mourning, he would not eat his fill, and if he should cry (at a funeral ceremony), he would not sing that day. When he saw people in mourning or passed by blind people, he would change his countenance, even though they were children. (He said) "I never take a walk in the company of three persons, without finding that one of them has something to teach me." "What concern or worry me are the following: that I have forgotten to cultivate my character, that I have neglected my studies, that I have not been able to follow the right course when I see it, and that I have not been able to correct my mistake." When he heard a man sing and liked it, he would ask for an *encore*, and then join in the refrain. He refused to discuss the mythological, exploits of physical prowess, unruly people, and the spirits.

Tsekung said of Confucius, "The Master taught us literature and scholarship; this we can learn from him. What we cannot learn from him or what he did not teach us was what he thought about Nature and the ways of Nature (or Heaven)." Yenyuan (or Yen Huei) sighed and said, "You look up to it and it seems so high. You try to drill through it, and it seems so hard.

You seem to see it in front of you, and all of a sudden it appears behind you. The Master is very good at gently leading a man along and teaching him. He taught me to broaden myself by the reading of literature and then to control myself by the observance of proper conduct. I just felt carried along, but after I have done my very best, or developed what was in me, there still remains something austerely standing apart, uncatchable. Do what I could to reach his position, I can't find the way." A young man of Tahsiang said, "Great is Confucius! He knows about everything and is an expert at nothing," and when Confucius heard this he said, "Now what am I going to specialize in? Shall I specialize in archery, or in driving a carriage?" Tselo said, "Confucius said of himself that he didn't go into the government, and that was why he had plenty of time to study the different arts and literature."

In the spring of the fourteenth year of Duke Ai of Lu (481 B.C.), there was a hunt in the state and Baron Shusun's driver, by the name of Chushang, caught a strange animal which was regarded as bad luck. Confucius looked at it and declared it was a unicorn, and then the people brought the animal home. Confucius then said, "Alas, no tortoise bearing magic anagrams has appeared in the Yellow River, and no sacred writings have come out of the River Lo. I have given up." When Yen Huei died, Confucius said, "I see Heaven is going to take away my mission from me." And when he saw the unicorn during the hunt in the Western countryside, he said, "This is the end of it all" And he heaved a sigh, saying, "There's no one in this world who understands me." And Tsekung said, "Why do you say that there is no one who understands you?" And Confucius said, "I don't blame Heaven, and I don't blame mankind. All I try to do is, my best to acquire knowledge, and to aim at a higher ideal. Perhaps Heaven is the only one who understands me!" He said of Poyi and Shuch'i that they did not compromise their principles, and were not disgraced (these persons and the following were famous scholars living as recluses); he said of Liuhsia Huei and Shaolien that they compromised their principles and were disgraced; he said of Yuchung and

Yiyi that they lived in seclusion and indulged in high talks of philosophy, but that these people were at least not materialistic and that they adjusted themselves to their circumstances according to the principle of expediency. "But I'm different from all of them. I decide according to the circumstances of the time, and act accordingly" (literally "not *may*, no *may not*").

Confucius said, "This won't do! This won't do! A gentleman is ashamed to die without having accomplished something. I realize that I cannot get into a position of power to put into effect my governmental ideal. How am I going to account for myself in the eyes of posterity?"" He therefore wrote the *Spring and Autumn* (Chronicles) on the basis of the existing histories, beginning from Duke Yin (722 B.C.) and coming down to the fourteenth year of Duke Ai (481 B.C.), thus covering the period of twelve Dukes (of Lu). He wrote from the point of view of Lu, but tried to show proper respect to the Chou Emperors, harking back to the Shang Dynasty and showing the changes in the systems of the Three Dynasties. He adopted a most concise style, but injected into it a profound meaning. That was why, although the rulers of Wu and Ch'u usurped the title of "kings," the *Spring and Autumn* degraded their ranks and simply called them "Barons." At a certain conference, the Emperor was actually summoned by the Dukes to appear, but the *Spring and Autumn*, in an effort to whitewash the matter, wrote, "The celestial emperor came to hunt at Hoyang." In this manner, he used different words implying approval or condemnation in criticism of the practices of his times, in the hope that should a great king appear in the future and open that book and adopt the principles implied therein, the unruly princes and robbers of power would be ashamed and restrain themselves. When Confucius was an official, he would go over the cases of lawsuits and official documents with his colleagues and seek their opinions, and not make his own decisions, but in writing the *Spring and Autumn*, he wrote down and deleted exactly as he thought fit, and the disciples like Tsehsia were not able to put in a word. When Confucius taught the

Spring and Autumn to his disciples, he said, "The future generations shall understand me through the *Spring and Autumn* and shall also judge me on the basis of the *Spring and Autumn*."

VIII. HIS DEATH (479 B.C.) AND POSTERITY

Next year (480 B.C.) Tselu died in Wei. Confucius himself also fell ill, and Tsekung come to visit him. Confucius was just then walking slowly around the door, supported by a walking stick, and said to him, "Ah Sze, why do you turn up so late?" Confucius then sighed and sang a song:

> "Ah! the T'aishan (Mountain) is crumbling down!
> The pillar is falling down!
> The philosopher is passing out!"

He then shed tears and spoke to Tsekung. "For a long time the world has been living in moral chaos, and no ruler has been able to follow me. The people of Hsia Dynasty kept their coffins before burial, above the eastern steps (of the Chinese courtyard), the people of Chou Dynasty kept their coffins above the western steps, and the people of Shang Dynasty kept them (in the main hall) between two pillars. Last night I dreamt I was sitting and receiving (or making) a libation between the two pillars. Perhaps it was because I am a descendant of the Shangs." Seven days afterwards he died, aged seventy three (or seventy-two according to English reckoning). This was on the day *chich'ou* of April, in the sixteenth year of Duke Ai (479 B.C.).

Duke Ai sent a prayer to the funeral of Confucius, which said, "Alas! Heaven has no mercy on me, and has not spared me the Grand Old Man. He has left me, the poor self, alone and helpless at the head of the state, and I am a sick person now. Alas! Father Ni (or Chung Ni, Confucius' name)! Great is my sorrow! Do not forget me (literally 'do not mind yourself')!" Tsekung said, "Did not Confucius die within the state of Lu?" (It was the Duke's fault that

Confucius was not put in power.) The Master said, 'When the ceremonies are improper, things become disorderly, and when the terminology used is incorrect, then things are out of place. Disorderliness means that a man who has lost his moral principles, and out of place means that a man does not get what he deserves (or is not placed in the right position).' When the Master was living, he could not use him, and waited till he is dead to send a prayer to his funeral, which is improper. In calling himself 'a poor self,' he also uses a wrong terminology."

Confucius was buried in Lu, on the River Sze in the north of the city. His disciples all observed the regular mourning of three years, and after the three years of mourning were over, they said good-bye to each other and left, weeping again at the grave before they departed. Some stayed on, but only Tsekung remained in a hut near the tomb for six years before he left. Over a hundred families, consisting of Confucius' disciples and natives of Lu, went to live near the tomb ground, and there grew up a village known as K'ungli, or "K'ung's Village." For generations sacrifices were offered at the Temple of Confucius at proper times, and the Confucianists also held academic discussions and village festivals and archery contests at the tomb. The tomb ground contained a hundred *mow*, and therefore could accommodate the disciples in its halls. The personal belongings of Confucius, his caps, gowns, string instruments, carriages and books, were preserved in the Confucian Temple by succeeding generations. This was kept up for over two hundred years down to the time of the First Emperor of the Han Dynasty (from 202 B.C.), who worshipped Confucius with grand offerings (of cows, sheep and pigs, a great honor). Whenever princes and high ministers arrived at the place, they first paid their respects at the Confucian Temple before assuming office.

Confucius begat Li, alias Poyu, who died before Confucius at the age of 50; Poyu begat Ch'i, alias Tsesze who died at 62, who was once arrested in Sung and who wrote the *Central Harmony*; Tsesze begat Po, alias Tseshang, who died at 47; Tseshang begat Ch'iu, alias Tsechia, who died at 45; Tsechia begat Ch'i, alias Tseching, who died at 46; Tseching begat Ch'uan, alias Tsekao, who died at 51; Tsekao begat Tseshen, who died at 57, who once became the minister of Wei; Tseshen begat Fu, who died at 57, who was once *poshih* (scholar or master of particular Classics) under King Ch'en Sheh and died at Ch'en; Fu's younger brother, Tsehsiang, who died at 57, once served as *poshih* under Emperor Hsiaohuei (of Han) and again as magistrate of Ch'angsha and was nine feet six inches tall; Tsehsiang begat Chung, who died at 57; Chung begat Wu; Wu begat Yen-nien and Ankuo; Ankuo was *poshih* under the present Emperor and was once magistrate of Linhuai and died young; Ankuo beget Ang and Ang begat Huan.

The Master Historian says: "The *Book of Songs* says, High is the mountain I look up to, and bright is his example for our emulation! Although I cannot reach the top, my heart leaps up to it." As I read the books of Confucius, I thought to myself how he must have looked. When visiting Lu, I saw the carriages, robes and sacred vessels displayed at the Temple, and watched how the Confucian students studied the historical systems at his home, and hung around, unable to tear myself away from the place. There have been many kings, emperors and great men in history, who enjoyed fame and honor while they lived and came to nothing at their death, while Confucius, who was but a common scholar clad in a cotton gown, became the acknowledged Master of scholars for over ten generations All people in China who discuss the six arts, from the emperors, kings and princes down, regard the Master as the final authority.

第三章 《中庸》

《中庸》在儒家哲学里之重要性，是显而易见的。我之所以把《中庸》这部书置诸儒家典籍之首，即因为研究儒家哲学自此书入手，最为得法。研究儒家哲学时，《中庸》一书本身，可说就是一个相当适宜而完整的基础。

《中庸》为《四书》之第二部，本书下一章《大学》，为《四书》之第一部。《中庸》在儒家哲学里之重要性，由下面文本看来，是显而易见的。我之所以把《中庸》这部书置诸儒家典籍之首，即因为研究儒家哲学自此书入手，最为得法。研究儒家哲学时，《中庸》一书本身，可说就是一个相当适宜而完整的基础。《中庸》这部书，据早期权威学者所说，其作者为孔子之孙，曾子之门人，孟子之师，名叫子思。此外，据说《礼记》中的《坊记》《表记》《缁衣》，也是出诸子思之手。若将《孟子》与《中庸》二书的风格与思想相比，尤其是《中庸》之第一、七、八三节，其相似之明显，实属有目共睹，不容误认。而该书第七节中一部分，在《孟子》一书中，竟完全重现。如果子思真是《中庸》的作者，他真不愧为孟子的良师，因为他的雏形观念之见于《中庸》者，竟生长成熟，在孟子的雄辩滔滔的口才中出现了。治学严谨之士，会在《中庸》与孟子的哲学中看出其脉络深深的关联。

【原文】

　　天命之谓性，率性之谓道，修道之谓教。道也者，不可须臾离也；可离，非道也。是故君子戒慎乎其所不睹，恐惧乎其所不闻。莫见乎隐，莫显乎微，故君子慎其独也。

　　喜怒哀乐之未发，谓之中；发而皆中节，谓之和。中也者，天下之大本也；和也者，天下之达道也。致中和，天地位焉，万物育焉。

【语译】

　　天所赋予人的禀赋叫本性，遵循本性处世做事叫正道，修明循乎本性的正道，使一切事物都能合于正道，叫作教化。这个正道，是人不能片刻离开的，若能离开，就不是正道了。所以君子在无人看到之处要警戒谨慎，在无人听到的地方要恐惧护持。须知道，最隐暗看不见的地方，也是最容易发现的，最微细得看不见的事物，也是最容易显露出来的。因此，君子一个人独居的时候，是要特别谨慎的。

　　喜怒哀乐的情感还没有发动之时，心是平静而无所偏倚的，这叫作中；如果情感发出来都能合乎节度，没有过与不及，就叫作和。中，是天下万事万物的大本；和，是天下共行的大道。人如能把中和的道理推而极之，那么，天地一切都各得其所，万物也都各遂其生了。

【原文】

　　仲尼曰："君子中庸，小人反中庸。君子之中庸也，君子而时中；小人之反中庸也，小人而无忌惮也。"

【语译】

孔子说："君子的所作所为都合乎中庸之道，小人的所作所为都违反中庸之道。君子之所以能合乎中庸之道，因为君子能随时居于中道，无过无不及；小人之所以违反中庸之道，因为小人不知此理，无戒慎恐惧之心，而无所不为。"

【原文】

子曰："中庸其至矣乎！民鲜能久矣。"

【语译】

孔子说："中庸的道理，真是至善至美啊！可惜一般人多不能实行这种道理，已经很久了。"

【原文】

子曰："道之不行也，我知之矣：知者过之，愚者不及也。道之不明也，我知之矣：贤者过之，不肖者不及也。人莫不饮食也，鲜能知味也。"

【语译】

孔子说："中庸的道理之所以不能实行，我已知道为什么了：聪明的人过于明白，以为不足行，而笨拙的人又根本不懂，不知道怎样实行。中庸的道理之所以不能显明，我已知道为什么了：有才智的人做得过分，而没有才智的人又做不到。犹之乎人没有不饮食的，但很少人能知道滋味。"

【原文】

子曰："道其不行矣夫！"

【语译】

　　孔子说："中庸之道恐怕不能够行了吧。"

【原文】

　　子曰："舜其大知也与！舜好问而好察迩言：隐恶而扬善，执其两端，用其中于民。其斯以为舜乎！"

【语译】

　　孔子说："舜可算得是有智慧的人吧！他喜欢问别人的意见，而且对于很浅近的话也喜欢仔细审度。把别人错的意见隐藏起来，把别人好的意见宣扬出来，并且把众论中之过与不及的予以折中，取其中道施行之于民众。这就是舜的道理吧！"

【原文】

　　子曰："人皆曰'予知'；驱而纳诸罟擭陷阱之中，而莫之知辟也。人皆曰'予知'；择乎中庸，而不能期月守也。"

【语译】

　　孔子说："人人都说'我是聪明人'，可是被别人驱入网内、驱入机槛中或陷坑里，却不知道避开。人人都说'我是聪明人'，可是自己选择的中庸之道，连一个月的时间还守不满呢。"

【原文】

　　子曰："回之为人也，择乎中庸，得一善，则拳拳服膺而弗失之矣。"

【语译】

　　孔子说："颜回的做人，能择取中庸之道，得到一善，就奉持固守而不再失掉。"

【原文】

子曰："天下国家可均也，爵禄可辞也，白刃可蹈也，中庸不可能也！"

【语译】

孔子说："天下国家（言其大）是可使之上轨道，官位和俸禄也可以辞掉不要，闪亮的刀也敢践踏上去，只是中庸之道不容易做到啊！"

【原文】

子路问"强"。子曰："南方之强与？北方之强与？抑而强与？宽柔以教，不报无道，南方之强也，君子居之。衽金革，死而不厌，北方之强也，而强者居之。故君子和而不流，强哉矫！中立而不倚，强哉矫！国有道，不变塞焉，强哉矫！国无道，至死不变，强哉矫！"

【语译】

子路问孔子什么是"强"。孔子说："你问的是南方人的强呢？北方人的强呢？还是你自己的所谓的强呢？以宽宏容忍的道理去教诲人，能忍受无理的欺负而不报复，是南方人的强，君子能安于此道。披戴兵器甲胄，坐卧不离，至死不厌倦，是北方人的强，勇武好斗的人能安于此道。可是君子与人和平相处，不随流俗转移，这才是真强！守中庸之道，而无所偏倚，这才是真强！国家政治上轨道时，不改变贫困时的操守，这才是真强！国家无道时，至死也不改变平生的志节，这才是真强！"

【原文】

子曰："素隐行怪，后世有述焉；吾弗为之矣。君子遵道而行，半途而废；吾弗能已矣。君子依乎中庸，遁世不见知而不悔，唯圣者能之。"

【语译】

孔子说："追求隐僻的生活，做些怪诞的事，用以欺世盗名，后世也会有人称道，我可不会这样做。有些君子遵循中庸之道，可是走到半路就停止了，我可不能中止。君子依照中庸之道而行，即使隐遁山林而不为世人所知，也不懊悔，这只有圣人才能做到。"

【原文】

君子之道，费而隐。夫妇之愚，可以与知焉；及其至也，虽圣人亦有所不知焉。夫妇之不肖，可以能行焉；及其至也，虽圣人亦有所不能焉。天地之大也，人犹有所憾。故君子语大，天下莫能载焉；语小，天下莫能破焉。《诗》云："鸢飞戾天，鱼跃于渊。"言其上下察也。君子之道，造端乎夫妇；及其至也，察乎天地。

【语译】

君子之道，用处很广，而道体隐微难见。即使没有知识的愚夫愚妇都可以知晓的道理，若讲到极精微之处，虽然是圣人，也有所不知。愚夫愚妇也是可以实行的道理，可是极精微之处，即使是圣人也有所不能。天地是这样的广博正大，而人遭到自然灾害时还感到不满。所以君子之道，讲到大处，天下都承载不了；讲到细微之处，天下也无人能识破其奥妙。《诗经》上说："鹯鹰一飞而上至天际，鱼儿一跃而下入深渊。"是说鹰与鱼上及于天下及于渊那自然而显著的性能。所以君子之道，自匹夫匹妇的简单生活起始，至其极致，能明察天地间的万事万物。

【原文】

子曰："道不远人；人之为道而远人，不可以为道。"《诗》云："伐柯伐柯，其则不远。"执柯以伐柯，睨而视之，犹以为远。故君子以人治人，改而止。忠恕违道不远，施诸己而不愿，亦勿施于人。

君子之道四，丘未能一焉："所求乎子以事父，未能也；所求乎臣以事君，未能也；所求乎弟以事兄，未能也；所求乎朋友先施之，未能也。庸德之行，庸言之谨；有所不足，不敢不勉；有余不敢尽。言顾行，行顾言，君子胡不慥慥尔！"

【语译】

孔子说："道是离人不远的；人好高骛远，反而使道与人远离，那就不足以为道。"《诗经》上说："伐柯伐柯，取法眼前。"若执斧柄来削制另一个斧柄，斜着眼睛看看，还是觉得不相似，那是偏差错误了。所以君子只拿别人能知能行且自身本有的道理作为法则去教别人，使他改正即可。能做到尽己之心推己及人，中庸之道就不远了，凡是别人加之于我自身而我自己不愿意的事，也不要加之于别人身上。

君子之道有四件事，我都没能做到一件："所求为子侍奉父母应做的那些事，我还没能完全做到；所求臣侍奉君王应做的事，我还没能够做到；所求做弟弟的敬兄长应做的事，我都没能够做到；所求对待朋友应做的，我也没有以身作则完全做到。平常的德行，应尽力实践，平常讲话，应力求谨慎，如有不周到之处，不敢不勉力去做；多余的话不敢全说出来。说话时要顾到能否做到，做事也要顾到所说的话，君子为何不努力笃行实践呢！"

【原文】

君子素其位而行，不愿乎其外。素富贵，行乎富贵；素贫贱，行乎贫贱；素夷狄，行乎夷狄；素患难，行乎患难。君子无入而不自得焉。

在上位，不陵下；在下位，不援上。正己而不求于人，则无怨。上不怨天，下不尤人。故君子居易以俟命，小人行险以侥幸。

子曰："射有似乎君子，失诸正鹄，反求诸其身。"

【语译】

君子就现在所处的地位做应做的事，不希望做本分以外的事。处在富贵的地位，做富贵时应做的事；贫贱时，做贫贱时应做的事；在夷狄的地位，做夷狄应做的事；处患难的地位，做患难时应做的事。君子守道安分，无论在何地位都是自得的。

（君子）处上位不欺侮在下位的人，处下位不攀附在上位的人。端正自己对别人无所要求，自然没有什么怨恨。上不怨恨天，下不怪罪他人。所以君子安于平易的地位以待天命到来，小人却要冒险妄求非分的利益。

孔子说："射箭像君子的做人之道，射不中正鹄，不怪别人，只反求诸己，怨自己的功力不够好。"

【原文】

君子之道，辟如行远，必自迩；辟如登高，必自卑。《诗》曰："妻子好合，如鼓瑟琴。兄弟既翕，和乐且耽。宜尔室家，乐尔妻孥。"子曰："父母其顺矣乎！"

【语译】

君子之道，如同走远路，必须从近处开始；如同登高处，必须从低处开始。《诗经》上说："妻子儿女感情和睦，像弹琴瑟一样和谐。兄弟感情投合，其乐融融。使家庭和顺皆得其宜，使你妻子快乐。"孔子赞叹说："这样，父母一定也很顺心乐意了！"

【原文】

子曰："鬼神之为德，其盛矣乎！视之而弗见，听之而弗闻，体物而不可遗。使天下之人，齐明盛服，以承祭祀，洋洋乎如在其上，如在其左右。

"《诗》曰：'神之格思，不可度思，矧可射思。'夫微之显，诚之不可掩如此夫！"

【语译】

孔子说："鬼神的性能，可算是到了极点！看他不见，听他无声，但他是无处不在，像是具有形体而不能遗忘一样。使天下人，斋戒沐浴穿着整齐衣服，承奉祭祀，到处充满鬼神的灵气，好像就在头顶上，又好像在身边左右。

"《诗经》上说：'神的来临，不可测度，怎么可以怠慢不敬呢？'鬼神之事本属隐微，却又如此明显，所以真实无妄的心，不能掩藏，必与此相同啊！"

【原文】

子曰："舜其大孝也与！德为圣人，尊为天子，富有四海之内，宗庙飨之，子孙保之。故大德，必得其位，必得其禄，必得其名，必得其寿。

故天之生物，必因其材而笃焉，故栽者培之，倾者覆之。

"《诗》曰：'嘉乐君子，宪宪令德。宜民宜人，受禄于天。保佑命之，自天申之。'故大德者必受命。"

【语译】

孔子说："舜可算是大孝的人吧！论他的德行，已为圣人，论他的尊贵，已为天子；论他的财富，已有四海之大，世世受宗庙的祭飨，子孙永久保持祭祀不绝。所以有大德之人，必定得到尊位，必定得到厚禄，必定得到美名，必定得到高寿。所以上天生育万物，一定因其材质而予以厚施，所以可栽种的予以培植，要倾倒的就只好任其倒下。

"《诗经》上说：'善良而快乐的君子，有明显的美德，适合于民众，有益于民众，所以能承受上天赐予的福禄，上天保佑他，并赋予他重大的使命。'所以有大德的人，必然能受天命而为天子。"

【原文】

子曰："无忧者，其惟文王乎！以王季为父，以武王为子，父作之，子述之。武王缵大王、王季、文王之绪，壹戎衣而有天下，身不失天下之显名，尊为天子，富有四海之内，宗庙飨之，子孙保之。

"武王末受命，周公成文、武之德，追王大王、王季，上祀先公以天子之礼。斯礼也，达乎诸侯大夫，及士庶人。父为大夫，子为士，葬以大夫，祭以士；父为士，子为大夫，葬以士，祭以大夫。期之丧，达乎大夫，三年之丧，达乎天子；父母之丧，无贵贱，一也。"

【语译】

孔子说："无忧无愁的人，算只有周文王了吧！有王季做他的父亲，有武王做他的儿子；父亲做好基业，儿子又能继志述德。周武王继承大王、王季、文王的基业，灭了殷而得了天下，自身没失掉天下显扬的名声，贵为天子，富有四海，世世受宗庙的祭飨，子子孙孙永久保持祭祀不绝。

"周武王在晚年才受天命做天子，到周公才完成文王武王的德业，追加大王、王季的帝王谥号，并以天子的礼节追祀以前的祖宗。这种礼节，从天子到诸侯大夫，一直适用到士人百姓。如果父亲做大夫，儿子是士人，葬时就用大夫的礼节，祭时用士人的礼节；父亲是士人，儿子为大夫，丧时就用士人的礼节，祭时用大夫的礼节。旁系亲属的一年之丧，只到大夫为止；直系亲属的三年之丧，天子也须遵守；至于父母之丧，无论尊贵和卑贱，完全一样。"

【原文】

子曰："武王、周公其达孝矣乎！夫孝者，善继人之志，善述人之事者也。春秋修其祖庙，陈其宗器，设其裳衣，荐其时食。

"宗庙之礼，所以序昭穆也；序爵，所以辨贵贱也；序事，所以辨贤也；旅酬下为上，所以逮贱也；燕毛，所以序齿也。

"践其位，行其礼，奏其乐；敬其所尊，爱其所亲；事死如事生，事亡如事存，孝之至也。

"郊社之礼，所以事上帝也；宗庙之礼，所以祀乎其先也。明乎郊社之礼、禘尝之义，治国其如示诸掌乎！"

【语译】

孔子说："周武王和周公算是天下通称为能尽孝道的了！所谓孝，就是能继承先人的遗志，完成先人的事业。春秋祭祀，修好祖宗的庙宇，陈列出祖宗所藏的重要器物，摆设祖宗穿过的衣服，并供献应时的食品。

"宗庙祭祀的礼节，就是要排列父子远近、长幼、亲疏的次序；排列爵位的次序，就是要分别官位的尊卑；排列各职事的次序，就是要分别子孙才能的高下；子弟们皆得举酒以敬长辈，就是要使卑下者也有居于先导的光荣。饮宴时，以毛发的颜色定座位的上下，就是要分别长幼的次序。

"站在排定的位置，行祭祀的礼节，奏着祭祀的音乐；敬奉那些应该尊重的，爱护那些应该亲近的；侍奉死者如同侍奉生者一样，侍奉逝去的如同侍奉现存的一样，这就是尽孝的极致。

"祭祀天地的礼节，是为了侍奉上帝；祭祀祖庙的礼节，是为了祭祀祖先。明白了祭天地的礼节，和天子宗庙大祭与秋祭的意义，治理国家，犹如把东西放在手掌上一样容易啊！"

【原文】

哀公问政。子曰："文武之政，布在方策。其人存，则其政举，其人亡，则其政息。人道敏政，地道敏树。夫政也者，蒲卢也。

"故为政在人，取人以身，修身以道，修道以仁。仁者，人也，亲亲为大。义者，宜也，尊贤为大。亲亲之杀，尊贤之等，礼所生也。

"故君子不可以不修身；思修身，不可以不事亲；思事亲，不可以不知人；思知人，不可以不知天。

"天下之达道五，所以行之者三。曰：君臣也，父子也，夫妇也，昆弟也，朋友之交也；五者，天下之达道也。知、仁、勇三者，天下之达德也。所以行之者一，一也。或生而知之，或学而知之，或困而知之，及

其知之，一也。或安而行之，或利而行之，或勉强而行之，及其成功，
一也。"

子曰："好学近乎知，力行近乎仁，知耻近乎勇。知斯三者，则知所
以修身；知所以修身，则知所以治人；知所以治人，则知所以治天下国
家矣。

"凡为天下国家有九经，曰：修身也，尊贤也，亲亲也，敬大臣也，体
群臣也，子庶民也，来百工也，柔远人也，怀诸侯也。修身，则道立；尊
贤，则不惑；亲亲，则诸父昆弟不怨；敬大臣，则不眩；体群臣，则士之
报礼重；子庶民，则百姓劝；来百工，则财用足；柔远人，则四方归之；
怀诸侯，则天下畏之。

"齐明盛服，非礼不动，所以修身也；去谗远色，贱货而贵德，所
以劝贤也；尊其位，重其禄，同其好恶，所以劝亲亲也；官盛任使，所
以劝大臣也；忠信重禄，所以劝士也；时使薄敛，所以劝百姓也，日省
月试，既禀称事，所以劝百工也；送往迎来，嘉善而矜不能，所以柔远
人也；继绝世，举废国，治乱持危，朝聘以时，厚往而薄来，所以怀诸
侯也。凡为天下国家有九经，所以行之者一也。凡事豫则立，不豫则
废。言前定，则不跲；事前定，则不困；行前定，则不疚；道前定，则
不穷。

"在下位，不获乎上，民不可得而治矣；获乎上有道，不信乎朋友，
不获乎上矣；信乎朋友有道，不顺乎亲，不信乎朋友矣；顺乎亲有道，反
诸身不诚，不顺乎亲矣。诚身有道，不明乎善，不诚乎身矣。

"诚者，天之道也，诚之者，人之道也。诚者，不勉而中，不思而得，
从容中道，圣人也。诚之者，择善而固执之者也。

"博学之，审问之，慎思之，明辨之，笃行之。有弗学，学之弗能弗

措也；有弗问，问之弗知弗措也；有弗思，思之弗得弗措也；有弗辨，辨之弗明弗措也；有弗行，行之弗笃弗措也。人一能之，己百之；人十能之，己千之。果能此道矣，虽愚必明，虽柔必强。"

【语译】

鲁哀公问为政之道。孔子说："周文王与武王的施政，都记载在典籍上。但全在乎施政的人。他们在位时，他们的政教就能施行；他们死后，他们的政教也就作废了。以人施政之道，在使政教能推行快速；以地种树之道，在使树木能生长快速。以人施政，易见成效，如同地上蒲苇的快速滋长一样。

"因此为政之道，在于得到人才，而得人才的方法在于修养自身，要修身必须重视天下人共守的法则，要修道必须依照万物得于天的自然本性。所谓仁，就是人性；以亲爱自己的亲人最为重大。所谓义，就是事事得其所宜，以尊敬贤德的人最为重大。亲爱亲人而有等差，尊敬贤者而有等级，就是从礼节所产生的。

"所以，要治国的君子不可不讲究修身；要想修身，不可不侍奉双亲；要想侍奉双亲，不可不知道尊贤爱人，要知道尊贤爱人，不可不知道天理。

"天下共同遵从的道路有五条，而用以实行的德行有三种。我们说：君臣、父子、夫妇、兄弟、朋友的交往，这五种就是天下人共同遵从的道路。智慧、仁爱、勇敢，是天下人应有的德行。用来实行的那就是一个'诚'字。

"这些道理，有些人天生不待学习就知道，有些人是经过学习才知道的，有些人则是经过勤勉苦学而后才知道的。等到知道时则都是一样。有些人心安理得去实行，有些人为了利益才去实行，有些人则需要勉强才能实行，但等到成功则都是一样。"

孔子说："喜爱研究学问接近智，能够努力行善接近仁，知道什么是羞耻接近勇。知道了这三样，就可以知道怎样去修身；知道怎样修身，就可以知道怎样治理别人；知道了怎样去治理别人，就可以知道怎样治理天下国家了。

"治理天下国家有九种不变的纲领，就是：修正己身，尊重贤人，亲近并爱护亲人，恭敬大臣，体恤众臣，爱民如子，招徕各种技工，善待远方来人，安抚列国诸侯。

"能修好己身，大道就可以树立；能尊重贤人，对于事理就不致疑惑；能亲爱亲人，伯叔兄弟们就不会有怨恨；能敬重大臣，临事就不会迷乱；能体恤臣下，才智之士就会竭力以图报效；能爱民如子，百姓就会自相效忠；能招徕各种工人，国家的财用就会充足；能善待远方的来人，四方的人自然都来归附了；能安抚列国诸侯，天下人自然畏服。

"斋戒明洁，正其衣冠，不合礼节的事不轻举妄为，就是修正己身的方法；不听诬陷好人的坏话，远离女色，轻视财物而重视道德，就是勉励贤人的方法；升高他的爵位，增加他的俸禄，同情他的爱好和厌恶，就是劝勉亲近亲人的方法；所属众多而便于差使，就是劝勉大臣的方法；待之以至诚，养之以厚禄，就是劝勉士众的方法；役使适时，少收赋税，就是劝勉百姓的方法；经常查考工作，给予报酬与其工作相称，就是劝勉工匠的方法；欢送去的，欢迎来的，对有善行的予以奖励，对于才能薄弱的加以矜恤，就是怀柔远方人的方法；延续已绝的世系，振兴废灭的国家，有乱事的将之治平，有危难的予以扶持，诸侯的朝聘之礼使有定时，赏赐厚而纳贡薄，就是安抚诸侯的方法。治理天下国家经常不变的纲领有九项，而用以实行的方法只是一个'诚'字。

"任何事情，事前有准备就可成功，没有准备就会失败。说话先有准备，就不会理由站不住；做事先有准备，就不会遭遇困难；行为先有定夺，就不会出毛病；做人的道理先有定则，就不会行不通。

"在下位时，若得不到上级的信任，人民就无法治理；要得到上级的信任有其方法，不为朋友所信任，就得不到上级的信任；要取得朋友的信任有其方法，若不能孝顺父母就不能为朋友所信任；孝顺父母是有方法的，若反省自身没有诚意，就不能孝顺父母。本身有诚意也有方法，若不明白至善之所在，自身也就不能有诚意了。

"诚，是天生的真理，实践此诚字，是人为的真理。所谓诚，是不需勉强而合，不需思维而得，一举一动都合乎道理，只有圣人才能做到。所谓实践之诚，那就要选择至善之道而坚守不渝才可以。

"要广博地学习，详细地求教，慎重地思考，明白地辨别，切实地力行。不学习则已，既学习，不到学识渊博不止；不求教则已，既求教，不到彻底明白不止；不思考则已，既思考，不到想出道理不止；不辨别则已，既辨别，不到辨别明白不止；不实行则已，既实行，不到切实做到不止。别人学一次就会了，我学一百次，别人学十回就会了，我学一千回。一个人如果真能照这样做，即使是个笨人也会聪明起来的，即使是个柔弱的人，也会坚强起来的。"

【原文】

自诚明，谓之性；自明诚，谓之教。诚则明矣，明则诚矣。

【语译】

由本性诚而自然明善，是天赋的本性；由明善而归于真诚，是人为的教化。有了诚就能明白道理，能够明白道理，也就做到诚了。

【原文】

唯天下至诚，为能尽其性；能尽其性，则能尽人之性；能尽人之性，则能尽物之性；能尽物之性，则可以赞天地之化育；可以赞天地之化育，则可以与天地参矣。

【语译】

只有天下之至诚圣人，能完全实行他天赋本性的极致；能尽他自己的本性，就能尽知他人的本性；能尽知他人的本性，就能尽知万物的本性；能尽知万物的本性，就可以赞助天地间万物的化育，能赞助天地间万物的化育，就可以与天地并立为三了。

【原文】

其次致曲，曲能有诚。诚则形，形则著；著则明，明则动；动则变，变则化。唯天下至诚为能化。

【语译】

次于圣人一等的贤人，如能完全发挥其本性之善，亦能达到诚的地步；诚于中就会表现于外；形于外就显而易见，就会光辉发越，光辉发越，就可以感动人心；感动人心，就能转移习俗，转移习俗，就能化育万物。只有天下最诚的人，能做到化育万物的地步。

【原文】

至诚之道，可以前知。国家将兴，必有祯祥；国家将亡，必有妖孽。见乎蓍龟，动乎四体。祸福将至，善，必先知之；不善，必先知之。故至诚如神。

【语译】

诚到极点，可以预知未来。国家将兴，必有吉兆；国家将亡，必有凶兆。发现在卜筮的蓍草和龟甲上，表现在人的动作仪态上。祸福将要来临，是福，必会先知道；是祸，也可预先知道。所以至诚之人，犹如神明一样。

【原文】

诚者，自成也；而道，自道也。诚者，物之终始，不诚无物。是故君子诚之为贵。诚者，非自成己而已也，所以成物也。成己，仁也；成物，知也。性之德也，合外内之道也，故时措之宜也。

【语译】

诚，为完成自己人格的要件；道，则是引导自己走向正当行的道路。诚，为自然之理，万事万物的始终本末都不能与之相离，没有"诚"，万事万物也就不存在了。所以君子把"诚"看得特别宝贵。诚，并不仅在完成自己，而是要成就万事万物。成就自己的人格叫作"仁"；成就万事万物，叫做"智"。仁与智植根于人的本性，因之，内外才能合而为一，随时施行都是适宜的。

【原文】

故至诚无息。不息则久，久则征，征则悠远，悠远则博厚，博厚则高明。博厚，所以载物也；高明，所以覆物也；悠久，所以成物也。博厚配地，高明配天，悠久无疆。如此者，不见而章，不动而变，无为而成。

天地之道，可一言而尽也：其为物不贰，则其生物不测。天地之道：博也，厚也，高也，明也，悠也，久也。今夫天，斯昭昭之多，及其无穷也，日月星辰系焉，万物覆焉。今夫地，一撮土之多，及其广厚，载华岳而不重，振河海而不泄，万物载焉。今夫山，一拳石之多，及其广大，草木生之，禽兽居之，宝藏兴焉。今夫水，一勺之多，及其不测，鼋鼍蛟龙鱼鳖生焉，货财殖焉。

《诗》云："维天之命，于穆不已。"盖曰，天之所以为天也。"于乎不显，文王之德之纯。"盖曰，文王之所以为文也，纯亦不已。

【语译】

所以至诚之道永不间断。不间断，自然会持久；诚于中者既久，自然征验于外；征验彰著，自会悠远而无穷；悠远无穷，则积为广博深厚；广博深厚，则高大而光明。博厚才能承载万物，高明才能覆盖万物，悠久才能化成万物。博厚可以比地，高明可以比天，悠久才能使万物发展无疆。厚博配地，高明配天，悠久配无疆之广。如此，不自我显示而自然彰明显著，不动作而自然感人化俗，不必有所施为，而自然有所成就。

天地之道，可以一句话说完，就是：造物者诚一不二，化生万物有难测之妙。天地之道是：广博、深厚、高大、光明、遥远、长久。现在比方说天，不过是光亮一点一点所积累，说到那无穷的天体，悬挂着日月星辰，覆盖着地上的万物。若说地，不过是一把泥土所积累，等到形成博厚的大地，却载着华岳那样的高山而不觉其重，收着河海那么多水而不泄漏，万物都载在上面。再说山，不过是拳大的石块所积累，等到形成广大之后，草木生长在上面，禽兽也栖止在上面，蕴藏的宝物也从中发掘出来。再说水，不过是一勺一勺的水所累积，可是等到大不可测，鼋鼍蛟龙鱼鳖都生长在里面，货物财富也生产出来。

《诗经》上说："上天的道理，是深奥而运转不息的啊！"这就是天之所以成为天的道理吧。又说："这不是很明显吗？文王的德行是如此纯一而彰著。"这就是文王所以尊谥为"文"的道理吧。纯一，也就是强健不息的意思。

【原文】

大哉圣人之道！洋洋乎，发育万物，峻极于天。优优大哉！礼仪三百，威仪三千，待其人而后行。故曰：苟不至德，至道不凝焉。故君子尊德性而道问学，致广大而尽精微，极高明而道中庸，温故而知新，敦厚以崇礼。是故居上不骄，为下不倍。国有道，其言足以兴；国无道，其默足以容。《诗》曰："既明且哲，以保其身。"其此之谓与！

【语译】

圣人的道理，真是伟大！充满于天地之间而发育万物，其崇高可与天相比。其大无所不包啊！包括了大的礼则有三百种之多，小的仪节有三千种之多，等待那有才有德的人出来而后实行。所以说：没有伟大德行的人，无法成就伟大的道理。因此，君子恭敬奉持着所禀赋于天的性理，同时讲求学问而求知，使德行与学问臻于广大精微的境界，虽然到达了高明的地步，而遵从中庸的大道。致知方面，从温习旧学而增进新知；修德方面，敦厚自身的纯一心志，以崇尚礼仪。所以，在上位而不骄傲，处卑贱也不犯上作乱。国家有道时，他的言论可以振兴国家；国家无道时，他的沉默足以见容于乱世。《诗经》上说："既明达而又有智慧，以保全自身。"就是这个意思吧！

【原文】

子曰："愚而好自用，贱而好自专，生乎今之世，反古之道；如此者，灾及其身者也。

"非天子，不议礼，不制度，不考文。今天下，车同轨，书同文，行同伦。虽有其位，苟无其德，不敢作礼乐焉；虽有其德，苟无其位，亦不敢作礼乐焉。"

子曰："吾说夏礼，杞不足征也；吾学殷礼，有宋存焉；吾学周礼，今用之，吾从周。"

【语译】

孔子说："笨拙的人偏偏自以为是，卑贱的人偏要任性而为，生在现代，要实行古法，这样的人，一定会自招其祸的。

"不是天子，不可议论礼法的是非，不可以创制法度，不可以校订文字。现今，天下一统，车辙宽度相同，写的文字相同，行为的法礼相同。即使在天子之位，如无圣人之德，也不敢制礼作乐的；即使有圣人之德，而不在天子之位，也是不敢制礼作乐的。"

孔子说："我喜研究夏代的礼法，可是夏代之后杞国所行的，不足以证明就是正确的夏礼。我学殷代的礼法，如今在宋国尚保存一部分。我也研究过周代的礼法，就是现在通行的，我依从现行的周礼。"

【原文】

王天下有三重焉，其寡过矣乎！上焉者，虽善无征；无征，不信；不信，民弗从。下焉者，虽善不尊；不尊，不信；不信，民弗从。故君子之道，本诸身，征诸庶民，考诸三王而不缪，建诸天地而不悖，质诸鬼神而无疑，百世以俟圣人而不惑。质诸鬼神而无疑，知天也；百世以俟圣人而不惑，知人也。

是故君子动而世为天下道，行而世为天下法，言而世为天下则。远之则有望，近之则不厌。

《诗》曰："在彼无恶，在此无射。庶几夙夜，以永终誉。"君子未有不如此，而早有誉于天下者也。

【语译】

君临天下有前述三件大事。做好这三件事，就不会有多大差错了。在上位的，夏、商两朝礼法虽然很好，但因年代久远，无从考证；既已无从考证，就无法使人相信；不能使人相信，百姓就不会遵从了。在下位的，虽然善于礼法，因为其位不尊，也不能取信于人，百姓也就不会遵从了。所以君临天下的人，必须以自身的德行为根本，再察看人民的信任，查考夏、商、周三代的制度而准确无误，建立于天地之间而不背逆天道，质问鬼神而无疑误，到百世以后圣人出来而无怀疑。质问鬼神而无疑心，知道已合乎天理；到百世以后圣人也不会疑惑，知道已顺乎人情了。因此君临天下者，其举动可以世世为天下的常道，其作为可以世世为天下人的法度，他的话可以世世做天下人的准则。远处的人仰慕他，近处的人不厌恶他。

《诗经》上说："彼处无人厌恶，此处无人怨恨，他能早晚不懈，永葆美誉。"君子不这样做而能在天下享有美好的名誉，是绝无此理的。

【原文】

仲尼祖述尧舜，宪章文武，上律天时，下袭水土。辟如天地之无不持载，无不覆帱；辟如四时之错行，如日月之代明。万物并育而不相害，道并行而不相悖。小德川流，大德敦化，此天地之所以为大也。

【语译】

孔夫子远绍唐尧虞舜之道，近宗文王武王之法，上顺天时自然运行的法则，下合水土滋生之本性。比如天地的无所不载，无所不覆；比如四季的更迭，日月的交替，万物同时生长而不相妨碍，道理一齐实行而彼此不相抵触。小的德行则协力分工，有如诸细水汇而为川；大的德行则敦厚化育。这足见天地之伟大。

【原文】

唯天下至圣，为能聪明睿智，足以有临也。宽裕温柔，足以有容也；发强刚毅，足以有执也；齐庄中正，足以有敬也；文理密察，足以有别也。

溥博渊泉，而时出之。溥博如天，渊泉如渊。见而民莫不敬，言而民莫不信，行而民莫不说。

是以声名洋溢乎中国，施及蛮貊。舟车所至，人力所通，天之所覆，地之所载，日月所照，霜露所队，凡有血气者，莫不尊亲。故曰配天。

【语译】

只有天下最伟大的圣人，能具有聪明睿智之才，始可以君临万民。宽柔温和，足以包容万物；刚强弘毅，足以坚持固执；庄严而能自省，持中而不偏，足以使人敬重；多才宏通，足以明辨是非。广博无所不包，渊深而富有活力，能应时施行。人见其仪容而无不敬仰，人闻其言论而无不听从。其声名洋溢中国，传及国外。凡舟车所至，人力所到之地，日月所照，霜露所沾之处，人人皆尊敬，人人皆爱戴。所以说其德行足以与天相比拟。

【原文】

唯天下至诚，为能经纶天下之大经，立天下之大本，知天地之化育，夫焉有所倚？肫肫其仁，渊渊其渊，浩浩其天。苟不固聪明圣知达天德者，其孰能知之？

【语译】

唯有天下极至诚的圣人，能定天下之常法，立天下之大德，通晓天地化育万物的真理，此乃至诚之力，难道还别有所依赖而后能吗？其仁心诚恳，其沉静如深渊，其广大如太空。若非聪明智慧有天赋圣德，何人能了解此等深奥道理呢？

【原文】

《诗》曰："衣锦尚絅。"恶其文之著也。故君子之道，暗然而日章；小人之道，的然而日亡。君子之道，淡而不厌，简而文，温而理，知远之近，知风之自，知微之显，可与入德矣。

《诗》云："潜虽伏矣，亦孔之昭。"故君子内省不疚，无恶于志。君子之所不可及者，其唯人之所不见乎！

《诗》云："相在尔室，尚不愧于屋漏。"故君子不动而敬，不言而信。

《诗》曰："奏假无言，时靡有争。"是故君子不赏而民劝，不怒而民威于鈇钺。

《诗》曰："不显惟德，百辟其刑之。"是故君子笃恭而天下平。

《诗》曰："予怀明德，不大声以色。"子曰："声色之于以化民，末也。"

《诗》曰："德輶如毛。"毛犹有伦。"上天之载，无声无臭。"至矣！

【语译】

《诗经》上说："穿彩色绸衣，外罩衣裳。"因嫌绸衣的纹彩太鲜明了。君子的为人之道，外表纹彩不露，日久自然渐渐露出来。小人的为人，外表纹彩鲜明，日子久了，就渐渐消亡了。君子做人，看来平淡，并不使人厌恶，看来简素却有文采，看来温和却明辨是非。知远事之近因，知风之来处，因微而知显。明白此等道理，就可进入道德之门了。

《诗经》上说："躲藏起来，似乎看不见了，其实，还是非常明显。"所以君子，无有过失，无愧于心。君子之令人比不上，正在别人看不见之处啊！

《诗经》上说："独居室内深处，依然无愧于心。"所以君子不必有行动，人就尊敬他；不必说话，人就信任他。

《诗经》上说："求神来享，肃然无言。"所以君子不必奖赏，而人民自知相勉向善，不必发怒，而人民畏惧，胜过畏惧刀斧。

《诗经》上说："彰明德行，诸侯自然效法。"故君子只要笃诚恭敬，天下自然太平。

《诗经》上说："我喜爱你以德化民，而不用厉声厉色。"孔子说："用厉声厉色去感化人，那是最下的办法。"

《诗经》上说："化民之德，轻如羽毛。"可是羽毛虽轻，还是有其大小可比。而《文王篇》所说："上天行四时化育万民，无声无味。"真是至高无上了。

Chapter Three   **CENTRAL HARMONY**

(*Chungyung*: originally *Liki*, Chapter XXXI)

This is the book of *Chungyung*, usually translated as "The Doctrine of the Mean," or "The Golden Mean." It constitutes the second of the "Four Books," the following chapter (IV) being the first. Its importance in the Confucian philosophy will be readily seen from the text itself. I have put it here at the beginning of the Confucian texts because it gives the best approach to Confucian philosophy. In itself it forms a fairly adequate and complete basis for the philosophy of Confucianism. The book, according to early authorities, was written by Tsesze, grandson of Confuicus, disciple of Tsengtse and teacher of Mencius. Besides this chapter, Tsesze is traditionally said to have been responsible for Chapters XXX, XXXII and XXXIII of *Liki* also. The identity in style and thought between Mencius and this essay, especially Sections 1, 7, 8, is unmistakable, and part of Section 7 is actually repeated in *Mencius*. But if Tsesze was responsible for this work, he was a worthy teacher of Mencius, for we find here certain germinal ideas which mature and ripen into the full eloquence of Mencius. Careful students will see a deep connection between this chapter and the philosophy of Mencius (Ch. XI).

This is the only chapter in which I have not made my own translation, the one used being by the late Ku Hungming. Ku's translation has merits which are sufficiently apparent to make any justification for its use here superfluous. It is interesting to note that Ku translates *jen* as "the moral sense," *yi* as "the sense of justice," *li* as "moral and religious institutions (of the Three Dynasties)," and elsewhere as "the laws and usages of social life," *tao* as "the moral law," *chuntse* as "the moral man," *hsiaojen* as "the vulgar man," and *chungyung* as the "universal moral order" and in another place as "to find the central clue in our moral being which unites us to the universal order." These renderings are essentially correct; some are even brilliant. I have, however, found it necessary to add, delete and substitute phrases or lines, bringing about, I believe, a closer adherence to the original, and have naturally changed certain spellings of Chinese names to make them uniform with the rest of the book.

Ku has made a rearrangement of the sections, which I have not followed. It is admitted in general that the different sections or "chapters" as they are called in Chinese, are put together without a pretense at a proper order, the most evident cases being the "Chapters" 6, 14, and 16 (numbers in the original, not indicated below). "Chapter 28" is a very bad chapter, with a clearly later interpolation, which I have deleted; the rest I have incorporated into "Chapter 29" in Section 7 here. It is not possible to go into detailed explanations here without taking up a great deal of space to discuss the internal evidences. For the convenience of students who have access to the Chinese text, I give below the numbers of the Chinese "chapters" and their present sequence as rearranged now under the different sections:

Section One: 1. *Section Two*: 2,3,4,5,7,8,9,10,11. *Section Three*: 12, 16. *Section Four*: 13, 15, 14. *Section Five*: 6, 17, 18, 19. *Section Six*: the greater part of 20, except the end. *Section Seven*: the end of 20, 21. *Section Eight*: 22, 23, 24, 25, 26. *Section Nine*: 27, 28 (partly deleted and partly combined with 29), 29, 30, 31, 32. *Section Ten*: 33.

I. THE CENTRAL HARMONY

What is God-given is what we call human nature. To fulfil the law of our human nature is what we call the moral law. The cultivation of the moral law is what we call culture.

The moral law is a law from whose operation we cannot for one instant in our existence escape. A law from which we may escape is not the moral law. Wherefore it is that the moral man (or the superior man) watches diligently over what his eyes cannot see and is in fear and awe of what his ears cannot hear.

There is nothing more evident than that which cannot be seen by the eyes and nothing more palpable than that which cannot be perceived by the senses. Wherefore the moral man watches diligently over his secret thoughts.

When the passions, such as joy, anger, grief, and pleasure, have not awakened, that is our *central* self, or moral being (*chung*). When these passions awaken and each and all attain due measure and degree, that is *harmony*, or the moral order (*ho*). Our central self or moral being is the great basis of existence, and *harmony* or moral order is the universal law in the world.

When our true central self and harmony are realised, the universe then becomes a cosmos and all things attain their full growth and development.

II. THE GOLDEN MEAN

Confuicus remarked: "The life of the moral man is an exemplification of the universal moral order (*chungyung*, usually translated as "the Mean"). The life of the vulgar person, on the other hand, is a contradiction of the universal moral order."

The moral man's life is an exemplification of the universal order, because he is a moral person who unceasingly cultivates his true self or moral being. The vulgar person's life is a contradiction of the universal order, because he is a vulgar person who in his heart has no regard for, or fear of, the moral law.

Confucius remarked: "To find the central clue to our moral being which unites us to the universal order, that indeed is the highest human attainment. For a long time, people have seldom been capable of it."

Confucius remarked: "I know now why the moral life is not practiced. The wise mistake moral law for something higher than what it really is; and the foolish do not know enough what moral law really is. I know now why the moral law is not understood. The noble natures want to live too high, high above their moral ordinary self; and ignoble natures do not live high enough, i.e., not up to their moral ordinary true self. There is no one who does not eat and drink. But few there are who really know flavor."

Confucius remarked: "There is in the world now really no moral social order at all."

Confucius remarked: "Men all say 'I am wise'; but when driven forward and taken in a net, a trap, or a pitfall, there is not one who knows how to find a way of escape. Men all say, 'I am wise'; but in finding the true central clue and balance in their moral being (i.e., their normal, ordinary, true self), they are not able to keep it for a round month."

Confucius remarked of his favorite disciple, Yen Huei: "Huei was a man who all his life sought the central clue in his moral being, and when he got hold of one thing that was good, he embraced it with all his might and never lost it again."

Confucius remarked: "A man may be able to put a country in order, be able to spurn the honors and emoluments of office, be able to trample upon bare, naked weapons: with all that he is still not able to find the central clue in his moral being."

Tselu asked what constituted strength of character.

Confucius said: "Do you mean strength of character of the people of the southern countries or force of character of the people of the northern countries; or do you mean strength of character of your type? To be patient and gentle, ready to teach, returning not evil for evil: that is the strength of character of the people of the southern countries. It is the ideal place for the moral man. To lie under arms and meet death without regret; that is the strength of character of the people of the northern countries. It is the ideal of brave men of your type. Wherefore the man with the true strength of moral character is one who is gentle, yet firm. How unflinching is his strength! When there is moral social order in the country, if he enters public life he does not change from what he was when in retirement. When there is no moral social order in the country, he is content unto death. How unflinching is his strength!"

Confucius remarked: "There are men who seek for the abstruse and strange and live a singular life in order that they may leave a name to posterity. This is what I never would do. There are again good men who try to live in conformity with the moral law, but who, when they have gone half way, throw it up. I never could give it up. Lastly, there are truly moral men who unconsciously live a life in entire harmony with the universal moral order and who live unknown to the world and unnoticed of men without any concern. It is only men of holy, divine natures who are capable of this."

III. MORAL LAW EVERYWHERE

The moral law is to be found everywhere, and yet it is a secret.

The simple intelligence of ordinary men and women of the people may understand something of the moral law; but in its utmost reaches there is something which even the wisest and holiest of men cannot understand. The ignoble natures of ordinary men and women of the people may be able to carry out the moral law; but in its utmost reaches even the wisest and holiest of men cannot live up to it.

Great as the Universe is, man is yet not always satisfied with it. For there is nothing so great but the mind of the moral man can conceive of something still greater which nothing in the world can hold. There is nothing so small but the mind of the moral man can conceive of something still smaller which nothing in the world can split.

The *Book of Songs* says: "The hawk soars to the heavens above and fishes dive to the depths below." That is to say, there is no place in the highest heavens above nor in the deepest waters below where the moral law is not to be found. The moral man finds the moral law beginning in the relation between man and woman; but ending in the vast reaches of the universe.

Confucius remarked: "The power of spiritual forces in the Universe—how active it is everywhere! Invisible to the eyes, and impalpable to the senses, it is inherent in all things, and nothing can escape its operation."

It is the fact that there are these forces which makes men in all countries fast and purify themselves, and with solemnity of dress institute services of sacrifice and religious worship. Like the rush of mighty waters, the presence of unseen Powers is felt; sometimes above us, sometimes around us.

In the *Book of Songs* it is said:

> "The presence of the Spirit:
> It cannot be surmised,
> How may it be ignored!

Such is the evidence of things invisible that it is impossible to doubt the spiritual nature of man.

IV. THE HUMANISTIC STANDARD

Confucius said: "Truth does not depart from human nature. If what is regarded as truth departs from human nature, it may not be regarded as truth. The *Book of Songs* says: 'In hewing an axe handle, the pattern is not far off.' Thus, when we take an axe handle in our hand to hew another axe handle and glance from one to the other, some still think the pattern is far off. Wherefore the moral man in dealing with men appeals to the common human nature and changes the manner of their lives and nothing more."

"When a man carries out the principles of conscientiousness and reciprocity he is not far from the moral law. What you do not wish others should do unto you, do not do unto them.

"There are four things in the moral life of a man, not one of which I have been able to carry out in my life. To serve my father as I would expect my son to serve me: that I have not been able to do. To serve my sovereign as I would expect a minister under me to serve me: that I have not been able to do. To act towards my elder brothers as I would expect my younger brother to act towards me: that I have not been able to do. To be the first to behave towards friends as I would expect them to behave towards me: that I have not been able to do.

"In the discharge of the ordinary duties of life and in the exercise of care in ordinary conversation, whenever there is shortcoming, never fail to strive for improvement, and when there is much to be said, always say less than what is necessary; words having respect to actions and actions having respect to words. Is it not just this thorough genuineness and absence of pretense which characterizes the moral man?"

The moral life of man may be likened to traveling to a distant place: one must start from the nearest stage. It may also be likened to ascending a height: one must begin from the lowest step. The *Book of Songs* says:

> "When wives and children and their sires are one,
> 'Tis like the harp and lute in unison.
> When brothers live in concord and at peace
> The strain of harmony shall never cease.
> The lamp of happy union lights the home,
> And bright days follow when the children come."

Confucius, commenting on the above, remarked: "In such a state of things what more satisfaction can parents have?"

The moral man conforms himself to his life circumstances; he does not desire anything outside of his position. Finding himself in a position of wealth and honor, he lives as becomes one living in a position of wealth and honor. Finding himself in a position of poverty and humble circumstances, he lives as becomes one living in a position of poverty and humble circumstances. Finding himself in uncivilized countries, he lives as becomes one living in uncivilized countries. Finding himself in circumstances of danger and difficulty, he acts according to what is required of a man under such circumstances. In one word, the moral man can find himself in no situation in life in which he is not master of himself.

In a high position he does not domineer over his subordinates. In a subordinate position he does not court the favors of his superiors. He puts in order his own personal conduct and seeks nothing from others; hence he has no complaint to make. He complains not against God, nor rails against men.

Thus it is that the moral man lives out the even tenor of his life, calmly waiting for the appointment of God, whereas the vulgar person takes to dangerous courses, expecting the uncertain chances of luck.

Confucius remarked: "In the practice of archery we have something resembling the principle in a moral man's life. When the archer misses the center of the target, he turns round and seeks for the cause of his failure within himself."

V. CERTAIN MODELS

Confucius remarked: "There was the Emperor Shun. He was perhaps what may be considered a truly great intellect. Shun had a natural curiosity of mind and he loved to inquire into ordinary conversation. He ignored the bad (words?) and broadcast the good. Taking two extreme counsels, he took the mean between them and applied them in dealings with his people. This was the characteristic of Shun's great intellect."

Confucius remarked: "The Emperor Shun might perhaps be considered in the highest sense of the word a pious man. In moral qualities he was a saint.

In dignity of office he was the ruler of the empire. In wealth all that the wide world contained belonged to him. After his death his spirit was sacrificed to in the ancestral temple, and his children and grandchildren preserved the sacrifice for long generations.

"Thus it is that he who possesses great moral qualities will certainly attain to corresponding high position, to corresponding great prosperity, to corresponding great name, to corresponding great age.

"For God in giving life to all created things is surely bountiful to them according to their qualities. Hence the tree that is full of life he fosters and sustains, while that which is ready to fall he cuts off and destroys.

The *Book of Songs* says:

> That great and noble Prince displayed
> The sense of right in all he wrought;
> The spirit of his wisdom swayed
> Peasant and peer; the crowd, the court.
> So Heav'n, that crowned his sires, restored
> The countless honors they had known;
> For Heav'n aye keepeth watch and ward,
> The Mandate gave to mount the throne.

It is therefore true that he who possesses exceedingly great moral qualities will certainly receive the divine mandate to the Imperial throne."

Confucius remarked: "The man perhaps who enjoyed the most perfect happiness was the Emperor Wen. For father he had a remarkable man, the Emperor Chi, and for son also a remarkable man, the Emperor Wu. His father laid the foundation of his House and his son carried it on. The Emperor Wu, continuing the great work begun by his ancestor, the great Emperor, his grandfather Chi and his father the Emperor Wen, had only to buckle on his armor and the Empire at once came to his possession. In dignity of office he was the ruler of the Empire; in wealth all that the wide world contained belonged to him. After his death his spirit was sacrificed to in the ancestral temple, and his children and grandchildren preserved the sacrifice for long generations.

"The Emperor Wu received Heaven's mandate to rule in his old age. His brother, Duke Chou, ascribed the achievement of founding the Imperial House equally to the moral qualities of the Emperors Wen and Wu. He carried the Imperial title up to the Great Emperor (Wen's grandfather) and the Emperor Chi (Wen's father). He sacrificed to all the past reigning Dukes of the House with imperial honors."

("This rule is now universally observed from the reigning princes and nobles to the gentlemen and common people. In the case where the father is a noble and the son is a simple gentleman, the father, when he dies, is buried with the honors of a noble, but sacrificed to as a simple gentleman. In the case where the father is a simple gentleman and the son a noble, the father, when he dies, is buried as a simple gentleman, but sacrificed to with the honors of a nobleman. The rule for one year of mourning for relatives is binding up to the rank of a noble, but the rule for three years of mourning for parents is binding for all up to the Emperor. In mourning for parents there is only one rule, and no distinction is made between noble and plebeian.")

Confucius remarked: "The Emperor Wu and his brother, Duke Chou, were indeed eminently pious men. Now, true filial piety consists in successfully carrying out the unfinished work of our forefathers and transmitting their achievements to posterity.

"In spring and autumn they repaired and put in order the ancestral temple, arranged the sacrificial vessels, exhibited the regalia and heirlooms of the family, and presented the appropriate offerings of the season.

"The principle in the order of precedence in the ceremonies of worship in the ancestral temple is, in the first place, to arrange the members of the family according to descent. Ranks are next considered, in order to give recognition to the principle of social distinction. Services rendered are next considered as a recognition of distinction in moral worth. In the general banquet those below take precedence of those above in pledging the company, in order to show that consideration is shown to the meanest. In conclusion, a separate feast is given to the elders, in order to recognize the principle of seniority according to age.

"To gather in the same places where our fathers before us have gathered; to perform the same ceremonies which they before us have performed; to play the same music which they before us have played; to pay respect to those whom they honored; to love those who were dear to them—in fact, to serve those now dead as if they were living, and now departed as if they were still with us: this is the highest achievement of true filial piety.

"The performance of sacrifices to Heaven and Earth is meant for the service of God. The performance of ceremonies in the ancestral temple is meant for the worship of ancestors. If one only understood the meaning of the sacrifices to Heaven and Earth, and the significance of the services in ancestral worship in summer and autumn, it would be as easy to govern a nation as to point a finger at the palm."

VI. ETHICS AND POLITICS

Duke Ai (ruler of Lu, Confucius' native state) asked what constituted good government.

Confucius replied: "The principles of good government of the Emperors Wen and Wu are abundantly illustrated in the records preserved. When the men are there, good government will flourish, but when the men are gone, good government decays and becomes extinct. With the right men, the growth of good government is as rapid as the growth of vegetation is in the right soil. Indeed, good government is like a fast-growing plant. The conduct of government, therefore, depends upon the men. The right men are obtained by the ruler's personal character. To cultivate his personal character, the ruler must use the moral law (*tao*). To cultivate the moral law, the ruler must use the moral sense (*jen*, or principles of true manhood).

"The moral sense is the characteristic attribute of man. To feel natural affection for those nearly related to us is the highest expression of the moral sense. The sense of justice (*yi* or propriety) is the recognition of what is right and proper. To honor those who are worthier than ourselves is the highest expression of the sense of justice. The relative degrees of natural affection we ought to feel for those who are nearly related to us and the relative grades of honor we ought to show to those worthier than ourselves: these give rise to the forms and distinctions in social life (*li*, or principles of social order). For unless social inequalities have a true and moral basis (or unless those being ruled feel their proper place with respect to their rulers), government of the people is impossibility.

"Therefore it is necessary for a man of the governing class to set about regulating his personal conduct and character. In considering how to regulate his personal conduct and character, it is necessary for him to do his duties toward those nearly related to him. In considering how to do his duties toward those nearly related to him, it is necessary for him to understand the nature and organization of human society. In considering the nature and organization of human society it is necessary for him to understand the laws of God.

"The duties of universal obligation are five, and the moral qualities by which they are carried out are three. The duties are those between ruler and subject, between father and son, between husband and wife, between elder brother and younger, and those in the intercourse between friends. These are the five duties of universal obligation. Wisdom, compassion and courage— these are the three universally recognized moral qualities of man. It matters not in what way men come to the exercise of these moral qualities, the result is one and the same.

"Some men are born with the knowledge of these moral qualities; some acquire it as the result of education; some acquire it as the result of hard experience. But when the knowledge is acquired, it comes to one and the same thing. Some exercise these moral qualities naturally and easily; some because they find it advantageous to do so; some with effort and difficulty. But when the achievement is made it comes to one and the same thing."

Confucius went on to say: "Love of knowledge is akin to wisdom. Strenuous attention to conduct is akin to compassion. Sensitiveness to shame is akin to courage.

"When a man understands the nature and use of these three moral qualities, he will then understand how to put in order his personal conduct and character. When a man understands how to put in order his personal conduct and character, he will understand how to govern men. When a man understands how to govern men, he will then understand how to govern nations and empires.

"For every one called to the government of nations and empires there are nine cardinal directions to be attended to:

1. Cultivating his personal conduct.
2. Honoring worthy men.
3. Cherishing affection for, and doing his duty toward, his kindred.
4. Showing respect to the high ministers of state.
5. Identifying himself with the interests and welfare of the whole body of public officers.
6. Showing himself as a father to the common people.
7. Encouraging the introduction of all useful arts.
8. Showing tenderness to strangers from far countries.
9. Taking interest in the welfare of the princes of the Empire.

"When the ruler pays attention to the cultivation of his personal conduct, there will be respect for the moral law. When the ruler honors worthy men, he will not be deceived (by the crafty officials). When the ruler cherishes affection for his kindred, there will be no disaffection among the members of his family. When the ruler shows respect to the high ministers of state, he will not make mistakes. When the ruler identifies himself with the interests and welfare of the body of public officers, there will be a strong spirit of loyalty among the gentlemen of the country. When the ruler becomes a father to the common people, the mass of the people will exert themselves for the good of the state. When the ruler encourages the introduction of all useful arts, there will be sufficiency of wealth and revenue in the country. When the ruler shows kindness to the strangers from far countries, people from all quarters of the world will flock to the country. When the ruler takes interest in the condition and welfare of the princes of the empire, he will inspire awe and respect for his authority throughout the whole world.

"By attending to the cleanliness and purity of his person and to the propriety and dignity of his dress, and in every word and act permitting nothing which is contrary to good taste and decency; that is how the ruler cultivates his personal conduct. By banishing all flatterers and keeping away from the society of women, holding in low estimation possession of worldly goods, but valuing moral qualities in men—that is how the ruler gives encouragement to worthy men. By raising them to high places of honor and bestowing ample emoluments for their maintenance; sharing and sympathizing with their tastes and opinions—that is how the ruler inspires love for his person among the members of his family. By extending the powers of their functions and allowing them discretion in the employment of their subordinates—that is how the ruler gives encouragement to the high ministers of state. By dealing loyally and punctually with them in all engagements which he makes with them and allowing a liberal scale of pay—that is how the ruler gives encouragement to men in the public service. By strictly limiting the time of their service and making all imposts as light as possible—that is how the ruler gives encouragement to the mass of the people. By ordering daily inspection and monthly examination and rewarding each according to the degree of his workmanship—that is how the ruler encourages the artisan class. By welcoming them when they come and giving them protection when they go, commending what is good in them and making allowance for their ignorance—that is how the ruler shows kindness to strangers from far countries. By restoring lines of broken succession and reviving subjugated states, putting down anarchy and disorder wherever they are found, and giving support to the weak against the strong, fixing stated times for their attendance and the attendance of their envoys at court, loading them with presents when they leave, while exacting little from them in the way of contribution when they come—that is how the ruler takes interest in the welfare of the princes of the empire.

"For every one who is called to government of nations and empire, these are the nine cardinal directions to be attended to; and there is only one way by which they can be carried out.

"In all matters success depends on preparation; without preparation there will always be failure. When what is to be said is previously determined, there will be no difficulty in carrying it out. When a line of conduct is previously determined, there will be no occasion for vexation. When general principles are previously determined, there will be no perplexity to know what to do."

VII. BEING ONE'S TRUE SELF

"If the people in inferior positions do not have confidence in those above them, government of the people is an impossibility. There is only one way to gain confidence for one's authority: if a man is not trusted by his friends, he will not have confidence in those above him. There is only one way to be trusted by one's friends: if a man is not affectionate toward his parents, he will not be trusted by his friends. There is only one way to be affectionate toward one's parents: if a man, looking into his own heart, is not true to himself, he will not be affectionate toward his parents. There is only one way for a man to be true to himself. If he does not know what is good, a man cannot be true to himself.

"Being true to oneself is the law of God. To try to be true to oneself is the law of man.

"He who is naturally true to himself is one who, without effort, hits upon what is right, and without thinking understands what he wants to know, whose life is easily and naturally in harmony with the moral law. Such a one is what we call a saint or a man of divine nature. He who learns to be his true self is one who finds out what is good and holds fast to it.

"In order to learn to be one's true self, it is necessary to obtain a wide and extensive knowledge of what has been said and done in the world; critically to inquire into it; carefully to ponder over it; clearly to sift it; and earnestly to carry it out.

"It matters not what you learn; but when you once learn a thing, you must never give it up until you have mastered it. It matters not what you inquire into, but when you inquire into a thing, you must never give it up until you have thoroughly understood it. It matters not what you try to think out, but when you once try to think out a thing you must never give it up until you have got what you want. It matters not what you try to sift out, but when you once try to sift out a thing, you must never give it up until you have sifted it out clearly and distinctly. It matters not what you try to carry out, but when you once try to carry out a thing you must never give it up until you have done it thoroughly and well. If another man succeed by one effort, you will use a hundred efforts. If another man succeed by ten efforts, you will use a thousand efforts.

"Let a man really proceed in this manner, and, though dull, he will surely become intelligent; though weak, he will surely become strong."

To arrive at understanding from being one's true self is called nature, and to arrive at being one's true self from understanding is called culture. He who is his true self has thereby understanding, and he who has understanding finds thereby his true self.

VIII. THOSE WHO ARE ABSOLUTE TRUE SELVES

Only those who are their absolute true selves in the world can fulfil their own nature; only those who fulfil their own nature can fulfil the nature of others; only those who fulfil the nature of others can fulfil the nature of things; those who fulfil the nature of things are worthy to help Mother Nature in growing and sustaining life; and those who are worthy to help Mother Nature in growing and sustaining life are the equals of heaven and earth.

The next in order are those who are able to attain to the apprehension of a particular branch of study. By such studies, they are also able to apprehend the truth. Realization of the true self compels expression; expression becomes evidence; evidence becomes clarity or luminosity of knowledge; clarity or luminosity of knowledge activates; active knowledge becomes power and power becomes a pervading influence. Only those who are absolutely their true selves in this world can have pervading influence.

It is an attribute of the possession of the absolute true self to be able to foreknow. When a nation or family is about to flourish, there are sure to be lucky omens. When a nation or family is about to perish, there are sure to be signs and prodigies. These things manifest themselves in the instruments of divination and in the agitation of the human body. When happiness or calamity is about to come, it can be known beforehand. When it is good, it can be known beforehand. When it is evil, it can also be known beforehand. Therefore he who has realized his true self is like a celestial spirit.

Truth means the fulfilment of our self; and moral law means following the law of our being. Truth is the beginning and end (the substance) of material existence. Without truth there is no material existence. It is for this reason that the moral man values truth.

Truth is not only the fulfilment of our own being; it is that by which things outside of us have an existence. The fulfilment of our being is moral sense. The fulfilment of the nature of things outside of us is intellect. These, moral sense and intellect, are the powers or faculties of our being. They combine the inner or subjective and outer or objective use of the power of the mind. Therefore, with truth, everything done is right.

Thus absolute truth is indestructible. Being indestructible, it is eternal. Being eternal, it is self-existent. Being self-existent, it is infinite. Being infinite, it is vast and deep. Being vast and deep, it is transcendental and intelligent. It is because it is vast and deep that it contains all existence. It is because it is transcendental and intelligent that it embraces all existence. It is because it is infinite and eternal that it fulfils or perfects all existence. In vastness and depth it is like the Earth. In transcendental intelligence it is like Heaven. Infinite and eternal, it is the Infinite itself.

Such being the nature of absolute truth, it manifests itself without being seen; it produces effects without motion; it accomplishes its ends without action.

The principle in the course and operation of nature may be summed up in one word: because it obeys only its own immutable law, the way in which it produces the variety of things is unfathomable.

Nature is vast, deep, high, intelligent, infinite and eternal. The heaven appearing before us is only this bright, shining mass; but in its immeasurable extent, the sun, the moon, stars and constellations are suspended in it, and all things are embraced under it. The earth, appearing before us, is but a handful of soil; but in all its breadth and depth, it sustains mighty mountains without feeling their weight; rivers and seas dash against it without causing it to leak. The mountain appearing before us is only a mass of rock; but in all the vastness of its size, grass and vegetation grow upon it, birds and beasts dwell on it, and treasures of precious minerals are found in it. The water appearing before us is but a ladleful of liquid; but in all its unfathomable depths, the largest crustaceans, dragons, fishes, and turtles are produced in them, and all useful products abound in them.

In the *Book of Songs* it is said:

> "The ordinance of God,
> How inscrutable it is and goes on for ever."

That is to say, this is the essence of God. It is again said:

> "How excellent it is,
> The moral perfection of King Wen."

That is to say, this is the essence of the noble character of the Emperor Wen. Moral perfection also never dies.

IX. EULOGY ON CONFUCIUS

Oh, how great is the divine moral law of the Sage. Overflowing and illimitable it gives birth and life to all created things and towers high up to the very heavens. How magnificent it is! How imposing the three hundred principles and three thousand rules of conduct! They await the man who can put the system into practice. Hence it is said: Unless there be the highest moral character, the highest moral law cannot be realized.

Wherefore the moral man, while honoring the greatness and power of his moral nature, yet does not neglect inquiry and pursuit of knowledge. While broadening the scope of his knowledge, he yet seeks to exhaust the mystery of the small things. While seeking to attain the highest understanding he yet orders his conduct according to the middle course (literally *"chungyung"*). Going over what he has already learned, he gains some new knowledge. Earnest and simple, he respects and obeys the laws and usages of social life (*li*).

Therefore, when in a position of authority, he is not proud; in a subordinate position, he is not insubordinate. When there is moral social order in the country, what he speaks will bring prosperity to the nation; and when there is no moral social order in the country, his silence will ensure forbearance for himself.

In the *Book of Songs* it is said:

> "With wisdom and good sense,
> He guards his life from harm."

That is the description of the moral man.

To attain to the sovereignty of the world, there are three important things necessary, which would make it perfect.

Although a man may occupy a position of authority, yet, unless he possesses the moral character fitting him for his task, he may not take upon himself to make changes in the established religious and artistic institutions (literally "ritual and music"). Although one may possess the moral character fitting him for his task, yet, unless he occupies the position of authority, he may not take upon himself to make changes in the established religious and artistic institutions.

Confucius remarked: "I have tried to understand the moral and religious institutions (*li*) of the Hsia Dynasty, but what remains of those institutions in the present state of Ch'i does not furnish sufficient evidence. I have studied the moral and religious institutions of the Shang (Yin) Dynasty; the remains of them are still preserved in the present state of Sung. I have studied the moral and religious institutions of the present Chou Dynasty, which being now in use, I follow in practice."

Coming from those in power, a system may be lacking in historical authority ("historic evidences"), however excellent it may be; what is lacking in historical authority cannot command credence; and what cannot command credence the people will never obey. Coming from those not in authority, a system may not command respect, however excellent it may be; what does not command respect cannot command credence; and what cannot command credence the people will never obey.

Therefore every system of moral laws must be based upon the man's own consciousness, verified by the common experience of mankind, tested by due sanction of historical experience and found without error, applied to the operations and processes of nature in the physical universe and found to be without contradiction, laid before the gods without question or fear, and able to wait a hundred generations and have it confirmed without a doubt by a Sage of posterity. The fact that he is able to confront the spiritual powers of the universe without any fear shows that he understands the laws of God. The fact that he is prepared to wait a hundred generations for confirmation from the Sage of posterity without any misgiving shows that he understands the laws of man.

Wherefore it is that it is true of the really great moral man that every move he makes becomes an example for generations; every act he does becomes a model for generations and every word he utters becomes a guide for generations. Those who are far away look up to him, while those who are near do not decrease their respect for him. In the *Book of Songs* it is said:

> "There they found no fault of him,
> Here they never tire of him;
> Thus from day to day and night to night
> They will perpetuate his praise!"

There never was a moral man who did not answer this description and who yet could obtain timely recognition throughout the world.

Confucius taught the truth originally handed down by the ancient Emperors Yao and Shun, and he adopted and perfected the system of social and religious laws established by the Emperors Wen and Wu. He shows that they harmonize with the divine order which governs the revolutions of the seasons in the Heaven above and that they fit in with the moral design which is to be seen in physical nature upon the Earth below.

These moral laws form one system with the laws by which Heaven and Earth support and contain, overshadow and canopy all things. These moral laws form the same system with the laws by which the seasons succed each other and the sun and moon appear with the alternations of day and night. It is this same system of laws by which all created things are produced and develop themselves each in its order and system without injuring one another, and by which the operations of Nature take their course without conflict or confusion; the lesser forces flowing everywhere like river currents, while the great forces of Creation go silently and steadily on. It is this (one system running through all) that makes the Universe so impressively great.

It is only the man with the most perfect divine moral nature who is able to combine in himself quickness of apprehension, intelligence, insight and understanding—qualities necessary for the exercise of command, magnanimity, generosity, benignity and gentleness—qualities necessary for the exercise of patience; originality, energy, strength of character and determination—qualities necessary for the exercise of endurance, piety, noble seriousness, order and regularity—qualities necessary for the exercise of dignity, grace, method, subtlety and penetration—qualities necessary for the exercise of critical judgment.

Thus all-embracing and vast is the nature of such a man. Profound it is and inexhaustible, like a living spring of water, ever running out with life and vitality. All-embracing and vast, it is like Heaven. Profound and inexhaustible, it is like the abyss.

As soon as such a man shall make his appearance in the world, all people will reverence him. Whatever he says, all people will believe it. Whatever he does, all people will be pleased with it. Thus his fame and name will spread and fill all the civilized world (literally "China"), extending even to savage countries, wherever ships and carriages reach, wherever the labor and enterprise of man penetrate, wherever the heavens overshadow and the earth sustain, wherever the sun and moon shine, wherever frost and dew fall. All who have life and breath will honor and love him. Therefore we may say: "He is the equal of God."

It is only he in this world who has realized his absolute self that can order and adjust the great relations of human society, fix the fundamental principles of morality, and understand the laws of growth and reproduction of the Universe.

Now, where does such a man derive his power and knowledge, except from himself? How simple and self-contained his true manhood! How unfathomable the depth of his mind! How infinitely grand and vast the moral height of his nature! Who can understand such a nature except he who is gifted with the most perfect intelligence and endowed with the highest divine qualities of character, and who has reached in his moral development the level of the gods?

X. EPILOGUE

In the *Book of Songs* it is said:

> "Over her brocaded robe,
> She wore a plain and simple dress,"

in that way showing her dislike of the loudness of its color and magnificence. Thus the ways of the moral man are unobtrusive and yet they grow more and more in power and evidence; whereas the ways of the vulgar person are ostentatious, but lose more and more in influence until they perish and disappear.

The life of the moral man is plain, and yet not unattractive; it is simple, and yet full of grace; it is easy, and yet methodical. He knows that accomplishment of great things consists in doing little things well. He knows that great effects are produced by small causes. He knows the evidence and reality of what cannot be perceived by the senses. Thus he is enabled to enter into the world of ideas and morals.

In the *Book of Songs* it is said:

> "How deep the fish may dive below,
> And yet it is quite clearly seen."

Therefore the moral man must examine into his own heart and see that he has no cause for self-reproach, that he has no evil thought in his mind. Wherein the moral man is superior to other men consists even in those things that people do not notice.

In the *Book of Songs* it is said:

> "In your secret chamber even you are judged;
> See you do nothing to blush for,
> Though but the ceiling looks down upon you."

Therefore the moral man, even when he is not doing anything, is serious; and, even when he does not speak, is truthful.

In the *Book of Songs* it is said:

> "All through the solemn rite not a word was spoken,
> And yet all strife was banished from their hearts"

Hence the moral man, without the inducement of rewards, is able to make the people good; and without the show of anger, to awe them into fear more than if he had used the most dreadful instruments of punishment.

In the *Book of Songs*, it is said:

> "He makes no show of his moral worth,
> Yet all the princes follow in his steps."

Hence the moral man, by living a life of simple truth and earnestness, alone can help to bring peace and order in the world.

> In the *Book of Songs*, it is said:
> "I keep in mind the fine moral qualities
> Which make no great noise or show."

Confucius remarked:"Among the means for the regeneration of mankind, those made with noise and show are of the least importance."

In another place in the *Book of Songs*, it is said:

> "His virtue is light as hair."

Still a hair is something material. "The workings of Almighty God have neither sound nor smell." That is the highest development of our moral nature.

第四章 《大学》

——伦理与政治

整个儒家的教育观点，似乎认为教育系为"士"（上等社会之知识分子）而设，以便日后为君主治理国家，或辅佐帝王以济世为政，因此在讨论教育时，始终皆以治国为宗旨。《大学》一书似乎是专为教育王子贵人而作，所以书名称为《大学》，而大学即王子贵人受教育之所。

《大学》原为《礼记》之一章，今列为《四书》之一部。因为列为《四书》中之一部，以前中国学童读《四书》时，皆自《大学》一书开始。《大学》与《中庸》背后的哲学意义，对学童并不重要，自然非七八岁的学童所能了解；然此书必须精读熟记，以备将来之用。关于本书之重要性，宋儒理学家程伊川曾说："《大学》孔氏之遗书，而初学入德之门也。于今可见古人为学次第者，独赖此篇之存，而《论》《孟》次之。学者必由是而学焉，则庶乎其不差矣。"

"大学"一词，理雅格（James Legge）氏英译为 The Great Learning；辜鸿铭译为 The Higher Education，意为"高等教育"，更为正确。以前

中国适于读"大学"的年龄，似乎相当于读美国的"专科学校"（Junior College）。《礼记》一书有一章把古时王子贵族的学制叙述得很明白，即本书中第九章。《礼记》之第八及第十二两章对古时教育制度犹有进一步的说明，本书并未选入。整个儒家的教育观点，似乎认为教育系为"士"（上等社会之知识分子）而设，以便日后为君主治理国家，或辅佐帝王以济世为政，因此在讨论教育时，始终皆以治国为宗旨。《大学》一书似乎是专为教育王子贵人而作，所以书名称为《大学》，而大学即王子贵人受教育之所。"君子"一词在大学中当然甚为通用，照字面看，"君子"者，"君王之子"也，亦即"王子"，后来渐渐为"士绅"（Gentleman）之称。此书内容所论，实际上，是以个人生活的修养（修身）与治国平天下为中心，也可以说以伦理与政治为主旨。

本书曾由宋儒朱熹改编，将一整节文字提到前面，使全文含义更为清楚。原来段落前后错乱，是早年将竹简误排之故，因以前竹简是用皮条穿入竹简洞口而成捆收存的。我认为朱熹的改编令人敬佩，故本书采用朱本。但他似乎不曾注意到原来错乱的缘故，以致在他调动顺序的一部分，转折之处遂显得不够自然，也因而有两行完全相同。那就是"此谓知本"这一句。此句之后，后来又有同样一句"此谓知本"，"此谓知之至也"。朱熹是把第二句"此谓知本"与随后的"此谓知之至也"看做是一段遗失文字的结语，于是他随即擅自代为补上那一段，借此机会把宋儒以冥想为格物致知的道理插入书中一些。也因此完全改变了格物致知的方法与对象，这也引起无尽无休的争辩与臆测。我曾将汉朝郑玄的《大学》原文与朱熹的版本比较，所得到的结论是，错误的由来是那相同的两句"此谓知本"，原来在那段文字里是分开的。但因为秦始皇焚书坑儒之后，那些幸未罹难得以硕果仅存的老儒生，是全凭心中记诵记录下来，因而联系错误，这也自然难免。就犹如现今排字房犯这类错误一样。由郑玄的版本中原有的错误推论起来，根本没有什么"阙文"，只是因文句错乱而起，在句中所讨论的"格物致知"只是限于人性与人心的活动，并未涉及物质界的宇宙。这一层由随后我改编的《大学》正文中即可一目了然。朱熹将全章予以前后调动，我仍保持其原来顺序，未予更动；只是把原来承上启下的那个雷同的句子，改放在我认为适当的所在而已。

【原文】

大学之道，在明明德，在亲民，在止于至善。

知止而后有定，定而后能静，静而后能安，安而后能虑，虑而后能得。物有本末，事有终始，知所先后，则近道矣。

古之欲明明德于天下者，先治其国；欲治其国者，先齐其家；欲齐其家者，先修其身；欲修其身者，先正其心；欲正其心者，先诚其意；欲诚其意者，先致其知；致知在格物。

物格而后知至，知至而后意诚，意诚而后心正，心正而后身修，身修而后家齐，家齐而后国治，国治而后天下平。自天子以至于庶人，壹是皆以修身为本。其本乱而末治者否矣；其所厚者薄，而其所薄者厚，未之有也。此谓知本。

【语译】

高等教育的目标在于保存人高尚的品格，在于赋予人民新的生命，在于止于完美之境。知道止于完美的境界之后，对人生才有固定的宗旨。对人生有了固定的宗旨，才能得到心境的宁静。得到心境的宁静之后，才能安然自处。能安然自处，才能用心思考；能思考才能有所知。物体之组织是由基础及高层所构成，而每件事务之演变上也是有其开始，有其终结的。因此了解事物之正常关联的顺序，乃是智慧之始。

先贤凡是要保存普天下人那清新的品德的，必要先把本国人民的生活纳入正轨。要想把本国人民的生活纳入正轨，必须先把家庭生活整顿好。要想把家庭生活整顿好，就须要先修养个人的生活。要修养个人的生活，必须先把心安放端正。要把自己的心安放端正，必须使自己的本意发乎真诚。要使自己的本意发乎真诚，必须获取真知；而真知在于研究万事万物。将万事万物研究之后，便有了真知；有了真知，其本意便能发乎真诚；本意能发乎真诚，内心便能放得端正；内心放得端正，个人的生活便可有了修养，个人的生活修养好，而后家庭生活才能整顿好；家庭生活整顿好之后，国民的生活才能上轨道；国民生活上了轨道，整个天下才能太平。上自帝王，下至庶民百姓，必须把个人生活的修养看做一切的基本。基本不好，其上层好者，是绝不可能的。树的主干瘦弱，而其上面枝叶茂密者，天下也绝无此事。这就叫作知道根本。

【原文】

《康诰》曰："克明德。"《太甲》曰："顾諟天之明命。"《帝典》曰："克明峻德。"皆自明也。

汤之《盘铭》曰："苟日新，日日新，又日新。"《康诰》曰："作新民。"《诗》云："周虽旧邦，其命维新。"是故君子无所不用其极。

《诗》云："邦畿千里，惟民所止。"《诗》云："缗蛮黄鸟，止于丘隅。"子曰："于止，知其所止。可以人而不如鸟乎？"《诗》云："穆穆文王，于缉熙敬止。"为人君，止于仁；为人臣，止于敬；为人子，止于孝；为人父，止于慈；与国人交，止于信。

《诗》云："瞻彼淇澳，菉竹猗猗。有斐君子，如切如磋，如琢如磨。瑟兮僩兮，赫兮喧兮。有斐君子，终不可喧兮。"如切如磋者，道学也；如琢如磨者，自修也；瑟兮僩兮者，恂慄也；赫兮喧兮者，威仪也；有斐君子，终不可喧兮者，道盛德至善，民之不能忘也。

《诗》云："于戏，前王不忘。"君子贤其贤，而亲其亲；小人乐其乐，而利其利。此以没世不忘也。

【语译】

什么是修养个人的生活？《尚书·康诰》说："唯我文王能使自己的品德清新。"《尚书·太甲》说："唯我先王成汤，常常顾念着上天的明命。"《尚书·尧典》说："唯我帝弟能使自己的崇高品德清新。"这些都是讲古代的帝王是从自明其德行开始的。

成汤的《盘铭》说："如果能够一天新，就应保持天天新，新了还要更新。"《康诰》说："使周人变成新民族。"《诗经·文王》说："周虽然是个旧国家，接受的天命是新的。"所以君子在所有时间都尽自己最大的力量。

什么是达到完美的境界？《诗经·玄鸟》说："王者的都城地方千里，百姓都居住在这里。"《诗经·缗蛮》说："嘤嘤鸣叫的黄鸟，都栖息在树多的小阜上。"孔子说："对于栖息，鸟都知道该栖息在什么地方，难道人可以不如鸟吗？"《诗经·文王》说："穆穆然深远的文王，他的德行总是光明，事事小心恭敬。"文王为人民的君王，保持着仁爱之心；为君王的臣，尽心奉职不敢疏忽；在家里是儿子，侍奉父母一片孝心；当父亲的时候，教诲儿子非常慈爱；与别人交往的时候，言语句句诚实。

　　《诗经·淇澳》说："看那淇水弯曲之处，青绿色的竹子多么美丽茂盛！我们那文采斐然的君子，学问何等精细，切削过似的，打磨过似的，严密刚强，威严光辉啊！文采斐然的君子，百姓终身不能忘记呀！"这如切如磋，说的是学习的道理；这如琢如磨，说的是自修的道理；瑟兮僴兮，是说战战兢兢，一刻不敢马虎；赫兮喧兮，是说恭敬之心在内，威仪表现于外；有斐君子，终不可喧兮，是说道德完善到了最高境界，百姓终身不能忘记。

　　《诗经·烈文》说："伟大啊！从前的文王和武王，虽然逝去久远了，后世人永远思念不忘！"后世君王尊敬前代贤明的模范，敬爱他们的亲人；后世人民享受太平的幸福，享受遗留的利益。这就是为什么后世追思不已的缘故。

【原文】

　　子曰："听讼，吾犹人也。必也使无讼乎？无情者，不得尽其辞，大畏民志。"此谓知本。此谓知之至也。

【语译】

　　什么是达到真知？孔子说："听断诉讼，我也和别人一样不算难事。我们的目的是要完全没有诉讼。于是那些犯了错误的人就会羞于为自己辩护，人民就怀着敬畏之心。"这就叫作知道事物的根本。这就叫作达到真知。

【原文】

　　所谓诚其意者，毋自欺也，如恶恶臭，如好好色。此之谓自谦，故君子必慎，其独也。小人闲居为不善，无所不至，见君子而后厌然，掩其不善，而著其善。人之视己，如见其肺肝然，则何益矣！此谓诚于中，形于外，故君子必慎其独也。曾子曰："十目所视，十手所指，其严乎！"富润屋，德润身，心广体胖，故君子必诚其意。

【语译】

所谓使自己的心意诚实，就是不要自己欺骗自己，如同厌恶恶劣像厌恶臭味一样，喜爱善良如同喜爱美人一样。这就叫做满足自己的心意。所以君子必然非常谨慎地对待他自己一个人独处的时候。普通的人在平时无人而独处时做坏事，可以无恶不作；看见诚实的君子就会内心不安，尽量掩饰，假装在做好事。其实别人看他，就像看清他的肝脏和肺脏一样，一目了然，这种欺骗有什么用呢！这就叫做内心是什么样的，表现出来的也会是那样，所以君子必然十分谨慎地对待他一人独处的时候。曾子说："不要说无人看见，十只眼睛看着呢；不要说没人指出，十只手指着呢。多么严格呀！"财富可以使屋子华美，德行可以使人身体充实，心地宽广。所以君子必然要使自己的心意出于至诚。

【原文】

所谓修身在正其心者，身有所忿懥，则不得其正；有所恐惧，则不得其正；有所好乐，则不得其正；有所忧患，则不得其正。心不在焉，视而不见，听而不闻，食而不知其味。此谓修身在正其心。

【语译】

为什么说修养个人的生活在于把自己的心安放端正呢？心里有愤怒，心就不能安放端正；心里有恐惧，心就不能安放端正；心里受着喜好的牵系，心就不能安放端正；心里有忧患，心就不能安放端正。

端正虚静的心已经不在了，就会看事物视而不见，听声音听而不闻，吃东西也不知道它的味道。这就是为什么修养个人的生活在于把心安放端正的原因。

【原文】

所谓齐其家在修其身者，人之其所亲爱而辟焉，之其所贱恶而辟焉，之其所畏敬而辟焉，之其所哀矜而辟焉，之其所敖惰而辟焉。故好而知其恶，恶而知其美者，天下鲜矣！故谚有之曰："人莫知其子之恶，莫知其苗之硕。"此谓身不修，不可以齐其家。

【语译】

为什么说整顿好他的家庭在于修养个人的生活呢？人对于他所亲爱的人会失之于偏颇，对于他所认为低贱厌恶的人会失之于偏颇，对于他所敬畏的人会失之于偏颇，对于他所怜悯的人会失之于偏颇，对于他所姑息或骄纵的人会失之于偏颇。所以说，喜爱的而又知道其中有恶劣之处，讨厌的而又知道其中有美好之处，这样无偏颇的态度天下少见！所以谚语说："人是没有知道自己的儿子的坏处的，是没有知道自己的庄稼茂盛的。"这就是说个人的生活没有修养好，是不可以整顿好他的家庭的。

【原文】

所谓治国必先齐其家者，其家不可教，而能教人者，无之。故君子不出家，而成教于国。孝者所以事君也，弟者所以事长也，慈者所以使众也。《康诰》曰："如保赤子。"心诚求之，虽不中，不远矣。未有学养子而后嫁者也。一家仁，一国兴仁；一家让，一国兴让；一人贪戾，一国作乱。其机如此。此谓一言偾事，一人定国。尧舜帅天下以仁而民从之；桀纣帅天下以暴而民从之；其所令反其所好，而民不从。是故君子有诸己而后求诸人，无诸己而后非诸人。所藏乎身不恕，而能喻诸人者，未之有也。故治国，在齐其家。

《诗》云："桃之夭夭，其叶蓁蓁。之子于归，宜其家人。"宜其家人，而后可以教国人。《诗》云："宜兄宜弟。"宜兄宜弟，而后可以教国人。《诗》云："其仪不忒，正是四国。"其为父子兄弟足法，而后民法之也。此谓治国在齐其家。

【语译】

为什么说治理国家的生活首先在于整顿好自己的家庭呢？他自己的家人都无法教育好，反而能教好别人的，没有这个道理。所以君子不一定走出自己的家庭，他的文化榜样延伸而感化一个国家。孝道是用来侍奉君主的，悌道是用以侍奉兄长的，慈爱是用来治理百姓的。《尚书·康诰》说："就像母亲爱护初生的婴儿一样。"从来没有一个姑娘是先学会养孩子而后嫁人的。如果你的本能是健全的，即使不能完全达到目标，也不会离得太远。一个家庭学会了仁爱，一个国家就会学到仁爱；一个家庭学会了谦让，一个国家就会学到谦让；一个家庭贪婪和狠戾，一个国家就会不守法纪。事物的法则就是如此。这就是所谓"一句话可以破坏一件事，一个人可以使国家安定"。尧舜为天下做出了仁爱的表率，人民就会学习他们；桀纣给天下做出了残酷的样子，人民也会模仿他们。他们的命令如果和他们的行为相反，百姓就不会听从。所以，君子必须先要求自己然后要求别人，自己没有过恶然后才去责备别人的过恶。在他自己的身上不采用推己及人的恕道，反而能影响别人明白宽恕的道理，这样的事情是不会有的。所以治理一个国家的生活在于整顿好自己的家庭。《诗经·桃夭》说："桃花那样的艳丽，桃叶婆娑多美盛！那个女儿嫁到了夫家，一家和睦真安宁。"做到了全家和睦安宁，然后有资格做一国的榜样教导别人。《诗经·蓼萧》说："和睦的家庭敬爱兄长、爱护弟弟。"敬爱兄长、爱护弟弟，然后有资格做一国的榜样教导别人。《诗经·鸤鸠》说："君主的礼仪丝毫不差，就能使一国井然有秩序。"君主的行为足够成为父亲、儿子、哥哥、弟弟的榜样，而后百姓自然会效法他。这就叫作治理一个国家的生活在于整顿好自己的家庭。

【原文】

所谓平天下在治其国者，上老老而民兴孝，上长长而民兴悌，上恤孤而民不倍。是以君子有絜矩之道也。

所恶于上，毋以使下；所恶于下，毋以事上；所恶于前，毋以先后；所恶于后，毋以从前；所恶于右，毋以交于左；所恶于左，毋以交于右。此之谓絜矩之道。

《诗》云："乐只君子，民之父母。"民之所好好之，民之所恶恶之。此之谓民之父母。

《诗》云："节彼南山，维石岩岩。赫赫师尹，民具尔瞻。"有国者不可以不慎，辟则为天下僇矣。

《诗》云："殷之未丧师，克配上帝。仪监于殷，峻命不易。"道得众，则得国；失众，则失国。

是故君子先慎乎德。有德此有人，有人此有土，有土此有财，有财此有用。德者本也，财者末也。外本内末，争民施夺。是故财聚则民散，财散则民聚。是故言悖而出者，亦悖而入；货悖而入者，亦悖而出。

《康诰》曰："惟命不于常。"道善则得之，不善则失之矣。《楚书》曰："楚国无以为宝，惟善以为宝。"舅犯曰："亡人无以为宝，仁亲以为宝。"

《秦誓》曰："若有一个臣，断断兮无他技，其心休休焉，其如有容焉。人之有技，若己有之，人之彦圣，其心好之，不啻若自其口出，实能容之，以能保我子孙黎民，尚亦有利哉！人之有技，媢疾以恶之，人之彦圣，而违之俾不通，寔不能容，以不能保我子孙黎民，亦曰殆哉！"唯仁人放流之，迸诸四夷，不与同中国。此谓唯仁人为能爱人，能恶人。见贤而不能举，举而不能先，命也。见不善而不能退，退而不能远，过也。好人之所恶，恶人之所好，是谓拂人之性，灾必逮夫身。是故君子有大道，必忠信以得之，骄泰以失之。

生财有大道，生之者众，食之者寡，为之者疾，用之者舒，则财恒足矣。仁者以财发身，不仁者以身发财。未有上好仁，而下不好义者也；未有好义，其事不终者也；未有府库财，非其财者也。

孟献子曰："畜马乘，不察于鸡豚；伐冰之家，不畜牛羊；百乘之家，不畜聚敛之臣。与其有聚敛之臣，宁有盗臣。"此谓国不以利为利，以义为利也。

长国家而务财用者，必自小人矣，彼为善之。小人之使为国家，灾害并至。虽有善者，亦无如之何矣。此谓国不以利为利，以义为利也。

【语译】

为什么说恢复天下太平在于治理国家的生活呢？当权的人尊敬老人，普通的人也就知道当好儿孙；当权的人敬重长辈，普通的人也就会知道尊重和友爱；当权的人仁爱幼弱和无助的人，普通的人也就不会做出与之相反的事情。这就叫做君子有规范自己的行为的测度的标准。一个人憎恶来自上面的东西，就不要用来对付自己的下面；憎恶来自下面的，就不要用来服侍自己的上面；憎恶来自前面的，就不要放在后面的前面；憎恶来自后面的，就不要放在前面的后面；憎恶自右面的，就不要用来对付左面；憎恶来自左面的，就不要用来对付右面。这就叫做絜矩之道。

《诗经·南山有台》说："人民悦乐的君主，是百姓的父母。"普通人喜欢的君主就喜欢，普通人憎恶的君主就憎恶。这就叫作人民的父母。

《诗经·节南山》说："庄严的南山啊，岩石莽莽。威严的师尹，人民瞻仰！"执掌国家的当权者万万不能不小心谨慎；一旦偏颇，就引起天下人的抨击。

《诗经·文王》说："殷朝还没有丧失人民的时候，能够配对上帝。应该吸取殷朝的教训，保持天命不容易。"这说的是得到人民的，就得到国家；丧失人民的，就会丧失国家。这就是为什么君子首先注重自己的德行。如果他有德行，就会有人民；如果有人民，就会有土地的权力；如果有土地的权力，就会有财富；有财富，就能有用度。德行是根本，财富是结果。如果君主忽视根本，而企求额外的财富，就会导致人民互相争夺和竞争利益。所以君主积累自己的财富，就会失去人民；君主分散个人的财富，就能获得人民。如果一个人言辞狡诈和欺骗，就会得到言辞狡诈和欺骗的回答；如果他的财富是欺骗得来的，也会由欺骗的方法而失去。

《尚书·康诰》说："天命不是固定不可改变的。"好的君主就能得到天命，不好的君主就会失去天命。《楚书》说："楚国没有财宝，做好事才是我们楚国的财宝。"逃亡的晋国公子的舅舅狐偃说："我们逃亡的公子没有财宝，只有对同宗人的感情联系是他的财宝。"

《尚书·秦誓》秦穆公说："我假若有那么一个大臣，朴实真纯，不假装有别的本领，心性淡然寡欲，豁达大度能包容一切。看见别人有才能，就像他自己有那种才能一般，看见别人英俊聪明，心里喜爱，不但能像从他的口里称赞的一样，而且确实能够容纳贤才，就将是一个能辅佐国家的人，他会保护我的子孙和黎民百姓。假若这个大臣，别人有才能，就妒忌和憎恨他，别人俊美聪明，就设法压抑他使他不能发达，实在不能容纳人，他就不能保护我的子孙和黎民百姓，这样的人对国家是很危险的。"只有仁德的君主才能驱逐那等邪恶的大臣，把他赶到四方夷狄地方，不让他和我们同住在中国。这就是说只有仁德的人才能爱别人，也才能恨别人。看到贤德的人君主不能任用，即使任用又不是尽早任用，就是怠慢或没有尽到君主的责任。看见坏人而不能退黜，退黜了又不能驱逐到远方，就是软弱。喜爱别人厌恶的，厌恶别人喜爱的，就叫作违反人的自然本性，灾难必然落在他的身上。于是我们看到做君主的基本原则：必定是忠实和诚信才能保持他的统治，骄傲而又生活放纵就会失去他的统治。

积累财富有其基本原则，即如果有很多财富的生产者，只有很少的消费者，如果人很快地挣钱，而花费缓慢，那么财富就总会是充足的。仁义的人用他的财富发展其人品，不仁义的人则发展财富用于他个人的消耗。从来不曾有过君主好仁德，而他的目标会失败于好义的臣民；从来不曾有过人民好义，而国家事务不能贯彻完成的；也从来不曾有过这样的国家财富集聚在国库里，君主不能继续占有的。

孟献子说："士人一变成大夫已经保有马匹和车辆，就不再照看鸡和猪了；丧祭用冰的卿大夫之家，就不再养牛和羊了；拥有百辆车子的贵族之家，在他的家里就不应该保有强夺收税的家臣。宁可有一个偷盗他的财货的管家人，也比有一个强夺收税的家臣为好。"这就是说的国家的物质兴旺不在于物质的兴旺，而在于正义的兴旺。

掌握政府的首脑依赖聚敛财富的，是因为任用小人而造成的。他想要做好，但是小人管理着国家，带来了国家的灾难，所有的善意都没有达到目的。这就是说国家的物质兴旺不在于物质的兴旺，而在于正义的兴旺。

Chapter Four ***ETHICS AND POLITICS***
(*Tahsueh*, *Liki*, Chapter XLII)

This essay, originally Chapter XLII of *Liki*, is now ranked among the *Four Books*, and as it stands first among these, all Chinese school children used to begin their first studies with this essay. The philosophy behind this essay and "Central Harmony," which used to come next, was of course entirely beyond the mental range of children of seven or eight. Nevertheless, they were studiously conned over and committed to memory so that the lines in these essays stuck in their minds for life, and served them usefully afterwards. Regarding the basic importance of this essay, the Sung Confucianist, Ch'eng Yich'uan, said, "This *Tahsueh* is a book in the surviving tradition of the Confucian school and constitutes the gateway through which beginners enter into the path of virtue. The fact that we can see now the order and sequence in which the ancients proceeded in their education, depends entirely on the existence of this essay, with the *Analects* and the *Book of Mencius* coming next. All students should begin their studies with this essay; then it may be hoped that they will not go far wrong."

The original title of this essay is *Tahsueh*, translated by James Legge as "The Great Learning," but more accurately translated by Ku Hungming as "The Higher Education." According to the school age defined for this "higher education," it seemed to correspond to the American junior college. This is made clear in another chapter of *Liki*, which I have translated here as Chapter IX, where the educational system for the princes and sons of aristocrats is more concretely described. (Chs. VIII and XII of *Liki*, not translated here, throw further light on the educational system.) The whole Confucian point of view regarding education seemed to be influenced by the basic assumption of an intellectual upper class, who were to be the rulers or who were to assist the rulers in the art of government; hence the always implicit assumption of preparing to govern a country in discussions on education. This essay seems to have been written expressly for the education of the princes (see especially Sec. 8), and this explains, I believe, its title *Tahsueh*, or "The College," where the princes were educated. The use of the word *chuntse* (literally "prince") must have been general at the College, and later became a more general term for "the gentlemen." In content, this essay actually deals with the connection between the cultivation of personal life and a general world order, or between ethics and politics.

The usual version of this essay has been re-edited by the Sung commentator Chu Hsi, resulting in the transposition of an entire section to an earlier part of the essay and in a much clearer arrangement of ideas. The disarrangement was said to be due to the mixing up of the strips of inscribed bamboo, which were perforated and tied together in bundles by leather straps. While I regard Chu Hsi's transposition as admirable and have adopted it, he did not seem to see why the original disarrangement took place. The result was, there was an awkward transition at the end of his transposed section, resulting in two identical lines coming together—"This is knowing the root. This is knowing the root. This is the perfection of knowledge." What Chu Hsi did was to regard the second of the identical lines and the third line as the conclusion of a separate "missing paragraph" and he proceeded to supply the "missing paragraph" himself, giving him an opportunity to put in a bit of Sung philosophy regarding meditation and the arrival at true knowledge.

This entirely changed the picture of the object and method of investigation of knowledge, which has caused unending dispute and no end of speculation. I have (by comparing the original version of the text of Cheng Hsuan, prior to the editing of Chu Hsi) come to the conclusion that the mistake was due to the existence of two identical lines originally apart in the same essay, and as these were learned by rote by old scholars who had survived the massacre of Ch'in Shih-huang, a wrong connection leading off from an identical line was perfectly natural—similar to what often happens in the composing room. The result of this perception of the original error, existing in Cheng Hsuan's text, leads me to believe that there was no "missing paragraph," but merely a wrong transposition, and that the object of investigation of knowledge discussed in that section was just human nature and the human heart, and not the physical universe. This will be quite plain in the following text, re-edited by myself. I have kept to Chu Hsi's transposition of an entire section, but have merely restored the original connecting identical lines to what I regard to be where they belong.

I. GENERAL IDEA OF THIS ESSAY

The principles of the higher education consist in preserving man's clear character, in giving new life to the people, and in dwelling (or resting) in perfecting, or the ultimate good. Only after knowing the goal of perfection where one should dwell, can one have a definite purpose in life. Only after having a definite purpose in life can one achieve calmness of mind. Only after having achieved calmness of mind, can one have peaceful repose. Only after having peaceful repose can one begin to think. Only after one has learned to think, can one achieve knowledge. There are a foundation and a superstructure in the constitution of things, and a beginning and an end in the course of events. Therefore to know the proper sequence or relative order of things is the beginning of wisdom.

The ancients who wished to preserve the fresh or clear character of the people of the world, would first set about ordering their national life. Those who wished to order their national life, would first set about regulating their family life. Those who wished to regulate their family life would set about cultivating their personal life. Those who wished to cultivate their personal life, would first set about setting their hearts right. Those who wished to set their hearts right would first set about making their wills sincere. Those who wished to make their wills sincere would first set about achieving true knowledge. The achieving of true knowledge depended upon the investigation of things. When things are investigated, then true knowledge is achieved; when true knowledge is achieved, then the will becomes sincere; when the will is sincere, then the heart is set right (or then the mind sees right); when the heart is set right, then the personal life is cultivated; when the personal life is cultivated, then the family life is regulated; when the family life is regulated, then the national life is orderly; and when the national life is orderly, then there is peace in this world. From the emperor down to the common men, all must regard the cultivation of the personal life as the root or foundation. There is never an orderly upshoot or superstructure when the root or foundation is disorderly. There is never yet a tree whose trunk is slim and slender and whose top branches are thick and heavy. This is called "to know the root or foundation of things."

II. ON THE MEANING OF CERTAIN EXPRESSIONS USED IN THE ABOVE SECTION

What is meant by "making clear man's character" is this: In the *Announcement to K'ang* (a document in the *Book of History*), it is said, "He was able to make his character clean." In *T'aichia* (another document in the same book), it said, "He contemplated the *clear* mandates of Heaven." In the *Canon of Yao* (another document), it is said, "He was able to make *clear* his great character." These all show that the ancient kings started by making their own characters *clear*.

What is meant by "giving new life to the people" is this: The inscription on the bath-tub of Emperor T'ang read, "If you make yourself fresh (or "renew yourself"), then daily make yourself fresh, and again make yourself every day fresh. The *Announcement to K'ang* said, "Become a *new* nation." The *Book of Songs* said, "Although the state of Chou is an old country, the mandates it has received from Heaven are forever *new*." Therefore the gentleman tries at all times to do his utmost.

What is meant by "resting, or dwelling, in perfection" is this: The *Book of Songs* says, "The Imperial domain of a thousand *li* is where the people *dwell*." It is again said in the *Book of Songs*, "The twittering yellow bird *rests* or alights on a little mound." And Confucius remarked, "When the bird *rests*, it knows where to *rest*. Should a human being be inferior to a bird in knowing where to *rest* (or in knowing what to *dwell in*)?" The *Book of Songs* again says, "How dignified and inspiring was King Wen! How bright was his virtue! He was careful in choosing that which he would *dwell in*." As a ruler, he dwelled in benevolence. As a minister, he dwelled in respectfulness. As a son, he dwelled in filial piety; as a father, he dwelled in kindness; and in his dealings with the people of the country, he dwelled in honesty.

The *Book of Songs* says, "Look at that curve in the River of Ch'i. How luxurious and green are the bamboo trees there! Here is our elegant and accomplished prince. He looks like a piece of jade, cut and filed and chiseled and polished. How grave and dignified in figure and majestic and distinguished! It is impossible to forget our elegant and accomplished prince!" The expression "cut and filed" refers to polishing his scholarship. The expression "chiseled and polished" refers to the cultivation of his character. The expression "grave and dignified" refers to his fear and caution, and the expression "majestic and distinguished" refers to his inspiring appearance. And the expression "it is impossible to forget our elegant and accomplished prince" means that the people could never forget his great character and his *perfection*.

The *Book of Songs* says, "Ah! The ancient kings are never forgotten by their people!" Future princes respected what they respected and loved what they loved, while the common people enjoyed what they enjoyed and benefited from their beneficial arrangements. That was why for generations the people could not forget them.

III. ON ACHIEVING TRUE KNOWLEDGE

What is meant by "achieving true knowledge" is this: Confucius said, "In presiding over lawsuits, I am as good as anyone. The thing is we should make it our aim that there may be no lawsuits at all, so that people who have actually done wrong will be too ashamed of themselves to indulge in words of self-defense. Thus the people are inspired with a great respect or fear (of the magistrate). That is called "to know the root (or bottom) of things." This is called "achieving true knowledge (or wisdom.)"

IV. ON MAKING THE WILL SINCERE

What is meant by "making the will sincere" is that one should not deceive oneself. This sincerity should be like the sincerity with which we hate a bad smell or love what is beautiful. This is called satisfying your own conscience. Therefore a superior man is watchful over himself when he is alone. The common man does wrong without any kind of self-restraint in his private life, and then when he sees the superior man, he is ashamed of himself and tries to hide the bad and show off the good in him. But what is the use? For people see into their very hearts when they look at them. That is what is meant when we say, "What is true in a man's heart will be shown in his outward appearance." Therefore the superior man (or the prince) must be watchful over himself when he is alone. Tsengtse said, "What ten eyes are beholding and what ten hands are pointing to—isn't it frightening?" Just as wealth beautifies a house, so character beautifies the body. A big-hearted man also has big proportions. (Probably a proverb, like "A fat man is good-natured.")

Therefore a superior man must make his will sincere.

V. ON SETTING THE HEART RIGHT AND PERSONAL CULTIVATION

What is meant by saying that "the cultivation of the personal life depends on setting one's heart right" is this: When one is upset by anger, then the heart is not in its right place; when one is disturbed by fear, then the heart is not in its right place; when one is blinded by love, then the heart is not in its right place; when one is involved in worries and anxieties, then the heart is not in its right place (or the mind has lost its balance). When the mind isn't there, we look but do not see, listen but do not hear and eat but do not know the flavor of the food. This is what is meant by saying that the cultivation of the personal life depends on setting the heart right.

VI. ON THE RELATIONSHIP BETWEEN PERSONAL AND FAMILY LIFE

What is meant by saying that "the regulation of the home life depends on the cultivation of one's personal life" is this: People usually lose their sense of judgment toward those whom they love, toward those whom they despise or dislike, toward those whom they fear, toward those whom they pity and toward those whom they pamper or are proud of. Therefore, there are few people in this world who can see the bad in those whom they like and see the good in those whom they dislike. Hence the saying that "People do not know their own children's faults, as they do not know the imperceptible growth of the rice plants in their fields." That is why it is said that those who do not cultivate their personal life cannot regulate their home life.

VII. ON THE RELATIONSHIP BETWEEN FAMILY AND NATIONAL LIFE

What is meant by the saying that "those who would order their national life must set about ordering their home life" is this: There is no one who fails in teaching the members of his own family and yet is capable of teaching others outside the family. Therefore the superior man spreads his culture to the entire nation by merely remaining at home. The teaching of filial piety is a preparation for serving the ruler of the state; the teaching of respect to one's elder brothers is a preparation for serving all the elders of the country; and the teaching of kindness in parents is a training for ruling over the people. In the *Announcement to K'ang*, it is said, "Act as if you were watching over an infant." No girl ever needs to learn about nursing a baby before she marries. If your instinct is correct (or sound or normal), you will not be far from the highest ideal, although you may not exactly achieve it. When the individual families have learned kindness, then the whole nation has learned kindness. When the individual families have learned courtesy, then the whole nation has learned courtesy. When one man is greedy or avaricious, then the whole country is plunged into disorder. Such is the law of things. That is why it is said that "A single word may spoil an affair, and a single man can set the country in order." The Emperors Yao and Shun set an example of kindness to the world and the people followed them. The Emperors Chieh and Chou set an example of cruelty to the world, and the people also followed them. The people did not follow what they commanded, if their command was contradicted by what they themselves did. Therefore, the superior man searches himself first before he demands it of others, and makes sure first that he himself is not a transgressor before he forbids transgressions to others. There is never a man who does not apply the principle of reciprocity (or the Golden Rule) in laying the foundation for his own personal conduct, and yet is able to influence others to his way of thinking. Therefore, the ordering of the national life depends on the regulation of one's home life.

The *Book of Songs* says, "Look at that peach tree, so fresh and pretty! How green and thick are its leaves! The girl (a princess) is going to her husband's house, and she will live in harmony with the people of her husband's home." By living in harmony with the people in one's home, one is qualified then to be an example to the people of the nation. Again the *Book of Songs* says, "They (the rulers) live in harmony with their elder brothers and their younger brothers." By living in harmony with their elder and younger brothers, they are then qualified to serve as examples to the people of the nation. The *Book of Songs* also says, "The deportment of the prince is all correct, and he sets a country in order." Because he himself served as a worthy example as a father, son, an elder brother and a younger brother, therefore the people took him for their model. That is why it is said the "Ordering of the national life depends upon regulating one's home life."

VIII. ON THE RELATIONSHIP BETWEEN NATIONAL LIFE AND WORLD PEACE

What is meant by saying that "the restoration of peace in the world depends on ordering the national life" is this: When those in authority are respectful toward the old people, then the common people learn to be good sons. When those in authority show respect to their superiors, then the common people learn respect and humility. When those in authority show kindness to the young and helpless, then the common people do not follow the opposite course. Therefore the superior man (or prince) has a principle with which, as with a measuring square, he may regulate his conduct.

What a man dislikes in his superiors, let him not display in his own dealings with his inferiors; what he dislikes in his inferiors, let him not display in his service to his superiors; what he dislikes in those in front of him, let him not display toward those behind; what he dislikes in those following behind, let him not display toward those in front; what he dislikes in those on his right, let him not display toward those on his left; and what he dislikes in those on his left, let him not display in those on his right. This is the principle of the measuring square (or footrule).

The *Book of Songs* says, "How the people are pleased with their ruler, who is like a parent to the people." The ruler loves what the common people love and hates what the common people hate. That is how to be a parent to the common people.

Again the *Book of Songs* says, "Oh, the magnificent Southern Mountains! How majestic are the rocks! How magnificent is the Grand Tutor Yin! The people look up to him." Thus those in a position of authority should never be careless; once they go wrong, the whole world will denounce them.

Again the *Book of Songs* says, "Before the sovereigns of the Shang Dynasty had lost the following of their people, they could appear before God in sacrifice. Take warning from the House of Shang. It is not easy to keep the Mandate of Heaven." This shows that those who have the people with them can keep their rule over a country, and those who have forfeited the following of their people thereby forfeit their rule over the country.

On this account, the superior man (or prince or ruler) will first be watchful over his own character. If he has character, then he has the people with him; if he has the people with him, then he has authority over a territory; if he has authority over a territory, then he has wealth; and having wealth, he then can get things done. Thus character is the foundation, while wealth is the result. If the ruler neglects the foundation and attends to the outward results, he will lead the people in mutual robbery or competition for profit. Therefore, when a ruler gains his personal wealth, he loses his people; and when he loses his personal wealth, he gains the following of his people. Therefore if a man is cunning or deceitful in his speech, he is answered by cunning or deceitful speech, and if his wealth comes in by crooked methods, it flows out again by crooked methods.

The *Announcement to K'ang* says, "The Mandate of Heaven is not fixed and unchangeable. The good rulers get it and the bad rulers forfeit it." The *History of Ch'u* says, "The state of Ch'u has no treasures; doing good is our only treasure." Tsefan (maternal uncle to a prince of Chin in exile) said, "Our exiled prince has no treasure; association with the kind people is his only treasure."

The *Oath of Duke Mu of Ch'in* (to his subjects) says, "Let me but have one minister, plain and sincere, not pretending to other abilities, but with a big simple heart, generous and tolerant toward others. When he sees another person has a certain kind of ability, he is pleased as if he had it himself; and when he sees another man who is handsome and wise, he likes him in his heart, as if he said so in so many words, thus showing that he can really tolerate them. Well may such a person be an asset to the nation, for he shall be able to protect my sons and grandsons and the black-haired people. But if a minister is jealous and hates a person, when he sees the latter has a certain ability, or tries to stand in the way of a handsome and wise man, when he sees one, such person can really not tolerate others, and he cannot protect my sons and grandsons and the black-haired people. Such a person is a danger to the country." It is only the truly great man who can send away such a minister and banish him, driving him to live among the barbarians and not allowing him to share China with us. It is only the truly great man who knows how to love and how to hate. To see men of worth and not recommend them to office, or to fail to be the first to do so—that is being disrespectful or negligent of one's duty toward his ruler. To see bad men and not be able to remove them from office and to fail to remove them as far away as possible— that is weakness. To love what the people hate and to hate what the people love—that is to act contrary to human nature, and disaster will overtake such a person. Thus we see there is a basic principle for the sovereign: Through sincerity and faithfulness, he maintains his rule, and through pride and self-indulgent living he loses it.

There is a basic principle in the accumulation of wealth and it is this: If there are many producers of wealth and few spenders, and if people are quick at earning money and slow at spending it, then wealth will always be sufficient. The true man develops his personality by means of his wealth, and the unworthy man develops wealth at the expense of his personality. There has never been a case of a ruler who loved benevolence, with his subjects failing to love righteousness, and there has never been a case where the people have come to love righteousness and the affairs of the state cannot be accomplished successfully. And there has never been a case where in such a state the wealth collected in the national treasury did not continue in the possession of the ruler.

Baron Hsien Meng said, "The scholars who have just become officials and begun to keep a horse and carriage do not look after poultry and pigs. The higher officials who use ice in their sacrifices do not keep cattle and sheep. And the nobles who can keep a hundred carriages do not keep rapacious tax-gatherers under them. It would be better to keep a minister who robbed them of their own treasury, than to keep such rapacious tax-gatherers. That is what is meant by saying that "the material prosperity of a nation does not consist in its material prosperity, but in righteousness."

He who is at the head of a government and is bent upon gathering wealth is forced to use petty persons in office. He may want to do good, but the petty officials rule the country and bring disaster to the state, and all his good intentions are to no purpose. That is why it is said that "the material prosperity of a nation does not consist in its material prosperity, but in righteousness."

第五章 《论语》
——孔子的格言

除去书中所见孔子的智慧之外,《论语》之美究竟何在?其美便在孔夫子的人品性格,以及他对同代人各种不同的评论;那美是传记文学的美,是孔夫子的语言之美,是随意漫谈,意在言外,而夫子的这些如珠的妙语出之以寥寥数语,自富有弦外之音。

《论语》一书,一般认为是儒家至高无上的经典,就犹如西洋基督教的《圣经》一样。其实这部书是未经分别章节、未经编辑的孔子混杂语录。所论涉及诸多方面;但对所论之缘起情况则概不叙明,而上下文之脉络又显然散乱失离。读《论语》,犹如读巴特莱(John Bartlett)之《引用名句集》(*Familiar Quotations*),令读者觉得那些警语名句津津有味,引起无限沉思想象,而对那些才子的文句,不禁讶异探索,窥求其真义之所在。如将《论语》的内容与《礼记》和《孟子》以及其他古籍各章相比,就会发现那些简洁精辟的文句都是从长篇论说文字中节录而来,而所以得存而不废者,正因为深受人们喜爱。比如说,读了《论语》的"吾未见好德如好色者也"，然后再读司马迁《史记·孔子世家》上记载的：

> 居卫月余。灵公与夫人同车，宦者雍渠参乘。出，使孔子为次乘，招
> 摇市过之。孔子曰："吾未见好德如好色者也。"于是丑之，去卫，过曹。

《论语》文本上并未提到孔子当时说些"吾未见好德如好色者也"的实际情况，只是把这句话作一句抽象的话来说的。另外，《论语》中颇多四五个字的短句，如"君子不器"，意思是说君子不是只有一种长处的技术人才。又如"乡愿者，德之贼也"。关于乡愿，我们幸而在《孟子》一书中找到了"乡愿"一词详细的解说。我想，谁也不会相信孔夫子每次说话只说三四个字就算了事。若说，有人向孔夫子发问，发问者整个的意思，读者若不了解较为充分，孔子所作的回答整个的含义就能充分了解，这也是无法相信的。清人袁枚曾经指出，《论语》这部书是孔子的语录，编纂者把弟子的问题部分尽量缩短了。因此在《论语》中发问都简单得只剩下一个字，如某某问"政"，某某问"仁"，某某问"礼"。于是，虽然是同一问题，因发问之人不同，孔夫子也就以各式各样的话回答。结果，为《论语》作注的学者也会因种种情况而误作注解，此种注解，自然不足以称公允之论。另有如下文：

> 子谓仲弓曰："犁牛之子，骍且角，虽欲勿用，山川其舍诸？"

注释《论语》的人解作"仲弓之贤，自当见用于世"。但袁枚则认为此系孔子与弟子凭窗外望，见牛犊行过，偶有所感而发，并非指仲弓而言。

那么，除去书中所见孔子的智慧之外，《论语》之美究竟何在？其美

便在孔夫子的人品性格，以及他对同代人各种不同的评论；那美是传记文学的美，是孔夫子的语言之美，是随意漫谈，意在言外，夫子的这些如珠的妙语却出之以寥寥数语，自富有弦外之音。《论语》之美正如英国十八世纪鲍斯韦尔（James Boswell）所写的《约翰逊传》(*Life of Samuel Johnson*)一书之美妙动人一样。而与孔夫子在一起的那批人物，他的弟子，他的朋友，也是与约翰逊周围那些人物一样富有动人之美。我们随时都可以翻开《论语》这部书，随便哪一页都会流露出智者的人品之美，纵然有时极其粗暴，但同时又和蔼可亲。这就是《论语》这部书对中国人所显示的魔力。至于武断偏执也自有其动人的力量，孔夫子与约翰逊的武断偏执之论，永远有动人的力量，因为这两位先哲把自己的见解都表现得那么断然无疑，那么坚定有力，其势堪称咄咄逼人。

《论语》这部书整个的特色只是阐释说明，并没有把孔子的思想系统作一个完备周全的叙述，孔子学说之真面目则端赖读者去深思明辨了。

孔夫子周围的人物，我们也可以借着《论语》这部书，得以略窥一斑。有时孔夫子与二三得意门生欢乐相处，夫子欣然，就单凭文中的只言片语，我们可以稍得一些暗示。与孔夫子的话混在一起的，有些是孔门几位大弟子如曾子、子夏、有子、子张等人的话。这是因为《论语》内那些章文字的来源不同，有若干章根本是孔门弟子的弟子所记载的。比如颜回，为孔门弟子之长，沉静而富有深思，孔子对他亦极爱慕，每每对他赞不绝口。另一方面，又有子路，等于耶稣的大弟子彼得，他时常对夫子大人的行为质疑问难，不稍宽容。在《论语》一书中，提到子路时，往往缺少恭维之辞，那是因为在《论语》这部书记录成文之时，子路已经去世，没有门徒替他辩护的缘故。还有能言善辩，但有些絮聒的子贡，还有比他们年纪颇轻但却恬静明达的曾子（将来弘扬孔教最为重要的就是他），还有文学气质最重的子夏，最为实际的政客冉求（最后孔子把他逐出了师门）。孔子的门墙之内广阔得无所不包，各式各样的学生都有，据说，每个弟子在学问上之所得，都只是孔子的一部分。后来，曾子、子思、孟子这个传统，发展成为儒家道统理想哲学的一面。子夏、荀子的儒学则顺着史学及学术的路线发展下去。正像基督教中圣约翰发展了耶稣教义的理想一面，当然其中也加上了圣约翰本人的一部分思想。所以，我们在《中庸》一书中可以看得出来，曾子把《中庸》里的哲学，人道精神，并中和诸重要性，予以发展引申了。一言以蔽之，我们可以把子思与孟子比做耶稣的门徒圣约翰，把子夏与荀子比做圣雅各（St. James）。

《论语》文本是属于零星断片而飞跳飘忽的风格，阅读时自然需要读者的凝神苦思。懒惰的读者往往需要作者谈论个没完没了，自己只采取消极的态度，若是那样来读《论语》，便得不到益处了。读《论语》时，读者必须全神贯注，文句中包含的真理必须凭读者自己的悟力才会彻底了解。读者必须凭自己的经验去印证，才能有所得。在古代那种教育制度之下，当然并不立即要学童了解世界上这种思想极为成熟的哲学。当年之所求，不过要学生精读，以便牢记在心永不忘记，是留到若干年后作为智慧的泉源而已。不过，儒家对这部书，仍然教人以适当的研读之法。宋儒就论到读《论语》的方法。程伊川就曾说，要把《论语》中的发问者的问题，当做你自己的问题，把孔子的答话当做对你而发，如此，必得到实在的益处。朱熹也曾说，先读《论语》，每日读一两段。不管难懂与否，也不管深奥不深奥。只将一段文字从开头读，若是读而不了解其含义，就思索一下，若思索之后仍然不能了解，就再读。反复阅读探索其滋味，长久之后，便了解其中的含义了。朱熹在给朋友的书信里曾说，在读书时，千万留心不要贪多，读少一点儿，便容易彻底了解。读书能悟到真义，都离不开这种方法。在他著的《语类》中也这样说，明白原文的字面是一件事，体会其意义又是一件事。一般读者最大的弱点就是只了解字表面，而未能把握住书中真正的好处。他又说，读书的正当办法是要费苦心思索。最初，你会觉得如此了解，是要大费思索与精力，但是等你一般的理解力够强大之后，再看完一本书，就轻而易举了。最初，一本书需要一百分精力去读，后来，只需八十、九十分精力就够了，再后只需六十或七十分就够了，最后，以四十、五十分的精力也就够了。把阅读与思索，在求知识的进程上看做相辅相成的两件事，这是儒家基本的教育方法。关于这两种方法，孔子本人也提到过，在《论语》上也有记载。

中国学者从未有人把《论语》再作一番校正工夫，或予以改编，以便使读者对《论语》的含义获致更精确的了解，这一点确实出人意料。当然有一些学人写过文章，论及《论语》书中若干不同的见解，如清人焦循著的《〈论语〉通释》，戴东原著的《〈孟子〉字义疏证》。但是除去西方学者外，没有中国学者编过一本孔子对"君子"一词的诸种解释。这个极为重要的描述"君子"的诸要素，会构成一个综合性的面貌。本章内选了《论语》文字约四分之一，而根据思想性质予以重编。如不特予注明，皆系《论语》原文。遇必要之处，如将"仁"字解释得更为清楚，我即从《礼记》上若干章内选出约十数节，以为补充。《礼记》中第三十二及三十三章，与《论语》的内容及风格相差不少，记载孔子的话特别丰富，当然对本书极为有用。

（一）夫子自述·旁人描写

叶公问孔子于子路，子路不对。子曰："汝奚不曰：'其为人也，发愤忘食，乐以忘忧，不知老之将至云尔？'"

子路宿于石门。晨门曰："奚自？"子路曰："自孔氏。"曰："是知其不可而为之者欤？"

微生亩谓孔子曰："丘何为是栖栖者欤？无乃为佞乎？"孔子曰："非敢为佞也，疾固也。"

颜渊季路侍，子曰："盍各言尔志？"子路曰："愿车马衣裘，与朋友共，敝之而无憾。"颜渊曰："愿无伐善，无施劳。"子路曰："愿闻子之志。"子曰："老者安之，朋友信之，少者怀之。"

子曰："吾十有五而志于学，三十而立，四十而不惑，五十而知天命，六十而耳顺，七十而从心所欲，不逾矩。"

逸民伯夷、叔齐、虞仲、夷逸、朱张、柳下惠、少连。子曰："不降其志，不辱其身，伯夷、叔齐欤？"谓柳下惠、少连，"降志辱身矣。言中伦，行中虑，其斯而已矣"。谓虞仲夷逸，"隐居放言，身中清，废中权"。"我则异于是，无可无不可。"

大宰问于子贡曰："夫子圣者欤？何其多能也？"子贡曰："固天纵之将圣，又多能也。"子闻之曰："大宰知我乎？吾少也贱，故多能鄙事。君子多乎哉？不多也！"牢曰："子云：'吾不试，故艺。'"

子曰："饭疏食饮水，曲肱而枕之，乐亦在其中矣。不义而富且贵，于我如浮云。"

子曰："君子道者三，我无能焉：仁者不忧，智者不惑，勇者不惧。"子贡曰："夫子自道也。"

子曰："文，莫吾犹人也。躬行君子，则吾未之有得。"

子曰："若圣与仁，则吾岂敢？抑为之不厌，诲人不倦，则可谓云尔已矣。"

子曰："十室之邑，必有忠信如丘者焉。不如丘之好学也。"

子曰："吾有知乎哉！无知也。有鄙夫问于我，空空如也；我叩其两端而竭焉。"

子曰："述而不作，信而好古，窃比于我老彭。"

子曰："默而识之，学而不厌，诲人不倦，何有于我哉？"

子曰："德之不修，学之不讲，闻义不能徙，不善不能改，是吾忧也。"

子曰："我非生而知之者。好古，敏以求之者也。"

子曰："赐也，汝以予为多学而识之者欤？"对曰："然。非欤？"曰："非也。予一以贯之。"

子曰："盖有不知而作之者，我无是也。多闻，择其善者而从之，多见而识之，知之次也。"

子曰："吾尝终日不食，终夜不寝，以思，无益，不如学也。"

子曰："三人行，必有我师焉。择其善者而从之，其不善者而改之。"

子曰："不愤不启，不悱不发，举一隅不以三隅反者，则不复也。'"

子曰："自行束脩以上，吾未尝无诲焉。"

互乡难与言。童子见，门人惑。子曰："与其进也，不与其退也。唯何甚？人洁己以进，与其洁也，不保其往也。"

子畏于匡。曰："文王既没，文不在兹乎？天之将丧斯文也，后死者不得与于斯文也，天之未丧斯文也，匡人其如予何？"

子曰："天生德于予，桓魋其如予何！"

子曰："加我数年，五十以学易，可以无大过矣。"

子不语怪力乱神。

子罕言利，与命，与仁。

子以四教：文、行、忠、信。

子钓而不纲，弋不射宿。

子绝四：毋意、毋必、毋固、毋我。

子温而厉，威而不猛，恭而安。

颜渊喟然叹曰："仰之弥高，钻之弥坚，瞻之在前，忽焉在后。夫子循循然善诱人，博我以文，约我以礼。欲罢不能，既竭吾才，如有所立卓尔，虽欲从之，末由也已。"

叔孙武叔语大夫于朝曰："子贡贤于仲尼。"子服景伯以告子贡。子贡曰："譬之宫墙，赐之墙也，及肩，窥见室家之好。夫子之墙，数仞，不得其门而入，不见宗庙之美，百官之富。得其门者，或寡矣。夫子之云，不亦宜乎？"

叔孙武叔毁仲尼。子贡曰："无以为也。仲尼不可毁也。他人之贤者，丘陵也，犹可逾也。仲尼，日月也，无得而逾焉。人虽欲自绝，其何伤于日月乎？多见其不知量也。"

（二）孔子的感情与艺术生活

颜渊死，子哭之恸。从者曰："子恸矣。"曰："有恸乎？非夫人之为恸而谁为？"

子食于有丧者之侧，未尝饱也。子于是日哭，则不歌。

子之所慎，斋、战、疾。

或问禘之说，子曰："不知也。知其说者，之于天下也，其如示诸斯乎？"指其掌。

祭如在，祭神如神在。子曰："吾不与祭，如不祭。"

王孙贾问曰："与其媚于奥，宁媚于灶，何谓也？"子曰："不然，获罪于天，无所祷也。"

子贡欲去告朔之饩羊。子曰："赐也，尔爱其羊，我爱其礼。"

子曰："敬鬼神而远之。"

子曰："甚矣！吾衰也。久矣，吾不复梦见周公。"

子在齐闻韶，三月不知肉味。曰："不图为乐之至于斯也。"

子曰："兴于诗，立于礼，成于乐。"

子曰："吾自卫返鲁，然后乐正，雅颂各得其所。"

颜渊问为邦。子曰："行夏之时，乘殷之辂，服周之冕，乐则《韶》舞。放郑声，远佞人；郑声淫，佞人殆。"

子曰："由之瑟，奚为于丘之门？"门人不敬子路。子曰："由也，升堂矣，未入于室也。"

君子不以绀緅饰，红紫不以为亵服。当暑袗绤，必表而出之。缁衣羔裘，素衣麑裘，黄衣狐裘。亵裘长，短右袂。必有寝衣，长一身有半。狐貉之厚以居。去丧，无所不佩。

食不厌精，脍不厌细。食饐而餲。鱼馁而肉败，不食。色恶不食，臭恶不食，失饪不食，不时不食。割不正不食，不得其酱不食。肉虽多，不使胜食气。唯酒无量，不及乱。沽酒市脯不食。不撤姜食，不多食。

迅雷、风烈，必变。

（三）谈话的风格

子路、曾皙、冉有、公西华侍坐。子曰："以吾一日长乎尔，毋吾以也。居则曰：'不吾知也。'如或知尔，则何以哉？"子路率尔而对曰："千乘之国，摄乎大国之间，加之以师旅，因之以饥馑，由也为之，比及三年，可使有勇，且知方也。"夫子哂之。"求，尔何如？"对曰："方六七十，如五六十，求也为之，比及三年，可使足民。如其礼乐，以俟君子。""赤，尔何如？"对曰："非曰能之，愿学焉。宗庙之事，如会同，端章甫，愿为小相焉。""点，尔何如？"鼓瑟希，铿尔，舍瑟而作。对曰："异乎三子者之撰。"子曰："何伤乎？亦各言其志也。"曰："暮春者，春服既成，冠者五六人，童子六七人，浴乎沂，风乎舞雩，咏而归。"夫子喟然叹曰："吾与点也。"

子曰："二三子，以我为隐乎？吾无隐乎尔。吾无行而不与二三子者，是丘也。"

子之武城，闻弦歌之声。夫子莞尔而笑曰："割鸡焉用牛刀？"子游对曰："昔者偃也，闻诸夫子曰：'君子学道则爱人，小人学道易使也。'"子曰："二三子，偃之言是也，前言戏之耳。"

达巷党人曰："大哉孔子！博学而无所成名。"子闻之，谓门弟子曰："吾何执？执御乎？执射乎？吾执御矣。"

陈司败问昭公知礼乎。孔子曰："知礼。"孔子退，揖巫马期而进之曰："吾闻君子不党，君子亦党乎？君取于吴为同姓，谓之吴孟子。君而知礼，孰不知礼？"巫马期以告。子曰："丘也幸，苟有过，人必知之。"

子贡曰："有美玉于斯，韫椟而藏诸？求善价而沽诸？"子曰："沽之哉！沽之哉！我待贾者也。"

或问子产，子曰："惠人也。"问子西，曰："彼哉！彼哉！"问管仲，曰："人也。夺伯氏骈邑三百，饭疏食，没齿无怨言。"

子问公叔文子于公明贾曰："信乎？夫子不言不笑，不取乎？"公明贾对曰："以告者过也。夫子时然后言，人不厌其言。乐然后笑，人不厌其笑。义然后取，人不厌其取。"子曰："其然？岂其然乎？"

子贡方人。子曰："赐也贤乎哉！夫我则不暇。"

子曰："饱食终日，无所用心，难矣哉！不有博弈者乎？为之，犹贤乎已。"

子曰："群居终日，言不及义，好行小慧，难矣哉！"

子曰："予欲无言。"子贡曰："子如不言，小子何述焉？"子曰："天何言哉？四时行焉，百物生焉，天何言哉？"

子曰："吾与回言终日，不违，如愚。退而省其私，亦足以发。回也不愚。"

（四）霸气

子曰："观过知仁。"

子贡问曰："何如斯可谓之士矣？"子曰："行己有耻，使于四方，不辱君命，可谓士矣。"曰："敢问其次？"曰："宗族称孝焉，乡党称弟焉。"曰："敢问其次？"曰："言必信，行必果，硁硁然，小人哉！抑亦可以为次矣。"曰："今之从政者何如？"子曰："噫！斗筲之人，何足算也。"

子疾病，子路使门人为臣。病间曰："久矣哉！由之行诈也。无臣而为有臣，吾谁欺？欺天乎？"

子见南子，子路不说。夫子矢之，曰："予所否者，天厌之！天厌之！"

宰予昼寝。子曰："朽木不可雕也，粪土之墙不可圬也。于予与何诛？"子曰："始吾于人也，听其言而信其行。今吾于人也，听其言而观其行。于予与改是。"

哀公问社于宰我。宰我对曰："夏后氏以松，殷人以柏，周人以栗。"

曰使民战栗。子闻之曰:"成事不说,遂事不谏,既往不咎。"

孺悲欲见孔子,孔子辞以疾。将命者出户,取瑟而歌,使之闻之。

阳货欲见孔子,孔子不见,归孔子豚。孔子时其亡也,而往拜之。遇诸途。谓孔子曰:"来,予与尔言。"曰:"怀其宝而迷其邦,可谓仁乎?"曰:"不可。""好从事,而亟失时,可谓智乎?"曰:"不可。""日月逝矣,时不我与。"孔子曰:"诺。吾将仕矣。"

陈成子弑简公。孔子沐浴而朝,告于哀公曰:"陈恒弑其君,请讨之。"公曰:"告夫三子。"孔子曰:"以吾从大夫之后,不敢不告也。君曰:'告夫三子'者。"之三子告,不可。孔子曰:"以吾从大夫之后,不敢不告也。"

原壤夷俟,子曰:"幼而不孙弟,长而无述焉,老而不死,是为贼。"以杖叩其胫。

季康子患盗,问于孔子。孔子对曰:"苟子之不欲,虽赏之不窃。"

季氏富于周公,而求也为之聚敛而附益之。子曰:"非吾徒也,小子鸣鼓而攻之可也。"

季氏将伐颛臾。冉有、季路见于孔子,曰:"季氏将有事于颛臾。"孔子曰:"求,无乃尔是过欤?夫颛臾,昔者先王以为东蒙主,且在邦域之中矣,是社稷之臣也。何以伐为?"冉有曰:"夫子欲之,吾贰臣者。皆不欲也。"孔子曰:"求,周任有言曰:'陈力就列,不能者止。'危而不持,颠而不扶,则将焉用彼相矣。且尔言过矣。虎兕出于柙,龟玉毁于椟中,是谁之过欤?"冉有曰:"夫颛臾,固而近于费,今不取,后世必为子孙忧。"孔子曰:"求,君子疾夫舍曰欲之,而必为之辞。丘也闻有国有家者,不患寡,而患不均,不患贫,而患不安。盖均无贫,和无寡,安无倾。夫如是,故远人不服,则修文德以来之;既来之,则安之。今由与求也,相夫子,远人不服,而不能来也,邦分崩离析,而不能守也。而谋动干戈于邦内，吾恐季孙氏之忧，不在颛臾，而在萧墙之内也。"

（五）急智与智慧

子曰："知之为知之，不知为不知，是知也。"

子曰："不曰'如之何？如之何？'者，吾末如之何也已矣。"

子曰："过而不改，是谓过矣。"

子曰："觚，不觚——觚哉！觚哉！"

季文子三思而后行，子闻之曰："再，斯可矣。"

子曰："圣人吾不得而见之矣。得见君子者，斯可矣。"

子曰："有德者必有言，有言者不必有德。仁者必有勇，勇者不必有仁。"

子曰："君子耻其言而过其行。"

子曰："知之者不如好之者，好之者不如乐之者。"

子曰："可与言而不与之言，失人；不可与言而与之言，失言。知者不失人，亦不失言。"

子曰："君子不以言举人，不以人废言。"

子贡问曰："乡人皆好之，何如？"子曰："未可也。""乡人皆恶之，何如？"子曰："未可也。不如乡人之善者好之，其不善者恶之。"

子曰："民之于仁也，甚于水火。水火吾见蹈而死者矣，未见蹈仁而死者也。"

子曰："贫而无怨难，富而无骄易。"

子曰："邦有道，贫且贱焉，耻也；邦无道，富且贵焉，耻也。"

子曰："鄙夫，可与事君也欤哉！其未得之也，患得之；既得之，患失之。苟患失之，无所不至矣。"

子曰："不患人之不己知，患己无能也。"

子曰："君子求诸己，小人求诸人。"

子曰："躬自厚而薄责于人，则远怨矣。"

子曰："人无远虑，必有近忧。"

子曰："巧言乱德，小不忍，则乱大谋。"

子曰："骥，不称其力，称其德也。"

子贡曰："以德报怨，何如？"子曰："何以报德？以直报怨，以德报德。"

子曰："以德报德，则民有所劝。以怨报怨，则民有所惩。"（《礼记》第三十二）

子曰："以德报怨，则宽身之仁也。以怨报德，则刑戮之民也。"（同前）

子曰："性相近也，习相远也。"

子曰："唯上知与下愚不移。"

子曰："苗而不秀者，有矣夫。秀而不实者，有矣夫。"

子曰："如有周公之才之美，使骄且吝，其余不足观也已。"

子曰："君子不重则不威，学则不固。主忠信，无友不如己者。过，则勿惮改。"

子曰："见贤思齐焉，见不贤而内自省焉。"

子曰："已矣乎！吾未见能见其过，而内自讼者也。"

子贡曰："贫而无谄，富而无骄，何如？"子曰："可也。未若贫而乐，富而好礼者也。"

子曰："三军可夺帅也，匹夫不可夺志也。"

（六）人道精神与仁

子曰："人能弘道，非道弘人。"

子曰："道不远人，远人非道也。"

季路问事鬼神。子曰："未能事人，焉能事鬼？"曰："敢问死。"曰："未知生，焉知死？"

厩焚。子退朝，曰："伤人乎？"不问马。

（七）以人度人

子曰："无欲而好仁者，无畏而恶不仁者，天下一人而已矣。是故君子议道自己，而置法以民。"（《礼记》第三十二）

子曰："仁之为器重，其为道远，举者莫能胜也，行者莫能致也。取数多者，仁也。夫勉于仁者，不亦难乎？是故君子以义度人，则难为人；以人望人，则贤者可知已矣。"（同前）

子曰："中心安仁者，天下一人而已矣。"（人同此心）（同前）

子贡曰："如有博施于民而能济众，何如？可谓仁乎？"子曰："何事于仁？必也圣乎，尧舜其犹病诸。夫仁者，己欲立而立人，己欲达而达人。能近取譬，可谓仁之方也已。"

子曰："仁远乎哉？我欲仁，斯仁至矣。"

恕　　道

仲弓问仁。子曰："出门如见大宾，使民如承大祭。己所不欲，勿施于人。在邦无怨，在家无怨。"

子贡曰："我不欲人之加诸我也，吾亦欲无加诸人。"子曰："赐也，非尔所及也。"

子曰："参乎，吾道一以贯之。"曾子曰："唯。"子出，门人问曰："何谓也？"曾子曰："夫子之道，忠恕而已矣。"

子贡问曰："有一言，而可以终身行之者乎？"子曰："其恕乎？己所不欲，勿施于人。"

论"仁"

子曰："仁之难成久矣。人人失其所好，故仁者之过易辞也。"(《礼记》第三十二)

子曰："仁之难成久矣。惟君子能之。是故君子不以其所能者病人，不以人之所不能者愧人。"(同前)

子曰："中庸之为德也，其至矣乎，民鲜久矣。"

颜渊问仁。子曰："克己复礼为仁。一日克己复礼，天下归仁焉。为仁由己，而由人乎哉！"

子曰："恭近礼，俭近仁，信近情。敬让以行此，虽有过，其不甚矣。夫恭寡过，情可信，俭易容也。以此失之者，不亦鲜乎？"(《礼记》第三十二)

子曰："回也，其心三月不违仁。其余，则日月至焉而已矣。"

子张问曰："令尹子文，三仕为令尹，无喜色，三已之，无愠色。旧令尹之政，必以告新令尹，何如？"子曰："忠矣。"曰："仁矣乎？"曰："未知，焉得仁？"

或曰："雍也，仁而不佞。"子曰："焉用佞？御人以口给，屡憎于人，不知其仁。焉用佞？"

孟武伯问子路仁乎。子曰:"不知也。"又问。子曰:"由也,千乘之国,可使治其赋也。不知其仁也。""求也何如?"子曰:"求也,千室之邑,百乘之家,可使为之宰也。不知其仁也。""赤也何如?"子曰:"赤也,束带立于朝,可使与宾客言也。不知其仁也。"

仁又释

子曰:"不仁者,不可以久处约,不可以长处乐。仁者安仁,知者利仁。"

子曰:"唯仁者能好人,能恶人。"

子曰:"君子去仁,恶乎成名?君子无终食之间违仁。造次必于是,颠沛必于是。"

子曰:"人而不仁,如礼何?人而不仁,如乐何?"

子曰:"知者不惑,仁者不忧,勇者不惧。"

子曰:"仁者其言也讱。"曰:"其言也讱,斯谓之仁已乎?"子曰:"为之难,言之得无讱乎?"

君子与小人

子曰:"君子喻于义,小人喻于利。"

子曰:"君子怀德,小人怀土。君子怀刑,小人怀惠。"

子曰:"君子周而不比,小人比而不周。"

子曰:"君子矜而不争,群而不党。"

子曰:"君子求诸己,小人求诸人。"

子曰:"君子易事而难说也;说之不以道,不说也。及其使人也,器之。小人难事而易说也;说之虽不以道,说也。及其使人也,求备焉。"

子曰："君子不可小知，而可大受也。小人不可大受，而可小知也。"

子曰："君子不器。"

子曰："君子和而不同，小人同而不和。"

（孔子）在陈绝粮。从者病，莫能兴。子路愠见。曰："君子亦有穷乎？"子曰："君子固穷。小人穷斯滥矣。"

子曰："君子谋道不谋食。耕也，馁在其中矣。学也，禄在其中矣。君子忧道不忧贫。"

子曰："君子坦荡荡，小人长戚戚。"

子曰："君子上达，小人下达。"

子曰："君子泰而不骄，小人骄而不泰。"

司马牛问君子。子曰："君子不忧不惧。"曰："不忧不惧，斯谓之君子已乎？"曰："内省不疚，夫何忧何惧？"

子曰："君子食无求饱，居无求安，敏于事而慎于言，就有道而正焉，可谓好学也已矣。"

子曰："士志于道，而耻恶衣恶食者，未足与议也。"

子曰："士而怀居，不足以为士矣。"

子曰："事君三违而不出竟，则利禄也。人虽曰不要，吾弗信也。"（《礼记》第三十二）

子曰："君子耻其言而过其行。"

孔子曰："君子有三戒。少之时，血气未定，戒之在色；及其壮也，血气方刚，戒之在斗；及其老也，血气既衰，戒之在得。"

（八）中庸为理想

夫子之所厌恶

子曰："不得中行而与之，必也狂狷乎？狂者进取，狷者有所不为也。"

子曰："乡愿，德之贼也。"

子在陈。曰："归欤！归欤！吾党之小子狂简，斐然成章，不知所以裁之。"

子贡问师与商也孰贤。子曰："师也过，商也不及。"曰："然则师愈欤？"子曰："过犹不及。"

子谓子夏曰："汝为君子儒，无为小人儒。"

子曰："质胜文则野，文胜质则史。文质彬彬，然后君子。"

子曰："先进于礼乐，野人也。后进于礼乐，君子也。如用之，则吾从先进。"

子曰："古者，民有三疾。今也，或是之无也。古之狂也，肆；今之狂也，荡。古之矜也，廉；今之矜也，忿戾。古之愚也，直；今之愚也，诈而已矣。"

子贡曰："君子亦有恶乎？"子曰："有恶。恶称人之恶者，恶居下流而讪上者，恶勇而无礼者，恶果敢而窒者。"曰："赐也，亦有恶乎？""恶徼以为知者，恶不孙以为勇者，恶讦以为直者。"

子曰："狂而不直，侗而不愿，悾悾而不信，吾不知之矣。"

孔子曰："恶似而非者。恶莠，恐其乱苗也。恶佞，恐其乱义也。恶利口，恐其乱信也。恶郑声，恐其乱乐也。恶紫，恐其乱朱也。恶乡愿，恐其乱德也。"（《孟子·尽心下》）

子曰："色厉而内荏，譬诸小人，其犹穿窬之盗也欤？"

子曰："唯女子与小人为难养也。近之不孙，远之则怨。"

子曰："巧言令色，鲜矣仁。"

子曰："君子不以辞尽人。故天下有道，则行有枝叶。天下无道，则辞有枝叶。"（《礼记》第三十二）

（九）论为政

为政之理想

子曰："道之以政，齐之以刑，民免而无耻。道之以德，齐之以礼，有耻且格。"

子曰："听讼吾犹人也。必也，使无讼乎。"

或谓孔子曰："子奚不为政？"子曰："《书》云孝子惟孝，友于兄弟，施于有政。是亦为政，奚其为为政？"

有子曰："其为人也孝悌，而好犯上者鲜矣。不好犯上而好作乱者，未之有也。"

以德行为政

子曰："为政以德，譬如北辰，居其所而众星拱之。"

季康子问政于孔子，曰："如杀无道以就有道，何如？"孔子对曰："子为政，焉用杀？子欲善，而民善矣。君子之德风也，小人之德草也，草上之风必偃。"

季康子问政于孔子。孔子对曰："政者，正也。子帅以正，孰敢不正？"

子曰："其身正，不令而行。其身不正，虽令不从。"

子曰："苟正其身矣，于从政乎何有？不能正其身，如正人何？"

为政要素

子贡问政。子曰："足食，足兵，民信之矣。"子贡曰："必不得已而去，于斯三者何先？"曰："去兵。"子贡曰："必不得已而去，于斯二者何先？"曰："去食。自古皆有死，民无信不立。"

（十）论教育、礼与诗

子曰："兴于诗，立于礼，成于乐。"

子曰："君子博学于文，约之以礼，亦可以弗畔矣夫。"

有子曰："礼之用，和为贵，先王之道，斯为美。小大由之。有所不行，知和而和，不以礼节之，亦不可行也。"

子曰："礼云，礼云，玉帛云乎哉！乐云，乐云，钟鼓云乎哉！"

子夏问曰："'巧笑倩兮，美目盼兮，素以为绚兮'，何谓也？"子曰："绘事后素。"曰："礼后乎？"子曰："起予者，商也。始可与言诗已矣。"

林放问礼之本。子曰："大哉问！礼与其奢也，宁俭。丧，与其易也，宁戚。"

子曰："知及之，仁不能守之，虽得之，必失之。知及之，仁能守之，不庄以莅之，则民不敬。知及之，仁能守之，庄以莅之，动之不以礼，未善也。"

子曰："诗三百，一言以蔽之，曰：思无邪。"

陈亢问于伯鱼曰："子亦有异闻乎？"对曰："未也。尝独立，鲤趋而过庭，曰：'学诗乎？'对曰：'未也。'曰：'不学诗，无以言。'鲤退而学诗。他日。又独立，鲤趋而过庭。曰：'学礼乎？'对曰：'未也。'曰：'不学礼，无以立。'鲤退而学礼。闻斯二者。"陈亢退而喜曰："问一得三。闻诗，闻礼，又闻君子之远其子也。"

子曰："学而不思则罔，思而不学则殆。"

子曰："学而时习之，不亦说乎？"

子曰："温故而知新，可以为师矣。"

子曰："记问之学，不足以为人师。"（《礼记》第十八）

子曰："古之学者为己，今之学者为人。"

子曰："由也，汝闻六言六蔽矣乎？"对曰："未也。""居，吾语汝。好仁不好学，其蔽也愚。好知不好学，其蔽也荡。好信不好学，其蔽也贼。好直不好学，其蔽也绞。好勇不好学，其蔽也乱。好刚不好学，其蔽也狂。"

孔子曰："生而知之者，上也。学而知之者，次也。困而学之，又其次也。困而不学，民斯为下矣。"

子曰："弟子入则孝，出则悌，谨而信，泛爱众，而亲仁，行有余力，则以学文。"

Chapter Five **APHORISMS OF CONFUCIUS**
(*The Analects*)

The *Analects* is generally regarded as the Confucian Bible, being a miscellaneous, unclassified and unedited collection of the remarks of Confucius on various occasions, mostly without any suggestion as to the circumstances in which the remarks were made, and certainly torn from their context. Reading the *Analects* is like reading Bartlett's *Familiar Quotations*, an exciting taste of bits of choice sayings, giving the reader plenty of room for meditation, imagination and wonder as to what the variety of brilliant writers really mean. A comparison with chapters of the *Liki*, *Mencius*, and other sources shows that the most pithy and epigrammatic sayings have been cut off from longer discourses and preserved because they were so much admired. It is illuminating, for instance, to read in the *Analects* the remark by Confucius that "I have never yet seen people attracted by virtuous scholars as they are by beautiful women," and then to learn from Ssŭma Ch'ien (see Ch. II) that he made this remark after he had paraded the streets of Wei in a carriage with a beautiful queen, and found the people looked at the queen but did not look at him. The text of the *Analects* itself does not mention the circumstance, and actually puts it in the form of a more abstract remark: "I haven't yet seen people who love virtue as they love beauty." The *Analects* is full of short sentences of four or five words, like the following: "The gentleman is not a vessel (has not only one particular ability)," or "The goody-goodies are the thieves of virtue." In the last instance, we are fortunate to have an amplification of this idea of the "goody-goodies" in the *Book of Mencius*. One cannot believe that Confucius talked in three or four syllables at a time. It is further impossible to believe that the full meaning of Confucius' replies to various questions can be understood without knowing more fully what the questioner asked. As Yuan Mei has pointed out, this was essentially a book of the sayings of Confucius, and therefore the questions of his disciples were cut as short as possible. Thus the only hint we get of the questions is mostly in one word: this man asked about "government," that man asked about "true manhood," and a third man asked about "*li*," and Confucius came out with the most diverse and contradictory answers to the same questions put by different people. Actually the commentators were sometimes misled into an interpretation that is not justifiable. Thus, once Confucius said to Chung Kung, "Look at that beautiful calf, with such a light brown skin and such pretty little horns! Even if I wanted to spare it, do you think the (spirits of the) mountains and rivers would spare it (for sacrifices to them)?" This is interpreted to mean that Chung Kung had such a beautiful character, fit to become a moral ruler, but Yuan Mei suggests that this was merely a casual remark of Confucius as he and his disciple were looking out of the window and saw a beautiful calf passing by.

What then is the chief charm of the *Analects*, apart from Confucian wisdom contained therein? Its charm centers around the character of Confucius and the different remarks he made upon his contemporaries, the charm of a biography and sayings of Confucius, disorderly, suggestive and done by a few impressionistic strokes. It is essentially like the charm of Boswell's *Johnson*, and of the entire Johnsonian circle, here represented by the circle of Confucius' disciples and friends. It can be opened and read from any page, revealing to us the charm of a wise, terribly rude and withal

an affable character. That is the fascination of the *Analects* for the Chinese.
For dogmatism has its charm, and one is always impressed by the dogmatic
judgments of Confucius and of Dr. Johnson because they both pronounced
their judgments with so much force and self-assurance. The entire character
of the *Analects* is therefore merely illustrative, and in itself gives us no well-
rounded view of the Confucian system of thought, except by some very hard
thinking on the part of the reader.

We also get a glimpse through the *Analects* of the Confucian circle.
Sometimes we get a suggestion by a mere word that Confucius was "happy"
when he was surrounded by two or three of his favorite disciples. Mixed,
of course, with the sayings of Confucius himself are also quite a few sayings
by his greater disciples, like Tsengtes, Tsehsia, Yutse, Tsechang, etc., for
the various chapters of the *Analects* are certainly of diverse origin, some
being recorded by the disciples of the disciples. We have Yen Huei, a quiet,
thoughtful person, the oldest of the disciples, whom Confucius admired
and praised in superlative terms. On the other hand, we have Tselu, the
Confucian St. Peter, who constantly questioned the Master's conduct. This
man receives very rough handling in the *Analects*, because he was dead and
there were no disciples to defend him at the time the *Analects* were recorded.
There were also the garrulous, fluent Tsekung, the very much younger,
but philosophic Tsengtse (who later became probably the most important
interpreter of Confucius), the more literary-minded Tsehsia, and the practical
politician Jan Ch'iu, whom Confucius finally disowned from his circle of
disciples. Confucius was, therefore, broad enough to be a teacher of all types
of persons, and it is said that each disciple was one "limb" of the "body of
the Sage." Later on, the Tsengtse-Tsesze-Mencius tradition developed the
idealistic-philosophic side of Confucianism, while the Tsehsia-Hsuntse
tradition developed along the line of historic learning and scholarship. Just as
St. John developed the idealistic side of Jesus' teachings and added a little of
his own, so we see, for instance in the chapter on "Central Harmony," how

Tsesze developed the philosophic significance of the Doctrine of the Golden Mean, of Humanism and of "the true self." Briefly, we may compare Tsesze and Mencius to St. John and Hsuntse to St. James.

The abrupt, jumpy style of the *Analects* requires of course some hard thinking on the part of the reader. It isn't the kind of book that can be read with profit by a lazy reader who expects the author to talk on and on, while he assumes an entirely passive role. The full participation of the reader is necessary and the truths must be apprehended by personal insight; the reader must draw upon his own personal experience. Of course the ancient Chinese school system did not expect young school children to master the philosophic meaning of one of the most mature philosophies of the world. What was expected, however, was mainly a thorough conning over of the text so that the lines would stick forever in their memory, a fountain of wisdom to be drawn upon later on. But then the Confucianists also taught the proper way of reading the *Analects*. These were the methods advised by the Sung scholars. Ch'eng Yich'uan said, "Regard the questions by the disciples in the *Analects* as your own questions, and the answers of Confucius as answers to yourself, then you will get some real benefit." Chu Hsi said, "Read the *Analects* first. Just take one or two sections a day. Never mind whether the passage is difficult or easy to understand, or whether it is a profound passage or not. Just read on from the beginning of the section, and you don't get the meaning by reading, then use some thinking, and if you don't get the meaning by thinking, then read again. Turn it back and forth and try to get its flavor. Thus after a long while, you will understand what is in it." In his letter to a friend, Chu Hsi said, "In reading be most careful not to read too much. Read a little and it will be easy to thoroughly master it. All real insight from studies is gained in this manner." Again in his *Yulei* or "Sayings," we read, "To understand the language of the text is one thing; to appreciate the beauty of its meaning is another. It is a great common weakness of readers to understand the superficial side without catching what is good in a book."

Again, "The proper method of reading is to spend some real thought on it. At first, you will find that this understanding requires a lot of time or energy, but (after you have gained enough general insight and understanding yourself), it will require little time to run through a book. At first, a book requires a hundred per cent energy in reading; afterwards it may require only eighty or ninety per cent, and later on, sixty or seventy per cent, and at last only forty or fifty per cent." To regard reading and thought as two necessary complementary elements in the progress of knowledge is basic in the Confucian system of education, and Confucius himself had something to say about these two elements, as will be seen in the last section of this chapter.

It is amazing that no Chinese scholar has tried to revise or re-edit the *Analects*, in order to give the reader a better conception of the contents, although a few have written essays on the different ideas dealt with in the book (for instance, the *Lunyu T'ungshih* "Studies on the *Analects*" by Ch'iao Hsun, 1763-1820, and the splendid work on the "Meaning of Words in Mencius," *Mengtse Tseyi Shucheng* by Tai Chen, 1724-1777). No one, apart from Western scholars, has even complied a collection of all Confucius' descriptions of "the superior man." This most important conception forms a composite picture of the qualities of this "superior man". In this chapter I have selected probably one-fourth of the contents of the *Analects* and regrouped them according to certain ideas. Unless otherwise indicted, the sayings are all by Confucius and are taken from the *Analects*. Where necessary, however (e.g., for a clearer statement of the humanistic position), I have drawn upon Chapters XXVIII, XXIX, XXX, XXXII, and XXXIII of the *Liki*—about a dozen passages, all told. Chapters XXXII and XXXIII, in particular differ not in the slightest as regards contents and style from the *Analects*, and are extremely rich in records of Confucius' sayings.

I. DESCRIPTION OF CONFUCIUS BY HIMSELF AND OTHERS

Duke Yeh (of Ch'u) asked Tselu about Confucius, and Tselu did not make a reply. Confucius said, "Why didn't you tell him that I am a person who forgets to eat when he is enthusiastic about something, forgets all his worries when he is happy, and is not aware that old age is coming on?"

Tselu was stopping for the night at the Stone Gate and the gate-keeper asked him, "Where are you from?" "I'm from Confucius," replied Tselu. "Oh, is he the fellow who knows that a thing can't be done and still wants to do it?"

Weisheng Mou said to Confucius, "Why are you so self-important and constantly rushing about? Don't you talk a little bit too much?" "It isn't that I want to talk. It's because I hate (the present moral chaos)."

Confucius said, "At fifteen I began to be seriously interested in study. At thirty I had formed my character. At forty I had no more perplexities. At fifty I knew the will of heaven. At sixty nothing that I heard disturbed me. At seventy I could let my thought wander without trespassing the moral law."

Yen Huei and Tselu were sitting together with Confucius, and Confucius said, "Why don't you each tell me your ambitions in life?" Tselu replied, "It is my ambition in life to go about with a horse and carriage and a light fur coat and share them with my good friends until they are all worn out without any regret." Yen Huei said, "It is my ambition never to show off and never to brag about myself." Then Tselu said, "May I hear what is your ambition?" And Confucius replied, "It is my ambition that the old people should be able to live in peace, all friends should be loyal and all young people should love their elders."

There were the famous recluses, Poyi, Shuch'i, Yuchung, Yiyi, Chuchang, Liuhsia Huei and Shaolien. Confucius said, "Not to compromise with their own ideals and not to be disgraced—these were Poyi and Shuch'i." He said of Liuhsia Huei and Shaolien that they compromised with their ideals and were disgraced, but that they managed to be able to maintain a standard in their words and their conduct. He said of Yuchung and Yiyi that they escaped from society and were unconventional or untrammeled in their speech, and that they were able to live a clean private life and to adjust themselves according to the principle of expediency in times of chaos. "I am different from these people; I decide according to the circumstances of the time, and act accordingly."

A great official asked Tsekung, "Is the Master a Sage? Why is it that he is so many-sided?" Tsekung replied, "Heaven has sent him to become a Sage, and he is many-sided, to boot." When Confucius heard this he said, "Perhaps this great official knows me well. I was a poor man's son and can therefore do many things that belong to a common man. Does a superior man have to learn all these things? No, he doesn't." Tsechang said, "Confucius said, I did not enter the government, that was how I had time for learning the arts."

Confucius said, "There is pleasure in lying pillowed against a bent arm after a meal of simple vegetables with a drink of water. On the other hand, to enjoy wealth and power without coming by it through the right means is to me like so many floating clouds."

Confucius said, "There are three things about the superior man that I have not been able to attain. The true man has no worries; the wise man has no perplexities; and the brave man has no fear." Tsekung said, "But, Master, you are exactly describing yourself."

Confucius said, "In the study of literature, I am probably as good as anyone, but personally to live the life of the superior man, I don't think I have succeeded."

Confucius said, "As to being a sage and a true man, I am not so presumptuous. I will admit, however, that I have unceasingly tried to do my best and to teach other people."

Confucius said, "Do you think I know a great deal? I don't. There was an uneducated man who asked me about something, and I couldn't say a word in reply. I merely discussed the two sides of the question and was at my wit's end."

Confucius said, "In every hamlet of ten families, there are always some people as honest and faithful as myself, but none who is so devoted to study."

Confucius said, "I may perhaps compare myself to my old friend Laop'eng. I merely try to describe (or carry on) the ancient tradition, but not to create something new. I only want to get at the truth and am in love with ancient studies."

Confucius said, "To silently appreciate a truth, to learn continually and to teach other people unceasingly—that is just natural with me."

"The things that trouble or concern me are the following: lest I should neglect to improve my character, lest I should neglect my studies, and lest I should fail to move forward when I see the right course, or fail to correct myself when I see my mistake."

Confucius said, "I'm not born a wise man. I'm merely one in love with ancient studies and work very hard to learn them."

Confucius said, "Ah Sze, do you suppose that I merely learned a great deal and tried to remember it all?" "Yes, isn't that what you do?" "No," said Confucius, "I have a system or a central thread that runs through it all."

Confucius said, "There are some people who do not understand a subject, but go ahead and invent things out of their own head. I am not like those people. One can come to be a wise man by hearing a great deal and following the good, and by seeing a great deal and remembering it."

Confucius said, "Sometimes I have gone the whole day without food and a whole night without sleep, occupied in thinking and unable to arrive at any results. So I decided to study again."

Confucius said, "Whenever walking in a company of three, I can always find my teacher among them (or one who has something to teach me). I select a good person and follow his example, or I see a bad person and correct it in myself."

Confucius said, "I won't teach a man who is not anxious to learn, and will not explain to one who is not trying to make things clear to himself. And if I explain one-fourth and the man doesn't go back and reflect and think out the implications in the remaining three-fourths for himself, I won't bother to teach him again."

Confucius said, "There was never yet a person who came to me with the present of dried meat (equivalent of tuition) that I have refused to teach something."

The young men of a certain village Hu were given to mischief, and one day some young people from that village came to see Confucius, and the disciples were surprised that Confucius saw them. Confucius said, "Don't be too hard on people. What concerns me is how they come, and not what they do when they go away. When a man approaches me with pure intentions, I respect his pure intentions, although I cannot guarantee what he does afterwards."

Confucius was in difficulties at K'uang and he said, "Since King Wen died, is not the tradition of King Wen in my keeping or possession? If it be the will of Heaven that this moral tradition should be lost, posterity shall never again share in the knowledge of this tradition. But if it be the will of Heaven that this tradition shall not be lost, what can the people of K'uang do to me?"

Confucius said, "Heaven has endowed me with a moral destiny (or mission). What can Huan T'uei (a military officer who was diving him away) do to me?"

Confucius said, "Give me a few more years to finish the study of the *Book of Changes*, then I hope I shall be able to be free from making serious mistakes (or error of judgment)."

These were the things Confucius often talked about: Poetry, history, and the performance of ceremonies—all these were what he often talked about.

Confucius seldom talked about profit or destiny or true manhood.

Confucius did not talk about monsters, physical exploits, unruly conduct and the heavenly spirits.

Confucius taught four things: Literature, personal conduct, being one's true self and honesty in social relationships.

Confucius fished with a fishing rod, but would not use a net. While shooting he would not shoot a bird at rest.

Confucius denounced or tried to avoid completely four things: arbitrariness of opinion, dogmatism, narrow-mindedness and egotism.

Confucius was gentle but dignified, austere yet not harsh, polite and completely at ease.

Yen Huei heaved a sigh and said, "You look up to it and it seems so high. You try to drill through it and it seems so hard. You seem to see it in front of you, and all of a sudden it appears behind you. The Master is very good at gently leading a man along and teaching him. He taught me to broaden myself by the reading of literature and then to control myself by the observance of proper conduct. I just felt being carried along, but after I have done my very best, or developed what was in me, there still remains something austerely standing apart, uncatchable. Do what I could to reach his position, I can't find the way."

Shusun Wushu said to the officials at court, "Tsekung is a better man than Confucius." Tsefu Chingpo told this to Tsekung, and Tsekung said, "It is like the matter of housewalls. My housewall comes up only to the shoulder, and the people outside are therefore able to see my beautiful house, whereas the wall of Confucius is twenty or thirty feet high, and unless you go right inside, you do not see the beauty of its halls and the grandeur of its furniture. But there are very few people who can penetrate inside that household. What Shusun says is therefore perfectly easy to understand."

Again Shusun Wushu tried to belittle the greatness of Confucius, and Tsekung said, "There's no use trying. Confucius cannot be belittled. Other great men are like mounds or hillocks which you can climb up, but Confucius is like the moon and the sun, which you can never reach. A man can shut his eyes to the sun and the moon, but what harm can it do to the sun and the moon? You are just trying to do the impossible."

II. THE EMOTIONAL AND ARTISTIC LIFE OF CONFUCIUS

When Yen Huei died, Confucius wept bitterly and his followers said, "You are all shaken up." Confucius said, "Am I all shaken up? But if I don't feel all shaken up at the death of this person, for whom else shall I ever feel shaken up?"

Confucius never ate his fill in the company of people in mourning. If he wept on that day, then he did not sing.

What Confucius took very seriously were: The ceremonial bath before religious worship, war, and sickness.

Someone asked Confucius about the meaning of the Grand Sacrifice to the Imperial Ancestors, and Confucius said, "I don't know. One who knows the meaning of the Grand Sacrifice would be able to rule the world as easily as pointing a finger at the palm."

When Confucius offered sacrifice to his ancestors, he felt as if his ancestors were present bodily, and when he offered sacrifice to the other gods, he felt as if the gods were present bodily. Confucius said, "If I don't offer sacrifice by being personally present, it is as if I didn't sacrifice at all."

Wangsun Chia asked, "Why do people say that it is better to get on good terms with the kitchen god than with the god of the southwestern corner of the house?" Confucius replied, "Nonsense, if you have committed sins against Heaven, you haven't got a god to pray to."

Tsekung wanted to do away with the ceremony of sacrificing the lamb in winter. Confucius said, "Ah Sze, you love the lamb, but I love the ritual."

Confucius said, "Respect the heavenly and earthly spirits and keep them at a distance."

Confucius said, "My, how old I have grown! For a long time I have not dreamed of Duke Chou again."

Confucius heard the music of *Hsiao* in Ch'i, and for three months he forgot the taste of meat, saying, "I never thought that music could be so beautiful." When Confucius was singing with some other men and liked the song, he always asked for an *encore* and then would join in the chorus.

Confucius said, "Wake yourself up with poetry, establish your character in *li* and complete your education in music."

Confucius said, "Since my return to Lu from Wei, I have been able to classify the different kinds of music, and the *ya* and the *sung* are restored to their proper place."

Yen Huei asked about running a government. Confucius replied, "Use the calendar of Hsia Dynasy (the Hsia year begins with "January," or about February in the solar calendar, while the Chou year begins with "November"), adopt the (heavy and strong and comparatively unadorned wooden) carriages of the Shang Dynasty, and use the imperial crown of the Chou Dynasty. For music, adopt the dance of *Hsiao*. Suppress the music of Cheng and keep away the petty flatterers. The music of Cheng is lascivious, and the petty flatterers are dangerous."

(Tselu was playing the *seh*, and) Confucius said, "How dare Ah Yu play such atrocious music in my house!" The disciples then began to look down upon Tselu and Confucius said, "Ah Yu has entered the hall, but he has not entered the inner room."

Confucius would not use navy blue or scarlet for the binding and collar of his dress. He would not have red or purple pajamas. In summer he would wear underclothes beneath the thin (transparent) coarse or fine linen gown. He would match a lamb coat with a black material; match a coat of white fawn with white material, and match a fox coat with brown (or yellow) material. He always wore a nightgown longer than his body by half. At home he used to wear a long-haired fox coat. Except during mourning, he wore all sorts of pendants (on his girdle).

For him rice could never be white enough and mince meat could never be chopped fine enough. When the food was mushy or the flavor had deteriorated, or when the fish had become bad or the meat was tainted, he would not eat. When its color had changed, he would not eat. When the smell was bad, he would not eat. When it was not cooked right, he would not eat. When food was not in season, he would not eat. When the meat was not cut properly, he would not eat. When a food was not served with its proper sauce, he would not eat. Although there was a lot of meat on the table, he would not take it out of proportion with his rice; as for wine, he drank without any set limit, except not to get drunk. Wine or shredded meat bought from the shops he would not eat. A meal without ginger on the table, he would not eat. He did not overeat.

During thunderstorms, his face always changed color.

III. THE CONVERSATIONAL STYLE

Tselu, Tseng Hsi, Jan Ch'iu and Kunghsi Hua were sitting together one day and Confucius said, "Do not think that I am a little bit older than you and therefore am assuming airs. You often say among yourselves that people don't know you. Suppose someone should know you, I should like to know how you would appear to that person." Tselu immediately replied, "I like to rule over a country with a thousand carriages, situated between two powerful neighbors, involved in war and suffering from famine. I like to take charge of such a country and in three years, the nation will become strong and orderly." Confucius smiled at this remark and said, "How about you, Ah Ch'iu?" Jan Ch'iu replied, "Let me have a country sixty or seventy *li* square or perhaps only fifty or sixty *li* square. Put it in my charge, and in three years, the people will have enough to eat, but as for teaching them moral order and music, I shall leave it to the superior man." (Turning to Kunghsi Hua) Confucius said, "How about you, Ah Ch'ih?" Kunghsi Hua replied, "Not that I say I can do it, but I'm willing to learn this. At the ceremonies of religious worship and at the conference of the princes, I should like to wear the ceremonial cap and gown and be a minor official assisting at the ceremony." "How about you, Ah Tien?" The latter (Tseng Hsi) was just playing on the *seh*, and with a bang he left the instrument and arose to speak. "You know my ambition is different from theirs." "It doesn't matter," said Confucius, "we are just trying to find out what each would like to do." Then he replied, "In late spring, when the new spring dress is made, I would like to go with five or six grown-ups and six or seven children to bathe in the River Ch'i, and after the bath go to enjoy the breeze in the Wuyi woods, and then sing on our way home." Confucius heaved a deep sigh and said, "You are the man after my own heart."

Confucius said, "Do you think that I have hidden anything from the two or three of you? No, I have hidden nothing from you. There is nothing that I do that I don't share with the two or three of you. That is I."

Confucius went to the city of Wu (where his disciple Tseyu had been made the magistrate), and heard the people singing to the accompaniment of string instruments. Confucius grinned and said to Tseyu, "You are trying to kill a chicken with a big cleaver for killing a cow." "But I heard from you," replied Tseyu, "that when the superior man had learned culture, he became kind to people, and when the common people learned culture, they would become well-disciplined." Confucius (turned to the other disciples and) said, "You fellows, what he says is right, I was only pulling his leg."

Some people of Tahsiang said, "Great indeed is Confucius! He knows about everything and is an expert at nothing." When Confucius heard this, he said, "Now what am I going to specialize in? Shall I specialize in archery, or in driving a carriage?"

The Secretary of Justice of Ch'en asked Confucius if Duke Chao of Lu understood propriety (or *li*) and Confucius replied that he did. After Confucius had left, the Secretary asked Wuma Ch'i to come in and said to him, "Is a superior man partial to his own country? I heard that a superior man should not be partial. Duke Chao married a princess of Wu, who was of the same family name, and called her Mengtse of Wu. Now if that man understands propriety, who doesn't?" Later on Wuma Ch'i told this to Confucius, and Confucius said, "How lucky I am! Whenever I make a mistake, people are sure to discover it."

Tsekung said, "Here is a beautiful piece of jade, kept in a casket and waiting for a good price for sale." Confucius remarked, "For sale! For Sale! I'm the one waiting for a good price for sale!"

Someone asked about Tsech'an (a good minister of Cheng) and Confucius said, "He is a kind man." The man then asked about Prince Tsehsi (of Ch'u), and Confucius said, "Oh, that fellow! Oh, that fellow!"

Confucius asked Kungming Chia about Kungsun Wentse, "Is it true that your Master doesn't talk, doesn't smile and doesn't take goods from the people?" Kungming Chia replied, "That is an exaggerated story. My Master talks only when he should talk and people are not bored with his talk. He smiles only when he is happy, and people are not bored with his smiles. And he takes goods from the people only when it is right to do so, and people do not mind his taking their goods." Confucius said, "Really! Is that so?"

Tsekung loved to criticize people, and Confucius said, "Ah Sze, you're clever, aren't you? I have no time for such things."

Confucius said, "I greatly admire a fellow who goes about the whole day with a well-fed stomach and a vacuous mind. How can one ever do it? I would rather that he play chess, which would seem to me to be better.

"I have seen people who gather together the whole day and never talk of anything serious among themselves, and who love to play little tricks on people. Marvellous, how can they ever do it!"

Confucius said, "I am going to remain quiet!" Tsekung remarked, "If you remain quiet, how can we ever learn anything to teach to the others?" And Confucius said, "Does Heaven talk? The four seasons go their way in succession and the different things are produced. Does Heaven talk?"

Confucius said, "I have sometimes talked with Huei for a whole day, and he just sits still there like a fool. But then he goes into his own room and thinks about what I have said and is able to think out some ideas of his own. He is not a fool."

IV. THE JOHNSONIAN TOUCH

Confucius said, "By looking at a man's faults, you know the man's character."

Tsekung asked Confucius, "What kind of a person do you think can be properly called a scholar?" Confucius replied, "A person who shows a sense of honor in his personal conduct and who can be relied upon to carry out a diplomatic mission in a foreign country with competence and dignity can be properly called a scholar" "What kind of a person would come next?" "One who is known to be a good son in his family and has a reputation for humility and respect in a village." "What kind of a person would come next after that?" "A person who is extremely careful of his conduct and speech and always keeps his word. That is a priggish, inferior type of person, but still he can rank below the above two types." "What do you think of the officials today?" "Oh!" said Confucius, "those rice-bags! They don't count at all."

Confucius was once seriously ill, and Tselu asked his disciples to serve as stewards (for his funeral to emulate the style of official families). When Confucius got a little better, he remarked, "The scoundrel! He has gone on preparing to do these things behind my back. I have no stewards in my house and he wants to pretend that I have stewards. Whom can I deceive? Can I deceive God?"

Confucius saw Queen Nancia and Tselu was displeased. Confucius swore an oath, "If I had said or done anything wrong during the interview, may Heaven strike me! May Heaven strike me!"

Tsai Yu slept in the daytime and Confucius remarked, "There is no use trying to carve on a piece of rotten wood, or to whitewash a wall made of earth from a dunghill. Why should I bother to scold him?" Confucius said, "At first when I heard a man talk, I expected his conduct to come up to what he said. But now when I hear a man talk, I reserve my judgment until I see how he acts. I have learned this lesson from Tsai Yu."

(*Confucius hates a bad pun.*) Duke Ai asked about the customs of the worship of the Earth, and Tsai Yu replied, "The Hsias planted pine trees on the altar, the Shangs used cypresses, and the Chous used chestnuts, in order to make the people nuts." (Literally "give the people the creeps," a pun on the Chinese word *li*.) When Confucius heard this, he said, "Oh, better forget your history! Let what has come, come! Don't try to remedy the past!"

Ju Pei wanted to see Confucius and Confucius declined by saying that he was sick. When the man was just outside the door, Confucius took a string instrument, the *seh*, and sang, in order to let him hear it (and know that he was not sick after all.)

Yang Ho wanted to see Confucius, and Confucius would not see him. Yang then presented Confucius with a leg of pork, and Confucius took care to find out when he would not be at home and then went to pay his return call, but met him on the way. Yang Ho said to Confucius, "Come, I want to talk to you!" And he said, "Can you call a man kind who possesses the knowledge to put the country in order, but allows it to go to the dogs?" "Of course not," said Confucius. "Can you call a man wise who loves to get into power and yet lets an opportunity pass by when it comes?" "Of course not," said Confucius. "But the time is passing swiftly by," said Yang Ho. Confucius replied (sarcastically), "Yes, sir, I'm going to be an official." (Yang Ho was a powerful but corrupt official in Lu, and Confucius refused to serve under him.)

Baron Ch'eng Ch'en assassinated Duke Chien (in Ch'i), and Confucius took a ceremonial bath and went to see the Duke of Lu and said, "Ch'en Heng has assassinated the Duke, his superior. We must send a punitive expedition." "You speak to the three Barons (of Lu)." Confucius replied, "You know in my capacity as an official, I have to inform you formally of this matter." "You speak to the three Barons," said the Duke again. Confucius then went to speak to the three Barons who disapproved, and Confucius said to them, "You know in the capacity of an official I have to inform you formally of this matter."

Yuan Jan (who was reputed to sing at his mother's death) squatted in

Confucius' presence and Confucius said, "As a child, you were impudent; after you are grown up, you have absolutely done nothing; and now in your old age you refuse to die! You're a thief!" And Confucius struck him in the shin with a cane.

Baron K'ang Chi was worried about thieves and burglars in the state and consulted Confucius about it. Confucius replied, "If you yourself don't love money you can give it to the thieves and they won't take it."

Baron K'ang Chi was richer than Duke Chou and Jan Ch'iu (Confucius' disciple who was his secretary) continued to tax the people in order to enrich the Baron. Confucius said (to his disciples), "He is not my disciple. You fellows may strike the drum and denounce him. You have my permission."

Baron K'ang Chi was going to attack Ch'uanyu and Jan Ch'iu and Tselu came to see Confucius and said, "The Baron is going to send an expedition against Ch'uanyu." Confucius said, "Ah Ch'iu, isn't this your fault? The town of Ch'uanyu was originally designated by the ancient emperors as a fief to maintain the worship of the Tungmeng Hill, and besides it is situated within the boundaries of Lu, and the ruler was directly appointed by the founder of the Dynasty. How can you ever think of sending an expedition to take it over (to enlarge the territory of the Baron)?" "The Baron wants it. We don't," replied Jan Ch'iu. "Ah Ch'iu," said Confucius, "the ancient historian Chou Jen said, 'Do your best according to your official capacity, and if you can't stop it, then you quit.' If a person is approaching danger and you do not assist him, or if a person is falling down and you do not support him, then what is the use of being an assistant or guide? What you have just said is wrong. When a tiger or a buffalo escapes from the fenced enclosure or when a piece of sacred jade is found broken in its casket, whose fault is it (but that of the keeper)?" "But this Ch'uanyu lies right next to Pi (city of the Baron)," said Jan Ch'iu, "and if we don't take it now, it will remain a constant threat to our defense in the future." Confucius replied, "Ah Ch'iu, a gentleman hates the person who is embarked upon a course for selfish gains and then tries to create all sorts of pretexts. I have heard that a man in charge of a state or a family doesn't worry about there being too few people in it, but about the unequal distribution of wealth, nor does he worry about poverty, but about general dissatisfaction. For when wealth is equally distributed, there is no poverty; when the people are united, you cannot call it a small nation, and when there is no dissatisfaction (or when people have a sense of security), the country is secure. Accordingly, if people in the neighboring cities do not pay homage to you, you attend to the civil development in your own country to attract them, and when they come, you make it so that they would like to settle down and live in peace. Now you two as secretaries assisting your chief, have not been able to induce people in the neighboring cities to pay homage and come to you. You see the state of Lu divided against itself without being able to do anything about it, and then you set about thinking of starting wars right inside the country. I'm afraid that what the Baron will have to worry about will not be the city of Ch'uanyu, but right within your own household."

V. WIT AND WISDOM

Confucius said, "To know that you know and know what you don't know is the characteristic of one who knows."

Confucius said, "A man who does not say to himself, 'What to do? What to do?'—indeed I do not know what to do with such a person!"

Confucius said, "A man who has committed a mistake and doesn't correct it is committing another mistake."

Confucius said, "A melon-cup that no longer resembles a melon-cup and people still say, 'A melon-cup! A melon-cup!'"

Confucius said: "It is said, 'It is difficult to be a king, but it is not easy to be a minister, either.'"

Baron Wen Chi said that he always thought three times before he acted. When Confucius heard this, he remarked, "To think twice is quite enough."

Confucius said, "I do not expect to find a saint today. But if I can find a gentleman, I shall be quite satisfied."

Confucius said, "A man who has a beautiful soul always has some beautiful things to say, but a man who says beautiful things does not necessarily have a beautiful soul. A true man (or truly great man) will always be found to have courage, but a courageous man will not always be found to have true manhood."

Confucius said, "A man who brags without shame will find great difficulty in living up to his bragging."

Confucius said, "The man who loves truth (or learning) is better than the man who knows it, and the man who finds happiness in it is better than the man who loves it."

Confucius said, "In speaking to a sovereign, one must look out for three things: To talk before you are asked is called 'impulsiveness.' To fail to talk when you are asked is called 'lack of candor.' And to talk without noticing the sovereign's mood is called 'blindness.'"

Confucius said, "When you find a person worthy to talk to and fail to talk to him, you have lost your man. When you find a man unworthy to talk to and you talk to him, you have lost (i.e., wasted) your words. A wise man neither loses his man, nor loses his words."

Confucius said, "A gentleman does not praise a man (or put him in office) on the basis of what he says, nor does he deny the truth of what one says because he dislikes the person who says it (if it is good)."

Tsekung asked Confucius, "What would you say if all the people of the village like a person?" "That is not enough," replied Confucius. "What would you say if all the people of the village dislike a person?" "That is not enough," said Confucius. "It is better when the good people of the village like him, and the bad people of the village dislike him." (When you are disliked by the bad persons, you are a good person.)

Confucius said, "The common man often gets in trouble because of his love for the water (literally "gets drowned" in it); the gentleman often gets into trouble because of his love for talking; and the great man often gets into trouble because of his love for the people. All of them get submerged in what they come close to or are familiar with. Water seems so familiar to the people, but easily drowns them because it is a thing that seems so easy to approach and yet is dangerous to get too near to. Talking easily leads one into trouble because when you talk, you use so many words, and it is easy to let them out of your mouth, but difficult to take them back. The people often get one into trouble because they are mean and not open-minded; you can respect them, but you must not insult or offend them. Therefore the gentleman must be very careful."

Confucius said, "The people who live extravagantly are apt to be snobbish (or conceited), and the people who live simply are apt to be vulgar. I prefer the vulgar people to the snobs."

Confucius said, "It is easy to be rich and not haughty; it is difficult to be poor and not grumble."

Confucius said, "When a country is in order, it is a shame to be poor and common man. When a country is in chaos, it is a shame to be rich and an official."

Confucius said, "Can you ever imagine a petty soul serving as a minister of the state? Before he gets his post, he is anxious to get it, and after he has got it, he is anxious about losing it, and if he begins to be anxious about losing it, then there is nothing that he will not do."

Confucius said, "Do not worry about people not knowing your ability, but worry that you have not got it."

Confucius said, "A gentleman blames himself, while a common man blames others."

Confucius said, "If a man would be severe toward himself and generous toward others, he would never arouse resentment."

Confucius said, "A man who does not think and plan long ahead will find trouble right by his door."

Confucius said, "Polished speech often confuses our notion of who is good and who is bad. A man who cannot put up with small losses or disadvantages will often spoil a big plan."

Confucius said, "In talking about a thoroughbred, you do not admire his strength, but admire his temper."

Someone said, "What do you think of repaying evil with kindness?" Confucius replied, "Then what are you going to repay kindness with?" "Repay kindness with kindness, but repay evil with justice (or severity)."

Confucius said, "When you repay kindness with kindness, then the people are encouraged to do good. When you repay evil with evil, then people are warned from doing bad."

Confucius said, "To repay evil with kindness is the sign of a generous character. To repay kindness with evil is the sign of a criminal." (*Liki*, Ch. XXXII.)

Confucius said, "Men are born pretty much alike, but through their habits they gradually grow further and further apart from each other."

Confucius said, "Only the highest and the lowest characters don't change."

Confucius said, "I have seen rice plants that sprout, but don't blossom, and I have seen rice plants that blossom, but don't bear grains."

Confucius said, "Even though a man had the beautiful talent of Duke Chou, but if he were proud and egoistic, he would not be worth looking at."

Confucius said, "If the superior man is not deliberate in his appearance (or conduct), then he is not dignified. Learning prevents one from being narrow-minded. Try to be loyal and faithful as your main principle. Have no friends who are not as good as yourself. When you have mistakes, don't be afraid to correct them."

Confucius said, "When you see a good man, try to emulate his example, and when you see a bad man, search yourself for his faults."

Confucius said, "Well, well! I have never yet seen a person who knows his own faults and accuses himself before himself!"

Confucius said, "Don't criticize other people's faults, criticize your own."

Tsekung said, "What do you think of a person who is not snobbish (or subservient to the great) when he is poor, and not conceited when he is rich?" Confucius replied, "That's fairly good. It would be better if he were happy when he was poor, and had self-discipline when he was rich."

Confucius said, "You can kill the general of an army, but you cannot kill the ambition in a common man."

VI. HUMANISM AND TRUE MANHOOD
Humanism:

Confucius said, "It is man that makes truth great, and not truth that makes man great."

Confucius said, "Truth may not depart from human nature. If what is regarded as truth departs from human nature, it may not be regarded as truth."

Tselu asked about the worship of the celestial and earthly spirits. Confucius said, "We don't know yet how to serve men, how can we know about serving the spirits?" "What about death?" was the next question, and Confucius said, "We don't know yet about life, how can we know about death?"

A certain stable was burned down. On returning from the court, Confucius asked, "Was any man hurt?" And he did not ask about the horses.

The measure of man is man:

Confucius said, "To one who loves to live according to the principles of true manhood without external inducements and who hates all that is contrary to the principles of true manhood without external threats of punishments, all mankind seems but like one man only. Therefore the superior man discusses all questions of conduct on the basis of himself as the standard, and then sets rules for the common people to follow." (*Liki*, Ch. XXXII.)

Confucius said, "True manhood requires a great capacity and the road thereto is difficult to reach. You cannot lift it by your hands and you cannot reach it by walking on foot. He who approaches it to a greater degree than others may already be called 'a true man.' Now is it not a difficult thing for a man to try to reach this standard by sheer effort? Therefore, if the gentleman measures men by the standard of the absolute standard of righteousness, then it is difficult to be a real man. But if he measures men by the standard of man, then the better people will have some standard to go by." (*Liki*, Ch. XXXII.)

Confucius said, "To a man who feels down in his heart that he is happy and natural while acting according to the principles of true manhood, all mankind seems like but one man." (What is true of the feelings of one person will serve as the standard of feelings for all people.) (*Liki*, Ch. XXXII.)

Tsekung asked, "If there is a man here who is a benefactor of mankind and can help the masses, would you call him a true man?" "Why, such a person is not only a true man," said Confucius, "he is a Sage. Even the Emperors Yao and Hsun would fall short of such a standard. Now a true man, wishing to establish his own character, also tries to establish the character of others, and wishing to succeed himself, tries also to help others to succeed. To know how to make the approach from one's neighbors (or from the facts of common, everyday life) is the method or formula for achieving true manhood."

Confucius said, "Is the standard of true manhood so far away, after all? When I want true manhood, there it is right by me."

The Golden Rule:

Chung Kung asked about true manhood, and Confucius replied, "When the true man appears abroad, he feels as if he were receiving distinguished people, and when ruling over the people, he feels as if he were worshipping God. What he does not want done unto himself, he does not do unto others. And so both in the state and in the home, people are satisfied."

Tsekung said, "What I do not want others to do unto me, I do not want to do unto them." Confucius said, "Ah Sze, you cannot do it."

Confucius said, "Ah Ts'an, there is a central principle that runs through all my teachings." "Yes," said Tsengtse. When Confucius left, the disciples asked Tsengtse what he meant, and Tsengtse replied, "It is just the principle of reciprocity (or *shu*)."

Tsekung asked, "Is there one single word that can serve as a principle of conduct for life?" Confucius replied, "Perhaps the word 'reciprocity' (*shu*) will do. Do not do unto others what you do not want others to do unto you."

True manhood:

Confucius said, "For a long time it has been difficult to see examples of true men. Everybody errs a little on the side of his weakness. Therefore it is easy to point out the shortcomings of the true man." (*Liki*, Ch. XXXII.)

Confucius said, "For a long time it has been difficult to find examples of true men. Only the superior man can reach that state. Therefore the superior man does not try to criticize people for what he himself fails in, and he does not put people to shame for what they fail in...." (*Liki*, Ch. XXXII.)

Confucius said, "To find the central clue to our moral being which unites us to the universal order (or to attain central harmony), that indeed is the highest human attainment. For a long time people have seldom been capable of it."

Yen Huei asked about true manhood, and Confucius said, "True manhood consists in realizing your true self and restoring the moral order or discipline (or *li*). If a man can just for one day realize his true self, and restore complete moral discipline, the world will follow him. To be a true man depends on yourself. What has it got to do with others?"

Confucius said, "Humility is near to moral discipline (or *li*); simplicity of character is near to true manhood; and loyalty is near to sincerity of heart. If a man will carefully cultivate these things in his conduct, he may still err a little, but he won't be far from the standard of true manhood. For with humility or a pious attitude, a man seldom commits errors; with sincerity of heart, a man is generally reliable; and with simplicity of character, he is usually generous. You seldom make a mistake when you start off from these points." (*Liki*, Ch. XXXII.)

Confucius said, "Yen Huei's heart does not leave the condition of true manhood for as long as three months. The others are able to live on that level only for a month or for a few days."

Someone said, "Would you call a man who has succeeded in avoiding aggressiveness, pride, resentment and greed a true man?" Confucius said, "I would say that he is a very rare person, but I do not know whether he can be called a true man."

Tsechang asked Confucius: "Secretary Tsewen (of Ch'u) was three times made a secretary and didn't seem to show particular satisfaction at his appointment, and three times he was relieved of his office and did not seem to show any disappointment. And when he was handing over the affairs of his office to his successors, he explained everything to the latter. Now what would you say about such a person?" Confucius said, "I would call him a sincere, faithful person." "Would you say that he is a true man?" "I do not know," said Confucius. "How should I call him a true man?"

Someone said that Chung Kung (a disciple of Confucius) was a true man and that he was not a glib talker. Confucius said, "What is the use of being a glib talker? The more you talk to defend yourself, the more the people hate you. I do not know about his being a true man. What is the use of being a glib talker?"

Count Wu Meng asked if Tselu was a true man, and Confucius said,

"I do not know." On being asked again, Confucius said, "You can put Yu in charge of a country with a thousand carriages and let him take care of its finance. But I do not know about his being a true man." "How about Ch'iu?" Confucius said, "You can put Ch'iu in charge of a township of a thousand families or make him the steward of a household with a hundred carriages (that is, of a minister), but I do not know about his being a true man." "How about Ch'ih (Kunghsi Hua)?" Confucius said, "You can let Ch'ih stand at court, dressed in his official gown and girdle and let him entertain the guests, but I do not know about his being a true man."

Further descriptions of the true man:

Confucius said, "One who is not a true man cannot long stand poverty, nor can he stand prosperity for long. A true man is happy and natural in living according to the principles of true manhood, but a wise man thinks it is advantageous to do so."

Confucius said, "Only a true man knows how to love people and how to hate people."

Confucius said, "How can the superior man keep up his reputation when he departs from the level of the true man? The superior man never departs from the level of true manhood for the time of a single meal. In his most casual moments, he lives in it, and in the most compromising circumstances, he still lives in it."

Confucius said, "If a man is not a true man, what is the use of rituals? If a man is not a true man, what is the use of music?"

Confucius said, "The wise man has no perplexities, the true man has no sorrow, and the brave man has no fear."

Confucius said, "A true man is very slow to talk." Someone asked, "Can a man who is slow to talk then be called a true man?" Confucius said, "Because it is so difficult for a man to do what he says, of course he would be very slow to talk."

VII. THE SUPERIOR MAN AND THE INFERIOR MAN

Confucius said, "The superior man understands what is right; the inferior man understands what will sell."

Confucius said, "The superior man loves his soul; the inferior man loves his property. The superior man always remembers how he was punished for his mistakes; the inferior man always remembers what presents he got."

Confucius said, "The superior man is liberal towards other's opinions, but does not completely agree with them; the inferior man completely agrees with others' opinions, but is not liberal toward them."

Confucius said, "The superior man is firm, but does not fight; he mixes easily with others, but does not form cliques."

Confucius said, "The superior man blames himself; the inferior man blames others."

Confucius said, "The superior man is easy to serve, but difficult to please, for he can be pleased by what is right, and he uses men according to their individual abilities. The inferior man is difficult to serve, but easy to please, for you can please him (by catering to his weaknesses) without necessarily being right, and when he comes to using men, he demands perfection."

Confucius said, "You can put a superior man in an important position with large discretionary powers, but you cannot give him a nice little job; you can give an inferior man a nice little job, but you cannot put him in an important position with great discretionary powers."

Confucius said, "The superior man is not one who is good for only one particular kind of position."

Confucius said, "The superior man is broad-minded toward all and not a partisan; the inferior man is a partisan, but not broad-minded toward all."

Confucius and his followers had to go for days without food in Ch'en, and some of his followers felt ill and were confined to bed. Tselu came to see Confucius in low spirits and asked, "Does the superior man also land in difficulties?" Confucius said, "Yes, the superior man also sometimes falls into difficulties, but when an inferior man falls into difficulties, he is likely to do anything."

Confucius said, "The superior man attends to the spiritual things and not to his livelihood. You let him cultivate a farm, and he will be starved, but if you let him attend to his studies, be will find riches in it. The superior man does not worry about his poverty, but worries about the spiritual things."

Confucius said, "The superior man is always candid and at ease (with himself or others); the inferior man is always worried about something."

Confucius said, "The superior man develops upwards; the inferior man develops downwards."

Confucius said, "The superior man is dignified, but not proud; the inferior man is proud, but no dignified."

Confucius said, "The superior man keeps to the standard of right, but does not (necessarily) keep his promise."

Ssŭma Niu asked Confucius about being a gentleman, and Confucius replied, "A gentleman has no worry and no fear." "Does having no worry and no fear then constitute a gentleman?" Confucius said, "If he looks within himself and is sure that he has done right, what does he have to fear or worry about?"

Confucius said, "The superior man goes through his life without anyone preconceived course of action or any taboo. He merely decides for the moment what is the right thing to do."

Confucius said, "The superior man doesn't insist on good food and good lodging. He is attentive to his duties and careful in his speech, and he finds a great man and follows him as his guide. Such a person may be called a lover of learning."

Confucius said, "A scholar who intends to follow the truth and is ashamed of his poor dress and poor food is not worth talking to."

Confucius said, "A scholar who is in love with living comforts is not worthy to be called a scholar."

Confucius said, "A man who serves his king and three times finds his advice rejected and still does not leave the country, is hanging on to his post for the sake of the salary. Even though he says that it is not the salary that attracts him, I won't believe him."(*Liki*, Ch. XXXII.)

Confucius said, "A gentleman is ashamed that his words are better than his deeds."

Confucius said, "A gentleman is careful about three things: In his youth, when his blood is strong, he is careful about sex. When he is grown up, and his blood is full, he is careful about getting into a fight (or struggle in general). When he is old and his blood is getting thinner, he is careful about money." (A young man loves women; a middle-aged man loves struggle; and an old man loves money.)

VIII. THE MEAN AS THE IDEAL CHARACTER AND TYPES OF PERSONS THAT CONFUCIUS HATED

The people of the mean:

Confucius said, "Since I cannot find people who follow the Mean (or Golden Mean) to teach, I suppose I will have to work with those who are brilliant or erratic (*k'uang*) and those who are a little dull but careful (*chuan*). The brilliant but erratic persons are always ready to go forward (or are too active), and the dull but careful persons always hold themselves back (or are not active enough)."

Confucius said, "The goody-goodies are the thieves of virtue."

Confucius said (when he was wandering in Ch'en and decided to return to his state to devote himself to editing books and teaching), "Let us go home! The scholars of our state are brilliant but erratic, but they are anxious to go forward, and have not lost their original simplicity of character."

Tsekung asked whether Shih (Tsechang) or Shang (Tsehsia) was the better man. Confucius said, "Ah Shih goes a little too far (or is above the normal) and Ah Shang doesn't go far enough (or is a little below the normal)." "Then is Ah Shih a better person?" Confucius said, "To go a little too far is as bad as not going far enough."

Confucius said to Tsehsia, "You must be a gentleman scholar and not a petty scholar."

Confucius said, "When a man has more solid worth than polish, he appears uncouth, and when a man has more polish than solid worth, he appears urbane. The proper combination of solid worth and polish alone makes a gentleman."

Confucius said, "The earlier generations were primitive or uncouth people in the matter of ritual and music; the later generations are refined (literally "gentlemen") in the matter of ritual and music. But if I were to choose between the two, I would follow the people of the earlier generations."

Types of persons that Confucius hated:

Confucius said, "The ancient people have three kinds of faults, and nowadays we haven't even got them. The ancient people who were impulsive were just unconventional in their ways, but today the impulsive people indulge themselves. The ancient people who were correct and smug were at least austere and careful in their conduct, but today the smug people are always condemning other people and are bad-tempered. The ancient lower class were simple and honest souls, but today the lower class are a deceitful lot."

Tsekung asked, "Does the superior man also have certain things that he hates?" "Yes, there are things that the superior man hates," said Confucius. "He hates those who like to criticize people or reveal their weaknesses. He hates those who, in the position of inferiors, like to malign or spread rumors about those in authority. He hates those who are chivalrous and headstrong but are not restrained by propriety. He hates those who are sure of themselves and are narrow-minded." "But what do you hate?" asked Sze. "I hate those who like to spy on others and think they are very clever. I hate those who think they are brave when they are merely unruly. And I hate the wily persons who pretend to be honest gentlemen."

Confucius said, "A man who is impulsive and headstrong without having the virtue of simple honesty, who doesn't know a thing and has not enough wit to speak or behave cautiously, or who has no particular ability and withal has not the virtue of honesty or faithfulness—why, there is nothing to be done about such a person."

Confucius said, "I hate things that resemble the real things but are not the real things. I hate cockles because they get mixed up with the corn. I hate the ingratiating fellows, because they get mixed up with the good men. I hate the glib talkers because they confuse us with honest people. I hate the music of Cheng, because it brings confusion into classical music. I hate the purple color, because it confuses us with the red color. I hate the goody-goodies because they confuse us with the virtuous people." (Mencius).

Confucius said, "A man who appears dignified and austere but is all hollow and weak inside seems to me to be like a little petty burglar who slips into the house through a hole at night."

Confucius said, "Women and the uneducated people are most difficult to deal with. When you are familiar with them, they become cheeky, and when you ignore them, they resent it."

Confucius said, "I hate the garrulous people."

Confucius said, "A glib talker with an ingratiating appearance is seldom a gentleman."

Confucius said, "The gentleman does not judge a person entirely by his words. Therefore in a cultured world, we have flowery conduct, and in an uncultured world, we have flowery speeches." (*Liki*, Ch. XXXII.)

IX. GOVERNMENT

The moral ideal of government:

Confucius said, "Guide the people with governmental measures and control or regulate them by the threat of punishment, and the people will try to keep out of jail, but will have no sense of honor or shame. Guide the people by virtue and control or regulate them by *li*, and the people will have a sense of honor and respect."

Confucius said, "When the kingdom of Ch'i moves a step forward, it will have reached the culture of the kingdom of Lu, and when the kingdom of Lu moves a step forward, it will have reached the stage of true civilization."

Confucius said, "In presiding over lawsuits, I'm as good as any man. The thing is to aim so that there should be no lawsuits."

Someone asked Confucius, "Why don't you go into the government?" Confucius replied, "Doesn't the *Book of History* speak about the good son? When the sovereign is a good son, and a good brother, and applies the same principles to the government of the nation, that is also what we call government. Why should I go into the government?"

Yutse said, "We seldom find a man who is a good son and a good brother that is disrespectful to authority, and we never find a man who is not disrespectful to authority wanting to start a rebellion."

Government by moral example:

Confucius said, "A sovereign who governs a nation by virtue is like the North Polar Star, which remains in its place and the other stars revolve around it."

Baron K'ang Ch'i asked Confucius concerning government, and Confucius replied, "Government is merely setting things right. When you yourself lead them by the right example, who dares to go astray?"

Baron K'ang Ch'i asked Confucius concerning government, saying, "If I kill off the bad citizens, and associate with the good citizens, what do you think?" Confucius replied, "What's the need of killing off people on the part of a ruler of a country? If you desire what is good, the people will become good also. The character of the ruler is like wind, and the character of the common people is like grass, and the grass bends in the direction of the wind."

Confucius said, "When the ruler himself does what is right, he will have influence over the people without giving commands, and when the ruler himself does not do what is right, all his commands will be of no avail."

Confucius said, "If a ruler rectifies his own conduct, government is an easy matter, and if he does not rectify his own conduct, how can he rectify others?"

Factors of government:

Tsekung asked about government, and Confucius replied: "People must have sufficient to eat; there must be a sufficient army; and there must be confidence of the people in the ruler." "If you are forced to give up one of these three objectives, what would you go without first?" asked Tsekung. Confucius said, "I would go without the army first." "And if you were forced to go without one of the two remaining factors, what would you rather go without?" asked Tsekung again. "I would rather go without sufficient food for the people. There have always been deaths in every generation since man lived, but a nation cannot exist without confidence in its ruler."

X. ON EDUCATION, RITUAL AND POETRY

Confucius said, "Education begins with poetry, is strengthened through proper conduct and consummated through music."

Confucius said, "The gentleman broadens himself by scholarship or learning, and then regulates himself by *li* (proper conduct or moral discipline). Then he will not fall away from the proper principles."

Yutse said, "Among the functions of *li*, the most valuable is that it establishes a sense of harmony. This is the most beautiful heritage of the ancient kings. It is a guiding principle for all things, big and small. If things do not go right, and you are bent only on having social harmony (or peace) without regulating the society by the pattern of *li* (or the principle of social order), still things won't go right."

Confucius said, "We are saying all the time, '*Li! Li!*' Does *li* mean merely a collection of jades and silks (in ceremonial use)? We are saying all the time 'Music! Music!' Does music merely mean playing about with drums and bells?"

Tseshia asked (concerning a passage in the *Book of Songs*), "What is the meaning of the passage, 'She has a winning smile, and her eyes are so clear and bright. Her dress is of a colored design on a plain background'?" Confucius said, "In painting, we must have a plain background." "Does that mean that the ceremonial forms of *li* must be based on a background of simplicity of character?" Confucius said, "Now you have contributed a fresh thought, Ah Shang! You are worthy to study the *Book of Songs*."

Lin Fang asked concerning the foundation of *li*, and Confucius replied, "You are asking an important question! In this matter of rituals or ceremony, rather than be extravagant, be simple. In funeral ceremonies, rather than be perfunctory, it is more important to have the real sentiment of sorrow."

Confucius said, "If you have the wisdom to perceive a truth, but have not the manhood to keep to it, you will lose it again, though you have discovered it. If you have the wisdom to perceive a truth, and the true manhood to keep to it, and fail to preserve decorum in your public appearance, you will not gain the people's respect for authority. If you have the wisdom to perceive a truth, the manhood to keep to it, and have decorum of appearance, but fail to be imbued with the spirit of *li* (or social discipline) in your actions or conduct, it is also not satisfactory."

Confucius said, "Ah Sze is worthy to discuss the *Book of Songs* with me. I tell him something, and he comes up with a fresh suggestion."

Confucius said, "One phrase will characterize all the three hundred poems (actually three hundred and five), and that is: Keep the heart right."

Ch'en K'ang asked Poyu (or Li, the name of Confucius' only son, meaning "a carp"), "Is there anything special that you were taught by your father?" Poyu replied, "No. One day he was standing alone and I ran past the court, and he asked me, 'Have you learned poetry?' And I said, 'Not yet.' He said, 'If you don't study poetry, your language will not be polished.' So I went back and studied poetry. Another day he was standing alone, and I went past the court, and he said to me, 'Have you studied the ceremonies?' And I said, 'Not yet.' And he said, 'If you don't study the ceremonies, you have no guide for your conduct.' And I went back and studied the ceremonies. I was taught to study these two things." Ch'en K'ang came away quite pleased and said, "I asked him one question and learned three things. I learned what Confucius said about poetry. I learned what he said about ceremonies. And I learned that the Master taught his own son in exactly the same way as he taught his disciples (was not partial to his son)."

Confucius said, "Reading without thinking gives one a disorderly mind, and thinking without reading makes one flighty (or unbalanced)."

Confucius said, "Isn't it a great pleasure to learn and relearn again?"

Confucius said, "A man who goes over what he has already learned and gains some new understanding from it is worthy to be a teacher."

Confucius said, "That type of scholarship which is bent on remembering things in order to answer people's questions does not qualify one to be a teacher."

Confucius said, "The ancient scholars studied for their own sake; today the scholars study for the sake of others (out of obligations to their teachers, their parents, etc.)."

Confucius said, "Ah Yu, have you heard of the six sayings about the six shortcomings?" "No," said Tselu. "Sit down, then, and I will tell you. If a man loves kindness, but doesn't love study, his shortcoming will be ignorance. If a man loves wisdom but does not love study, his shortcoming will be having fanciful or unsound ideas. If a man loves honesty and does not love study, his shortcoming will be a tendency to spoil or upset things.

If a man loves simplicity but does not love study, his shortcoming will be sheer following of routine. If a man loves courage and does not love study, his shortcoming will be unruliness or violence. If a man loves decision of character and does not love study, his shortcoming will be self-will or headstrong belief in himself."

Confucius said, "Those who are born wise are the highest type of people; those who become wise through learning come next; those who learn by sheer diligence and industry, but with difficulty, come after that. Those who are slow to learn, but still won't learn, are the lowest type of people."

Confucius said, "The young people should be good sons at home, polite and respectful in society; they should be careful in their conduct and faithful, love the people, and associate themselves with the kind people. If after learning all this, they still have energy left, let them read books."

第六章　儒家社会秩序三论（一）
——《礼记·经解》第二十六

礼实际上包括了中国古代社会上整个道德宗教的组织，而具体见之于宗教性崇拜、祭祀婚丧等庆典的仪式，以及一般的社会交往的礼俗，由历史上的记载即可见出，并且以孔子的哲理为基础。

以下包含三篇论说，为《礼记》中之第二十六《经解》，第二十七《哀公问》，第九《礼运》。此数篇文字精练，但文章中有数处很难判定是孔子本人的话，还是写定此数章的作者所说的话。实际上，此三篇皆论礼在哲学上之重要。关于礼字，在本书前之导言中已稍作解释，在此三篇内又再三将礼字看做是为政的要件，为政的基本，绝不可只看做遵守仪礼之意，而是代表社会秩序与社会法规的哲理。礼实际上包括了中国古代社会上整个道德宗教的组织，而具体见之于宗教性崇拜、祭祀婚丧等庆典的仪式，以及一般的社会交往的礼俗，由历史上的记载即可见出，并且以孔子的哲理为基础。礼教目的在于恢复古代的封建制度，使尊卑阶级制度显而易见，不过这种组织的原理又推展到家庭、社会、政治的基本关系上去。

因此，礼之目的，是将社会地位与明确的义务，予以清楚而简明的解释之后，使之构成一套完整的道德秩序，以为国家的政治秩序之道德基础。这种和谐的人际关系的哲理，对中国仍然有其益处——因为它仍然是中国社会风气的基石；当然，孔子志在恢复的古代的封建制度，则是不合时宜了。

不过，必须说明的是，就孔子所说的封建制度，分明是具有宗教性质，非常讲究其哲学的意义，祭祀上的规矩及其他礼节仪式。《礼记》上若干章全部讨论礼服式样，描写祭器，有七八章单讨论丧礼（此数章在《大戴礼记》中缺）。但是耐人寻味的是，礼的观念在论宗教崇拜仪式之余，却不知不觉延伸至农村中的舞蹈、打猎、宴饮、射箭，及一般的社交应酬。由此显而易见礼之含义包括了社会秩序、社会规范、典礼仪式的社会传统。孔子曾提醒弟子子张，他说礼并不在使用那些祭器，正如音乐并不在打钟打鼓而已；礼乐来自一种心境，而且创造一种心境，是在举行此仪礼时内心的虔敬，是在演奏音乐时内心的幸福和谐。

其实，这只是儒家对宗教崇拜仪式的虔诚所致，如祭天，祭地，皇家的祭祖、祭日、祭月、祭山、祭河，祭灶神，祭房子的西南角，以及所有的民间节日，这都是由于宗教心境的虔诚的缘故，所以我常常想把中国礼字在英文里只译成religion（宗教），不过只是想如此译而已，并未真如此译。将礼字译成宗教在以下句中非常适宜，如"博我以文，约我以礼"（这是孔子言求仁之法）。礼字内的宗教特点是毋庸置疑的。甚至今天中国人还把儒家的道理称之为"礼教"。我们在此还是要避免"宗教"（religion）这一名词，因为很容易令人联想到基督教，而基督教是把宗教的与世俗的之间划有鸿沟的。此一分别在中国古代并没有。当然，在墨子的理论中也没有此一区别，墨子把所有的社会行为与宗教行为，都看作是宗教性的。现代人已不生活在那种神权社会或半神权社会，也就难以了解"典礼的选择""杀牲""视察动物""饭前的净手"等与宗教有何关系。现在把饭前洗手只视为是讲求卫生了。但是在墨子看来，卫生也是宗教，因为宗教是无所不包的。把礼字译为宗教当然是有点儿费解，但是在儒家思想里确实如此。从心理上说，人的宗教性的心境，在希伯来文说是"敬畏上帝"，在基督教里说为"虔诚"，其实也是儒家这个宗教在人生活中的目的，不过这种心境在儒家称之为"敬"，在日常生活中表现在对社会秩序与道德纪律上。我常把儒家的"敬"译成英文的piety（虔敬），因为我觉得译为respect是完全不妥的。

儒家"礼"字的中心观念的含义可作以下解释：作宗教解，作社会秩序原则解（其中包括宗教），作理性化的封建秩序解，作社会、道德、宗教习俗的整体解（一如孔子以之教人，一如孔子之予以理性化）。于是，又作一套历史学问解。又可解作宗教崇拜，国之仪礼，民间节庆，婚礼，丧礼，男女到达成年时之加冠与梳发的仪礼（古礼男人成年为二十岁，女为十五岁），军中纪律，学校制度，男女的性行为，家庭生活，饮食，运动（尤指射箭、驾车、打猎），音乐，舞蹈。礼也可解作意义分明的社会关系，彼此以适当的态度相对待：为父母者要慈爱，为子女者要孝顺；为弟者要敬兄长；为兄长者要爱护弟弟；对友人要忠诚；为臣民者要敬尊长；为首长者要仁爱。礼是一种诚敬的心境，是行为的道德纪律。作为人行为的原则时，是指处世行事皆得其宜（propriety）。作为广义的社会原则解时，其义为"物皆有序"，为"万物各得其所"。是礼仪，是遵守法则制度。是继往开来。最后，是礼貌，是风度。

我深信，孔子在当代声誉之隆，都是由于他之传授古礼以及他那套丰富的史学知识之所致。易言之，就是说，他所知之博，正是他同代的一般学者所望尘莫及的，这才使人对他如此之尊敬。人总是对自己所不知的怀有敬意。一个人越多谈论众人所不知者，众人对他所怀的敬意也越大。孔子若徒有机智而缺乏实学，充其量，他只不过像英国的萧伯纳（Bernard Shaw），切斯特顿（G．K．Chesterton），绝不能成为托马斯·阿奎那（Thomas Aquinas）。总之，历史方面的学问之于孔子，正犹如美国语文那套学问之于门肯（H．L．Mencken）一样，那套专门学问都是他们受人仰望不可或缺的条件。

【原文】

孔子曰："入其国，其教可知也。其为人也，温柔敦厚，《诗》教也。疏通知远，《书》教也。广博易良，《乐》教也。絜静精微，《易》教也。恭俭庄敬，《礼》教也。属辞比事，《春秋》教也。故《诗》之失愚，《书》之失诬，《乐》之失奢，《易》之失贼，《礼》之失烦，《春秋》之失乱。其为人也，温柔敦厚而不愚，则深于《诗》者也。疏通知远而不诬，则深于《书》者也。广博易良而不奢，则深于《乐》者也。絜静精微而不贼，则深于《易》者也。恭俭庄敬而不烦，则深于《礼》者也。属辞比事而不乱，则深于《春秋》者也。"

【语译】

孔子说："到一个国家，就可以了解这个国家的教化。国民若温柔敦厚，便是诗的教化。若开通而富有历史知识，便是历史的教化。若爽快而平和，那就是音乐的教化。若宁静而敏于观察，那就是《易经》的教化。若恭俭庄敬，那就是礼的教化。若巧于言辞，长于判别，便是《春秋》的教化。所以，诗的教化的缺点，是使人弱于理性。历史的教化的缺点，是使人失之于妄信传闻。音乐教化的缺点是使人奢侈放纵。哲学教化的缺点是使人狡猾奸诈。礼之教化的缺点是烦琐复杂。《春秋》教化的缺点是乱法悖德。人若是温柔敦厚，而不缺乏理性，他是深于诗教了。若胸襟开朗，熟于历史，但不盲信逸闻故事，则是深于书教了。慷慨温和而不奢侈放纵，则是深于乐教了。若宁静深思，敏于观察，而不狡猾奸诈，就是深于哲学的研究了。若是谦恭斯文，习于节俭，而不烦琐复杂，则是深于礼教了。若是巧于辞令，善于譬喻，而不惑于流俗悖乱，则是深于《春秋》的教化了。"

【原文】

天子者，与天地参，故德配天地，兼利万物，与日月并明，明照四海而不遗微小。其在朝廷，则道仁圣礼义之序；燕处，则听雅颂之音；行步，则有环佩之声；升车，则有鸾和之音。居处有礼，进退有度，百官得其宜，万事得其序。《诗》云："淑人君子，其仪不忒。其仪不忒，正是四国。"此之谓也。发号出令而民说，谓之和。上下相亲，谓之仁。民不求其所欲而得之，谓之信。除去天地之害，谓之义。义与信，和与仁，霸王之器也。有活民之意而无其器，则不成。

【语译】

天子的地位与天地同等，其有利于万物之运行演化上之支配作用，也与天地相同。他与日月同发光辉，照耀四季，虽微细不遗。在朝廷上，他与群臣讨论道德之理想与社会的秩序。在家则听雅颂之乐，步行之时，发环佩之声；升车时，发出鸾凤和鸣声。在家庭生活上，其举止也是彬彬有礼。因此，由他一人之举止言谈，百官也得以自知其职分，社会上亦遵从正当之礼法。《诗经》上说："在仪表与行为上，有德之君是完美无瑕的，因此是为国民之楷模。"对他的命令，国人心悦诚服，此即吾人所谓之"和睦"，或是"和谐"。执政者与国民互相亲爱，即所谓"仁"。国民不必表示有所要求即能得到，自然对国家有"信心"。君王为民众兴利除弊，他的施政即合乎"义"。义与信，是霸主为政之法；和与仁，是王者的为政之法。为政者若徒具信心，而不用这等方法，也不能达到目的。

【原文】

礼之于正国也，犹衡之于轻重也，绳墨之于曲直也，规矩之于方圆也。故衡诚县，不可欺以轻重。绳墨诚陈，不可欺以曲直。规矩诚设，不可欺以方圆。君子审礼，不可诬以奸诈。

是故隆礼由礼，谓之有方之士。不隆礼，不由礼，谓之无方之民。敬让之道也，故以奉宗庙则敬；以入朝廷，则贵贱有位；以处室家，则父子亲、兄弟和；以处乡里，则长幼有序。孔子曰："安上治民，莫善于礼。"此之谓也。

【语译】

礼法制度之于国家，犹如秤之称轻重，木匠之用绳墨之定直线，规矩之定方圆。秤正确无误，在轻重上人不受欺骗；绳墨无误，则线条弯直不会错误；规矩无误，则方圆不会错误；为帝王者熟于礼法制度，则不为奸诈所欺。所以遵守礼法之民称之为方正之民，不遵守礼法之民称之为无礼法之民。

礼是互相敬让之道。在宗庙祭祀时，要虔敬；在朝廷上要百官尊卑有序；在家庭生活上，则父子亲爱，兄弟和睦；在乡里聚会上则长幼有序。孔子说："统治者要安于上位以治理百姓，没有再善于遵守礼法的了。"

【原文】

故朝觐之礼，所以明君臣之义也。聘问之礼，所以使诸侯相尊敬也。丧祭之礼，所以明臣子之恩也。乡饮酒之礼，所以明长幼之序也。婚姻之礼，所以明男女之别也。夫礼，禁乱之所由生，犹坊止水之所自来也。故以旧坊为无所用而坏之者，必有水败。以旧礼为无所用而去之者，必有乱患。

故婚姻之礼废，则夫妇之道苦，而淫辟之罪多矣。乡饮酒之礼废，则长幼之序失，而争斗之狱繁矣。丧祭之礼废，则臣子之恩薄，而倍死忘生者众矣。聘觐之礼废，则君臣之位失，诸侯之行恶，而倍畔侵陵之败起矣。故礼之教化也微，其止邪也于未形，使人日徙善远罪而不自知也。是以先王隆之也。《易》曰："君子慎始。差若毫厘，缪以千里。"此之谓也。

【语译】

朝见皇帝的礼仪，是用表示君臣的身份。各国使节之交互访问，是用以表示各国元首之间的相互尊敬。丧礼与祭礼是用以表示为人臣及为人子者的感恩。乡村中饮酒之礼是表示长辈与晚辈的上下辈分。婚姻之礼是表示男女两性的区别。礼是防乱于未然，犹如堤防是防御水灾。若以为以前的堤防无用而拆除之，必有水患。若以为以前的礼教无用而废除之，必起祸乱。所以婚姻之礼一经荒废，则夫妇之间的生活必有苦恼，而淫邪之罪便会发生不已。乡村饮酒之礼一经荒废，则长幼之间的辈分便失其顺序，而争夺涉讼之事必多。丧祭之礼废除，为臣与子者对父母与君之感恩必致微薄，后辈对死者必致背叛，滋肆放纵。朝见皇帝之礼荒废之后，君臣的身份必致失去，各国元首必致傲慢不法，侵夺交战必然发生。

因此可见，礼的教化作用虽然不易见出，但能防止邪恶于未然，并且使人不知不觉中趋善避恶，所以前代的帝王无不重视礼的教化。《易经》上说："为君者当慎乎始。开始时若有些微的差错，以后便错误不堪了。"正是此意。

Chapter Six **FIRST DISCOURSE: ON EDUCATION THROUGH THE SIX CLASSICS**
(*Chingchieh*, *Liki*, Chapter XXVI)

The following three discourses constitute Chapters XXVI, XXVII and IX of *Liki*. There is a stylistic elaboration in these records and in certain places it is impossible to decide whether the words were those of Confucius or those of the authors of the different chapters. Practically all three discourses deal with the philosophic significance of *li*. As has been partly explained in the introduction, this conception of *li*, which is again and again said in these discourses to be the essence, the *sine qua non*, the foundation, or the indispensable principle, of government, cannot merely mean the observance of ritual, but represents a philosophy of social order and social control. *Li* practically covers the entire social, moral and religious structure of ancient Chinese society, as shown and regulated by forms of religious worship and social intercourse, revealed by history and rationalized by Confucius. Specifically, its aim was to restore the ancient feudal order, with a clear hierarchy of ranks, but this principle of social order was extended and broadened to cover the essential human relationships in the family and social and political life. It was therefore to establish a complete moral order in the nation by a clear and simple, but sharp, definition of social status and its specific obligations, thus providing the moral basis for political order. This philosophy of harmony of essential human relationships remains good today for modern China—in fact it is the foundation for the Chinese *ethos*—while the ancient feudal order which was Confucius' aim to restore is definitely out of date.

It must be noted, however, that the feudal system, as Confucius conceived it, was of a clearly religious character and was very much occupied with discussions of the philosophic meaning, as well as the actual rules and practices, of public worship. Whole chapters, for instance, in the *Liki* are devoted to the discussion of ceremonial robes, and to a description of sacrificial vessels, and seven or eight chapters cover the funeral rites alone (absent in the "Great Tai" collection). But then the curious aspect of it was, the conception of *li* dealt with the rites of religious worship at one end, and imperceptibly extended to the rites of village dance and hunting and drinking and archery and general social intercourse at the other end. Hence it is easy to see why the conception of *li* embodies at the same time a philosophy of social order and social control and a historical tradition of rites and ceremonies. Confucius himself warned his disciple Tsechang that *li* did not consist in playing about with sacrificial vessels, just as music did not consist in the mere beating of bells and drums; but that both ritual and music emanated from, and created, a state of mind, a state of God-fearing piety in the performance of ritual and a state of happiness and harmony in the performance of music.

In fact, such was the Confucian preoccupation with the rituals of religious worship—worship of Heaven, of Earth, of Imperial ancestors, of the sun and moon, and mountains and rivers, the kitchen god, the god of the southwestern corner of the house, and all folk festivals—and such was its preoccupation with the religious state of mind that I have often been tempted to translate *li* as merely "religion," which I have not done. Such a translation would make it perfect in passages like the following: "Broaden your knowledge with learning, and then control your conduct with religion," and "Realize your true self and return to religion" (a formula for achieving true manhood given by Confucius). The religious character of *li* cannot be doubted, and the Chinese have actually called Confucianism "the religion of *li*." a current term even today. But the term "religion" must be avoided here, because it suggests a type of religion such as we see in Christianity, which draws a sharp distinction between religious and secular affairs. Such a distinction was not made in ancient China, and certainly not in the laws of Moses, where all laws of social, as well as religious, conduct were regarded as of a religious character. Modern men no longer live in that age of theocracy or semi-theocracy, and it is difficult for them to realize what the ceremonial selection, killing, and inspection of animals and ceremonial washing of hands before eating their meat had to do with "religion." We delegate the washing of hands before meals strictly to the sphere of "hygiene." But for Moses, hygiene was also religion, for religion was all-inclusive. Such was exactly the position of Confucianism. Were it not so difficult to bear in mind this interpretation of "religion," there would be no objection to simply rendering *li* as the "religion" of Confucianism as Confucius taught it. Psychologically, the religious condition of mind—the Hebrew "fear of God" and the Christian "piety"—was also the aim of the Confucian religion in man's personal life, but again this state of mind, expressed as *ching* and usually translated as "respect," included both the condition of religious piety at worship and the God-fearing attitude in common, everyday life, as seen in respect for social order and moral discipline. I have therefore often translated *ching* by the word "piety," for I have often found the term "respect" wholly inadequate.

Li, the central conception of Confucian teachings, therefore, means the following things: It means religion; it means the general principle of social order, religion included; it means the rationalized feudal order; it means the entire body of social, moral and religious practices, as taught and rationalized by Confucius. Consequently, it also means historical scholarship. It means the study of the ritualism of religious worship, state ceremonies, folk festivals, the marriage ceremony, funerals, "capping" and "coiffure" ceremonies for boys and girls reaching maturity (at the age of twenty for boys and fifteen for girls), army discipline, the educational system, conduct of the sexes and home life, eating and drinking and sports (especially archery, carriage driving, and the hunt), music and dance. It means a system of well-defined social relationships with definite attitudes towards one another, love in the parents, filial piety in the children, respect in the younger brothers, friendliness in the elder brothers, loyalty among friends, respect for authority among subjects and benevolence in the rulers. It means the mental state of piety. It means moral discipline in man's personal conduct. As a broad principle of personal conduct, it means "propriety" in everything, or doing the proper thing. As a broad social principle, it means "the order of things," or "everything in its right place." It means ritualism and the observance of forms. It means continuity with the past. Finally, it means courtesy and good manners.

I have the definite feeling that it was the teaching of *li* and this tremendous body of historic scholarship that was back of Confucius' great prestige in his times. In other words, he knew so many things that the average scholars of his day did not know about—the usual basis for "respect." The public always respect what they don't understand. The more you talk about what most people don't understand, the greater is their respect for you. With his wit and without his scholarship, Confucius would have been at best a Bernard Shaw, or a G. K. Chesterton, instead of a Thomas Aquinas. After all, this body of historic scholarship was to Confucius what "the American language" is to H. L. Mencken—within the scope of their respective personalities.

FIRST DISCOURSE

Confucius said: When I enter a country, I can easily tell its type of culture. When the people are gentle and kind and simple-hearted, that shows the teaching of poetry. When people are broad-minded and acquainted with the past, that shows the teaching of history. When the people are generous and show a good disposition, that shows the teaching of music. When the people are quiet and thoughtful, and show a sharp power of observation, that shows the teaching of the philosophy of mutations (*Book of Changes*). When the people are humble and respectful and frugal in their habits, that shows the teaching of *li* (the principle of social order). When the people are cultivated in their speech, ready with expressions and analogies, that shows the teaching of prose, or *Spring and Autumn*. The danger in the teaching of poetry is that people remain ignorant, or too simple-hearted. The danger in the teaching of history is that people may be filled with incorrect legends and stories of events. The danger in the teaching of music is that the people grow extravagant. The danger in the teaching of philosophy is that the people become crooked. The danger in the teaching of *li* is that the rituals become too elaborate. And the danger in the teaching of *Spring and Autumn*, is that the people get a sense of the prevailing moral chaos. When a man is kind and gentle and simple-hearted, and yet not ignorant, we may be sure he is deep in the study of poetry. When a man is broad-minded and acquainted with the past, and yet not filled with incorrect legends or stories of events, we may be sure he is deep in the study of history. When a man is generous and shows a good disposition and yet not extravagant in his personal habits, we may be sure he is deep in the study of music. When a man is quiet and thoughtful and shows a sharp power of observation, and yet is not crooked, we may be sure that he is deep in the study of philosophy. When a man is humble and polite and frugal in his personal habits and yet not full of elaborate ceremonies, we may be sure he is deep in the study of *li*. And when a man is cultivated in his speech, ready with expressions and analogies and yet is not influenced by the picture of the prevailing moral chaos, we may be sure that he is deep in the study of *Spring* and *Autumn*.

The Emperor ranks in his position with the Heaven and the Earth, and therefore his moral function or significance is equal to that of the Heaven and the Earth in presiding over the course of the myriad things for their benefit. He shines with the sun and the moon, and casts his light over the Four Seas, not excluding the smallest objects. At the court, he discusses the ideal of moral manhood and the principles of social order. At home, he listens to the music of *ya* (classical songs) and *sung* (sacred anthems). When he walks on foot, we hear the jingle of jade hangings and when he mounts a carriage, we hear the music of "phoenix bells." His home life is decorous and his deportment is in accordance with good form. Thus through him the officials find their proper functions and the entire course of social life finds its order. The *Book of Songs says*, "The virtuous sovereign is immaculate in his external conduct and appearance, and being immaculate in his external conduct and appearance, he serves as the example for the country." When he gets willing obedience to his commands, he achieves what we call "harmony" in the nation. When the rulers and the ruled are kind and friendly to each other, he achieves what we call "an atmosphere of friendliness." When people are enabled to get what they want, without having to ask for it, he achieves what we call "confidence" in the nation. And when he removes the causes of unhappiness in his people, he achieves what we call "decent living" in the nation. "General harmony" and "an atmosphere of friendliness" are the means by which the rulers by force (*pa*) and the rulers by virtue (*wang*) rule their countries. With the determined purpose, but without these means, of ruling the country, they will not be able to attain their object.

　　Li, the principle of social order, is to a country what scales are to weight and what the carpenter's guideline is to straightness, and what the square and the compasses are to squares and circles. Therefore, when the scales are exact, one cannot be deceived in respect to weight; when the guideline is properly laid, one cannot be deceived in respect to straightness; when the squares and compasses are properly used, one cannot be deceived in respect to the right angle and the circular line; and when the sovereign is familiar with the principle of social order (*li*), he can not be deceived by cunning and crooked manipulations. Therefore, a people who respect and follow *li* are called "a people with a definite principle," and a people who do not respect and follow *li* are called "a people without a definite principle."

Li is the principle of mutual respect and courtesy. Therefore when it is applied to worship at the temples, we have piety; when it is applied to the court, we have order in the official ranks; when applied to the home, we have affection between parents and children and harmony between brothers; when applied to the village, we have respect for order between the elders and the juniors. That is the meaning of Confucius' saying that "there is nothing better than *li* for the maintaining of authority and the governing of the people."

Therefore, the rituals concerning a court audience are for the purpose of defining the proper relationships between the rulers and the ministers. The rituals of exchange of visits by diplomats are for the purpose of maintaining mutual respect among the rulers of the different states. The funeral ceremonies and rituals of sacrifice are for the purpose of showing the gratitude of children and subjects. The ceremonies of "the village wine feast" are for the purpose of defining order and discipline between the elders and the juniors. The marriage ceremonies are for the purpose of defining the distinction between the sexes.

Li, or the principle of social order, prevents the rise of moral or social chaos as a dam prevents flood. Just as people who think that they can destroy an old dam because they think it is useless will certainly meet a flood disaster, so will a people who do away with the old principle of social order because they think it is useless certainly meet a moral disaster. It follows, therefore, that when marriage ceremonies are taken lightly or disregarded, then marital relationships become difficult and promiscuity will become rampant. When the ceremonies of the "village wine feast" are disregarded, then the sense of order and discipline between elders and juniors is lost, and cases of fights and encroachments will be common. When the funeral and sacrificial rites are disregarded, then the sense of gratitude in children and subjects toward their parents and deceased spirits will decay, and there will be many who turn against the dead in their conduct and indulge themselves. When the ceremonies of diplomatic visits are disregarded, then the relations between fealties and sovereigns will be threatened and the different rulers will become arrogant or licentious, and wars of invasion will arise.

Therefore the cultural work of *li* is imperceptible. It prevents the rise of indulgent conduct beforehand and leads people gradually toward virtue and away from vice without their knowing it. That was why the ancient great kings placed such an importance on *li*. That is the meaning of the passage in the *Book of Changes*: "The sovereign is careful at the inception of things. A difference of a hundredth or a thousandth of an inch at the start results in a divergence of a thousand miles at the end."

第七章　儒家社会秩序三论（二）
——《礼记·哀公问》第二十七

礼之目的，是将社会地位与明确的义务，予以清楚而简明的解释之后，使之构成一套完整的道德秩序，以为国家的政治秩序之道德基础。这种和谐的人际关系的哲理，对中国仍然有其益处——因为它仍然是中国社会风气的基石。

【原文】

哀公问于孔子曰："大礼何如？君子之言礼，何其尊也？"孔子曰："丘也小人，不足以知礼。"君曰："否！吾子言之也。"孔子曰："丘闻之，民之所由生，礼为大。非礼无以节事天地之神也，非礼无以辨君臣上下长幼之位也，非礼无以别男女父子兄弟之亲、昏姻疏数之交也；君子以此之为尊敬然。然后以其所能教百姓，不废其会节。有成事，然后治其雕镂文章黼黻以嗣。其顺之，然后言其丧算，备其鼎俎，设其豕腊，修其宗庙，岁时以敬祭祀，以序宗族。即安其居，节丑其衣服，卑其宫室，车不雕几，器不刻镂，食不贰味，以与民同利。昔之君子之行礼者如此。"

【语译】

　　鲁哀公向孔子请教，说："何谓大礼？有知识的人何以那么重视'礼'呢？"孔子答道："我很平凡，不够了解大礼。"哀公说："不！请先生说吧。"孔子这才答道："我听说，在人类生活中，礼最重要。没有礼，便不能正当地敬拜天地神明；没有礼，便不能分别君臣及贵贱长幼的辈分；没有礼，便不能区别男女、父子、兄弟的亲情，以及婚姻上、社会上彼此的关系。因此，有知识的人把礼看得十分重要。而后以他所了解的来教导百姓，使他们不致弄坏了彼此的关系。到有了成效，再加以文采修饰，使在文采不同的情形中区别出长辈和小辈的等级，并依照此种等级讨论丧祭之事，如何备办食品，陈列牲体干货，修建祠庙，按时节举行祭祀，并排定亲属的秩序。自己要习于这种礼俗，穿衣服要俭朴，住房屋要低小，乘车不雕饰图案，用具不镂刻花纹，吃简单的食物，剩余的利益和人民同享。古之君长，是这样行礼。"

【原文】

　　公曰："今之君子，胡莫之行也？"孔子曰："今之君子，好实无厌，淫德不倦，荒怠傲慢，固民是尽，午其众以伐有道：求得当欲，不以其所。昔之用民者由前，今之用民者由后。今之君子，莫为礼也。"

【语译】

　　哀公说："今之君长何以无人行这礼呢？"孔子说："今之君长，贪图物质享受，不知满足，过分地贪求利益，不肯罢手。心荒体懒，态度傲慢，非要刮尽人民的资财不可，而且违反众意，侵害好人，只求个人欲望满足，不择手段。古之君子，是照前面的做法，而今之君子，则是照刚才所说的做法。今之君子岂肯行此古礼！"

【原文】

孔子侍坐于哀公，哀公曰："敢问人道谁为大。"孔子愀然作色而对曰："君之及此言也，百姓之德也！固臣敢无辞而对？人道，政为大。"公曰："何谓为政？"孔子对曰："政者正也。君为正，则百姓从政矣。君之所为，百姓之所从也。君所不为，百姓何从？"公曰："敢问为政如之何？"孔子对曰："夫妇别，父子亲，君臣严。三者正，则庶物从之矣。"公曰："寡人虽无似也，愿闻所以行三言之道，可得闻乎？"孔子对曰："古之为政，爱人为大。所以治爱人，礼为大。所以治礼，敬为大。敬之至矣，大婚为大。大婚至矣！大婚既至，冕而亲迎，亲之也。亲之也者，亲之也。是故，君子兴敬为亲；舍敬，是遗亲也。弗爱不亲，弗敬不正。爱与敬，其政之本与？"

【语译】

孔子陪伴哀公谈话时，哀公说："请问做人的道理，什么最重要？"孔子听了，肃然答道："君长提到这个问题，真是人民的福气。鄙人岂敢不好好答复？做人的道理，以政务最为重要。"哀公说："请问政的含义。"孔子说："政就是正，国君做得正，百姓就跟着做得正。因为国君所做，百姓跟着做榜样，国君不做，百姓就无楷模可尊。"哀公又说："政务该怎样办呢？"孔子说："夫妇有分别，父子相亲爱，君臣相敬重。此三事做好，其他事情都跟着做好了。"哀公说："像我虽然不够贤明，但愿听听怎样实行那三句话。"孔子说："古代负责政务的人，最重要的在于爱别人。做到爱别人，最重要的则在于礼。要行礼，最重要的在于敬。充分做到敬，最重要的在婚姻之事

上。婚姻是敬意中最难做到的！在婚姻大事上，要穿戴大礼服，亲往
女家迎接，以表示爱她。所谓爱她，应该是敬慕，所以做君长，当以
敬慕之心与她相爱，若抛开敬意，就失去爱慕的诚意了。无爱慕便不
能相亲，亲而无敬意，便不是正当的婚姻。因此，第一就是爱自己
最亲近的妻子，对妻子能有爱有敬，才是爱别人的开始，亦即政务的
开始。"

【原文】

公曰："寡人愿有言。然冕而亲迎，不已重乎？"孔子愀然作色而对
曰："合二姓之好，以继先圣之后，以为天地宗庙社稷之主，君何谓已
重乎？"公曰："寡人固！不固，焉得闻此言也。寡人欲问，不得其辞，
请少进！"孔子曰："天地不合，万物不生。大婚，万世之嗣也。君何
谓已重焉！"孔子遂言曰："内以治宗庙之礼，足以配天地之神明；出
以治直言之礼，足以立上下之敬。物耻，足以振之；国耻，足以兴之。
为政先礼，礼，其政之本与？"孔子遂言曰："昔三代明王之政，必
敬其妻子也，有道。妻也者，亲之主也，敢不敬与？子也者，亲之后
也，敢不敬与？君子无不敬也。敬身为大。身也者，亲之枝也，敢不
敬与？不能敬其身，是伤其亲；伤其亲，是伤其本；伤其本，枝从而
亡。三者，百姓之象也。身以及身，子以及子，妃以及妃，君行此三
者，则忾乎天下矣，大王之道也。如此，国家顺矣。"

【语译】

哀公说："我还想问一句，你说，王侯娶亲，也要穿大礼服去迎
接女人，不太隆重了吗？"孔子听了，皱眉正色回答道："婚姻之事
是结合不同的血统，以承继祖宗的后嗣，做天地宗庙社稷的主人，怎

能说过于隆重呢？"哀公赶忙说："我真笨，若不笨也听不到这些话
了。刚才我想问，一时话说得不得体，现在请继续说吧！"孔子接着
说："气候土壤不相合，万物不能生长。王侯婚礼是要传宗接代以至
万万代，怎能说太隆重呢！"于是孔子再往下说："夫妇在内主持宗
庙之礼，敬礼天地神明；在外主持号令，做上下相敬的模范。有此模
范，臣子失职时，可凭此纠正；国君失职时，可凭此辅导。施政必
定先有此礼，所以称夫妇之礼为政务之始。"孔子又往下说："从前，
夏、商、周三代的贤君，施政时必敬重妻子，自有其道理。因为是奉
事宗祧的主体，岂可不敬？子是传宗接代的，岂可以不敬？所以君子
无不敬，而敬自己，尤为重要。因为自己是承先启后的关键，岂可以
不敬？若不敬自身，就是伤害血统，伤害血统，就是毁灭根本，毁灭
根本，枝属亦随之而灭绝了。此三项：自身、妻、子，国君有，百姓
也有。由己身推到百姓之身，由己子推到百姓之子，由自己之配偶推
到百姓的配偶。所以国君行此三敬，则天下都行此三敬了。这就是周
代祖先大王所实行的道理。能够这样，则整个国内莫不依从了。"

【原文】

公曰："敢问何谓敬身？"孔子对曰："君子过言，则民作辞；过动，
则民作则。君子言不过辞，动不过则，百姓不命而敬恭。如是，则能敬其
身。能敬其身，则能成其亲矣。"公曰："敢问何谓成亲？"孔子对曰："君
子也者，人之成名也。百姓归之名，谓之君子之子。是使其亲为君子也，
是为成其亲之名也已！"孔子遂言曰："古之为政，爱人为大。不能爱人，
不能有其身。不能有其身，不能安土。不能安土，不能乐天。不能乐天，
不能成其身。"

【语译】

　　哀公说："请问何谓敬身？"孔子答道："君长若说错了话，人民会跟着说错话；做错了事，人民也会跟着模仿。所以君王说话不能有错，做事不能没规律。能这样，则不待发号施令人民便跟着敬而有礼了。这是敬身。能敬自身，也成就了上代人的名誉。"哀公又问："何谓成就上代人呢？"孔子答道："所谓君子，是别人所给的称呼。百姓归向他而给他的名称，叫做君子之子，他的上代便是君子了。这样就成就了上代人的名誉。"孔子又往下说："古代负责施政者，皆以爱人为首要。不能爱别人，别人也不能成就他了。不能保全其自身，就不能安享土地。不能安享土地，也就不能安乐天命。不能安乐天命，也就不能成就其自身了。"

【原文】

　　公曰："敢问何谓成身？"孔子对曰："不过乎物。"公曰："敢问君子何贵乎天道也？"孔子对曰："贵其不已。如日月东西相从而不已也，是天道也；不闭其久，是天道也；无为而物成，是天道也；已成而明，是天道也。"公曰："寡人蠢愚，冥烦，子志之心也。"孔子蹴然辟席而对曰："仁人不过乎物，孝子不过乎物。是故，仁人之事亲也如事天，事天如事亲，是故孝子成身。"公曰："寡人既闻此言也，无如后罪何！"孔子对曰："君之及此言也，是臣之福也。"

【语译】

　　哀公说："请问何谓成就自身？"孔子答道："自己的一切作为，都不逾越礼法，就叫成就自身了。不逾越礼法，也是自然的法则。"哀公又问："君子何以要尊重自然的法则呢？"孔子答道："是对自然的运行不息表示敬意。日月从东到西运行不息，是自然法则。既而运行无阻而又永远如一，也是自然法则。不显出能干而能完成一切，也是自然法则。再者完成一切而又明显可见，这也是自然法则。"哀公说："我很愚昧，幸承教诲。"孔子听了，赶忙离开座位回答说："仁人遵守自然之道，孝子遵守自然之道。因此，仁人孝敬父母就如同孝敬天，孝敬天就如同孝敬父母。效法天的无过无不及，力行不息，所以孝子能成就自身。"哀公说："我听了这些大道理，怕将来还有差错，该怎样办好？"孔子说："您会提到将来，是臣的福气。"

Chapter Seven **SECOND DISCOURSE: AN INTERVIEW WITH**
DUKE AI
(*Aikung Wen*, *Liki*, Chapter XXVII)

Duke Ai asked Confucius, "What is this great *li*? Why is it that you talk about *li* as though it were such an important thing?"

Confucius replied, "Your humble servant is really not worthy to understand *li*."

"But you do constantly speak about it," said Duke Ai.

Confucius: "What I have learned is this, that of all the things that the people live by, *li* is the greatest. Without *li*, we do not know how to conduct a proper worship of the spirits of the universe; or how to establish the proper status of the king and the ministers, the ruler and the ruled, and the elders and the juniors; or how to establish the moral relationships between the sexes, between parents and children and between brothers; or how to distinguish the different degrees of relationships in the family. That is why a gentleman holds *li* in such high regard, and proceeds to teach its principles to the people and regulate the forms of their social life. When these are established, then he institutes different insignia and ceremonial robes as symbols of authority to perpetuate the institutions. When everything is in order, then he proceeds to fix the periods of burial and mourning, provide the sacrificial vessels and the proper offerings, and beautify the ancestral temples. Every year sacrifices are made in their proper seasons, in order to bring about social order in the clans and tribes. Then he retires to his private dwelling where he lives in simple contentment, dressed simply and housed simply, without carved carriages and without carved vessels, sharing the same food and the same joys with the people. That was how the ancient princes lived in accordance with *li*."

Duke Ai: "Why don't the princes of today do the same?"

Confucius: "The princes of today are greedy in their search after material goods. They indulge themselves in pleasure and neglect their duties and carry themselves with a proud air. They take all they can from the people and invade the territory of good rulers against the will of the people, and they go out to get what they want without regard for what is right. This is the way of the modern rulers, while that was the way of the ancient rulers whom I just spoke of. The rulers of today do not follow *li*."

Confucius was sitting in the company of Duke Ai, and the Duke asked: "What, in your opinion, is the highest principle of human civilization?" Confucius looked very grave and replied: "It is the good fortune of the people that Your Highness has asked this question. I must do my best to answer it. The highest principle of human civilization is government."

The Duke: "May I ask what is the art of government?"

Confucius: "The art of government simply consists in making things right, or putting things in their right places. When the ruler himself is "right," then the people naturally follow him in his right course. The people merely follow what the ruler does, for what the ruler himself does not do, wherewithal shall the people know how and what to follow?"

The Duke: "Tell me more in detail about this art of government."

Confucius: "The husband and wife should have different duties. The parents and children should be affectionate toward each other. The king and his subjects should have rigid discipline. When these three things are right, then everything follows."

The Duke: "Can you enlighten me a little more on the method to carry out these three things, unworthy as I am?"

Confucius: "The ancient rulers regarded loving the people as the chief principle of their government, and *li* as the chief principle by which they ruled the people they loved. In the cultivation of *li*, the sense of respect is the most important, and as the ultimate symbol of this respect, the ceremony of royal marriage is the most important. The ceremony of royal marriage is the ultimate symbol of respect, and as it is the ultimate symbol of respect, the king goes with his crown to welcome the princess from her own home personally because he regards the bride as so close in relationship to him. He goes personally because the relationship is regarded as personal. Therefore the sovereign cultivates the sense of respect and personal relationship. To neglect to show respect is to disregard the personal relationship. Without love, there will be no *personal* relationship, and without respect, there will be no *right* relationship. So love and respect are the foundation of government."

Duke Ai: "I want to say something. Isn't it making the royal marriage a little too serious by requiring a king to wear his crown and welcome the princess from her own home?"

Confucius looked very grave and replied: "Why do you say so? A royal marriage means the union of two ruling houses for the purpose of carrying on the royal lineage and producing offspring to preside over the worship of Heaven and Earth, of the ancestral spirits, and of the gods of land and grains."

Duke Ai: "Excuse me for pressing the question, for if I do not persist, I shall not be able to hear your opinions on this point. I want to ask you something, but do not know how to put it. Will you please proceed further?"

Confucius: "You see, if Heaven and Earth (representing *yin* and *yang*) do not come together, there is no life in this world. A royal marriage is for the purpose of perpetuating the ruling house for thousands of generations. How can one take it too seriously?"

Confucius then said: "In the art of government, *li* comes first. It is the means by which we establish the forms of worship, enabling the ruler to appear before the spirits of Heaven and Earth at sacrifices on the one hand; and on the other, it is the means by which we establish the forms of intercourse at the court and a sense of piety or respect between the ruler and the ruled. It revives or resuscitates the social and political life from a condition, of disgraceful confusion. Therefore *li* is the foundation of government."

Confucius then went on to say: "The ancient great kings always showed respect or proper consideration to their wives and children in accordance with a proper principle. How can one be disrespectful (or show disregard) toward one's wife since she is the center of the home? And how can one be disrespectful toward (or be lacking in regard for) one's children, since the children perpetuate the family? A gentleman is always respectful or always shows regard for everything. First of all he is respectful, or shows a pious regard toward himself. How dare he be disrespectful or have no pious regard for himself since the self is a branch of the family line? Not to show regard for one's self is to injure the family, and to injure the family is to injure the root, and when the root is injured, the branches die off. These three things, the relationship toward one's wife, toward one's children and toward one's self, are a symbol of the human relationships among the people. By showing respect for his own self, he teaches the people respect for their selves; by showing regard for his own children, he teaches the people regard for their children; and by showing regard for his own wife, he teaches the people regard for their wives. When a sovereign carries out these three things, his example will be imitated by the entire country. This is the principle of King T'ai (grandfather of King Wen). Thus harmonious relationships will prevail in the country."

Duke Ai: "May I ask what is meant by 'showing respect for one's self'?"

Confucius: "When the sovereign makes a mistake in his speech, the people quote him, and when a sovereign makes a mistake in his conduct, the people imitate him. When a sovereign makes no mistakes in his speech or his conduct, then the people learn respect for him without any laws or regulations. In this way the sovereign shows respect for himself, and by showing respect for himself, he glorifies his ancestors."

Duke Ai: "May I ask what you mean by 'glorifying one's ancestors'?"

Confucius: "When a man becomes famous, we call him 'a prince' or 'a princely man,' and the people gladly follow him and honor him, saying that he is 'a prince's son' (or 'son of a gentleman'). Thus his own father is called a 'prince' through him and his name is glorified."

Confucius went on to say: "The ancient rulers considered loving the people as the first thing in their government. Without loving the people, the ruler cannot realize his true self, and without realizing or taking possession of his true self, he cannot establish peace in his land; without peace in his land, he cannot enjoy life in conformity with God's law; and being unable to enjoy life in conformity with God's law, he cannot live a full life."

Duke Ai: "May I ask what you mean by 'living a full life'?"

Confucius: "Just follow the natural law of things."

Duke Ai: "May I ask why the gentleman lays such stress on the laws of God?"

Confucius: "The gentleman lays such stress upon God's law, because it is eternal. For instance, you see the sun and the moon eternally following one another in their courses—that is God's law. Life in this universe never stops and continues forever—that is God's law. Things are created or produced without any effort or interference—that is God's law. When the things are created or produced, the universe is illuminated—that is God's law."

Duke Ai: "I'm stupid and confused. Will you make it clearer and simplify it so that I can remember?"

A change came over Confucius' countenance. He rose from his seat and said: "A great man simply follows the natural law of things. A good son simply follows the natural law of things. Therefore, a great man feels he is serving God when he serves his parents, and feels he is serving his parents when he serves God. Therefore, a good son lives a full life."

Duke Ai: "I am extremely fortunate to have heard these words from you, and I crave your pardon if I fail to live up to them hereafter."

Confucius: "The pleasure is mine."

第八章 儒家社会秩序三论（三）

——《礼记·礼运》第九

在大同世界，孔子所提倡之礼及其中之人道主义，已全无用处，而次一理想的小康世界则与礼大有关系……既知道有一个道德完美的世界理想存在，又敢毅然以我们这样不完美的人类而创立一个次一等的世界，这也是孔子的智慧另一面。

本文为《礼记》中若干重要章节之一，大概由孔子弟子冉求（字子有）所记。本章前段把孔子的理想社会"大同世界"与次一理想"小康世界"予以区别。在大同世界，孔子所提倡之礼及其中之人道主义，已全无用处，而次一理想的小康世界则与礼大有关系。在孔子理想中有一个世界，其中男女大致上近乎完美，而使礼的种种约束已无必要，这一点颇堪玩味，并因此令人觉得孔子的憧憬具有道不远人之意，这一段文字也暗示如不能达到大同世界，降而求其次，小康世界也可差强人意了。既知道有一个道德完美的世界理想存在，又敢毅然以我们这样不完美的人类而创立一个次一等的世界，这也是孔子的智慧另一面。近代中国学者受了西洋乌托邦理想主义的影响，孔子这种理想国越发受到他们的重视。有人向孙中山先生请赐墨宝之时，他常爱写"天下为公"四个字相赠，这四个字便是从本章文字中摘录下来的。礼这个字，也可以说是一种社会秩序原理，以及社会上一般的习俗，在本章中讲得十分清楚，也发挥得堪称完备。在本章我们可以看出礼是包括民俗、宗教风俗规矩、节庆、法律、服饰、饮食居住，也可以说是"人类学"一词的内涵。在这些原始存在的习俗上，再加以理性化的社会秩序的含义，对礼字全部的意义就能把握住了。

本章曾将孔子想恢复之古代封建制度数段文字，略而未录，此数段虽对研究中国古代语言学者颇为有趣，但本书重在阐述广义的孔子遗教，故不列入。孔子再三强调在生活中要广读博学，但莫忘融会贯通而能以一贯之。孔子认为学与思兼顾方为真正的"士"。西汉学者对儒家典籍致力于其语文之钻研，颇为精细，但于其中一贯的哲理则诸多忽略；宋儒深受佛学哲理与冥思主静之影响，而忽略儒学中之文字研究，以致读书不能把握其精义。后世有专研究语文细节之评注家，竟有以三万字专文解释"书经"二字者。《周礼》《仪礼》《礼记》三书为研究中国古代民风者，自系一丰富宝藏，但与本书则迹近风马牛。

【原文】

昔者仲尼与于蜡宾，事毕，出游于观之上，喟然而叹。仲尼之叹，盖叹鲁也。言偃在侧曰："君子何叹！"孔子曰："大道之行也，与三代之英，丘未之逮也，而有志焉。"

【语译】

从前，孔子受邀请参加蜡祭，充任来宾。祭事完毕后，他出游到大门楼上，唉声叹气，是因鲁国而起。当时子游随侍在侧，问道："老师为何叹气？"孔子说："大道实行的时代，和夏、商、周几位英明的君主当政的时代，我都来不及看到，所看到的只剩一些记载而已。"

【原文】

大道之行也，天下为公。选贤与能，讲信修睦，故人不独亲其亲，不独子其子，使老有所终，壮有所用，幼有所长，鳏寡孤独废疾者，皆有所养。男有分，女有归。货恶其弃于地也，不必藏于己；力恶其不出于身也，不必为己。是故，谋闭而不兴，盗窃乱贼而不作，故外户而不闭。是谓大同。

今大道既隐，天下为家，各亲其亲，各子其子，货力为己。大人世及以为礼，城郭沟池以为固，礼义以为纪；以正君臣，以笃父子，以睦兄弟，以和夫妇，以设制度，以立田里，以贤勇知，以功为己。故谋用是作，而兵由此起。禹、汤、文、武、成王、周公，由此其选也。此六君子者，未有不谨于礼者也。以著其义，以考其信，著有过，刑仁讲让，示民有常。如有不由此者，在执者去，众以为殃。是谓小康。

【语译】

在大道实行的时代，天下为天下人所共有。选举贤能者共同治理，人人注重信用，彼此和好，于是人不仅爱自己的父母，不仅爱自己的儿女，更能使社会上的老人都能安享天年，壮年人各能贡献才力，儿童能受良好的教育，鳏寡孤独以及残废的人都得到供养。男人各有职业，女的都正式婚配。既不以大好的资源委弃而不用，也不占为己有；有力的出力，但也不必为自己。阴谋不生，偷窃杀人也不再出现。门窗不必关闭，也平安无事。那样的世界叫作大同世界。

现在大道既已消失，天下成了一家一姓的私产，各人只爱自己的父母，自己的儿女；资源劳力都成为私人所有，而且还成为世袭的，旁人不得分享。要保有私产，就不能没有城郭沟池牢牢的防守，拟订仪式理论等纪律，以确定君臣的名分，强调父子的慈孝，加强兄弟的友爱，加深夫妇的恩情。如此立定制度，划分田地，尊重勇为智能，把功绩作为个人所有。因而诈巧的奸谋就随之发生，而争夺交战便由此而起。在此一时代，禹、汤、文王、武王、成王、周公算是最出色的人物了。这六位君子，都颇守礼法。发扬正义，考验信实，明示错误，行仁讲让，以正轨昭示于人。若有不遵礼法者，虽有权势，也予以斥逐，使人人知其为灾祸之根源。这就是小康时代。

【原文】

言偃复问曰："如此乎礼之急也？"孔子曰："夫礼，先王以承天之道，以治人之情。故失之者死，得之者生。《诗》曰：'相鼠有体，人而无礼。人而无礼，胡不遄死！'是故夫礼，必本于天，淆于地，列于鬼神，达于丧、祭、射、御、冠、昏、朝聘。故圣人以礼示之，故天下国家可得而正也。"

【语译】

言偃又问道："礼真是此等重要吗？"孔子说："礼本来是先王用以代表天道而治理人类的行为的。违背这法则便不能生存；合乎这法则才不消灭。《诗经·相鼠》说：'老鼠还有老鼠的形体，人怎能没有人的礼貌？人若不像人，不如早点死吧！'所以礼必顺乎天，合乎地，配合着鬼神之道，而表现于丧、祭、射、御、冠、婚、朝聘礼仪上！圣人用此等礼仪代表天道和人情，而天下国家才能正常发展。"

【原文】

言偃复问曰："夫子之极言礼也，可得而闻与？"孔子曰："我欲观夏道，是故之杞，而不足征也；吾得《夏时》焉。我欲观殷道，是故之宋，而不足征也；吾得坤乾焉。《坤乾》之义，《夏时》之等，吾以是观之。"

【语译】

言偃又问："老师说礼是那么重要，可否请老师告诉我们？"孔子说："我以前看夏代的礼仪，所以到杞国去考察，因为年代久远，那种礼仪已不可靠，我只得到他们的历书，名为《夏时》。我又想去看殷代的礼，于是到宋国去，但是也所见不多，只得到《乾坤》一书，讲的是阴阳变化，是夏时的历书。"

【原文】

夫礼之初，始诸饮食，其燔黍捭豚，汙尊而抔饮，蒉桴而土鼓，犹若可以致其敬于鬼神。及其死也，升屋而号，告曰：皋！某复。然后饭腥而苴孰。故天望而地藏也；体魄则降，知气在上。故死者北首，生者南乡，皆从其初。

【语译】

最古的礼仪，从饮食开始。饮食时，把黍子放在火上烤，把小猪放在火上烤；挖地当做酒壶，用两手捧着水当酒杯；用蒉草扎成的槌子敲地面当作鼓，照样可以敬鬼神。人死时，活人登屋顶向天喊叫。他们喊道：某人你回来吧！他们用生米塞在死者嘴里，埋葬时又给死者用草叶包的熟食。如此望天招魂，在地下埋葬。肉体入地，灵魂上天。死人的头向北，活人以南为尊。都是从古代流传下来的。

【原文】

昔者先王，未有宫室，冬则居营窟，夏则居橧巢。未有火化，食草木之实、鸟兽之肉，饮其血，茹其毛。未有丝麻，衣其羽皮。后圣有作，然后修火之利，范金合土，以为台榭宫室牖户；以炮以燔，以亨以炙，以为醴酪；治其麻丝，以为布帛。以养生送死，以事鬼神上帝，皆从其朔。

【语译】

上古先王之时，还没有宫殿房屋，冬天住在土窟里，夏天居柴巢上；不知道用火除去腥气，生吃草木的果实和鸟兽的肉，吸饮鲜血，连毛生吞；又不知用荨麻和蚕丝织布，只披鸟羽兽皮作衣服。到圣人出现，利用火做模型铸造金属，和泥土烧砖瓦，用以建筑台榭宫室门窗；同时又用火炮烤煮炙各种食物，酿造醴酒乳酪；同时又用丝麻织成麻布丝绸，以应日常生活及办理丧事、祭祀鬼神上帝，这与原始时代相同。

【原文】

故玄酒在室，醴盏在户，粢醍在堂，澄酒在下。陈其牺牲，备其鼎俎，列其琴瑟管磬钟鼓，修其祝嘏，以降上神与其先祖。以正君臣，以笃父子，以睦兄弟，以齐上下，夫妇有所。是谓承天之祜。

【语译】

因为事事皆依古制，所以祭祀时，玄酒反而在室，醴酒和盏酒在户，齐醍酒在堂，清酒在堂下。并陈列供祭的牺牲，备齐鼎俎，安排琴瑟管磬钟鼓，预备祝辞祭辞，以迎接神和先祖的降临。在祭祀进行时，辨正君臣之义，增厚父子之情，和睦兄弟之谊，沟通上下的情感，而主人夫妇各有应处的地位。此种祭祀，可称为承受了上天的降福。

【原文】

作其祝号，玄酒以祭。荐其血毛，腥其俎，孰其殽。与其越席，疏布以幂，衣其浣帛，醴盏以献，荐其燔炙。君与夫人交献，以嘉魂魄，是谓合莫。然后退而合亨，体其犬豕牛羊，实其簠簋笾豆铏羹，祝以孝告，嘏以慈告。是谓大祥。此礼之大成也。

【语译】

作祝辞的名称，设玄酒祭神，献刚宰的牺牲血和毛，再献生肉俎，再献半熟的牲礼。行礼时，主人主妇亲践蒲席，端着粗麻布覆盖的酒樽，穿着新染的绸衣，献了醴酒，又献盏酒；进了烤肉，又进烤肝。主人先献，主妇次献，一前一后，献了再献，使祖先的幽灵非常愉快，这叫人神相通。正祭完毕，然后把半生的牲肉在一起烹煮，再分别犬豕牛羊的骨体，盛在大盘小碗中，分敬众人。祝辞写的是"孝子孝孙"，嘏辞是"祝福子孙平安如意"。这是大吉大祥，是礼之大成。

【原文】

孔子曰："呜呼哀哉！我观周道，幽、厉伤之，吾舍鲁何适矣！"

【语译】

孔子说："可悲啊！我看周代的制度，厉王、幽王破坏尽了。目前，除鲁国之外，还能到何处去找呢？"

【原文】

是故，礼者君之大柄也。所以别嫌明微，傧鬼神，考制度，别仁义；所以治政安君也。故政不正，则君位危；君位危，则大臣倍，小臣窃。刑肃而俗敝，则法无常。法无常，而礼无列。礼无列，则士不事也。刑肃而俗敝，则民弗归也。是谓疵国。

【语译】

所以说，礼为君主治国的工具。用以判断是非洞察明微，敬事鬼神，考校制度，确保伦常；是用来推行政事巩固君权的。政事不上轨道，君权必发生动摇；君权动摇，则大臣背叛，小臣偷窃。虽有严刑峻罚，他们反而利用刑罚取巧作恶，风气败坏。因为法令漏洞百出，要时常改变，礼节也随之纷乱。礼节既乱，则士人必无所适应。再加刑罚峻严，风气败坏，民心尽失。此种国家，叫作疵国。

【原文】

何谓人情？喜、怒、哀、惧、爱、恶、欲，七者，弗学而能。何谓人义？父慈、子孝、兄良、弟弟、夫义、妇听、长惠、幼顺、君仁、臣忠，十者，谓之人义。讲信修睦，谓之人利。争夺相杀，谓之人患。故圣人所以治人七情，修十义，讲信修睦，尚辞让，去争夺，舍礼何以治之？饮食

男女，人之大欲存焉。死亡贫苦，人之大恶存焉。故欲恶者，心之大端
也。人藏其心，不可测度也；美恶皆在其心，不见其色也。欲一以穷之，
舍礼何以哉？

【语译】

何谓人情？喜、怒、哀、惧、爱、恶、欲，是人的本能，称为
人情。何谓人义呢？为父要慈，为子要孝，为兄要友爱，为弟要敬
兄，为丈夫要有义，为妻者要顺从，为长者要体恤下情，年幼者要听
从教训，皇帝要仁，为臣要忠，这十种叫作人义。此外，大家讲究信
用，保持和睦，叫作人利。若彼此争夺杀害，就是人祸了。所以圣人
协调七情，建立十义，讲信修睦，提倡辞让，摒弃争夺。要达到这些
目标，除去礼教，还有什么好方法呢？饮食男女本是人类最基本的欲
望，死亡贫苦，也是人类最怕的事。这种爱好与嫌恶，在人心理上是
很强烈的。人把这两种藏在内心，别人无从察觉；爱恶也藏在心中，
而不表现于形貌上。要使全部表露出来，除去用礼，还有什么好方
法呢？

【原文】

故人者，其天地之德，阴阳之交，鬼神之会，五行之秀气也。故人
者，天地之心也，五行之端也，食味、别声、被色而生者也。

【语译】

所以人类是天地的产物，阴阳的配合，为诸种元素的精华。
所以人类实为宇宙的心灵，五行所结的果实，生而要享受饮食声
色的。

【原文】

故先王患礼之不达于下也，故祭帝于郊，所以定天位也；祀社于国，所以列地利也；祖庙，所以本仁也；山川，所以傧鬼神也；五祀，所以本事也。故宗祝在庙，三公在朝，三老在学。王，前巫而后史，卜筮瞽侑皆在左右。王中心无为也，以守至正。

故礼行于郊，而百神受职焉；礼行于社，而百货可极焉；礼行于祖庙，而孝慈服焉；礼行于五祀，而正法则焉。故自郊社、祖庙、山川、五祀，义之修而礼之藏也。

【语译】

先王恐怕礼不能普行于天下，所以祭祀天帝于南郊，明定天的权位。祭地于国，表明生命所需之物资都来自大地。祭祖庙是表示尊亲之意，祭祀山川表示敬事鬼神。五种祭祀是表示纪念人在大地生存的本源。宗祝在庙，三公在朝，三老在学。帝王前有掌神事的巫，后有记人事的史官，乐师和谏官分守左右，王者居中央，宁静大公，以其至为纯正的态度为万民之主而已。像这样，礼行于郊以祭天则诸神各尽其职，祭地则万物滋生，祭祖庙，则慈孝蔚然成风；礼行于五祀，则使人人能善尽本分，礼之作用也就在于此了。

【原文】

是故夫礼，必本于大一，分而为天地，转而为阴阳，变而为四时，列而为鬼神。其降曰命，其官于天也。

【语译】

礼本于原始之浑元一体，此一体分化而为天地，进而旋转成为阴

阳，再变而为四季，又分任各职而为鬼神。鬼神之意志乃表现为命运
并受制于上天。

【原文】

故礼义也者，人之大端也。所以讲信修睦，而固人之肌肤之会，筋骸
之束也。所以养生送死事鬼神之大端也。所以达天道，顺人情之大窦也。
故唯圣人为知礼之不可以已也。故坏国，丧家，亡人，必先去其礼。故礼
之于人也，犹酒之有糵也，君子以厚，小人以薄。故圣王修义之柄，礼之
序，以治人情。故人情者，圣王之田也。修礼以耕之，陈义以种之，讲学
以耨之，本仁以聚之，播乐以安之。

【语译】

礼义是人生的本分，用以促进人类之间彼此的信任，社会生活的
和睦，加强社会生活的关系。并且为养生送死敬拜神灵的基本礼法，
也为上遵天理下达人情的原则。所以只有圣人才知道礼之不可废。因
此，若想灭亡一个国，破坏一个人家，或毁坏一个人，必先使之丧失
礼义的荣誉感。

礼之于人，就像酿酒用的曲糵。君子醇厚，因对礼注重；小人薄
劣，因不注重礼。所以古代圣王要培养义，建立礼的秩序，用以辅导
人性。因此，人性犹如圣王所耕种的田地，用礼为工具以耕之，用义
为种子以种之，用教育以除恶草，用仁爱来收络之，用音乐来使人
愉悦。

【原文】

故礼也者，义之实也。协诸义而协，则礼虽先王未之有，可以义起

也。义者，艺之分，仁之节也。协于艺，讲于仁，得之者强。仁者，义之本也，顺之体也，得之者尊。

故治国不以礼，犹无耜而耕也。为礼不本于义，犹耕而弗种也。为义而不讲之以学，犹种而弗耨也。讲之于学而不合之以仁，犹耨而弗获也。合之以仁而不安之以乐，犹获而弗食也。安之以乐而不达于顺，犹食而弗肥也。

【语译】

所以礼者，是正义之果。凡合乎理性的行为，虽在前代所未曾有，亦可视为正当。理性是人类的天赋，循正途必表现出仁德，能如此必然强大。仁心，是正当行为的根本，又是顺天理合乎人情的具体表现，能如此，则无人不敬服尊仰。

所以治国而不用礼，就犹如没有农具而耕田。制礼而不本于正义，就犹如耕了田不播种。行义而不说明，就像播种而不除草。说明其含义而不合乎仁爱，就像除草而不收成。合乎仁爱而不得其喜悦于音乐，就像收获了而不食用。得喜悦于音乐而不到心安理得的地步，就犹如食而得不到健康。

【原文】

四体既正，肤革充盈，人之肥也。父子笃，兄弟睦，夫妇和，家之肥也。大臣法，小臣廉，官职相序，君臣相正，国之肥也。天子以德为车，以乐为御；诸侯以礼相与；大夫以法相序；士以信相考；百姓以睦相守，天下之肥也。是谓大顺。

【语译】

四肢既已发育，而皮肤又复丰满，就是生活健康。父子相亲，兄弟和睦，夫妇相爱，就是家庭健康。大官奉公守法，小官方正廉洁，职务分工合作，君臣互相匡正，这是国家健康。天子以其德行为车，以音乐推行德政。诸侯以礼让相交往，大夫依法合作，士人以诚相勉，百姓和平共处，这是世界健康，可称之为大顺。

Chapter Eight   *THIRD DISCOURSE: THE VISION OF A SOCIAL ORDER*

(*Liyun*, *Liki*, Chapter IX)

This is one of the most important chapters in *Liki*, probably recorded by Tseyu, a disciple of Confucius. The first section makes an important distinction between a Confucian Utopia, the *tat'ung*, in which none of the humanistic distinctions in *li* would be necessary, and the second best type of culture, the culture of *li* or of a social order, practical and attainable in the present world, the *hsiaok'ang*, with which practically all the teachings of Confucius about *li* are concerned. The fact that Confucius did have a vision of a world of more or less perfect human beings in which *li* would not be necessary, is interesting and gives his teachings concerning the principle of attainable social order a quality of practical common sense and an implied meaning of resignation to the second best. To know that a world of moral perfection exists, but to go along bravely establishing a social order with the imperfect human beings that we know we are today, is the part of wisdom. This vision of the Confucian Utopia has gained increased prominence among recent Chinese scholars who have somehow been influenced by reading of Western Utopias and Western idealism in general. Dr. Sun Yat Sen's favorite phrase, the one that he most frequently used when asked to inscribe an autograph for his friends, consisted of the four words "*t'ien hsia tat'ung*" or "the world of *tat'ung*" taken from this section.

The meaning of *li*, or the principle of social order, and its identity with a general body of social practices are quite clear and most completely developed in this chapter. *Li* is here seen to include folkways, religious customs, festivals, laws, dress, food and housing, such as are usually included under the term "ethnology." Add to these original existing practices a conception of a *rationalized* social order, and you have *li* in its most complete sense.

In the following translation, I have omitted several paragraphs which concern strictly the details of the ancient feudal order which Confucius was trying to restore. Interesting as these details are for the students of ancient Chinese philology and comparative religion, they do not fall within the scope of this book, which deals more with the broader significance of Confucian teachings. Confucius himself emphasized again and again the importance of being widely read and learned in all aspects of life without forgetting the importance of having a philosophic principle that runs through all these details of scholarship. Only one who is able to couple thought with scholarship is a really educated man, according to Confucius. The early Han scholars, occupied with philological research, did involve themselves in such details to the exclusion of central philosophic principles, while the Sung philosophers, influenced by the Buddhistic bent for philosophy and meditation, on the other hand neglected this philologic scholarship and even developed the habit of "reading a book without knowing exactly what it means." An extreme example of mere occupation with philologic details was the case of a later commentator who wrote a treatise of over 30,000 words on two words of the *Shuking*. The three books on *li* (*Chouli*, *Yili*, and *Liki*) contain of course a rich field of material for the study of ancient Chinese folkways, but they cannot possibly be covered or even suggested in this book. I have also supplied sectional headings for the convenience of the reader.

I. THE TWO ORDERS OF HUMAN SOCIETY

One day Confucius went to see the ceremony of *tsa* (a winter folk festival at the end of the year at which the people offered a general sacrifice to all the animals and inanimate creation and of course indulged in dancing). After the ceremony was over, Confucius took a walk. He stopped at a roadhouse on the side of the city gate (overlooking the suburb) and heaved a deep sigh. Confucius was sighing over the social conditions in his state Lu. Yen Yen (Tseyu) was with him, and asked Confucius, "Why are you sighing?" And Confucius replied, "Oh, I was thinking of the Golden Age and regretting that I was not able to have been born in it and to be associated with the wise rulers and ministers of the Three Dynasties. How I would have loved to have lived in such an age!"

"When the great Tao prevailed (*i.e.*, in the Golden Age), the world was a common state (not belonging to any particular ruling family), rulers were elected according to their wisdom and ability and mutual confidence and peace prevailed. Therefore people not only regarded their own parents as parents and their own children as children. The old people were able to enjoy their old age, the young men were able to employ their talent, the juniors had the elders to look up to, and the helpless widows, orphans and cripples and deformed were well taken care of. The men had their respective occupations and the women had their homes. If the people didn't want to see goods lying about on the ground, they did not have to keep them for themselves, and if people had too much energy for work, they did not have to labor for their own profit. Therefore there was no cunning or intrigue and there were no bandits or burglars, and as a result, there was no need to shut one's outer gate (at night). This was the period of *tat'ung*, or the Great Commonwealth.

"But now the great Tao no longer prevails, and the world is divided up into private families (or becomes the possession of private families), and people regard only their own parents as parents and only their own children as children. They acquire goods and labor each for his own benefit. A hereditary aristocracy is established and the different states build cities, outer cities and moats each for its own defense. The principles of *li* (or forms of social intercourse) and righteousness serve as the principles of social discipline. By means of these principles, people try to maintain the official status of rulers and subjects, to teach the parents and children and elder brothers and younger brothers and husbands and wives to live in harmony, to establish social institutions and to live in groups of hamlets. The physically strong and the mentally clever are raised to prominence and each one tries to carve his own career. Hence there is deceit and cunning and from these wars arise. (The great founders of dynasties like) Emperors Yu, T'ang, Wen, Wu and Ch'eng and Duke Chou were the best men of this age. Without a single exception, these six gentlemen were deeply concerned over the principle of *li*, through which justice was maintained, general confidence was tested, and errors or malpractices were exposed. An ideal of true manhood, jen, was set up and good manners or courtesy was cultivated, as solid principles for the common people to follow. A ruler who violates these principles would then be denounced as a public enemy and driven off from his office. This is called the Period of *Hsiaok'ang* or "The Period of Minor Peace."

II. THE EVOLUTION OF *LI*, OR SOCIAL ORDER

"Is *li* so very important as all that?" asked Tseyu again.

"This *li*," replied Confucius, "is the principle by which the ancient kings embodied the laws of heaven and regulated the expressions of human nature. Therefore he who has attained *li* lives, and he who has lost it, dies. The *Book of Songs* say,

> See even the mouse has a *t'i* (body)
> And a human being has no *li*!
> A human being has no *li*—
> Why doesn't he go off and die?

Therefore *li* is based on heaven, patterned on the earth, deals with the worship of the spirits and is extended to the rites and ceremonies of funerals, sacrifices to ancestors, archery, carriage driving, 'capping,' marriage, and court audience or exchange of diplomatic visits. Therefore the Sage shows the people the principle of a rationalized social order and through it everything becomes right in the family, the state and the world."

"Can you explain to me, fully and completely, this *li*?" asked Tseyu once more.

Confucius: I wanted to see the ancient practices of the Hsia Dynasty (2070 B.C.-1600 B.C.), and that was why I went to visit the city of Chi (where the descendants of the Hsia rulers lived), but I found there weren't enough surviving customs left. There I secured, however, a copy of the book *Hsiashih*. And I wanted to see the ancient practices of the Shang Dynasty (or Yin, 1600 B.C.-1046 B.C.), and for this purpose I went to visit the city of Sung (where the descendants of the Shang rulers lived), but found there were not enough surviving customs left. There, however, I secured a copy of *K'unch'ien* (a version of the *Book of Changes*). With the help of these two books, the *Hsiashih* and *K'unch'ien*, I tried to study the ancient customs.

In the beginning, *li* (civilization) started with food or drink. People baked millets and pork, torn apart with the hand, on heated slabs of stone. They dug holes in the ground to serve as jars and drank out of the palms of their hands. They kneaded clay into drums and drum sticks. And yet this seemed to have been worthy materials for them to worship the spirits. When a relative died, they went up on the roof and cried aloud to the spirit, saying to him, "Ahooooooooo! So-and-So, will you please return to your body?" (If the spirit failed to return, and the man was really dead) then they used uncooked rice and baked meats for sacrifice, and they turned their heads toward the sky to "see at a distance" (*wang*) the spirit and buried the body in the earth. The material spirit then descended (to the earth), while the conscious spirit went up (to the air). Therefore the dead were buried with their heads toward the north, while the living had their houses facing the south. These were the early customs.

In the ancient times, the rulers did not have houses, and they lived in dug-out caves or in piled-up mounds in winter and on "nests" made of dry branches (on top of trees) in summer. They did not know the use of fire, but ate fruits and the flesh of birds and animals, drinking their blood, including the hair in it. They did not have hemp cloth or silk and were clothed in feathers and animal skins. Later came the Sages who taught them the use of fire, and to cast metalware by pouring it into bamboo moulds and to mould clay into earthenware. Then they built terraces and houses with doors and windows, and began to bake and broil and cook and roast by means of a spit, and made wine and vinegar. They began also to use hemp and silk and weave them into cloth for the use of the living and sacrifices to the dead and the worship of the spirits and God. These ancient practices were also handed down from the early times. Therefore, the black wine was kept in the inner room, the white wine was kept near the (southern) door, the red wine was kept in the hall and the heavy wine was kept still further outside. The meat offerings were then displayed and the round tripod and the square vessel were laid in order, and the musical instruments, the *ch'in*, *seh*, the flute, the *ch'ing* (musical stone suspended from a string and struck like bells), the bell and the drum were arranged in their places, and the sacrificial prayer to the dead and the answer from the dead were carefully prepared and read, that the celestial and the ancestors' spirits might descend to the place of worship. All these practices were for the purpose of maintaining the proper status of rulers and subjects, maintaining the love between parents and children, teaching kindness between brothers, regulating relationships between superiors and inferiors, and establishing the respective relationships of husband and wife, to the end that all might be blessed by Heaven. They then prepared the sacrificial lamentations. The black or dark wine was used for sacrifice, and the blood and hair of the animals were used in offering, and the raw meat was placed in a square vessel. Burnt meat was also offered, a mat was spread out and a piece of coarse cloth was used for covering the vessels, and silk ceremonial robes were used. The different wines, *li* and *chien*, and baked and broiled meats were also offered. The sovereign and the queen made the offerings alternately, that the good spirits might descend and they might be united with the occult world. After the sacrifices were over, they then gave a feast to the guests, dividing up the dogs, pigs, cows and lambs at the offering and placing them in various vessels. The prayer to the dead declared the gratitude or loyalty of the living, and the answer from the dead declared the continued affection of the deceased. This was the great blessing and accomplishment of *li*.

Confucius: "Alas! I have studied the practices of the Chou Dynasty (in which Confucius lived), but (the bad Emperors) Yu and Li have completely destroyed them. Where can I turn to except to the state of Lu?" (*Here follows a brief description of the prevailing chaos in the social and religious life of his time.*)

Therefore *li* is the great weapon or means of power of a sovereign, with which to expose malpractices and beginnings of disorder, offer sacrifices to the spirits, establish the systems of social life, differentiate the uses of love and duty. It is the means by which a country is governed and the sovereign maintains the security of his position. Therefore, if the government is not "right," then the sovereign's position is threatened, and when the sovereign's position is threatened, the powerful officials become arrogant and the minor officials begin to steal. We should then see criminals punished by severe sentences and the general morality of the people degenerates and there would be a general absence of standards. With a general absence of standards, the general social order would be upset; and with the upset of the general social order, the gentry would not be able to attend to their proper professions. And when the criminals are punished with severe penalties and the general morality of the people degenerates, then the people will not be loyal to the sovereign, or will go away to other countries. This is called "a sickly state."

(*Here follows a description of the proper functions of the sovereign.*)

III. *LI* BASED ON HUMAN NATURE

The reason the Sage is able to regard the world as one family and China as one man (what is true of human nature in one man is true for all), is that he does not make arbitrary rules, but on the other hand tries to understand human nature, define the human duties and come to a clear realization of what is good and what is bad for mankind. It is through this that he is able to do so. What is human nature? It consists of the seven things, joy, anger, sorrow, fear, love, hatred and desire, all of which do not have to be learned (*i.e.*, they are natural instincts). What are the human duties? Kindness in the father, filial piety in the son, gentility in the elder brother, humility and respect in the younger brother, good behavior in the husband, obedience in the wife, benevolence in the elders, and obedience in the juniors, benevolence in the ruler and loyalty in the ministers—these ten are the human duties. What is good for mankind means general confidence and peace, and what is bad for mankind means struggle for profit, robbery and murder. Therefore how can the Sage, or ideal ruler, dispense with *li* in his efforts to cultivate the seven emotions and the ten duties, and to promote mutual confidence and peace and courtesy and discourage the struggle for profit and robbery? Food and drink and sex are the great desires of mankind, and death and poverty and suffering are the great fears or aversions of mankind. Therefore desires and fear (or greed and hatred) are the great motive forces of the human heart. These, however, are concealed in the heart and are not usually shown, and the human heart is unfathomable. What other principle is there besides *li* which can serve as the one all-sufficient principle to explore the human heart?

Therefore man is the product of the forces of heaven and earth, of the union of the *yin* and the *yang* principles, the incarnation of spirits and the essence of the five elements (metal, wood, water, fire and earth). Therefore man is the heart of the universe, the upshot of the five elements, born to enjoy food and color and noise....

IV. *LI* BASED ON HEAVEN, OR NATURE

The worship of Heaven is for the purpose of recognizing the supreme rulership of Heaven. The worship of the god of Earth is for the purpose of displaying the productivity of the earth. Worship at the ancestral temple is for the purpose of recognizing the ancestry of man. The worship of the mountains and rivers is for the purpose of serving the different spirits. The five sacrifices are for the purpose of commemorating the origin of human occupations. Therefore there are priests at the temple, the Three High Ministers at the court, and the Three Elders at the College. The soothsayer stands in front of the king and the official historian at his back, while the priest in charge of divination and the blind music master and his assistants are scattered on his right and his left, while the king sits in the middle, maintaining calm in his heart, a guardian (or symbol) of the ultimate rightness of things.

Therefore when *li* is observed at the worship of Heaven, then the different gods attend to their duties. When *li* is observed at the worship of Earth, then things grow and multiply. When *li* is observed at the ancestral temple, then filial piety and affection prevail. When *li* is observed at the five sacrifices, then standards of measurements are established. Therefore the worship of Heaven, of Earth, of the ancestors, the mountains and rivers, and the five sacrifices are for the keeping up of the human duties and constitute the embodiment of *li*.

Therefore, this *li* originates in T'aiyi (Primeval Unity), which was divided into the Heaven and the Earth, transformed into the *yin* and the *yang*, operating as the seasons, and assuming shape as the different spirits. The will of the gods is expressed as destiny, and is controlled from Heaven.

Thus *li* must be based on Heaven, shows its action on the Earth, and is applied to the different human occupations, changing according to the seasons and fitted into the different crafts. In man, it emerges as the principle of livelihood and is shown in trade, labor, social intercourse, eating and drinking, and in the ceremony of "capping," marriage, burial and sacrifice to the dead, archery, carriage driving, and audience at court.

Therefore the duties of *li* are the main principles of human life, serving the purpose of promoting mutual confidence and social harmony and strengthening the socialties and bonds of friendship. They are the main principles for worshipping the spirits and feeding the living and sacrificing to the dead. *Li* is a great channel through which we follow the laws of Heaven and direct to proper courses the expressions of the human heart. Therefore, only the Sage knows that *li* is indispensable. Therefore, to destroy a kingdom, upset a family or ruin a man, you must first take away from him this sense of *li*.

V. THE METHOD OF CULTIVATING *LI*

Therefore *li* is to man as the yeast is to wine; the superior man has a little more of it, and the inferior man has a little less of it. Therefore the Sage, or saintly ruler, cultivates the proper approach to duties and the order of *li*, as a means of controlling or regulating human nature. Therefore, human nature is the field cultivated by the Sage or saintly ruler. He ploughs it with *li*, sows it with the seeds of duties, weeds it by education and learning, harvests it with true manhood, and enjoys it with music. Therefore *li* is but the crystallization of what is right. If a thing is in accordance with the standard of what is right, new social practices may be instituted, although they were not known to the rulers of the past. The standard of right is the following of each class of people in its proper course and true manhood become articulate. Those who have followed the right, observing the proper course and cultivating true manhood, will become powerful administrators. True manhood is the foundation for proper conduct and the embodiment of conformity with the standard of right. Those who have achieved true manhood become the rulers of man.

It follows, therefore, that to govern a country without *li* is like tilling a field without a plough. To observe *li* without basing it on the standard of right is like tilling the field and forgetting to sow the seeds. To try to do right without cultivating knowledge is like sowing the seeds without weeding the field. To cultivate knowledge without bringing it back to the aim of true manhood, is like weeding the field without harvesting it. And to arrive at the aim of true manhood without coming to enjoy it through music, is like harvesting and forgetting to eat the harvest. To enjoy true manhood through music and not arrive at complete harmony with nature is like eating and not becoming well-fed, or healthy.

When the four limbs are well developed and the skin is clear and the flesh is full, that is the health of human life. When the parents and children are affectionate, the brothers are good toward one another and the husband and the wife live in harmony, that is the health of the home life. When the higher officials obey the law and the lower officials are clean, the officials have regulated and well-defined functions and the king and the ministers help one another on the right course, that is the health of the national life. When the Emperor rides in the carriage of Virtue, with Music as his driver, when the different rulers meet each other with courtesy, the officials regulate each other with law, the scholars urge one another by the standard of honesty, and the people unite with one another in peace, that is the health of the world. This is called the Grand Harmony (*Tashun*)....

第九章　论教育

——《礼记·学记》第十八

　　玉不加磨琢，不会成为美术品；人若不学习，亦不会明白道理。所以古代君王建国为政，总是以教育为先。《尚书·兑命》说："永远要念念不忘教育。"正是此意。

【原文】

　　发虑宪，求善良，足以谀闻，不足以动众；就贤体远，足以动众，未足以化民。君子如欲化民成俗，其必由学乎！

【语译】

　　发愿为善，只能让人小有声望，尚不足感动群众。与贤能者结交，欢迎远方的来人，虽能感动群众，但还不能化育人民。君子若要化育人民，培养良好风俗，一定要从教育入手吧。

【原文】

　　玉不琢，不成器；人不学，不知道。是故古之王者建国君民，教学为先。《兑命》曰："念终始典于学。"其此之谓乎！

【语译】

　　玉不加磨琢，不会成为美术品；人若不学习，亦不会明白道理。所以古代君王建国为政，总是以教育为先。《尚书·兑命》说："永远要念念不忘教育。"正是此意。

【原文】

　　虽有佳肴，弗食，不知其旨也；虽有至道，弗学，不知其善也。是故学然后知不足，教然后知困。知不足，然后能自反也；知困，然后能自强也。故曰：教学相长也。《兑命》曰："学学半。"其此之谓乎？

【语译】

　　虽然有好菜，不去吃，就不能知道味道美。虽然有好学说，不去学，就不知道好在何处。所以，研究学问之后，才知道自己所知不足。教导别人，才知道困难何在。知道自己所知不足，才能反省有自知之明。知道有困难，才能努力进修。所以说，教学相长。《尚书·兑命》上说："教为学之一半。"正是此意。

【原文】

　　古之教者，家有塾，党有庠，术有序，国有学。比年入学，中年考校。一年视离经辨志，三年视敬业乐群，五年视博习亲师，七年视论学取友，谓之小成；九年知类通达，强立而不反，谓之大成。夫然后足以化民易俗，近者说服，而远者怀之。此大学之道也。记曰："蛾子时术之。"其此之谓乎？

【语译】

　　古时教学的处所，二十五家的一村里有一个塾，有五百家的一镇有一个庠，二千五百家的郡有序，国的首都有学，每年有新生入学，隔一年考试一次。入学一年考经文句读，辨别志向；三年考查学生的读书习惯与团体生活情形。五年考查学生是否博学敬师；七年考查学生在学术上的见解，及对朋友的选择，这叫小成；九年而通晓各科，临事不惑，坚定不移，这叫大成。这时，才能化育百姓，改变风俗，近处的人心悦诚服，远方的人都来归附，这是大学教育的道理。古书上说："蚂蚁时时学习不息。"正是此意。

【原文】

　　大学始教，皮弁祭菜，示敬道也；宵雅肄三，官其始也；入学鼓箧，孙其业也；夏楚二物，收其威也；未卜禘，不视学，游其志也；时观而弗语，存其心也；幼者听而弗问，学不躐等也。此七者，教之大伦也。记曰："凡学，官先事，士先志。"其此之谓乎！

【语译】

　　大学开学时，士子穿礼服，用素菜祭祀，表示敬学之意；练习唱《小雅》上三首诗歌，是学做官的初步。先击鼓召集学生，然后打开书箧，使学生敬业；夏楚两物用以鞭策学生，使之敦品励行。夏天谛祭以前，无人到学校视察，是使学生自行发展；教师只观察学生，必要时才加以训教，是使学生自己思维。年幼的学生，听讲而不发问，则因学习有一定程序。这七项，是教学的主要方法。古书上说："凡学习做官，先学管事，要做学者，先立定志向。"正是此意。

【原文】

大学之教也时，教必有正业，退息必有居。学，不学操缦，不能安弦；不学博依，不能安诗；不学杂服，不能安礼；不兴其艺，不能乐学。故君子之于学也，藏焉，修焉，息焉，游焉。夫然，故安其学而亲其师，乐其友而信其道。是以虽离师辅而不反也。《兑命》曰："敬孙务时敏，厥修乃来。"其此之谓乎！

【语译】

大学按时序施教，有正常学科，下课及休假时，有课外研究。学习的方法，如果不学"操""缦"这些小曲调，指法不熟，弹琴弹不好；不学举譬喻，诗作不好，不学服饰用途，行礼也行不好；不喜爱这些小技艺，就无法对学习有兴趣。所以君子学习时，内藏于心，而发于外，休息或游乐时，都念念不忘。能如此，才能专心学习，亲爱师长，与同学相处融洽深信真理。虽离开了师长同学，也不会违背道义。《尚书·说命》说："恭敬谦顺，努力不懈，进修便可成功。"正是此意。

【原文】

今之教者，呻其占毕，多其讯言，及于数进而不顾其安，使人不由其诚，教人不尽其材；其施之也悖，其求之也佛。夫然，故隐其学而疾其师，苦其难而不知其益也，虽终其业，其去之必速。教之不刑，其此之由乎！

【语译】

今之教师，胡言乱语，用陈腐的问题困扰学生，呶呶不休。结果使学生没有诚意，教育的人也不能因材施教，学生只好假装用功。所教的课业先错，所希望于学生者自然也错。这样，学生昧于学习，憎恶师长，只觉学习困难，不知有什么益处。虽然学完一科，也就很快忘光。教育之不能成功，正是由于此种原因。

【原文】

大学之法，禁于未发之谓豫，当其可之谓时，不陵节而施之谓孙，相观而善之谓摩。此四者，教之所由兴也。

【语译】

大学教育方法，在恶念发生前，用礼约束禁止，叫作准备；在适宜教导时才教导，这叫合乎时宜；根据学生的能力，不跨越程度教导，叫作顺序；使学者互相观摩而收到益处，叫做切磋。这四种就是使教育发展的方法。

【原文】

发然后禁，则扞格而不胜；时过然后学，则勤苦而难成；杂施而不孙，则坏乱而不修，独学而无友，则孤陋而寡闻；燕朋逆其师；燕辟废其学。此六者，教之所由废也。

【语译】

恶念已经发生才加以禁止，因坚不可入，教育也难有作用。过了适当的学习时期才学习，纵然努力也难有成就。不按着进度学习，只使脑筋混乱而不成功。独自学习，不与同学研究，必然浅陋而见闻不广。结交损友会违背师长的教训；有不良的习惯会荒误学业。这六项是教育失败的原因。

【原文】

君子既知教之所由兴，又知教之所由废，然后可以为人师也。故君子之教喻也，道而弗牵，强而弗抑，开而弗达。道而弗牵则和，强而弗抑则易，开而弗达则思；和易以思，可谓善喻矣。

【语译】

君子既然知道了教育兴起的原因，又知道了教育衰落的原因，然后可以为人师。君子的教育方法是晓谕别人，以引导而不强迫别人服从；对学生刚严，并不抑制其个性发展；启发学生，而不将结论道破无余。引导而不强迫，使学生易于亲近。教师刚严而不抑制，学生才能自由发展。启发而不必说个净尽，学生才能思考。使学生亲近而又能自由思考，才是善于晓谕。

【原文】

学者有四失，教者必知之。人之学也，或失则多，或失则寡，或失则易，或失则止。此四者，心之莫同也。知其心，然后能救其失也。教也者，长善而救其失者也。

【语译】

学习的人会犯四种过错，教导的人必须知道。人在学习时，有的贪多而不求甚解；有的囿于一隅，而所知太少；有的见异思迁而学不专一；有的故步自封，不求进步。这四种心理各自不同，先明白这些心理，才能补救那些毛病。教育之目的，是在培养良善挽救过失。

【原文】

善歌者，使人继其声；善教者，使人继其志。其言也约而达，微而臧，罕譬而喻，可谓继志矣。

【语译】

善于唱歌的人，能引人随同他歌唱；善于教学的人，能使人继续他的思想。教师的言语简约而明达，含蓄而精当，少用譬喻也容易了解，这样才能使人继续其理想。

【原文】

君子知至学之难易，而知其美恶，然后能博喻；能博喻然后能为师；能为师然后能为长；能为长然后能为君。故师也者，所以学为君也。是故择师不可不慎也。记曰："三王四代惟其师。"此之谓乎？

【语译】

君子知道求学上的深浅难易，个人品性上的优劣，然后能广举晓谕，如此才有能力为人师。能为人师，始能做官长，能做官长，才能做君主。所以学为人师，就是学做君主。所以择师不可不慎。古书说："虞、夏、殷、周四代，择师都很慎重。"正是此意。

【原文】

凡学之道，严师为难。师严然后道尊，道尊然后民知敬学。是故君之所不臣于其臣者二：当其为尸则弗臣也，当其为师则弗臣也。大学之礼，虽诏于天子，无北面，所以尊师也。

【语译】

求学时最难做到的，就是尊师。老师受到尊敬，然后真理才受到

重视；真理受到重视，然后人民才知道重视学术。所以君主不以臣事
君之礼要求他的臣子，有两种情形：一种就是在祭祀中，臣子代表死
者魂灵之时；另一种就是臣子做君主老师之时。在大学里的礼法中，
对天子讲课时，臣下不必面北居臣位，这就是表示尊师。

【原文】

善学者，师逸而功倍，又从而庸之；不善学者，师勤而功半，又从而
怨之。善问者，如攻坚木，先其易者，后其节目，及其久也，相说以解；
不善问者反此。善待问者，如撞钟，叩之以小者则小鸣，叩之以大者则大
鸣，待其从容，然后尽其声；不善答问者反此。此皆进学之道也。

【语译】

学生善于学习，老师很轻松，而教育效果加倍，更得到学生的尊
敬；学生不善于学习，老师督促严厉，而效果只到一半，学生怨恨老
师过于严格。善发问的人，像砍坚硬的木头，先从软的部位开始，再
到硬节，久了，木头自然脱落；不善发问的人刚好相反。善于答问的
人，有如撞钟，轻敲钟声小，重敲钟声大，从容不迫地敲，钟声会余
韵悠扬；不善答问的人刚好相反。这都是教与学的方法。

【原文】

记问之学，不足以为人师。必也其听语乎。力不能问，然后语之；语
之而不知，虽舍之可也。

【语译】

只记忆材料以备回答别人发问的人，不够资格做别人的老师。好
老师一定注意学生的见解。学生已经尽力而不得要领时，老师再予以

指导；老师指导，学生仍然不明白，只暂时搁置。

【原文】

良冶之子，必学为裘；良弓之子，必学为箕；始驾马者反之，车在马前。君子察于此三者，可以有志于学矣。

【语译】

好铁匠的儿子，自然也能补缀皮袍。好弓匠的儿子，自然也能做畚箕。初学驾车的小马都先系在车子后面，而车就在面前。君子观察这三件事，就可学得教学的正当方法。

【原文】

古之学者，比物丑类。鼓无当于五声，五声弗得不和。水无当于五色，五色弗得不章。学无当于五官，五官弗得不治。师无当于五服，五服弗得不亲。

【语译】

古代学者，比较事物的异同而归成类别。鼓的声音并不同于五音之任何一种，但是五音不得鼓的调节就不和谐。水的颜色并不同于五色中任何一色，然而五色没有水调匀就不鲜明。学者并不等于政府任何官员，然而任何官员没经过教育就不会办事。老师不是人伦中的任何一种，但五伦没有老师的教诲就也不懂得人伦了。

【原文】

君子曰：大德不官，大道不器，大信不约，大时不齐。察于此四者，可以有志于学矣。

【语译】

　　君子说：伟大的德行，不专任一种职务。伟大的道理，不局限于一事一物。最大的信用，不必见于盟誓立约。恒久的天时，也不专属暑天或冬天。了解了这四种情形，就能立志学做大事了。

【原文】

　　三王之祭川也，皆先河而后海；或源也，或委也。此之谓务本。

【语译】

　　夏商周三代王者祭祀河川时，都是先祭河而后祭海。原委由此即可分明了。知道此一分别，就知道什么是要点了。

Chapter Nine **ON EDUCATION**

(*Hsuehchi*, *Liki*, Chapter XVIII)

I. THE NEED FOR EDUCATION

To desire to do right and to seek what is good would give a person a little reputation but would not enable him to influence the masses. To associate with the wise and able men and to welcome those who come from a distant country would enable a person to influence the masses, but would not enable him to civilize the people. The only way for the superior man to civilize the people and establish good social customs is through education. A piece of jade cannot become an object of art without chiselling, and a man cannot come to know the moral law without education. Therefore the ancient kings regarded education as the first important factor in their efforts to establish order in a country. That is the meaning of the passage in the *Advice to Fu Yueh* (by King Kaotsung of the Hsia Dynasty, now a chapter of *Shuking*) which says, "Forever occupy your thoughts with education." Just as one cannot know the taste of food without eating it, however excellent it may be, so without education one cannot come to know the excellence of a great body of knowledge, although it may be there.

Therefore only through education does one come to be dissatisfied with his own knowledge, and only through teaching others does one come to realize the uncomfortable inadequacy of his knowledge. Being dissatisfied with his own knowledge, one then realizes that the trouble lies with himself, and realizing the uncomfortable inadequacy of his knowledge, one then feels stimulated to improve himself. Therefore it is said, "The processes of teaching and learning stimulate one another." That is the meaning of the passage in the *Advice to Fu Yeuh* which says, "Teaching is the half of learning."

II. THE ANCIENT EDUCATIONAL SYSTEM

The ancient educational system was as follows: There was a primary school in every hamlet of 25 families, a secondary school in every town of 500 families, an academy in every county of 2500 families, and a college in the capital of every state (for the education of the princes and sons of nobles and the best pupils from the lower schools). Every year new students were admitted, and every other year there was an examination. At the end of the first year, and effort was made to see how the pupils were able to punctuate their sentences and to find out their natural inclinations. At the end of three years, an effort was made to find out their habits of study and their group life. At the end of five years, they would try to see how well read in general the pupils were and how closely they had followed their teachers. At the end of seven years, they would try to find out how their ideas had developed and what kind of friends they had selected for themselves. This is called the Minor Graduation (*hsiaoch'eng*—from the lower grades). At the end of nine years, they were expected to know the various subjects and have a general understanding of life and to have laid a firm foundation for their character from which they could not go back. This was called the Major Graduation (*tach'eng*—from the higher grades).

By such an educational system only is it possible to civilize the people and reform the morals of the country, so that the local inhabitants will be happy and those in distant lands will love to come to the country. This is the principle of *tahsueh*, or higher education. That is the meaning of the passage in the *Ancient Records* which says, "The ants are busy all the time" (*the importance of continuous study*).

In the college, the students begin to study the proper use of ceremonial robes and vegetable offerings at sacrifices, in order to learn the principle of respect or piety. They are made to sing the first three songs of *Hsiaoya*, in order to learn the first elements of official life.

On entering the college, a drum is beaten before the students unpack their books, so as to teach discipline at their studies. The ferule or hickory stick is used in order to regulate their external behavior. No inspector is sent to the college except on the occasion of the Grand Sacrifice to the royal ancestors, that the students may be left alone to develop themselves. The teacher observes but does not constantly lecture to them, so that the students have time to think out things for themselves. The young ones are supposed to listen and not to ask questions, so that they may know their own place. These seven things are the main methods of teaching. That is the meaning of the passage in the *Ancient Records* which says, "At the college, those who already have an office make studies relative to their respective departments, while those who do not yet have an office study what they want to do afterwards."

III. EXTRA-CURRICULAR STUDIES

In the educational system of the college, there are regular studies in class and collateral studies when the students are in their own rooms. Without the practice of fingering, one cannot learn to play the string instrument smoothly. Without wide observation of things, one cannot learn poetry easily. Without acquaintance with the different ceremonial robes, one cannot master the study of rituals. Without learning the different arts (like archery and carriage driving), one cannot enjoy study at school. Therefore in the education of the superior man (or the intellectual upper class), one is given time to digest things, to cultivate things, to rest and to play. In this way the students learn to feel at home at college and establish a personal relationship with their teachers, enjoy friendship and acquire conviction in ideas. They then may leave their teachers without turning their backs on their studies. This is the meaning of the passage in the *Advice of Fu Yueh*, which says, "Respectfully keep at your studies constantly, and then you will have results."

The teachers of today just go on repeating things in a rigmarole fashion, annoy the students with constant questions, and repeat the same things over and over again. They do not try to find out what the students' natural inclinations are, so that the students are forced to pretend to like their studies, nor do they try to bring out the best in their talents. What they give to the students is wrong in the first place and what they expect of the students is just as wrong. As a result, the students hide their favorite readings and hate their teachers, are exasperated at the difficulty of their studies and do not know what good it does them. Although they go through the regular course of instruction, they are quick to leave it when they are through. This is the reason for the failure of education today.

IV. THE IDEAL TEACHER

The principles of college education are as follows: First, prevention, or preventing bad habits before they arise. Secondly, timeliness, or giving the students things when they are ready for them. Thirdly, order, or teaching the different subjects in proper sequence. Fourthly, mutual stimulation (literally "friction"), or letting the students admire the excellence of other students. These four things ensure the success of education.

On the other hand, to forbid them after they have already acquired bad habits would seem to make everything go against their grain and efforts at correction would be without success. To teach them after the young age is past would make their learning difficult and futile. To fail to teach the different subjects in their proper order would bring about chaos in their studies, without good results. To study a subject all alone without friends would make a student too narrow in scope, lacking in general knowledge.

Bad company would encourage them to go against their teachers and bad pastimes would cause them to neglect their studies. These six things cause the breakdown of a college education.

With the knowledge of the reasons for success in education and the causes of its failure, the superior man is then qualified to be a teacher.

Therefore in his teaching the superior man guides his students but does not pull them along; he urges them to go forward and does not suppress them; he opens the way, but does not take them to the place. Guiding without pulling makes the process of learning gentle; urging without suppressing makes the process of learning easy; and opening the way without leading the students to the place makes them think for themselves. Now if the process of learning is made gentle and easy and the students are encouraged to think for themselves, we may call the man a good teacher.

There are four common errors in education which the teacher must beware of. Some students try to learn too much or too many subjects, some learn too little or too few subjects, some learn things too easily and some are too easily discouraged. These four things show that individuals differ in their mental endowments, and only through a knowledge of the different mental endowments can the teacher correct their mistakes. A teacher is but a man who tries to bring out the good and remedy the weaknesses of his students.

A good singer makes others follow his tune, and a good educator makes others follow his ideal. His words are concise but expressive, casual but full of hidden meaning, and he is good at drawing ingenious examples to make people understand him. In this way, he may be said to be a good man to make others follow his ideal.

The superior man knows what is difficult and what is easy, what is excellent and what is deplorable in the things to be learned, and then he is good at drawing examples. Being good at drawing examples, he then knows how to be a teacher. Knowing how to be a teacher, he then knows how to be an elder. And knowing how to be an elder, he then knows how to be a ruler of men. Therefore, the art of being a teacher is the art of learning to be a ruler of men. Therefore one cannot be too careful in selecting one's teacher. That is the meaning of the passage in the *Ancient Records* which says, "The Three Kings and the Four Dynasties (Yu, Hsia, Shang and Chou) laid the greatest emphasis upon the selection of teachers."

In this matter of education, the most difficult thing is to establish a respect for the teacher. When the teacher is respected, then people respect what he teaches, and when people respect what he teaches, then they respect learning or scholarship. Therefore there are only two classes of persons that the king dare not regard as his subjects: his teacher and the *shih* (child representing the spirit of the deceased at a sacrifice). According to the customs of the college, a teacher doesn't have to stand facing north even when receiving an edict from the king, which shows the great respect for the teacher.

V. THE PROCESS OF LEARNING

With a good student, the teacher doesn't have much to do and the results are double, besides getting the student's respect. With a bad student, the teacher has to work hard and the results are only half of what is to be expected, besides getting hated by the student. A good questioner proceeds like a man chopping wood—he begins at the easier end, attacking the knots last, and after a time the teacher and student come to understand the point with a sense of pleasure. A bad questioner does just exactly the opposite. One who knows how to answer questions is like a group of bells. When you strike the big bell, the big one rings, and when you strike the small bell, the small one rings. It is important, however, to allow time for its tone gradually to die out. One who does not know how to answer questions is exactly the reverse of this. These are all suggestions for the process of teaching and learning.

That type of scholarship which is bent on remembering things in order to answer questions does not qualify one to be a teacher. A good teacher should observe the students' conversations. When he sees a student is doing his best but is lost, then he explains it to him, and if after the explanation, the student still does not understand, he may as well leave the matter alone.

The son of a tinker naturally learns how to mend fur coats, and the son of a good maker of bows naturally learns how to make a bamboo *chi* (shallow pan made of woven sliced bamboo for holding grain), and a man breaking in a horse first puts the horse behind the carriage. A gentleman can learn from these three things the proper method of education. The scholars of ancient times learned the truth about things from analogies.

The drum itself does not come under any of the five modes of music, and yet the five modes cannot succeed in harmony without the drum. Water itself does not belong to any of the five colors, and yet (in painting) the five colors would lack brightness without the use of water. Learning itself does not come under any of the five senses, and yet the five senses cannot be properly trained without learning. The teacher does not come under the five degrees of clan kinship, and yet the five degrees of clan kinship would not love one another without the teacher.

The gentleman says, "A great personality does not (necessarily) fit one for any particular office. A great character does not (necessarily) qualify one for any particular service. Great honesty does not (necessarily) make a man keep his word. Great regard for time does not (necessarily) make one punctual." To know these four things is to know the really fundamental things in life.

In offering sacrifices to the river gods, the ancient kings always began with worshipping the gods of the rivers before worshipping the gods of the seas. A distinction was made between the source and the outlet, and to know this distinction is to know how to attend to the essentials.

第十章　论音乐

——《礼记·乐记》第十九

音乐出于人的内心。人有感于心，就表现于声音便有了节奏，便是乐。所以，太平盛世的音乐安详而愉快，政治也清平。乱世的音乐怨恨而愤怒，即因其政治之错乱。亡国的音乐悲哀而愁思，当时的人民必流离困苦。由此看来，音乐的道理与政治是密切相关的。

【原文】

凡音之起，由人心生也。人心之动，物使之然也。感于物而动，故形于声。声相应，故生变；变成方，谓之音；比音而乐之，及干戚羽旄，谓之乐。

【语译】

人心自外界接受到刺激，音乐便自内发生。人心受到外物的刺激而起反应，即表现于声音。因反应不同，所发的声音也不同。不同的声音相应和，就显出变化。将此变化列成一定的节奏，则成为歌声。比照歌声而配合以乐器以及跳舞用的道具，就是"乐"。

【原文】

乐者，音之所由生也；其本在人心之感于物也。是故其哀心感者，其声噍以杀。其乐心感者，其声啴以缓。其喜心感者，其声发以散。其怒心感者，其声粗以厉。其敬心感者，其声直以廉。其爱心感者，其声和以柔。六者，非性也，感于物而后动。

是故先王慎所以感之者。故礼以道其志，乐以和其声，政以一其行，刑以防其奸。礼乐刑政，其极一也；所以同民心而出治道也。

【语译】

"乐"是由声音所构成，对内心之刺激而来。所以心里悲哀时起的反应，则发出焦急低沉的声音。快乐时起的反应，则发出宽裕徐缓的声音。喜悦时的反应，则发出兴奋爽快的声音。愤怒时的反应，则发出粗野凄厉的声音。恭敬的反应，则发出虔诚而清纯的声音。恋爱的反应，发出体贴温柔的声音。这六种反应，不是人之天性不同，而是因不同的刺激所引起的。因此古代圣王非常重视人心所受的"刺激"。要用礼诱导人心，用乐调和人声，用政令划一行为，用刑罚防止社会的邪恶。礼、乐、刑、政其终极目的是相同的；全是要齐一人心而实现政治清平的理想。

【原文】

凡音者，生人心者也。情动于中，故形于声。声成文，谓之音。是故，治世之音安以乐，其政和。乱世之音怨以怒，其政乖。亡国之音哀以思，其民困。声音之道，与政通矣。宫为君，商为臣，角为民，徵为事，羽为物。五者不乱，则无怗懘之音矣。宫乱则荒，其君骄。商乱则陂，其官坏。角乱则忧，其民怨。徵乱则哀，其事勤。羽乱则危，其财匮。五者皆乱，迭相陵，谓之慢。如此，则国之灭亡无日矣。郑卫之音，乱世之音也，比于慢矣。桑间濮上之音，亡国之音也，其政散，其民流，诬上行私而不可止也。

【语译】

音乐出于人的内心。人有感于心，就表现于声音便有了节奏，便是乐。所以，太平盛世的音乐安详而愉快，政治也清平。乱世的音乐怨恨而愤怒，即因其政治之错乱。亡国的音乐悲哀而愁思，当时的人民必流离困苦。由此看来，音乐的道理与政治是密切相关的。若以五音之宫为君，商为臣，角为民，徵为事，羽为物，而此五音协调不乱，就不会有不和谐的声音。宫音乱时，显得慌乱，有如国君骄恣而贤者去位。商音乱则显得倾颓，有如官常败坏而国事贴危。角音乱则显得忧愁，有如人民愁想而隐忧四伏。徵音乱则显得悲哀，有如百事须苦而勤劳无功。羽音乱则显得危迫，有如物资匮乏而民用匮乏。若五音全乱而交相侵犯，国家也就行将灭亡了。古代郑、卫地方的音乐，是乱世的音乐，几乎完全错乱。师涓从濮水上听到的音乐，就是殷纣亡国之音乐。当时政事荒废，人民流离，不知爱国家只图私欲，败坏无度。

【原文】

凡音者，生于人心者也。乐者，通伦理者也。是故，知声而不知音者，禽兽是也；知音而不知乐音，众庶是也。唯君子为能知乐。是故，审声以知音，审音以知乐，审乐以知政，而治道备矣。是故，不知声者不可与言音，不知音者不可与言乐。知乐，则几于知礼矣。礼乐皆得，谓之有德。德者，得也。

【语译】

声音生于人心，而音乐则通于人伦物理。所以，只听声而不知文理的，是禽兽。只懂声音而不懂得音乐效用的，便是一般大众。唯有君子能懂音乐。因此，从分辨声而懂得音；从分辨音而懂得音乐的道理；从分辨音乐的道理而懂得政治的道理，这才会有全盘治国的计划。所以不知声的人，不可和他讨论音，不知音的人，不可和他讨论"乐"。如果懂得"乐"的功能，大概也懂得礼的意义了。若深通礼和乐，就可称为有德之君。德就是心得。

【原文】

是故，乐之隆，非极音也。食飨之礼，非致味也。清庙之瑟，朱弦而疏越，一倡而三叹，有遗音者矣。大飨之礼，尚玄酒而俎腥鱼，大羹不和，有遗味者矣。是故先王之制礼乐也，非以极口腹耳目之欲也，将以教民平好恶，而反人道之正也。

【语译】

所以最精美的音乐，不见得就是最复杂的音乐。最盛大的宴席，不见得就是最讲究的酒席。譬如周代大祭，伴奏清庙乐章所奏的乐器瑟，只有朱红的弦和稀疏的底孔，一人唱诗，三人和声，所弹所唱的甚为简单，其目的不在于美好的音乐。大祭享之礼，水首要，而盘里只是生肉生鱼，羹汤也没调味，可知其目的不在于口味了。因此，可知先王制订礼乐，不在于满足人口腹耳目之欲。恰恰相反，其宗旨是用礼乐教导人民，使人分辨爱与憎以恢复到天性的真纯。

【原文】

人生而静，天之性也；感于物而动，性之欲也。物至知知，然后好恶形焉。好恶无节于内，知诱于外，不能反躬，天理灭矣。夫物之感人无穷，而人之好恶无节，则是物至而人化物也。人化物也者，灭天理而穷人欲者也。于是有悖逆诈伪之心，有淫泆作乱之事。是故，强者胁弱，众者暴寡，知者诈愚，勇者苦怯，疾病不养，老幼孤独不得其所，此大乱之道也。

【语译】

人的思考力受了外界的刺激，才有了爱好或厌恶两种欲念。好恶的欲念没有节制，而外物又引诱不停，人若不能反省，以良知抑制冲动，则天生的理性就要毁灭了。外界不断刺激人，人若随其刺激而生好恶的反应，不以理性制衡，那就是接触外物也随之改变了。随外物改变，就是灭绝理性而追随人欲。于是便生有悖道诈伪的心，做出淫泆乱法的事，终致强者胁迫弱者，多数欺压少数，智者诈骗愚者，勇者欺负懦怯者，有病者无人照顾，老幼孤独者流离失所，这就天下大乱了。

【原文】

是故先王之制礼乐，人为之节；衰麻哭泣，所以节丧纪也；钟鼓干戚，所以和安乐也；婚姻冠笄，所以别男女也；射乡食飨，所以正交接也。礼节民心，乐和民声，政以行之，刑以防之，礼乐刑政，四达而不悖，则王道备矣。

【语译】

先王创作礼乐，是使人有所节制，比如披麻戴孝时的哀哭，是使人节哀，钟鼓干戚之设，用以庆祝安乐；婚姻冠笄之事，用以区别男女；射乡食飨之礼，用以纠正社交礼俗。用礼调节人的性情，用乐调和人的声音，用政令实行，用刑罚防治违法。礼乐刑政，四方面相辅而行，毫无冲突，政治之道便完备了。

【原文】

乐者为同，礼者为异。同则相亲，异则相敬。乐胜则流，礼胜则离。合情饰貌者，礼乐之事也。礼义立，则贵贱等矣；乐文同，则上下和矣；好恶著，则贤不肖别矣。刑禁暴，爵举贤，则政均矣。仁以爱之，义以正之，如此，则民治行矣。

【语译】

音乐使众人结合，礼仪使众人区别。因其结合，故使人彼此亲近；因其区别，故使人彼此尊敬。太重视乐，容易使人松弛；过分讲究礼，会使人隔阂而不亲。所以，礼与乐，是用以保持正当的感情与仪表。有一定的礼仪，就会显出贤能者贵，不贤能者贱的等级；有相同的音乐，居上位者与在下位者情感即可交流；有好坏的标准，才会显出谁贤谁不贤。不贤的，禁之以刑；贤能的，以爵赏推举；政治自然修明了。以仁心爱民，以正义治之，民治的理想即可实现了。

【原文】

乐由中出，礼自外作。乐由中出故静，礼自外作故文。大乐必易，大礼必简。乐至则无怨，礼至则不争。揖让而治天下者，礼乐之谓也。暴民不作，诸侯宾服，兵革不试，五刑不用，百姓无患，天子不怒，如此，则乐达矣。合父子之亲，明长幼之序，以敬四海之内。天子如此，则礼行矣。

【语译】

乐发自内心，礼自外来。乐发自内心，所以平静。礼自外来，所以表现于仪式。盛大的音乐必然平易，最大的典礼必须简单。乐教实行，人的情思都表达于外，心内便无怨恨；礼教流行，人的举动皆有定规，言行上便无冲突。所说"揖让而治天下"，即指礼乐的政治。要使无暴民作乱，远近诸国都来朝拜，无须动兵作战，不动用刑罚而百姓无忧，天子不怒，便是乐通行了。普天之下，父子相亲，长幼有序，国民敬爱。天子能做到这样，这就是礼通行了。

【原文】

大乐与天地同和，大礼与天地同节。和故百物不失，节故祀天祭地。明则有礼乐，幽则有鬼神。如此，则四海之内，合敬同爱矣。礼者殊事，合敬者也；乐者异文，合爱者也。礼乐之情同，故明王以相沿也。故事与时并，名与功偕。

【语译】

雄伟的音乐与自然和谐，隆重的礼仪与自然的节奏配合。因为和谐，故能不失万物之本性；有固定程序，故有祀天祭地之礼。明处用礼乐，暗处有鬼神。如此，天下之人，皆能相敬相爱。换言之：礼的仪式有所不同，但其宗旨在于相敬；乐也有所不同，但其宗旨皆在于相爱。因为礼乐是使人相敬相爱，故历代英明之主一贯以礼乐施政。政事历代不同，礼乐也因君王成就之庆典而异。

【原文】

乐者，天地之和也；礼者，天地之序也。和故百物皆化；序故群物皆别。乐由天作，礼以地制。过制则乱，过作则暴。明于天地，然后能兴礼乐也。

【语译】

乐表现宇宙的和谐；礼表现宇宙的秩序。因和谐故能化生万物；因秩序故能显出品级。乐由于自然而来，礼因社会的生活而作。礼逾越了秩序则乱，乐逾越了和谐则暴乱。知道天地的关系，而后才能创制礼乐。

【原文】

故圣人作乐以应天，制礼以配地。礼乐明备，天地官矣。

【语译】

所以圣哲作乐以应天，制礼以配地。礼乐分明而且完备之后，天地各尽其功能了。

【原文】

天尊地卑，君臣定矣。卑高已陈，贵贱位矣。动静有常，小大殊矣。方以类聚，物以群分，则性命不同矣。在天成象，在地成形；如此，则礼者天地之别也。地气上齐，天气下降，阴阳相摩，天地相荡，鼓之以雷霆，奋之以风雨，动之以四时，煖之以日月，而百化兴焉。如此，则乐者天地之和也。

【语译】

天尊而在上，地卑而在下，正似君与臣。高低分列，贵贱则各有其位了。动静各有定律，大小随以分别。万物以类而分，动物亦各自成群。在天为星球，在地成山河。而礼亦即据差别而定的。地气上升，天气下降，天地阴阳互相摩荡，雷霆鼓动，风雨滋润，四时周流，日月照耀，而万物化育生长。所以乐是与宇宙自然之理并行不悖的。

【原文】

乐著大始，而礼居成物。著不息者天也，著不动者地也。一动一静者，天地之间也。故圣人曰礼乐云。

【语译】

乐显示宇宙原始的力量，而礼则反应于创造的形体。显示不停的动是天；显示凝定的静是地；又动又静的则在天地之间，即圣人所论的礼乐。

【原文】

故观其舞，知其德。

【语译】

看到一个国家的舞，就知道此一国家的特性。

【原文】

夫民有血气心知之性，而无哀乐喜怒之常，应感起物而动，然后心术形焉。是故志微噍杀之音作，而民思忧。啴谐慢易，繁文简节之音作，而民康乐。粗厉猛起，奋末广贲之音作，而民刚毅。廉直劲正庄诚之音作，而民肃敬。宽裕肉好顺成和动之音作，而民慈爱。流辟邪散狄成涤滥之音作，而民淫乱。

【语译】

　　人虽皆有血气心知的本性，但哀乐喜怒的心情，则随境况而变。必待外物刺激而引起欲望。而低沉的声音引起人感伤忧愁。倦怠平易而音调慢长的声音，引起宁静喜悦。强而有力声音，发与收皆猛壮而昂奋的声音，引起刚强坚毅之心。清纯正直而庄严诚恳的声音，引起肃穆而虔敬。发出宽舒清润平静的声音，引起慈爱之心。淫荡刺激的声音，引人心情邪乱而悖德。

【原文】

　　土敝则草木不长，水烦则鱼鳖不大，气衰则生物不遂，世乱则礼慝而乐淫。是故其声哀而不庄，乐而不安。

【语译】

　　土壤瘠敝，草木不生。渔捞无时，鱼鳖不大；气温不正，生物不长；社会浊乱，则礼失其常，音乐淫靡。因此音虽悲哀而不庄重，虽喜悦而不安详。

【原文】

　　德者，性之端也。乐者，德之华也。金石丝竹，乐之器也。诗，言其志也，歌，咏其声也，舞，动其容也。三者本于心，然后乐器从之。是故情深而文明，气盛而化神。和顺积中而英华发外，唯乐不可以为伪。

【语译】

　　德是人性的基本；乐是德的光华。至于金石丝竹制成的是乐的工具。诗抒发心思，歌表现人的声音，舞则表现人的动作。诗、歌、舞，都是发于人心，而佐以乐器。因此，乐所表达的心志虽然幽深，而形象却是明白；气氛使人兴奋，感化效用却有力量。精神的和谐来自心灵而表现于音乐，所以在音乐上不可以作伪。

【原文】

魏文侯问于子夏曰："吾端冕而听古乐，则惟恐卧；听郑卫之音，则不知倦。敢问：古乐之如彼何也？新乐之如此何也？"子夏对曰："今夫古乐，进旅退旅，和正以广。弦匏笙簧，会守拊鼓，始奏以文，复乱以武，治乱以相，讯疾以雅。君子于是语，于是道古，修身及家，平均天下。此古乐之发也。今夫新乐，进俯退俯，奸声以滥，溺而不止；及优侏儒，獶杂子女，不知父子。乐终不可以语，不可以道古。此新乐之发也。今君之所问者乐也，所好者音也！夫乐者，与音相近而不同。"

【语译】

魏文侯向子夏问道："我穿着官服，衣冠整齐听古典音乐时，就一直想睡觉；但是，听到郑卫的音乐时，却精神振奋。请问：古乐为什么会使人那样，而新乐又为什么会使人这样呢？"子夏回答道："所谓古乐，是大众共同动作，或进或退，步调齐一，配以和平纯正而宽缓的乐声。弦乐管乐，都按'拊'与'鼓'的节拍。开始时击鼓，收场时鸣钟。用'相'调节收场，用'雅'调节快速动作，有君子解说叙述，全是关于修身、齐家、安定社会的事。古乐的表演是如此。至于新乐，舞与弯腰屈脊，淫声浪语，无限诱惑。还有俳优丑角，男女混杂，父子不分，歌舞终了仍不知内容为何，更无古事古训。这就是新乐的演奏。现在大人问的是乐，但大人爱好的却是音。乐虽也有音，彼此相近，但实际却是两件事。"

【原文】

文侯曰："敢问何如？"子夏对曰："夫古者，天地顺而四时当，民有德而五谷昌，疾疢不作而无妖祥，此之谓大当。然后圣人作，为父子君臣，以为纪纲。纪纲既正，天下大定。天下大定，然后正六律，和五声，弦歌诗颂，此之谓德音；德音之谓乐。《诗》云：'莫其德音，其德克明。克明克类，克长克君，王此大邦；克顺克俾，俾于文王，其德靡悔。既受帝祉，施于孙子。'此之谓也。今君之所好者，其溺音乎？"

【语译】

文侯又问道："这是怎么说呢？"子夏回答道："在古时，风调雨顺，四季平安，人民有德，农产丰盛，没有疾疫灾祸，也没有妖怪异象发生，这叫大当。然后圣人制订父子君臣的名分，作为人与人关系的纲纪。纲纪既定，社会便有了秩序。社会安定之后，便稽考音律，调和五音，用乐器伴奏歌谣舞曲，叫作德音。这种德音才叫乐。《诗经》里有诗云：'德音虽静，德行却表现得明白，而且合乎德行。适于做领袖，做君主，为大国的国王。能遵循前代遗风，上配文王，从不做懊悔的事。受蒙上帝降福，直到他的后代。'此乃德音的真义。大王既不喜欢德音，喜爱的是那些靡靡之音吧。"

Chapter Ten *ON MUSIC*
(*Yochi*, *Liki*, Chapter XIX)

I. THE ORIGIN AND FUNCTION OF MUSIC

Music rises from the human heart when the human heart is touched by the external world. When touched by the external world, the heart is moved, and therefore finds its expression in sounds. These sounds echo, or combine with, one another and produce a rich variety, and when the various sounds become regular, then we have rhythm. The arrangement of tones for our enjoyment in combination with the military dance, with shields and hatchets, and the civil dance, with long feathers and pennants of ox-tails, is called music.

Music is the form wherein tones are produced, because it takes its rise from the human heart when the heart is touched by the external world. Therefore when the heart's chord of sorrow is touched, the sounds produced are sombre and forlorn; when the heart's chord of satisfaction is touched, the sounds produced are languorous and slow; when the chord of joy is touched, the sounds produced are glowing and expansive; when the chord of anger is touched, the sounds produced are harsh and strong; when the chord of piety is touched, the sounds produced are simple and pure; and when the chord of love is touched, the sounds produced are sweet and gentle. These six kinds of emotion are not spontaneous, but are moods produced by impact from the external world.

Therefore the ancient kings were ever careful about things that affected the human heart. They tried therefore to guide the people's ideals and aspirations by means of *li*, establish harmony in sounds by means of music, regulate conduct by means of government, and prevent immorality by means of punishments. *Li*, music, punishments and government have a common goal, which is to bring about unity in the people's hearts and carry out the principles of political order.

Music rises from the human heart. When the emotions are touched, they are expressed in sounds, and when the sounds take definite forms, we have music. Therefore the music of a peaceful and prosperous country is quiet and joyous, and the government is orderly; the music of a country in turmoil shows dissatisfaction and anger, and the government is chaotic; and the music of a destroyed country shows sorrow and remembrance of the past, and the people are distressed. Thus we see music and government are directly connected with one another.

The mode of C is the symbol of the king; the mode of D is the symbol of the minister; the mode of E is the symbol of the people; the mode of G is the symbol of the affairs of the country; and the mode of A is the symbol of the natural world, When the five keys are arranged in order, we do not have discordant sounds. When the key of C loses its tonality, then the music loses its fundamental and the king neglects his duties. When the key of D loses its tonality, then the music loses its gradation, and the ministers become unruly. When the key of E loses its tonality, then the music is sorrowful and the people feel distressed. When the key of G loses its tonality, then the music is mournful and the affairs of the country become complicated. When the key of A loses its tonality, then the music suggests danger, and the people suffer from poverty. When all the five keys lose their tonality and upset one another, we have a general discord, and the nation will not have long to live. The music of the states of Cheng and Wei is the music of countries in turmoil, coming very near to a general discord. The music of "In the Mulberry Field," upon the banks of River P'u (in Wei) is the music of a destroyed country, whose government is tottering and whose people are dispersed or live in constant insecurity, calumniating their rulers and pursuing their selfish ends without restraint.

Tones rise from the human heart, and music is connected with the principles of human conduct. Therefore the animals know sounds but do not know tones, and the common people know tones but do not know music. Only the superior man is able to understand music. Thus from a study of the sounds, one comes to understand the tones; from a study of the tones, one comes to understand music; and from the study of music, one comes to understand the principles of government and is thus fully prepared for being a ruler. It is therefore impossible to talk to a man about tones who does not understand sounds, and impossible to talk to a man about music, who does not understand tones. He who understands music comes very near to understanding *li*, and if a man has mastered both *li* and music, we call him virtuous, because virtue is mastery (or fulfilment).

Hence, when we say that music is well cultivated in a country, we do not mean that its music is elaborate or complicated; nor do the ceremonies of feasting have sophisticated flavors. As we hear the music of the *seh* at the *Chou* ancestral temple, with its red strings and perforated resonance board, and only one man singing and three men joining in the chorus, we feel a certain restraint in its sounds; and as we see the ceremonies at the royal feast, with black wine and raw fish and unsavored soup, we feel there is a restraint in the use of flavors. Therefore the ancient kings did not institute rituals and music for the mere purpose of satisfying the desires of our senses ("the mouth, the stomach, the ear and the eye"), but rather for teaching the people the right taste and the return to normality.

The nature of man is usually quiet, but when it is affected by the external world, it begins to have desires. With the thinking mind becoming conscious of the impact of the material world, we begin to have likes and dislikes. When the likes and dislikes are not properly controlled and our conscious minds are distracted by the material world, we lose our true selves and the principle of reason in Nature is destroyed. When man is constantly exposed to the things of the material world which affect him and does not control his likes and dislikes, then he becomes overwhelmed by the material reality and becomes dehumanized or materialistic. When a man becomes dehumanized or materialistic, then the principle of reason in Nature is destroyed and man is submerged in his own desires. From this arise rebellion, disobedience, cunning and deceit, and general immorality. We have then a picture of the strong bullying the weak, the majority persecuting the minority, the clever ones deceiving the simple-minded, the physically strong going for violence, the sick and crippled not being taken care of, and the aged and the young and helpless not cared for. This is the way of chaos.

The people are therefore controlled through the rituals and music instituted by the ancient kings. The weeping and wailing and wearing of the dress of mourning, made of hemp and without hemming, are for the purpose of regulating sorrow at funerals. The bell, the drum, the shield and the hatchet (in dance and music) are for the purpose of celebrating peace and happiness. The marriage ceremony and "capping" ceremony for boys reaching maturity and the "coiffure" ceremony for girls reaching maturity are for the purpose of establishing distinctions between the sexes. The archery contests and feasting at the village are for the purpose of normalizing social intercourse. The rituals regulate the people's feelings; music establishes harmony in the sounds of the country; the government orders their conduct and the punishments prevent crimes. When rituals, music, punishments and governments are all in order, then the principles of political order are complete.

II. A COMPARISON OF RITUALS AND MUSIC, BOTH BASED ON HARMONY WITH THE COSMIC ORDER

Music unites, while rituals differentiate. Through union the people come to be friendly toward one another, and through differentiation the people come to learn respect for one another. If music predominates, the social structure becomes too amorphous, and if rituals predominate, social life becomes too cold. To bring the people's inner feelings and their external conduct into balance is the work of rituals and music. The establishment of rituals gives a well-defined sense of order and discipline, while the general spread of music and song establishes the general atmosphere of peace in the people. When good taste is distinguished from bad taste, then we have the means of distinguishing the good from the bad people, and when violence is prevented by the criminal law and the good men are selected for office, then the government becomes stable and orderly. With the doctrine of love for teaching affection, and the doctrine of duty for teching moral rectitude, the people will then have learned to live in a moral order.

Music comes from the inside, while rituals come from the outside. Because music comes from the inside, it is characterized by quiet and calm. And because rituals come from the outside, they are characterized by formalism. Truly great music is always simple in movement, and truly great rituals are always simple in form. When good music prevails, there is no feeling of dissatisfaction and when proper rituals prevail, there is no strife and struggle. When we say that by mere bowing in salute the king can rule the world, we mean thereby the influence of rituals and music. When the violent elements of a nation are kept quiet, the different rulers come to pay homage, the military weapons are locked up, the five criminal laws are not brought into use, the people have no worries and the Emperor has no anger, then truly music has prevailed. When the parents and children are affectionate toward one another, the juniors respect the elders and this respect is extended to all people in the country and the Emperor himself lives such an exemplary life, then we may truly say that *li* has prevailed.

Truly great music shares the principles of harmony with the universe, and truly great ritualism shares the principles of distinctions with the universe. Through the principles of harmony, order is restored in the physical world, and through the principles of distinctions, we are enabled to offer sacrifices to Heaven and Earth. We have, then, rituals and music in the material world and the different gods in the spiritual world, and thus the world will come to live in love and piety. Rituals teach piety under different circumstances, and music teaches love in varying forms. When this moral condition is established through rituals and music, then we have a continuity of culture through the rise of different wise rulers. The political events differ with (the rulers of) the different generations, and the rituals and music celebrating the events are given names appropriate to the different accomplishments of the rulers.

Music expresses the harmony of the universe, while rituals express the order of the universe. Through harmony all things are influenced, and through order all things have a proper place. Music rises from heaven, while rituals are patterned on the earth. To go beyond these patterns would result in violence and disorder. In order to have the proper rituals and music, we must understand the principles of Heaven and Earth....

Therefore the Sage creates music to correlate with Heaven and creates rituals to correlate with the Earth. When rituals and music are well established, we have the Heaven and Earth functioning in perfect order. The Heaven is high and the Earth is low, and we have there the established relationship between the king and the ministers. When the high and low are arranged in different ranks, we have the principle of social ranks. When we have the law governing action and reaction, we have as the result the distinctions between the great and the small. And when the myriad things are grouped and classified according to their natural class, we recognize the principle of diversity in animal life. Thus are brought about the symbolic constellations of the stars in heaven and the different shapes of mountains and rivers and things on earth. This shows that *li* proceeds upon the principle of distinctions in the universe.

When the gases on the earth's surface go up and the gases in the upper atmospheres come down, when the principles of *yin* and *yang* meet and produce friction and the Heaven and the Earth interact upon one another, and when quickened by thunder and lightning, aroused into life by the lashing of wind and rain, stimulated by the rotation of the seasons and warmed by the sun and the moon, things grow and prosper. This shows that music proceeds upon the principle of harmony in the universe....

Music illustrates the primordial forces of nature, while *li* reflects the products of the creation. Heaven represents the principle of eternal motion, while Earth represents the principle of remaining still, and these two principles of motion and rest permeate life between Heaven and Earth. Therefore, the Sage talks about rituals and music.

III. MUSIC REVEALS MAN'S CHARACTER

When you see the type of a nation's dance, you know its character....

Man is gifted with blood and breath and a conscious mind, but his feeling of sorrow and happiness and joy and anger depend on circumstances. His definite desires arise from reactions toward the material world. Therefore, when a sombre and depressing type of music prevails, we know the people are distressed and sorrowful. When a languorous, easy type of music with many long-drawn-out airs prevails, we know that the people are peaceful and happy. When a strong and forceful type of music prevails, beginning and ending with a full display of sounds, we know that the people are hearty and strong. When a pure, pious and majestic type of music prevails, we know that the people are pious. When a gentle, lucid and quietly progressing type of music prevails, we know that the people are kind and affectionate. When lewd, exciting and upsetting music prevails, we know that the people are immoral....

When the soil is poor, things do not grow, and when fishing is not regulated according to the seasons, then fishes and turtles do not mature; when the climate deteriorates, animal and plant life degenerates, and when the world is chaotic, the rituals and music become licentious. We find then a type of music that is rueful without restraint and joyous without calm....

Therefore, the superior man tries to create harmony in the human heart by a rediscovery of human nature, and tries to promote music as a means to the perfection of human culture. When such music prevails and the people's minds are led toward the right ideals and aspirations, we may see the appearance of a great nation.

Character is the backbone of our human nature, and music is the flowering of character. The metal, stone, string and bamboo instruments are the instruments of music. The poem gives expression to our heart, the song gives expression to our voice, and the dance gives expression to our movements. These three arts take their rise from the human soul, and then are given further expression by means of the musical instruments. Therefore, from the depth of sentiment comes the clarity of form and from the strength of the mood comes the spirituality of its atmosphere. This harmony of spirit springs forth from the soul and finds expression or blossoms forth in the form of music. Therefore music is the one thing in which there is no use trying to deceive others or make false pretenses....

IV. ON CLASSICAL AND MODERN MUSIC

Baron Wen of Wei asked Tsehsia, the disciple of Confucius, "Why is it that I feel sleepy every time I listen to classical music in my offcial dress, and never feel tired when I listen to the music of (the states of) Cheng and Wei? Why is it that the classical music is like that and this new music is like this?"

"In the ancient music," replied Tsehsia, "the dancers move in formation forward and backward in an atmosphere of peace and order and a certain luxury of movement. The *hsuan* (a string instrument) the gourd and the *sheng* (a kind of mouth organ with bamboo reed-pipes, resembling bagpipes in principle) are held in readiness until the drum gives the signal for the start. The music begins with the civil dance movements and ends with the military dance movements, and there is a continuity of movement from

the beginning to the end, while the measure of the classical music prevents
or checks the dancers who are inclined to go too fast. After listening to such
music, the superior man will be in a proper atmosphere to discuss the music
and the ways of the ancients, the cultivation of personal life and the ordering
of national life. This is the main sentiment or character of ancient music. Now
in this new music, people bend their bodies while they move back and forth,
there is a deluge of immoral sounds without form or restraint, and the actors
and dwarfs dressed like monkeys mix (or mix with) the company of men and
women, behaving as if they didn't know who were their parents or children. At
the end of such a performance it is impossible to discuss music or the ways of
the ancients. This is the main sentiment or character of the new music. Now
you asked me about music, but what you are really interested in is just sounds.
Music and sounds are of course related, but they are two different things."

"What do you mean?" asked Baron Wen.

"In the ancient times," said Tsehsia, "the forces of nature were in
harmony and the weather was in accord with the four seasons; the people
were good in character and the harvests were plentiful; there were no
epidemics and no monsters of bad omen appeared. That was the time when
everything was right. So then the Sages (or priests) arose and established
social discipline in the relationships between parents and children and kings
and their ministers. With the establishment of social discipline, the world was
brought into order, and after the world was brought into order, the Sages set
the right standards for the six pitch-pipes and the five keys. People then began
to sing songs and anthems to the accompaniment of *hsuan* string instruments,
and these were called sacred music (literally "virtuous sounds") and sacred
music was music.... But what your Highness is interested in is merely a
jumble of lewd sounds."

"May I ask, where do the lewd sounds come from?" asked the Baron.

"The music of Cheng," replied Tsehsia, "is lewd and corrupting,
the music of Sung is soft and makes one effeminate, the music of Wei is

repetitious and annoying, and the music of Ch'i is harsh and makes one haughty. These four kinds of music are all sensual music and undermine the people's character, and that is why they cannot be used at the sacrifices. The *Book of Songs* says, 'The harmonious sounds are *shu* and *yung* and my ancestor listened to them.' *Shu* means 'pious' and *yung* means 'peaceful.' If you have piety and peacefulness of character, you can do everything you want with a country.

"All that a king needs to do is to be careful with regard to his likes and dislikes. What the king likes, that the people will do, and what the king does, that the people will follow. That is the meaning of the passage in the *Book of Songs* which says, 'It is very easy to guide the people'."

In accordance with this idea, therefore, the sages (or priests) made the musical instruments, the *yao* (a small drum with two beads suspended on both sides and a handle—when the handle is rolled between the palms, the beads strike the drum itself), the drum, the *k'ung* and the *ch'ia* (varieties of square wooden drums with wooden tops with a hole in the center), the *hsuan* and the *ch'ib* (varieties of mouth organs, the *hsuan* being a broad oval-shaped clay pot with six holes and the *ch'ih* being made of bamboo with different pipes provided with reeds). These six instruments produce sounds used in sacred music. In addition, they are accompanied by the bells, the *ch'ing* (a stone slab suspended in a stand), the *yu* (a kind of bagpipe with 36 reeds) and the *seh* (a long horizontal string instrument with fifty strings), and with the dance with shields and hatchets (military dance) and with pennants of ox-tail and long pheasant tails ("civil dance"). This is the kind of music used at the worship of ancient kings and at the drinking ceremonies. It is the kind of music by which a sense of social order between the different ranks was established and the sense of discipline between elders and juniors and superiors and inferiors was taught to the following generations.

The sound of the bell is clear and resonant; its clarity and resonance make it especially suitable for serving as signals, such signals create an impression of majesty, and the impression of majesty inspires a sense of the military power. Therefore when the sovereign hears the bell, he thinks of his military officials. The sound of the musical stone is sharp and clear-cut; its sharpness and clear-cut quality tend to foster the sense of decision, and the sense of decision makes it easy for the generals to die in battle. Therefore when the sovereign hears the musical stone, he thinks of his military officers who died in battle at the border. The sound of the string is plaintive; its plaintive quality cleanses the soul, and the cleansed state of mind makes for a sense of righteousness. Therefore, when the sovereign hears the sound of the string instrument, the *ch'in* and the *seh* (both horizontal string instruments on a flat sounding board) he thinks of his righteous ministers. The sound of bamboo (corresponding to the Western wood-wind instruments) has a floating quality; its floating quality tends to spread everywhere and bring together the masses of the people. Therefore when the sovereign hears the sound of bamboo instruments, he thinks of his ministers of the interior. The sound of the big and small drums is noisy; its noisy quality tends to arouse and excite, and the excitement tends to prepare the masses for action. Therefore when the sovereign hears the sound of the big and small drums, he thinks of his great generals. It is seen, therefore, that in hearing music, the sovereign does not hear their sounds only, but also hears the significance proper to the different sounds.

V. CONFUCIUS ON THE DIFFERENT MOVEMENTS OF THE INTERPRETATIVE DANCE MUSIC OF EMPEROR WU

Pinmou Chia was talking one day with Confucius, and they began to disuss music, and Confucius asked, "Why is it that at the beginning of this Dance of Wu, the dancers stand a long time holding themselves in readiness before they begin, while the drum is being played?"

"Because it symbolizes the fact that Emperor Wu waited a long time and did not launch out on the conquest of the *Shang* Emperor (Chou, whom he overthrew) until he was assured of the support of the other rulers," replied Pinmou Chia.

"What is the meaning again of the singing and the sighing of the dancers, with the movements slowly and gradually growing in intensity?"

"Because Emperor Wu was still waiting to assure himself of the support of the other rulers."

"What is the meaning again of the dance and the stamping on the ground early in the dance?" asked Confucius again.

"Because it was a time to act."

"Why is it that the dancers then begin to squat on the ground, with their right knees touching the ground and their left knees lifted?"

"They should not squat on the ground in the Dance of Wu."

"Why is it that in between we hear the characteristic melody of the Shangs (the enemy)?"

"That melody doesn't properly belong in this music of Wu."

"Then what melody is it, if it doesn't belong in the music of Wu?"

"The masters of music have forgotten its original meaning.... If this weren't a later interpolation (*i.e.*, if it was the melody of Emperor Wu), then Emperor Wu must have been a cruel king."

"I have heard this interpretation from Ch'ang Hung (an official at the Chou capital)," said Confucius, "which essentially agrees with yours."

Pinmou Chia rose from his seat and said, "We all understand the meaning of that long preliminary waiting. But, may I ask, why the delay and waiting of the dancers at the start, and such a long delay?"

"Sit down and I will tell you," said Confucius. "This music is a symbolic interpretation of the historical events. That the dancers stand in long lines with their shields like a solid wall (literally "like a mountain") symbolizes the events of Emperor Wu. That the dancers start to stamp the ground at an early part of the dance symbolizes the agitations or ambitions of Emperor Wu's great-grandfather, King T'ai. The dancers then squat down on the ground to symbolize the rule of peace by the Dukes Chou and Shao (brothers of Emperor Wu later assisting his son in pacifying the country and founding the governmental system of the Chou Dynasty, after the overthrow of the previous dynasty). Besides, the dancers of Wu start out in the first movement from the south facing north (advancing to the second position and symbolizing the setting out of his army, *according to the commentators*). In the second movement, the Shangs are defeated (advancing to the third position, *according to the commentators*). In the third movement, the dancers turn South again (taking the fourth position). In the fourth movement, the establishment of his rule over the Southern countries is symbolized (taking the second position again). In the fifth movement, the dancers divide themselves, signifying the rule of Duke Chou on the left and Duke Shao on the right (taking the third position again). In the sixth movement, the dancers return to their original positions again to symbolize the homage of the entire country to the Emperor. The advancing of the dancers in formation, with the players of the wooden resonance box at their sides and their breaking up into the spear dance facing four directions (or repeating the dance of spears four times, *according to another interpretation*) show the spread of the military power of Emperor Wu over China. The advance in two parallel columns with the players of the wooden resonance box at their side shows their easy victory. Their long waiting in formation symbolizes the waiting for the armies of the allied rulers to arrive.

"Furthermore, haven't you heard the story about what Emperor Wu did at the suburb of the capital of the defeated dynasty? When Emperor Wu had defeated the Shangs and arrived at their capital, he made the descendants of Huangti (the Yellow Emperor) rulers of Chi, made the descendants of Emperor Yao rulers over Chu, and made the descendants of Emperor Shun rulers over Ch'en. This was done before the campaign was finished, and after the campaign was finished, he made the descendants of Emperor Yu rulers over Chi (*different from the 'Chi' above*) and degraded the descendants of the

Shang Emperors and put them in Sung. He also gave a posthumous rank to the tomb of Prince Pikan, released Chitse from prison and allowed him to continue to live according to the customs of the Shangs, and restored his rank. The people were freed from the army service and the knights were given double salaries. After he crossed the Yellow River westwards, he set the army horses free to pasture on the south of the Hua Mountains and did not ride them again. He set the buffaloes free on the plains of the Peach Grove and did not keep them again; and he had the chariots and armors smeared with blood and kept in the Imperial Treasury and did not use them again. The spears and shields were carried backwards (with the handles first) and wrapped in tiger skins, and the generals were made rulers over cities. This was called the disarmament (literally "locking up the arrow-bag"). So then it was made known to the world at large that Emperor Wu was not going to use his military weapons any more. The army was disbanded and made to take up the sport of archery in the suburbs. In the eastern suburb, the ceremony of archery contests was accompanied with the song *Lishou*, and in the western suburb, the ceremony of the archery contests was accompanied with the song *Tsouyu*. The practice of shooting to penetrate the target was discontinued. Ceremonial robes and audience tablets (held between the hands by the ministers when seeing the Emperor) were used and the knights were relieved of their swords. Sacrifices were made at the Grand Temple (the Mingt'ang or "Hall of Clear Virtue"), in order that the people might understand filial piety. The ceremonies of the court audience were established so that the different dukes might know how to show their homage. The ceremony of the Emperor tilling the field himself was established, so that the people might understand respect toward Nature. These five institutions were the five great cultural institutions of the world.

"At the Imperial College, the Three Elders and Five Superiors were maintained; the Emperor bared his left arm to cut the sacrificial animal and gave it to these Elders; he held the pot of gravy in his hands, and presented it to them; he held the wine cup and made them drink (literally "gargle"); and he wore a crown and held a shield in his hand. These were done that the different dukes might be taught the general virtue of humility and respect. In this way the culture of the Chous was spread to entire China, and rituals and music prevailed throughout the country. Don't we understand now why at the beginning of the Dance of Wu, the dancers waited so long in formation (*i.e.*, for the other rulers to follow Emperor Wu)?"...

第十一章　孟子

　　研究孔子思想之特点时，须略知儒家思想经过孟子又有了何等发展。这一点之重要，一因经孟子的阐释，儒家思想的哲学价值才更为清楚，二因儒家思想的哲学价值因孟子而发生了实际的影响。孟子代表了儒家的正统发展。

　　研究孔子思想之特点时，须略知儒家思想经过孟子又有了何等发展。这一点之重要，一因经孟子的阐释，儒家思想的哲学价值才更为清楚，二因儒家思想的哲学价值因孟子而发生了实际的影响。孟子代表了儒家的正统发展。《孟子》全书共七篇，每篇分为上下两章，比《论语》几乎厚了三分之一。以散文的文学价值论，也是《论语》所不及的。孟子是个雄辩滔滔的作家，真是辩才无碍，口若悬河，每篇都是气势如虹的长论，可以说段段精彩，使选辑儒家文字的人往往无法割爱。

　　孟子既然代表了孔子学说一方面重要的发展，如果不读孟子的文章，对儒家的精义便不足以窥其全貌。儒家学说包罗至广，其门人实不能全部精通。所以孔氏早期的门人皆仅就其资禀之所近，对孔门学说予以发扬。

后来，弟子散处四方，定居各国，以其所长传授弟子，遂与孔氏学说之真面目，相距愈远。唯孟子受业于子思，子思为曾子之弟子。故自孔子亡后，传孔学之正统者，唯孟子一人。故后人欲研究圣人之道，必自孟子入手。在解释孔氏学说上，"孟氏，醇乎醇者也。荀与扬（雄），大醇而小疵"（韩退之《读荀子》）。

本书所选孟子为《告子篇》，我认为它是《孟子》一书中最为重要，因而也最具有代表性的一篇。孟子思想中最重要处为以下各点——人性善，恢复性本善之重要，文化与教育之功用在防止人性为恶的环境所泯没，培养"浩然之气"〔相当于法国哲学家柏格森所说的"蓬勃的生气"（elan vital）〕。最后一点为：人人都是"性本善"，所以"人人可以为尧舜"。孟子也发挥了"王道"与"霸道"差异之所在。王道指仁政，霸道指专政。他进而将孔子所倡导的为政须以身作则的学说，发展到一个界说分明的体系，并首次用"仁政"一词，孔子则从未用过。孟子在其时大概是最渊博的史学家，关于征税制度、农业制度、封建制度，他都有明确的认识。至于他由孔子的"正己以为政"发展而来的"仁政"之道，我们未得其详，但是在他的文章里，我们分明见到他的"性善"说与"养其大者为大人"之重要。以上皆孟子独特之见解。

（一）性善说

告子曰："性，犹杞柳也。义，犹桮棬也。以人性为仁义，犹以杞柳为桮棬。"

（孟子曰：）"子能顺杞柳之性而以为桮棬乎？将戕贼杞柳而后以为桮棬也？如将戕贼杞柳而以为桮棬，则亦将戕贼人以为仁义欤？率天下之人而祸仁义者，必子之言夫。"

告子曰："性犹湍水也，决诸东方则东流，决诸西方则西流；人性之无分善与不善也，犹水之无分于东西也。"

孟子曰："水信无分于东西。无分于上下乎？人性之善也，犹水之就下也。人无有不善，水无有不下。今夫水搏而跃之，可使过颡，激而行之，可使在山，是岂水之性哉？其势则然也。人之可使为不善，其性亦犹是也。"

告子曰："生之谓性。"

孟子曰："生之谓性也，犹白之谓白欤？"

（告子）曰："然。"

（孟子曰：）"白羽之白也，犹白雪之白；白雪之白，犹白玉之白欤？"

（告子）曰："然。"

（孟子曰：）"然则犬之性犹牛之性，牛之性犹人之性欤？"

告子曰："食色，性也。仁内也，非外也。义外也，非内也。"

孟子曰："何以谓仁内义外也？"

（告子）曰："彼长而我长之，非有长于我也。犹彼白而我白之，从其白于外也，故谓之外也。"

（孟子）曰："异于白马之白也，无以异于白人之白也。不识长马之长也，无以异于长人之长欤？且谓长者义乎？长之者义乎？"

（告子）曰："吾弟则爱之，秦人之弟则不爱也，是以我为悦者也，故谓之内。长楚人之长，亦长吾之长，是以长为悦者也，故谓之外也。"

（孟子）曰："耆秦人之炙，无以异于耆吾炙。夫物则亦有然者也。然则耆炙亦有外欤？"

孟季子问公都子曰："何以谓义内也？"

（公都子）曰："行吾敬，故谓之内也。"

（孟季子）曰："乡人长于伯兄一岁，则谁敬？"

（公都子）曰："敬兄。"

（孟季子）曰："酌则谁先？"

（公都子）曰："先酌乡人。"

（孟季子）曰："所敬在此，所长在彼，果在外，非由内也。"

公都子不能答，以告孟子。

孟子曰："敬叔父乎？敬弟乎？彼将曰：'敬叔父。'曰：'弟为尸，则谁敬？'彼将曰：'敬弟。'子曰：'恶在其敬叔父也？'彼将曰：'在位故也。'子亦曰：'在位故也。庸敬在兄，斯须之敬在乡人。'"

季子闻之曰："敬叔父则敬，敬弟则敬。果在外，非由内也。"

公都子曰："冬日则饮汤，夏日则饮水。然则饮食亦在外也。"

公都子曰："告子曰：'性无善无不善也。'或曰性可以为善，可以为不善，是故文武兴，则民好善；幽厉兴，则民好暴。或曰有性善，有性不善。是故以尧为君而有象，以瞽瞍为父而有舜。以纣为兄之子且以为君而有微子启，王子比干。今曰性善，然则彼皆非欤？"

孟子曰："乃若其情，则可以为善矣，乃所谓善也。若夫为不善，非才之罪也。恻隐之心，人皆有之；羞恶之心，人皆有之；恭敬之心，人皆有之；是非之心，人皆有之。恻隐之心，仁也；羞恶之心，义也；恭敬之心，礼也；是非之心，智也。仁义礼智，非由外铄我也，我固有之也。弗思耳矣。故曰：求则得之，舍则失之。或相倍蓰而无算者，不能尽其才者也。《诗》曰：'天生蒸民，有物有则。民之秉夷，好是懿德。'孔子曰：'为此诗者，其知道乎！'故有物必有则，民之秉夷也，故好是懿德。"

孟子曰："富岁子弟多赖，凶岁子弟多暴，非天之降才尔殊也，其所以陷溺其心者然也。今夫麰麦，播种而耰之。其地同，树之时又同。浡然而生，至于日至之时皆熟矣。虽有不同，则地有肥硗雨露之养，人事之不齐也。故凡同类者，举相似也，何独至于人而疑之。圣人与我，同类者。故龙子曰：'不知足而为屦，我知其不为蒉也。'屦之相似，天下之足同也。口之于味，有同耆也，易牙先得我口之所耆者也。如使口之于味也，其性与人殊，若犬马之与我不同类也，则天下何耆皆从易牙之于味也？至于味，天下期于易牙，是天下之口相似也。惟耳亦然。至于声，天下期于师旷，是天下之耳相似也。惟目亦然。至于子都，天下莫不知其姣也。不知子都之姣者，无目者也。故曰，口之于味也，有同耆焉。耳之于声也，有同听焉。目之于色也，有同美焉。至于心，独无所同然乎？心之所同然者？何也？谓理也，义也。圣人先得我心之所同然耳。故理义之悦我心，犹刍豢之悦我口。"

（二）本性之破坏

孟子曰："牛山之木尝美矣。以其郊于大国也，斧斤伐之，可以为美乎？是其日夜之所息，雨露之所润，非无萌蘗之生焉，牛羊又从而牧之，是以若彼濯濯也。人见其濯濯也，以为未尝有材焉，此岂山之性也哉！虽存乎人者，岂无仁义之心哉！其所以放其良心者，亦犹斧斤之于木也。旦旦而伐之，可以为美乎？其日夜之所息，平旦之气，其好恶与人相近也者几希。则其旦昼之所为，有梏亡之矣。梏之反覆，则其夜气不足以存。夜气不足以存，则其违禽兽不远矣。人见其禽兽也，而以为未尝有才焉者，是岂人之情也哉？故苟得其养，无物不长；苟失其养，无物不消。孔子曰：'操则存，舍则亡。出入无时，莫知其乡。'惟心之谓欤？"

孟子曰："无或乎王之不智也。虽有天下易生之物也，一日暴之，十日寒之，未有能生者也。吾见亦罕矣，吾退而寒之者至矣。吾如有萌焉何哉！今夫弈之为数，小数也，不专心致志则不得也。弈秋，通国之善弈者也。使弈秋诲二人奕。其一人专心致志，惟弈秋之为听。一人虽听之，一心以为有鸿鹄将至，思援弓缴而射之。虽与之俱学，弗若之矣。为是其智弗若欤？曰，非然也。"

（三）人性中之贵贱大小

孟子曰："鱼，我所欲也，熊掌亦我所欲也。二者不可得兼，舍鱼而取熊掌者也。生，亦我所欲也，义亦我所欲也。二者不可得兼，舍生而取义者也。生亦我所欲，所欲有甚于生者，故不为苟得也。死亦我所恶，所恶有甚于死者，故患有所不辟也。如使人之所欲莫甚于生，则凡可以得生者，何不用也？使人之所恶莫甚于死者，则凡可以辟患者，何不为也？由是则生而有不用也，由是则可以辟患而有不为也。是故所欲有甚于生者，所恶有甚于死者，非独贤者有是心也，人皆有之；贤者能勿丧耳。一箪食，一豆羹，得之则生，弗得则死。呼尔而与之，行道之人弗受；蹴尔而与之，乞人不屑也。万钟则不辨礼义而受之，万钟于我何加焉？为宫室之美，妻妾之奉，所识穷乏者得我欤？乡为身死而不受，今为宫室之美为之；乡为身死而不受，今为妻妾之奉为之；乡为身死而不受，今为所识穷乏者得我而为之，是亦不可以已乎？此之谓失其本心。"

孟子曰："仁，人心也；义，人路也。舍其路而弗由，放其心而不知求，哀哉！人有鸡犬放，则知求之；有放心而不知求。学问之道无他，求其放心而已矣。"

孟子曰："今有无名之指，屈而不信，非疾痛害事也。如有能信之者，则不远秦、楚之路，为指之不若人也。指不若人，则知恶之；心不若人，则不知恶。此之谓不知类也。"

孟子曰："拱把之桐梓，人苟欲生之，皆知所以养之者。至于身而不知所以养之者，岂爱身不若桐梓哉？弗思甚也。"

孟子曰："人之于身也，兼所爱。兼所爱，则兼所养也。无尺寸之肤不爱焉，则无尺寸之肤不养也。所以考其善不善者，岂有他哉？于己取之而已矣。体有贵贱，有大小。无以小害大，无以贱害贵。养其小者为小人，养其大者为大人。今有场师，舍其梧槚，养其樲棘，则为贱场师焉。养其一指而失其肩背而不知也，则为狼疾人也。饮食之人，则人贱之矣，为其养小以失大也。饮食之人无有失也，则口腹岂适为尺寸之肤哉？"

公都子问曰："钧是人也，或为大小，或为小人，何也？"

孟子曰："从其大体为大人，从其小体为小人。"

（公都子问）曰："钧是人也，或从其大体，或从其小体，何也？"

（孟子）曰："耳目之官不思，而蔽于物，物交物，则引之而已矣。心之官则思。思则得之，不思则不得也。此天之所与我者。先立乎其大者，则其小者不能夺也。此为大人而已矣。"

孟子曰："有天爵者，有人爵者。仁义忠信，乐善不倦，此天爵也。公卿大夫，此人爵也。古之人修其天爵，而人爵从之。今之人修其天爵，以要人爵；既得人爵，而弃其天爵，则惑之甚者也。终亦必亡而已矣。"

孟子曰："欲贵者，人之同心也。人人有贵于己者，弗思耳。人之所贵者，非良贵也。赵孟之所贵，赵孟能贱之。《诗》云：'既醉以酒，既饱以德。'言饱乎仁义也。所以不愿人之膏粱之味也。令闻广誉施于身，所以不愿人之文绣也。"

孟子曰："仁之胜不仁也，犹水之胜火。今之为仁者，犹以一杯水救一车薪之火也。不熄，则谓之水不胜火。此又与于不仁之甚者也。亦终必亡而已矣。"

孟子曰："五谷者，种之美者也。苟为不熟，不如荑稗。夫仁亦在乎熟之而已矣。"

孟子曰："羿之教人射，必志于彀，学者亦必志于彀。大匠诲人，必以规矩，学者亦必以规矩。"

Chapter Eleven MENCIUS
(The *Book of Mencius*, Book VI, Part I)

In the study of the character of Confucian thought, it is important to have some ideas of its chief developments in Mencius, because of the clearer exposition of philosophic values in Mencius and because of their actual influence. Mencius represents the "orthodox" development of the Confucian school. The *Book of Mencius*, in seven books, each divided into two parts, is thicker than the *Analects* by almost one-third, and is incomparably better prose than the *Analects*. Mencius was an eloquent writer and speaker, good at debates, and the passages often consist of long and sustained discourses, and there are so many brilliant passages that it is difficult to make a selection in a volume devoted to Confucius.

Nevertheless, the ideas of Mencius represent such an important development of one side of Confucius' teachings, that it is impossible to get a fair conception of the Confucian ideas without reading something from Mencius. Hantse said, "The teachings of Confucius were broad and covered a wide scope, and it was impossible for any of his disciples to master the whole field. Therefore the early students of Confucianism developed each that side of his teachings which lay closest to him mental equipment. These disciples later on dispersed and settled in different countries and began to teach their disciples what they themselves had mastered, and the farther they were separated from the original source, the more divergent became their views or lines of study. Only Mencius studied under Tsesze, whose knowledge of Confucius' teachings came from Tsengtse. Since Confucius' death, only Mencius was able to carry on the orthodox tradition. Therefore, in order to study the teachings of the Sage, one must begin with Mencius." Hantse also said, "Mencius was the purest of the pure in the interpretation of Confucius; Hsuntse and Yangtse were on the whole pure, with certain adulterations."

I have selected for translation, a whole part of one of the Books of Mencius, in my opinion the most important and representative one. The most important ideas in Mencius are, the goodness of human nature, consequently the importance of recovering that original good nature, the recognition that culture or education merely consists in preventing the good nature in us from becoming "beclouded" by circumstances, the theory of nourishing what amounts to an equivalent of Bergson's *elan vital* (the *haojan chih ch'i*), and finally the declaration that all men are equal in their inherent goodness, and that since the Emperors Yao and Shun were also human beings, "any man could become a Yao or Shun." Mencius also developed the distinction between the ruler by virtue (*wang*) and the ruler by force or cunning (*pa*)— roughly, the distinction between "a kingly ruler" and "a dictator." He further developed Confucius' idea of government by example into a well-defined system, and for the first time used the phrase "benevolent government" which Confucius never used. (*Jen* definitely means "benevolence" in *Mencius*.) He was also probably the best historical scholar of his days and had definite ideas about taxation systems, agricultural systems and the feudal system. We do not get a clear idea of his theory of "benevolent government," developed from Confucius' government by moral example, but in this essay we find practically all his ideas about the goodness of human nature and the importance and method of finding one's "greater self." This essay is translated in full without omissions.

I. THE GOODNESS OF HUMAN NATURE

Kaotse said, "Human nature is like the willow tree, and righteous conduct or character is like a wicker basket (made of the willow branches). To make human nature follow benevolence and righteousness is like making willow branches into wicker baskets." Mencius said, "Now in making a wicker basket, don't you try to follow the nature of the willow branches (in bending them), or are you going to violate the nature of the willow branches? If you are going to violate the nature of the willow branches in order to make wicker baskets, then you are also going to violate human nature in order to make it benevolent and righteous. Your teachings are going to mislead the entire world and ruin the teachings of benevolence and righteousness."

Kaotse said, "Human nature is like water in the gulley. You guide it toward the East and it flows eastwards, and you guide it toward the West, and it flows westwards. There is no distinction between goodness and badness in human nature, as there is no distinction between East and West in water." "It is true," said Mencius, "that the water has no preference for the East or the West, but doesn't it make a distinction between 'up' and 'down' or a 'higher' and a 'lower' level? Human nature follows the good as water seeks the lower level. There is no man who is not good, as there is no water which does not flow downwards. Now you can strike the water and it splashes upwards above your forehead, or you can force it up the hills. But is this the original nature of water and not just due to the circumstances? And you can make human nature turn to evil in the same way."

Kaotse said, "What is born in us is called our nature." And Mencius replied, "When you say that nature is what is born in us, do you mean that it is like saying that a white substance is called 'white'?" "Yes," replied Kaotse. "Then do you consider the whiteness of a white feather the same as the whiteness of white snow, or again, consider the whiteness of white snow the same as the whiteness of a piece of white jade?" "Yes," said

Kaotse. "Then do you consider the nature of dogs the same as the nature of cows, or again consider the nature of cows the same as the nature of human beings?"

Kaotse said, "The desires for food and sex are born in us. Benevolence comes from within and is not something external, while righteousness is something external, and does not come from within." Mencius replied, "What do you mean by saying that benevolence comes from within while righteousness (or righteous conduct) is something external?" "When I see a tall man and call him tall," Kaotse replied, "it is not I who am tall (or that tallness is not within me), just as when something is white and I call it white, I observe its external white appearance merely. Therefore, I say righteous conduct is external." "Now," said Mencius, "the whiteness of a white horse in no way differs from the whiteness of a white person. But do you think that the tallness of a tall horse is in no way different from the tallness of a tall person? Now is the tall person or horse *right* (same word as *righteous*) or the man who calls it tall or regards it as tall *right* (*the right conception of 'tallness' is a subjective element belonging to the observer*)?" "But," said Kaotse, "I love my own brother, but I don't love the brother, say, of a man from the country of Ch'in. That shows that love comes from myself and is therefore regarded as something from within. On the other hand, I equally respect the elders of Ch'u as well as my own elders. That shows that what pleases me is the fact of their being eiders, and this respect (a virtue of righteous conduct) is therefore something external." Mencius replied, "But we love the roast pork of the Ch'in people as much as we love our own roast pork. That is so even with respect to material things. Then are you going to say that this love of roast pork is also something external?"

Baron Chi Meng asked Kungtutse, "What does Mencius mean by saying that righteous conduct is internal or comes from within?" The latter replied, "Righteous conduct is merely the showing of my inner respect. That is why it is considered to come from within." "If you have a person in the same village who is one year older than your elder brother, whom are you going to serve with respect?" asked the Baron. "Of course I will serve my elder brother with respect first." "But in offering wine at a feast, whom are you going to offer it to first?" "Of course I will offer wine first to the villager," was the reply. "Then you see you serve with respect one person, while you honor another person, which shows conduct is something external (depending on external circumstances) and not something internal." To this Kungtutse could not make a reply, and he told Mencius about it. Mencius said, "If you ask him whether he will serve with respect his uncle or his younger brother, he will say that he will serve with respect his uncle. Then you ask him, in case his younger brother is acting at a sacrifice as the representative of the deceased, then to whom is he going to show greater respect? He will then say he will show greater respect to his younger brother. Then you say to him, 'Where then is your respect for your uncle?' He will reply, of course, that in this case his younger brother represents the spirit in an official capacity. Then you can say to him, 'Exactly. In our everyday life we serve with respect our own elder brothers, but on special occasions we honor the villager.'" When the Baron heard this, he said, "Now in one case you respect the uncle, and in the other case you respect the younger brother. That shows clearly respect is dependent upon external circumstances." Kungtutse replied, "You take hot soup on a winter day and take cold water on a summer day. Then would you also say that (our desire for) food and drink is also something external (though it differs with varying circumstances)?"

Kungtutse said, "Kaotse says that the original human nature is neither good nor bad. Some people say that human nature can be either good or bad; therefore when the Emperors Wen and Wu were in power, the people loved virtue, and when the Emperors Yu and Li were in power, the people loved violence. Again other people say that some natures are good, while other natures are bad, and that therefore even under the rule of Emperor Yao, there was a bad man Hsiang, and even with a bad father, Kusou, there was produced a good son, Shun, and there were the good princes Ch'i and Pikan with such a bad man as Chou for their uncle and king. Now if you say that human nature is (always) good, then are all those people wrong?" "If you let them follow their original nature," replied Mencius, "then they are all good. That is why I say human nature is good. If men become evil, that is not the fault of their original endowment. The sense of mercy is found in all men; the sense of shame is found in all men; the sense of respect is found in all men; the sense of right and wrong is found in all men. The sense of mercy is what we call benevolence or charity. The sense of shame is what we call righteousness. The sense of respect is what we call propriety. The sense of right and wrong is what we call wisdom, or moral consciousness. Charity, righteousness, propriety and moral conciousness are not something that is drilled into us; we have got them originally with us, only we often forget about them (or neglect or ignore them). Therefore it is said, 'Seek and you will find it, neglect and you will lose it.' This moral consciousness is developed in different persons to different degrees, some five times, some ten times and some infinitely more than others, because people have not developed to the full extent what is in them. The *Book of Songs* says, 'Heaven created the common people with laws governing their affairs. When the people keep to the central (or common) principles, they will love a beautiful character.' Confucius commented upon this poem, saying, 'The writer of this poem understood the moral law, and therefore he recognized that there were laws governing human affairs. Because the people keep to the central principles, therefore they have come to love beautiful character.' "

Mencius said, "In years of prosperity, most of the young people are well behaved, and in bad years, most of the young people turn to violence. This is not due to a difference in their natural endowments from Heaven, but because something has happened to lead their hearts astray. Take, for instance, the growing of wheat. You sow the seeds and till the field. The different plants are planted at the same time and grow from the same piece of land, and soon they sprout beautifully from the earth. When the time for harvest comes, they are all ripe, and although there is a difference between the different stalks of wheat, it is due to the difference in the soil, in the obtaining of moisture from the rain and the dew, and to differences in human care. Therefore, all who belong to the same species are essentially alike. Why should you doubt that this holds true also of human beings? The Sages belong to the same species as ourselves. As Lungtse has said, 'A man who proceeds to make a pair of shoes without knowing the feet measurements will at least not end up by making a wicker basket.' Shoes are alike because the people's feet are alike. There is a common taste for flavor in our mouths. Yiya (a famous gourmet) is but one who has discovered our common taste for food. If, for instance, one man's taste for flavors should differ from that of another man, as the taste of dogs and horses, who belong to a different species, differs from the human taste, then why should the whole world follow the judgment of Yiya in regard to flavor? Since in the matter of flavor the whole world regards Yiya as the ultimate standard, we must admit that our tastes for flavors are alike. The same thing is true of our ears. In the matter of sounds, the whole world regards Master K'uang as the ultimate standard, and we must admit that our ears are alike. The same thing is true of our eyes. In regard to Tsetu, the whole world considers him a handsome man, and whoever cannot see his handsomeness may be said to have no eyes. Therefore I say there is a common love for flavors in our mouths, a common sense for sounds in our ears, and a common sense for beauty in our eyes. Why then do we refuse to admit that there is something common in our souls also? What is that thing that we have in common in our souls? It is reason and a sense of right. The Sage is the man who has first discovered what is common to men's souls. Therefore, reason and the sense of right please our minds as beef and mutton and pork please our palates."

II. HOW OUR ORIGINAL NATURE IS DESTROYED

Mencius said, "There was once a time when the forests of the Niu Mountain were beautiful. But can the mountain any longer be regarded as beautiful, since being situated near a big city, the woodsmen have hewed the trees down? The days and nights gave it rest, and the rains and the dew continued to nourish it, and a new life was continually springing up from the soil, but then the cattle and the sheep began to pasture upon it. That is why the Niu Mountain looks so bald, and when people see its baldness, they imagine that there was never any timber on the mountain. Is this the true nature of the mountain? And is there not a heart of love and righteousness in man, too? But how can that nature remain beautiful when it is hacked down every day, as the woodsman chops down the trees with his axe? To be sure, the nights and days do the healing and there is the nourishing air of the early dawn, which tends to keep him sound and normal, but this morning air is thin and is soon destroyed by what he does in the day. With this continuous hacking of the human spirit, the rest and recuperation obtained during the night are not sufficient to maintain its level, and when the night's recuperation does not suffice to maintain its level, then the man degrades himself to a state not far from the beast's. People see that he acts like a beast and imagine that there was never any true character in him. But is this the true nature of man? Therefore with proper nourishment and care, everything grows, and without the proper nourishment and care, everything degenerates or decays. Confucius said, 'Keep it carefully and you will have it, let it go and you will lose it. It appears and disappears from time to time in we do not know what direction.' He was talking about the human soul."

Mencius said, "Do not think that King (Hsuan of Ch'i) is lacking in wisdom or moral consciousness (as a man). Even in the case of the things that grow most easily in this world, they would never grow up properly if for one day of sunshine they get ten days of cloudy (or chilly) weather. He seldom sees me, and when I leave, the people who are the 'cloudy days' for him arrive. Even if what I say to him is taking root (literally 'sprouting') in his mind, what can he do about it? Even in a trivial thing like playing chess, one cannot learn it unless he concentrates his mind on learning it. You let Chess-Player Ch'iu, who is the best chess player of the state, teach two persons how to play chess. One man will concentrate his mind and energy on it and listen carefully to Chess-Player Ch'iu's explanations and advice, and another man will hear the same explanations, but his mind will be thinking of how a wild goose is going to pass by and how he is going to take a bow and shoot at it. Now although the second man studies under the same master, he will never be equal to the other man. But if you say that this man is lacking in original talent of intelligence, you know it isn't true."

III. THE HIGHER LIFE AND THE GREATER SELF

Mencius said, "I like fish, but I also like bear's paw, but if I can't have both at the same time, I will forego the fish and eat the bear's paw. I love life, but I also love righteousness, and if I can't have both at the same time, I will sacrifice life to have righteousness. I love life, but there is something that I love more than life, and therefore I would not have life at any price. I also hate death, but there is something that I hate more than death, and therefore I would not avoid danger at any price. If there is nothing that man loves more than life, then does he not permit himself to do anything in order to save it? And if there is nothing that man hates more than death, then why does he not always avoid dangers that could be avoided? And so there are times when a man would forsake his life, and there are times when a man would not avoid danger. It is not only the good men who have this feeling that there are times when they would forsake life and there are times when they would not avoid danger. All men have this feeling, only the good men have been able to preserve it." A man's life or death may sometimes depend on a bamboo basket of rice and a bowl of soup, but if you say to a starving man passing by, "Hey, Mister!" and offer them to him in the most insulting manner, he would refuse to take them, or if you offer them to a beggar with a kick, the beggar would not receive them.

"What is a salary of ten thousand bushels to me, if I come by it against my principles? Shall I take this position because it offers me beautiful mansions and the service of a wife and concubines, or because I shall be able to help my friends who knew me when I was poor? If formerly I refused to accept the post in the face of death (or starvation), and now I accept it in order to have a fine residence, if formerly I refused to accept this post in the face of death, and now I accept it in order to have the service of a wife and concubines, if formerly I refused this post in the face of death, and now I accept it in order to be able to help my friends who knew me when I was poor, would that not be something totally unnecessary? This is called 'losing one's original heart.' "

Mencius said, "Charity is in the heart of man, and righteousness is the path for men. Pity the man who has lost his path and does not follow it and who has lost his heart and does not know how to recover it. When people's dogs and chicks are lost, they go out and look for them, and yet the people who have lost their hearts (or original nature) do not go out and look for them. The principle of self-cultivation consists in nothing but trying to look for the lost heart."

Mencius said, "Suppose there is a man who has a crooked ring finger which cannot stretch out straight. It isn't painful and it doesn't cause him any inconvenience. And yet, if there was someone who could straighten out the finger for him, he would not mind going as far as Ch'in or Ch'u because he is ashamed that his finger is not like that of other men (or not normal). Now a man is wise enough to be ashamed of a finger that is not normal, and yet he is not wise enough to be ashamed of his heart, when his heart is not normal. We say such a man has no sense of the relative importance of things."

Mencius said, "People know that if they want a lindera tree whose circumference is a fathom long to grow and live, they must take proper care of it. But as to their own selves, they do not know how to take proper care of them. Can it be that they love their selves less than they love a lindera tree? It is mere thoughtlessness."

Mencius said, "There is not a part of the body that a man does not love. And because there is not a part that he does not love, there is not a part of it that he does not nourish. Because there is not an inch of his skin that he does not love, there is not an inch of his skin that he does not take care of. The thing that determines whether a thing is good or bad depends only on his regard for it or the value he places upon it. Now in our constitution there is a higher and a lower nature, and a smaller and a greater self. One should not develop the lower nature at the expense of the higher nature, or develop the smaller self at the expense of the greater self. He who attends to his smaller self becomes a small man, and he who attends to his greater self becomes a great man. A gardener who attends to thorns and bramble to the neglect of his lindera trees will be regarded as a bad gardener. A man who takes good care of his finger and suffers an injury to his shoulder blade is deformed. People look down upon the matter of food and drink because food nourishes our smaller self and does nothing to our greater self. If a man attends to his food, without forgetting about his greater self, then it may be said that the food taken indeed does not only go to nourish any particular small part of the body (an inch of his skin)."

Kungtutse asked Mencius, "We are all human beings. Why is it that some are great men and some are small men?" Mencius replied, "Those who attend to their greater selves become great men, and those who attend to their smaller selves become small men." "But we are all human beings. Why is it that some people attend to their greater selves and some attend to their smaller selves?" Mencius replied, "When our senses of sight and hearing are distracted by the things outside, without the participation of thought, then the material things act upon the material senses and lead them astray. That is the explanation. The function of the mind is thinking;

when you think, you keep your mind, and when you don't think, you lose your mind. This is what heaven has given to us (for the purpose of thinking or knowing what is right and wrong). One who cultivates his higher self will find that his lower self follows in accord. That is how a man becomes a great man."

Mencius said, "There is the heaven-made nobility, and there is the man-made nobility. The people who are kind, righteous, faithful and love virtue without fail belong to the heaven-made nobility (or the nobility of God), and the *kung*, *ch'ing*, and *taifu* (different ranks of officials) belong to the man-made nobility. The ancient people cultivated what belonged to God's noblemen and they obtained without conscious effort the ranks of man-made nobility. People today, on the other hand, cultivate what belongs to this heaven-made nobility in order to secure man-made honors (or man-made nobility), and after they have secured man-made honors, they forsake the things that make for heaven-make nobility. Thus they are led grievously astray and must soon perish after all."

Mencius said, "All people have the common desire to be elevated in honor, but all people have something still more elevated in themselves without knowing it. What people usually consider as an elevated rank or honor is not true honor, for he whom Chao Meng (a powerful ruling family of Chin) has honored, Chao Meng can also bring into dishonor. The *Book of Songs* says, 'I am drunk with wine, and I am filled with virtue.' This figurative expression means that a man is 'filled' with kindness and righteousness, and when he is so filled, he does not care for the flavors of delicate food. And when a man wears a mantle of fame, he does not care for the embroidered gowns."

Mencius said, "The five kinds of grains are considered good plants, but if the grains are not ripe, they are worse than cockles. It is the same with regard to kindness, which must grow into maturity."

Mencius said, "When Yi (a famous archer) taught people to shoot, he

told them to pull the string on the bow its full length. The man who wants
to cultivate himself must also develop himself to the full extent. A great
carpenter teaches his apprentice to use squares and compasses. The man
who wants to cultivate himself, must also have squares and compasses for his
conduct."